# THE KOREAN WAR

## 1950–53

# THE KOREAN WAR
## 1950–53

BRIAN CATCHPOLE

Carroll & Graf Publishers, Inc.
NEW YORK

Carroll & Graf Publishers, Inc.
19 West 21st Street
New York
NY 10010-6805

First published in the UK by Constable 2000

First Carroll & Graf edition 2000

Copyright © Brian Catchpole 2000

ISBN 0-7867-0780-1

Printed and bound in the EU

951.9042
C

# Contents

# Contents

# List of Illustrations

# List of Maps

# Acknowledgements

It is just over 50 years since the conflict in Korea began and all who write on Korean studies have benefited from the new sources of information released from the archives of the People's Republic of China and the Russian Federation, and I freely acknowledge my debt to these. Equally valuable were the many friends who helped me during my research and I thank them for the efforts they have made on my behalf. I can name but a few. Ivy Chou translated the US propaganda leaflets dropped on the Chinese and North Korean forces; Barbro Farrar gave me free access to Peter Farrar's collection of documents and transcripts; Daphne Rowland provided several vital references. Mary Eaton allowed me to quote from her husband's superbly written *Something Extra*; Warren Thompson kindly permitted me to quote from his invaluable articles in *Wings of Fame*. The Fleet Air Arm Museum, Major M.B. Murphy, Curator of the Royal Ulster Rifles Regimental Museum, and Dr J. E. Hoare at the Foreign Office were especially helpful.

Danny Crawford at the Marine Corps Historical Center, Washington, DC, located source materials as did Randy W. Hoickenburg of the US Army Military History Institute. I am grateful to Her Majesty's Stationery Office for permission to quote from General Sir Anthony Farrar-Hockley's *An Honourable Discharge* (Volume II of the Official History); and to the Australian War Memorial, Canberra, for permission to quote copyright material.

Veterans were unstinting in their assistance. John Murphy, Norman 'Taff' Davies, Colin Ross, Ian Stratford, Ashley Cunningham-Boothe MBE, Roy Williams, John Martin and Ron Larby all obliged me with their memories, photographs and local colour. Reuben Holroyd BEM, a signaller in Korea, provided contact with the Duke of Wellington's Regimental Headquarters Museum and allowed me to quote freely from *The Morning Calm*, Journal of the British Korean Veterans Association, of which he is editor. Ashley Cunningham-Boothe generously gave me permission to quote from *British Forces in Korea* and from other Korean writings he has edited. Members of the American Mosquito Association sent me unit transcripts of CBS broadcasts during 1950–1, while Richard Tripp, Jerry Allen in California and Colonel Sidney F. Johnston, Jr, in New Mexico, provided data that may be new to British readers. Publishers in the UK and the United States were always helpful. I have acknowledged my debt to them elsewhere.

# Introduction

The war in Korea was the first war waged against an aggressor state by the United Nations in the twentieth century. It was unlike any other major conflict in that there was no formal declaration of war to mark its beginning and no peace treaty to mark its end. Casualties for the Korean people and for the United States and communist armed forces were horrific; and for the British and Commonwealth forces it was their third biggest conflict in the twentieth century. Unlike any previous war, Korea provided a complicated scenario of advance and retreat during 1950–1, followed by a deliberate decision to fight a 'static war' throughout 1951–3 while negotiations between the delegates of the armed forces proceeded fitfully, first at Kaesong and then at Panmunjom. These negotiations often revolved around the prisoner-of-war issue, for Korea was the first war in which westerners were subjected to barbaric forms of imprisonment ameliorated only when they responded positively to intensive indoctrination. Many writers on the Korean War, when commenting on overall strategy and tactics employed by the two sides, lament the absence of a positive victory. However, it is important to stress the effective domination of the coasts of Korea by United Nations' navies throughout the war; and the overwhelming victory achieved by United Nations' air power, a victory that helped to bring an end to the conflict. There is much that we still do not fully understand: the real motives of the Chinese in 1950 when they suddenly withdrew from the battlefields of North Korea; and when they hesitated to prevent the withdrawal of X Corps from north-eastern Korea in December 1950. Most of all, for many years, there was an extraordinary lack of recognition the political masters of both sides accorded to the men who had fought for principles enshrined in the constitutions of communist nations and the Charter of the United Nations. I have tried to recognize the sacrifice of those who fought in Korea.

Brian Catchpole
Goodmanham 1999

# CHAPTER I

# The Outbreak of War

'Mr President, I have very serious news. The North Koreans have invaded South Korea.' Secretary of State Dean Acheson was calling President Truman at his home in Independence, Missouri, just before lunch on Saturday 24 June 1950. Some eight hours had already passed since the first North Korean troops had blasted their way into South Korea on 25 June 1950, thirteen hours ahead of America's Eastern Standard Time. Acheson recommended that the United Nations Security Council should meet to confirm that communist troops had committed an act of aggression against the Republic of Korea. Harry Truman agreed and said he would fly back to Washington the following day. He left Kansas Airport in his personal aircraft *Independence* and during the three hour flight to Washington he reflected on events in Korea since he had become President of the United States of America, following the death of Franklin Delano Roosevelt in April 1945.

## THE OCCUPATION OF KOREA

Prior to the end of the Second World War, Americans had little knowledge of Korea. The Allies had agreed at the 1943 Cairo Conference that Korea should be freed from Japanese occupation; at Potsdam in 1945 they noted that Korea would be the demarcation area for Soviet and American air and sea operations once Stalin had entered the war against Japan. It was not anticipated that Allied ground troops would ever be involved in Korea. However, the sheer speed of the Red Army advance after 8 August 1945 led to the Soviet occupation of Manchuria, the capture of four Japanese islands in the Kuriles and the penetration of north-east Korea. Stalin's tactics had transformed the situation in East Asia and Truman promptly issued General Order No. 1 defining the 38 degree Parallel as the line separating the interests of Russia and the United States in Korea. Stalin accepted this arrangement and the first American troops arrived in Inchon, Korea under the command of Lt General John Reed Hodge, US military governor, on 8 September 1945.

Hodge was a veteran of the war in the Pacific and had led XXIV Corps through the Okinawa campaign during 1945. He was appointed military governor of the island and was still based there when he was transferred to Korea as the nearest available senior officer. He had no experience of either politics or Korea. His Russian counterpart was Colonel General Ivan Chistiakov, a veteran of Stalingrad and formerly based in the Soviet Far East. Both men encouraged the formation of political parties in their respective zones, though Hodge refused to tolerate the 'People's Republic' movement, even though it encompassed most shades of political opinion and was a possible vehicle for the ultimate independence of a united Korea. Similarly, both military governors encouraged the return of Korean political leaders in 1945: Kim Il Sung, destined to become the first Premier of North Korea; and Syngman Rhee, who would become the President of South Korea. Chistiakov and Hodge first met in the Joint Commission in Seoul on 16 January 1946, charged with the creation of 'democracy' in Korea but neither could agree on a definition of the term. It soon became clear to Truman that Chistiakov was creating a communist state north of the 38 degree Parallel. Truman's personal adviser, Edwin A. Pauley, entered the Soviet zone May-June 1946 and reported that Russian propaganda was brainwashing the Korean people with slogans such as, 'The Soviet government is the highest form of democracy' and, 'For the Fatherland, for the party, for Stalin.' The Red Army was running the country's transport and economic infrastructure and was promising the people a golden future under communism. Pauley was convinced that, because most people were peasant farmers who had previously been denied the right to vote, they would back the North Korean Communist Party. According to Pauley, communism had a better chance of establishing itself in North Korea than anywhere else in the world.

Truman feared that Russian propaganda might even undermine the military government he had established under Hodge in South Korea.

Syngman Rhee warned Hodge that this propaganda, coupled with the failure to deal with the effects of floods, poor harvests and the mass exodus of refugees from the North, could lead to civil war. Indeed, there were many violent demonstrations in South Korea against the American presence and in favour of independence during 1946–7. Not all of these could be attributed to communist agitation. Truman had to balance such difficulties against his wish to contain the danger of communist expansion in Korea, and this was why he proposed to the Russians that a Joint Conference be held with the aim of creating a united Korea as speedily as possible. He offered to hold secret elections with universal suffrage for the Korean people. Naturally, the Russians refused to accept the terms of the proposal (August 1947) because they knew they would be defeated in a secret ballot: they assumed that as most Koreans lived south of the Parallel the majority would vote for a western-style democratic government. Russia's response was to accuse the Americans of being in breach of existing agreements, reminding them that in Moscow on 27 December 1945 the United States had agreed to establish a 'democratic government' for all of Korea prior to the recognition of Korean independence. But neither side could agree on a political process to achieve a democratically elected Korean government. However, the Russians did propose that all occupation troops be removed from Korea during 1948. Truman's Chiefs of Staff gave tacit approval to this by stating that there was little strategic interest in maintaining 45,000 troops and their expensive bases in South Korea.

## THE CREATION OF TWO KOREAS

In a final effort to hold elections before pulling out US troops, Truman took the problem to the United Nations which in turn created the United Nations Temporary Commission on Korea (later replaced by UNCOK – United Nations Commission on Korea). This commission met in Seoul on 12 January 1948 but the Russians refused to let it cross the Parallel to hold elections in the North. It therefore supervised free elections in South Korea (10 May 1948) and the newly-elected National Assembly in turn selected Syngman Rhee as President of the Republic of Korea. On 15 August, with General MacArthur, Supreme Commander Allied Powers, in attendance, the new republic came into being with its capital at Seoul. This event terminated the American military government and General Hodge, having overseen the transition to civilian political control, left Korea for a new command at Fort Bragg, North Carolina. In the North the communists proclaimed the Democratic People's Republic of Korea (9 September 1948) with its capital at Pyongyang. Russian armed forces withdrew from Korea in December and in June 1949 all US troops (apart from a 480-strong US Korea Military Advisory Group) left the South. So the attempt to create a united Korea had totally failed; instead there now existed two ideologically-opposed Koreas divided by the 38 degree Parallel, both the protegés of the two most powerful nations in the world and separated by a profound disagreement over the meaning of the word 'democracy'.

Truman had been far from happy with the outcome. He had very little confidence in Syngman Rhee's narrow-minded right-wing beliefs and realized that South Korea was rapidly turning into a police state controlled by a dictator with a large armed National Constabulary and a small but growing army. But Korea was just one of many locations where the tensions of the Cold War nagged upon his mind and so he remained anxious to prop up Syngman Rhee's South Korea with economic and military aid. Congress was less willing and deliberately dragged its feet so that US military support to South Korea was minimal during this period. That it was needed was clear from reports of border clashes along the 38 degree Parallel, uprisings on the Cheju Island troublespot off the southern coast and guerrilla warfare in the Cholla and Kyonsang provinces. Most of these conflicts were sparked by peasant hostility towards local landlords but they could easily be penetrated and redirected by communist agitators already well-organized in the South. Kim Il Sung had despatched Pak Hon Yong, leader of the Korean Workers' Party, to train guerrilla forces and lay plans to overthrow Syngman Rhee. It was little comfort to know that parts of North Korea were similarly beset by guerrilla groups opposed to the new communist regime. However, the Americans were confident that the small and ill-equipped Republic of Korea Army (ROK) they had bequeathed to Syngman Rhee was capable of dealing with any communist infiltration across the 38 degree parallel.

Thus the news that North Koreans with tanks and air support had crossed the 38 degree parallel and were rapidly advancing on Seoul was a considerable shock to President Truman. There had been earlier rumours of war: in March 1950 the Central Intelligence Agency had spoken of a possible North Korean invasion in June 1950. This obviously made little impact on Truman for on 1 June he had told the Press that conditions for world peace were better than they had been since the end of the Second World War; and Dean Rusk, the State Department's expert on the Far East, had said there was no evidence of war starting in East Asia. Now Truman was both surprised and worried. During the flight to Washington he sent a radio message for Dean Acheson and the relevant State and Defense Department staff to meet him when he landed.

## TRUMAN'S DECISIONS

He held his first war conference on the crisis in Korea after dinner at Blair House, a mansion being used by his family while apartments in the White House were undergoing renovation. US Ambassador John J. Muccio had sent a report from Seoul based on information filtered through from members of the US Korean Military Advisory Group: Ongjin, Kaesong and Chunchong had all been attacked and there had been a North Korean amphibious landing near Kangnung. Muccio was certain that the attack had been initiated by North Korea. Truman also had a message from John Foster Dulles who was in Tokyo and had just returned from Korea. He was in no doubt that North Korea was the aggressor and urged the immediate use of American armed forces, suggesting that the Security Council of the United Nations should call for UN members to aid South Korea. Truman agreed. North Korean aggression had to be blocked, and blocked quickly. He had been contemptuous of British and French appeasement of Nazi Germany in the 1930s. If Kim Il Sung were appeased this could mark the beginning of a Third World War. So to prevent the further expansion of communist power, Truman was ready to change American foreign policy. He authorized the use of US air power against the invading North Korean tanks and ordered the US Navy to patrol the straits between Taiwan (Formosa) and main-land China. Next day, on 27 June, Truman and Acheson met US Congressional leaders and confirmed that America would defend South Korea. As a member of the United Nations and of the Security Council it was America's duty so to do. At that stage, when diplomatic and military intelligence available to the President was, to say the least, imperfect, both Truman and Acheson instinctively held the Soviet Union responsible for the North Korean attack. Acheson advised

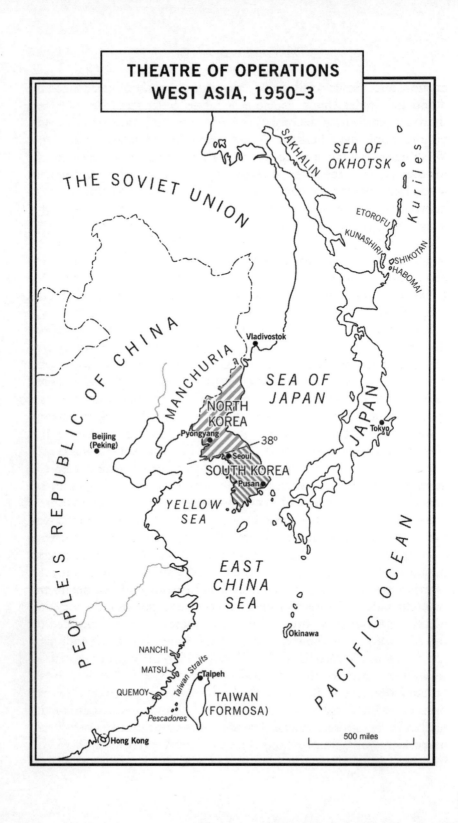

# THEATRE OF OPERATIONS
## WEST ASIA, 1950–3

THE SOVIET UNION

SAKHALIN

SEA OF
OKHOTSK

Kuriles

ETOROFU

KUNASHIRI

SHIKOTAN

HABOMAI

PEOPLE'S REPUBLIC OF CHINA

MANCHURIA

Vladivostok

SEA OF
JAPAN

Beijing
(Peking)

NORTH
KOREA

Pyongyang

38°

Seoul

SOUTH KOREA

Pusan

JAPAN

Tokyo

YELLOW
SEA

EAST
CHINA
SEA

Okinawa

PACIFIC OCEAN

NANCHI

MATSU

Taiwan Straits

Taipeh

QUEMOY

Pescadores

TAIWAN
(FORMOSA)

Hong Kong

500 miles

caution and recommended that the President should not publicly brand the Soviet Union as the evil genius behind the invasion but should try to contain the crisis as a 'local war' in the Far East.[1] When, on the same day, Stalin received a polite diplomatic note from Washington asking him to confirm that he had no responsibility for the invasion, the Soviet dictator responded simply by saying that it was improper for 'foreigners' to become involved in Korea's internal matters. Acheson was not impressed: he privately believed that Kim Il Sung was 'a proxy of the Soviet Union.' But in the light of Stalin's reply and in the interests of world peace both Truman and he favoured handling the Korean affair as a local issue. Such a policy, unprecedented in the brief history of the Cold War, might prevent its sparking a Third World War against the Soviet Union and the newly-established People's Republic of China.[2]

Some historians, notably I. F. Stone in the 1950s and G. Kolko in the 1960s, were tempted to revise the opinion that North Korea was the aggressor. Stone[3] claimed that the US had foreknowledge of the North Korean military build-up; Kolko[4] suggested that the North Korean attack was merely a response to a previous South Korean incursion across the border with the intention of luring the North Koreans into a trap. Later, distinguished revisionists such as Bruce Cumings, writing in the 1980s, accepted that the Korean war began when the North Koreans initiated a full-scale attack with barely any attempt to claim provocation by the South Koreans.[5] This did not persuade critics who had adopted a consistently anti-American stance. Dora Russell, wife of Bertrand Russell, remained convinced that it was the United States that called for a hasty meeting of the Security Council, which imposed on other UN members a requirement to give military aid to South Korea and the United States in a war against the North. She was certain that the North Koreans had not begun the war.[6] In fact, the United Nations' immediate response to the invasion was to call for a cease-fire in Korea, a request that went unheeded by the North Koreans. This was its first resolution on the Korean War (25 June 1950) when India (a non-aligned country unconnected by treaty with either of the superpowers) provided the President of the Security Council, Sir Benegal Rau. He supported the resolution on the basis of an UNCOK cable (dated 25 June 1950) from Seoul where he had an Indian representative. The text of the resolution is significant, based as it was on a previous General Assembly resolution dated 21 October 1949 defining the Republic of Korea as a lawfully established government, The Security Council now viewed 'with grave concern the armed attack upon the Republic of Korea by forces from North Korea.'

It stated that North Korea's action constituted a breach of the peace. Its resolution:

> I   Calls for the immediate cessation of hostilities; and calls upon the authorities of North Korea to withdraw forthwith their armed forces to the 38th parallel.
>
> II  Requests the United Nations Commission on Korea:
>     (a) To communicate in fully considered recommendations on the situation with the least possible delay,
>     (b) To observe the withdrawal of the North Korean forces to the 38th parallel, and
>     (c) To keep the Security Council informed on the execution of this resolution.
>
> III Calls upon all members to render every assistance to the United Nations in the execution of this resolution and to refrain from giving assistance to the North Korean authorities.

Voting was 9–0 in favour, with one abstention (Yugoslavia) and one member absent (USSR).

Two days later (27 June), when Dean Rusk had stated that 'a South Korea absorbed by the Communists would be a dagger pointed at the heart of Japan,' the Americans did bring pressure on the Security Council to act in this emergency according to UN principles. America's representative informed the Council that the President of the United States had authorized US naval and air forces to give cover and support to ROK troops resisting the invasion. Moreover, the US Seventh Fleet was now patrolling the straits between the People's Republic of China and Taiwan (Formosa). He then provided a draft resolution adopted by the Security Council – now in receipt of three further UNCOK cables. This was adopted by the Security Council which then invited General Assembly members to 'furnish such assistance to the Republic of Korea as may be necessary to repel the armed attack and restore international peace and security in the area.' Normally, this would have failed, vetoed by the Soviet Union. However, the Soviet delegate, Jacob Malik, had been conspicuously absent since February 1950 in protest against the UN refusal to admit the unrepresented People's Republic of China in place of the Chinese Nationalist Government on Taiwan, then occupying a permanent seat on the Security Council. Russia's Foreign Minister Andrei Gromyko advised Stalin to send Malik and the Soviet delegation back to the Security Council where the Soviet Union would be able to accuse South Korea of starting the invasion. But Stalin refused, the delegation did not return and the Security Council's request for international assistance was not vetoed. It passed with two abstentions (India and Egypt) and one vote against (Yugoslavia). India did not vote as her delegate had received no specific instructions. Rau mentioned on 29 June that he was much influenced by an UNCOK cable from UN field observers, notably two Australian officers, Major F.S.B. Peach and Squadron Leader R.J. Rankin, who had spent fourteen days (9–23 June 1950) inspecting the South Korean positions. They reported that the South Korean Army was entirely organized for defence and, from a logistical point of view, was unable to undertake an offensive war across the border. Freely admitted to all ROK positions and command posts, they saw no signs of air support potential, no arms dumps, no petrol stores, no armour, no heavy artillery and no troop concentrations. Front-line commanders were under orders to maintain a 'vigilant defence' and to retire if attacked. On 30 June India accepted the resolution of 27 June and in the following month it promised a Field Ambulance Unit to serve in Korea.[7]

It was a Franco-British draft resolution to the Security Council on 7 July that proposed a Unified Command to oversee developments in Korea; and asked that the United States should provide the commander of the United Nations' forces. This draft resolution was adopted; it noted that governments and peoples of the UN, in support of the two resolutions 25 and 27 June, wished to help South Korea in defending itself against armed attack and have made offers of assistance. Later, the Soviet Union's delegate, Foreign Minister Gromyko, returned to the Security Council (1 August 1950) and argued that the Council's resolutions were null and void because of their earlier absence. However, the Security Council held that if a member wished to block a resolution it must be present to veto it. To be absent was to decline to use the veto and in that sense, an absent member was held to concur in the passing of a resolution. On 3 August 1950, the Soviets changed their tack: their argument was that the Korean War was really a civil war being fought to secure the unification of that country. UN intervention was therefore illegal, a point that the Security Council found untenable.

Meanwhile, in South Korea Ambassador Muccio ordered the evacuation of American women and children from Seoul and Kimpo and they left on freighters from Inchon on 26 June. Air cover was provided by F-82G Twin Mustangs without incident apart from one unsuccessful sortie from a lone North Korean La-7 fighter. Next day President Truman issued a press release stating that he had ordered US air and sea forces to give the Korean government troops 'cover and support.' General MacArthur had visited Korea, assessed the situation and requested the immediate despatch of a Regimental Combat Team; thereafter he stated it would take two infantry divisions to stem the North Korean advance. On 30 June the first US ground troops flew into Pusan and on 1 July the 24th Infantry Division arrived in Korea. General MacArthur informed the President that he was planning counter-measures against the North Koreans but desperately needed more troops. Truman promptly alerted the 2nd Infantry Division and the 1st Marine Division for service in Korea. He then presented a resolution to the UN offering to name a commander for UN forces in Korea and suggesting that these forces should fight under the blue banner of the United Nations. The resolution passed. General MacArthur advised the US Joint Chiefs of Staff of his plan to land UN troops behind the advancing North Koreans and cut off their supplies; whereupon Truman, at the request of the UN, appointed him UN Commander in Korea on 7 July.


THE EXTENT OF SOVIET-NORTH KOREAN COLLUSION

At the time the United States had little comprehension of the extent of North Korean and Soviet planning prior to the invasion. Kim Il Sung was dedicated to the reunification of Korea and believed that this could only come about through the military defeat of the South. He had suggested this to Stalin in Moscow (March 1949) but the Soviet leader, with defeat over the Berlin Airlift staring him in the face, warned him that the moment was not propitious and suggested that Kim restrict himself to guerrilla activities across the 38 degree parallel. Kim persisted with his ideas both with the Soviet ambassador in Pyongyang and during a second meeting with Stalin in March 1950. Stalin now relented, promised military aid but insisted that Kim receive approval from Mao Zedong, Chairman of the Central Government of the People's Republic of China. Stalin's relations with Mao at this stage were far from amicable as the Soviet leader distrusted the long-term ambitions of this new communist power in the east. Nevertheless, he had entertained Mao in Moscow (December 1949) and signed the Sino-Soviet Treaty of Friendship, Alliance and Mutual Assistance in February 1950. Mao had returned to Beijing, thrilled with his achievement and confident that the Chinese were now members of a great international communist brotherhood with the prospect of co-operation with one of the world's superpowers over the next thirty years. He had no objection to Stalin's offer of military assistance to North Korea.

Thus Stalin was ready to integrate a war in Korea with his overall plans for East Asia: the subordination of Mao Zedong's policies to a dominant Soviet strategy; the support of Ho Chi Minh in Vietnam (Indo-China) and the infiltration of the Communist Party in Japan. By creating new flashpoints in the east, Stalin would compel the United States to take on new and expensive defence commitments around the globe. These might not win the approval of the American people; and they might help reduce the US commitment to the 1949 North Atlantic Treaty Organization. Stalin must have been delighted when MacArthur had stated in March 1949 that the US defence perimeter in the Pacific ran from the Philippines to Okinawa and then bent back through Japan, excluding Korea; and when Dean Acheson excluded both Taiwan and Korea from the US Pacific defence perimeter on 12 January 1950. So Stalin was now ready to help Kim Il Sung though he warned him that Soviet armed forces would not be directly involved in an invasion of South Korea. However, he promised that 14,000 Koreans who had fought in the Chinese People's Liberation Army would be returned with battle equipment to the North. Moreover, there would be a total re-fit of the North Korean People's Army (NKPA) with Second World War surplus T-34/85 tanks, armoured personnel carriers, anti-aircraft defences, trucks, aircraft and the famous automatic 7.6 mm PPSh 41 sub-machine-guns, or 'burp guns;' a Soviet team would provide weapon and vehicle training; and, crucially, Soviet staff officers would draw up the overall plan for an invasion and conquest of South Korea. The plan's objective was to occupy all of South Korea within 14–15 days of an invasion and unify the peninsula under communist control.

Stalin also advised Kim that military preparations should be carefully camouflaged first by a radio propaganda war against South Korea, stressing that guerrilla raids would intensify with the objective of reuniting Korea. Then during April and May 1950, by which time Stalin would have formally approved the attack, the North Koreans must significantly reduce their activity along the 38 degree parallel. This would lull the South Koreans into a false sense of security. Simultaneously, North Korean propaganda teams should canvass a mythical election to be held in the North and the South. It must be 'scheduled' for August 1950 – by which time the communist occupation of South Korea should be complete! – and be followed by the promise of a National Assembly representing the whole of a united Korea. Stalin also advised Kim to consult directly with Mao. The North Korean Premier visited Beijing in May 1950 when Mao may have promised him back-up support in the form of three Chinese divisions north of the border on the Yalu River. Certainly, Stalin was positive that if the North Koreans needed additional ground troops these would have to come from China rather than from the Soviet Union.

By 25 June 1950 the communist propaganda war and the secret military preparations had met every one of their objectives and completely deceived the South Koreans and the various military and United Nations observers in Korea. On the parallel, no one anticipated an attack. All but one of the US military advisers were absent and their commanding officer was in Tokyo; most of the ROK divisions charged with frontier defence were then located south of their battle positions. Many ROK officers were enjoying extended weekend leave. No one was prepared when the North Korean T-34 tanks smashed their way into the Uijongbu corridor, the natural age-old route south, and headed for Seoul. Simultaneously, North Korean soldiers were actually leaving their trains and forming into battle squads in the centre of Kaesong. However, the North Koreans did not enjoy total success in the first hours of the invasion: they ran into spirited opposition from ROK artillery and infantry units at Chunchon; while their amphibious landings on the east coast were only partially successful. A daring attempt by 600 troops to capture Pusan was frustrated. Crammed into small armed steamship, they were intercepted by the South Korean patrol boat PC701 which sank the enemy vessel.

However, the North Korean tanks proved unstoppable and behind them came the NKPA's infantry. Communist soldiers of the 2nd and 7th Divisions hurled themselves against the dazed and bewildered troops of the 1st and 6th ROK Divisions. Enveloped on both flanks,

6th ROK was forced to retreat thus causing a general collapse along the front line. These tactics were to become standard NKPA practice over the next few days. Meanwhile, 1st ROK, commanded by General Paik Sun Yup, carried out a fighting retreat to protect Seoul and Kimpo airport for as long as possible. Then came the disastrous destruction of the main bridges across the Han River. Apart from the deaths of many refugees who were actually on the bridges, the demolition had cut off thousands of ROK troops north of the capital, occupied by the NKPA on 28 June only three days after their invasion began.

## THE NEED FOR GROUND TROOPS

MacArthur witnessed the carnage and pandemonium around Seoul. Escorted by four Mustangs, his C-54 Skymaster *Bataan* flew into Suwon on 29 June. He and his staff drove up to the outskirts of Seoul and saw for themselves the retreat of the surviving ROK troops. He realized that the South Koreans had neither the will nor the staff leadership and resources to contain the NKPA advance. It would take months to re-equip and train the ROK army and time was of the essence. Unless the United States intervened Korea would be lost with all its new strategic implications. Moreover, the NKPA could not be stopped by the use of air power or naval bombardment alone, invaluable though they were. Ground troops were the answer and they would have to be provided by America. To add point to MacArthur's feelings, NKPA units captured Yongdungpo and Inchon shortly after his return to Tokyo. The South Korean government fled south to Taejon; the American military advisory group abandoned Suwon; and the whole of central Korea now lay before the NKPA so that Taejon, Taegu and even Pusan were at risk.

The first American troops to go into action had arrived by air on 1 July under the command of Lt Col Charles B. Smith. This combat team of 403 men – the famous 'Task Force Smith' – was followed by Major General William F. Dean, commander of the US Army in Korea, with his headquarters staff in Taejon. He ordered Task Force Smith to block NKPA units driving south along the highway from Suwon. The combat team dug in at Osan, eight miles south of the city. Lt Col Miller O. Perry had moved up with Task Force Smith, bringing his six 105mm howitzers; behind them were two battalions of the 34th

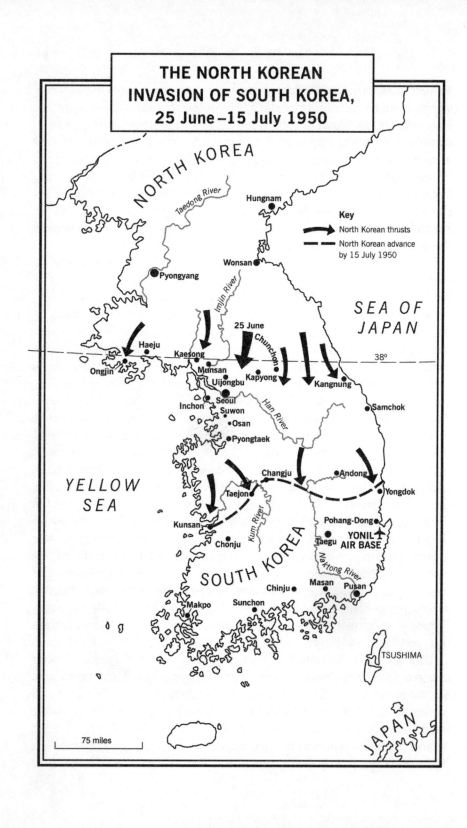

Infantry Regiment covering Pyongtaek and Ansong where they spent a sleepless night during 4/5 July. Next morning the riflemen of Task Force Smith at Osan found themselves staring at 33 T-34 tanks rumbling along the highway. The Americans fired everything in their armoury but their bazookas, mortar fire and howitzer shells simply bounced off the heavily-armoured T-34s. Scores of trucks brought the NKPA infantry into the battle and these were immediately engaged by the Americans. Outnumbered and taking heavy casualties, Task Force Smith had to fall back. They had fought the first US delaying action of the war but had no hope of stopping the NKPA.

General Dean's sole intent was to hold up the NKPA advance so that more American troops and better military equipment could reach Korea in time to save Pusan. His next line of resistance was the arc between Pyongtaek and Ansong but his riflemen were ill-equipped to deal with T-34s and their 85mm guns. The American Army was paying a heavy price for its years of indolence and self-indulgence in Japan. Outfought and out-manoeuvred by the NKPA, the Americans were forced to retreat amidst a worrying decline in unit morale, compounded when one of their own aircraft machine-gunned them. The defence of Chonan was the next priority and the hard-pressed infantry now had the support of the 63rd Field Artillery. Its guns put down a cover of white phosphorus shells under which some soldiers managed to escape from the devastating barrages from the NKPA tanks and artillery. Chonan fell to the NKPA after fierce firefights in the streets between NKPA infantry and the 3rd Battalion of the US 34th Regiment. Somewhat late in the day, General Dean confessed that the Americans had underestimated the fighting ability of the North Korean soldier, the level of training and the quality of his equipment. Meanwhile, ROK forces had virtually abandoned the western half of Korea to the communists and were now moving across to the east, tasked with defending the northern approach to Pusan. It was vital that the American defence give the ROK forces time to cross the Kum River.

This was why the battered 34th and 21st Infantry Regiments were ordered to hold at Chochiwon for the next four days. They were given air support and artillery with superior anti-tank shells and took up positions on high ground east of Chonui. The NKPA 4th Division began its assault and drove Colonel Jensen's 3rd Battalion 21st Infantry from its defences along the ridges. The 3rd Battalion slithered down into the paddy fields but was then ordered to retake its lost position. This it did and managed to hold the ridges all day before retreating to prepared foxholes nearer the river. Here it suffered total defeat at the hands of the NKPA 3rd Division. Jensen was killed and his command dispersed. Everything now depended on the survivors of the two hard-pressed American infantry divisions fighting, in MacArthur's words, 'a desperate rearguard action.' The 21st moved across the Kum River followed by the 34th and the artillery. They had held the NKPA for three days, wrecked the enemy timetable and given General Dean the chance to create a defensive perimeter in south-west Korea.

But Dean desperately needed more troops. British and Commonwealth forces had begun to swell the UN strength in Korea. Australia deployed 77 Fighter Squadron equipped with F-51 Mustangs from Japan; later in July the Royal Canadian Air Force allocated 426 (Transport) Squadron to operate an airlift between the USA and Japan; while the British Admiralty placed naval units in Japanese waters under US Navy command 'for operations in support of Security Council resolutions.' The Royal Navy contributed the Fleet Carrier *Triumph*, two cruisers, *Jamaica* and *Belfast*, four destroyers, *Cossack*, *Consort*, *Comus* and *Cockade*, and three frigates, *Black Swan*, *Alacrity* and *Hart*. The Royal Australian Navy despatched the destroyer *Bataan* and the frigate *Shoalhaven*, the Royal Canadian Navy provided three destroyers, *Athabaskan*, *Cayuga* and *Sioux*, and from the Royal New Zealand Navy came two frigates, *Pukaki* and *Tutira*.

## BRITISH CAUTION

This was an impressive naval contribution but what was needed above all and as quickly as possible was manpower – a few battalions would suffice to stem the enemy advance. Britain's Prime Minister Clement Attlee hesitated to send British troops to Korea, pleading heavy commitments in Malaya against insurgent communist guerrilla forces and a fear that a Chinese attack upon Hong Kong was imminent. Attlee was already doubtful that he could honour his promises to France to send military equipment to help in its struggle against Ho Chi Minh in Indo-China, let alone equip a British force for Korea. He was also doubtful about Commonwealth participation because of the problems that member states were currently facing. His attitude towards China was also different from Truman's: he had informed the People's Republic of China that Britain was willing to support her membership of the UN Security Council.

On 6 July, the Cabinet decided that neither the British Army nor the Royal Air Force should be committed to serve in Korea; and a fortnight later the Foreign Office was still exercising itself over the implications of current American policies. While US soldiers were dying in South Korea, a Foreign Office minute of 21 July was worried about the possibility of UN forces pushing back the North Koreans to the 38 degree parallel. What is to happen then, it asked. However, there was a growing awareness among British diplomats in Washington that the Americans were looking for help from their British ally and that the provision of ground troops would be the most powerful expression of solidarity with the USA. Above all, this would show the Americans that they were not alone in this venture to draw the line against communist aggression. British ground troops in Korea would encourage other western and Commonwealth countries to make a similar gesture. Attlee was persuaded and on 25 July, when the NKPA had conquered most of South Korea, his government recommended that a UK Independent Brigade Group should be sent there from Britain and placed under United States command. This would be in addition to two battalions, then stationed in Hong Kong. Attlee had Foreign Secretary Bevin's full support and a public announcement of the British decision was finally made on 20 August. By 26 July the governments of Australia and New Zealand had followed suit and promised an infantry battalion and an artillery regiment respectively. On 20 August the French promised to send one battalion and next day the Canadians stated that a Canadian Special Service Force would be assembled. Belgium, the Netherlands and Turkey would also send infantry battalions to fight in Korea. India's Field Ambulance was on the way. The United Nations force in Korea was gradually becoming representative of the free world.

# CHAPTER 2

# The Defence of
# the Pusan Perimeter, 1950

On 9 July General Walton Harris Walker transferred his advance headquarters staff to Taegu. As commander of the US Eighth Army, the ground component of General MacArthur's Far East Command based in Japan, he was now appointed commander of ROK and US units in Korea. He was a distinguished officer, having led XX Corps in its 'great swan' across northern France in 1944 when it won the nickname 'Ghost Corps' because of the speed of its advance. It fought its way across Europe, liberated Buchenwald, crossed the Danube and entered Austria. He had the reputation of being a resourceful and courageous leader; he would need these qualities when he took up his command at Eighth Army's new headquarters on 13 July 1950.

He was charged with stabilizing the front line to protect the south-east corner of the Korean peninsula and to guarantee the survival of Pusan. MacArthur assured him that much more military support – far more than General Dean had ever received – would be forthcoming. On 10 July MacArthur had convinced two representatives of the Joint Chiefs of Staff, Generals Collins and Vandenburg, that he would win the war in Korea and that this unhappy country would be reunited under the leadership of Syngman Rhee. The great issue, he said, was not just the defeat of North Korea; it was the containment of communism. If Korea were lost, the world might be lost to communism. His words seemed to impress the generals for they returned to Washington to urge the Joint Chiefs and the President to support MacArthur, expand the armed services and dispatch infantry, armoured and specialist units to Korea as a matter of urgency.

In fact some were already passing through Pusan. The 25th Division was commanded by Major General William B. Kean. His 27th Infantry Regiment led by Lt Col John H. Michaelis was moving into position to defend Taegu. It was understrength, unlike the 24th Infantry Regiment commanded by Colonel Horton V. White – the first all-black unit to arrive in Korea – and the 35th Infantry Regiment under the command of Colonel Henry G. Fisher. The time won by General Dean's 24th Division north of the Kum River and the massive effort made by ROK forces to defend Yongdok gave these reinforcements their chance to take up defensive positions. Walker now had some 18,000 US troops – increasing daily – and 58,000 ROK soldiers to break the NKPA attacks.

The NKPA offensive began on 13 July – the same day that Walker arrived in Taegu. US defenders, strung along the southern bank of the Kum River, watched the NKPA assemble its artillery and mortar units on the opposite bank. Next morning and entirely unopposed, 500 enemy troops with mortars came across on barges and headed directly for US artillery positions. They killed the commander of the 63rd Field Artillery Battalion, captured the guns and forced the Americans to flee. The NKPA then formed a beachhead on the south bank, brought their tanks across on barges and consolidated their gains. Their engineers repaired the blown bridges across the Kum River and brought in more tanks, troops and equipment from across the Han to the north, so that by 18 July they were ready to begin the Battle of Taejon. Walker decided that the 24th Division and the ROK forces in the east should hold on to the Kum River line and Taejon for as long as possible. He was waiting for the 1st Cavalry Division to come ashore at Pohangdong and dig in along the Naktong River as the second main line of defence. He wanted Dean's 24th Division to stem the NKPA attack for at least two days once the assault on Taejon began; the 21st Infantry Regiment would have to keep the escape road out of Taejon open. He could not afford to have his troops surrounded.

On 19 July North Korean Yak fighter-bombers came in low to attack a bridge south of Taejon to cut off the escape route, a broad hint that the NKPA would adopt its well-tried tactics and envelop Taejon on both sides. As Taejon was a large city served by many roads it was not easy to predict the precise line of NKPA attack. In fact, the North Koreans stationed their 3rd Division north of the city and allocated the main attack to the 4th Division, well-equipped with tanks. These rumbled down the main Seoul–Pusan highway, accompanied by infantry who systematically outflanked American defenders, cutting them off and creating large gaps in the defences. The intelligence system operated by the North Koreans was so efficient that Walker believed that it was fed by South Korean civilian agents working for the US and ROK forces. There was no other explanation for the precise targeting of US gun pits, mortar positions and headquarter posts. When the NKPA tanks entered Taejon on 20 July they immediately destroyed the food stores, trucks and ammunition dumps belonging to the 34th Infantry, established sniper units at keypoints in the streets and then went on to capture Taejon airstrip. Great gaps now existed in General Dean's formations though they did not appear on his battle maps. Radio communication between scattered units was non-existent. He was unaware that the 34th Infantry had lost its 1st Battalion or that the 19th Infantry had lost its 2nd Battalion. Both had been surrounded and forced to escape into the mountains. Dean was far more concerned with maintaining the morale of his troops in Taejon itself. He took charge of a bazooka team and went out into the city hunting T-34 tanks. The 3.5-inch bazookas were the first that proved effective against the communists' armoured fighting vehicles in Korea and every T-34 that entered Taejon fell victim to this new American weapon. But the real threat came from overwhelming NKPA forces advancing on three fronts around the city. Dean, who had given Walker the two days he had demanded, now decided it was time to withdraw.

As the US defenders began moving out of Taejon they were first hit by artillery and machine-gun fire and then had to run the gauntlet of NKPA roadblocks and ambushes. Organized American resistance collapsed. Units lost their way, burnt their vehicles and escaped into the mountains. General Dean was in his jeep when it headed the wrong way down the Kumsan road. When it came under fire he abandoned the jeep and that night took refuge in a mountain village. As he tried to find fresh water for wounded US soldiers he fell down a hillside and became unconscious. He came to and spent the next five weeks in the mountains before being betrayed to the NKPA by two South Korean peasants. So the Americans had lost a general; and of the 4,000 American troops engaged in the Battle of Taejon 50 had been killed and some 200 wounded. However, over 900 soldiers were missing in action and many of these were never seen again. There is evidence that it was NKPA practice to execute prisoners during and in the immediate aftermath of intensely fought battles.

For some commanders fighting a defensive war in the south of a peninsula, the disaster at Taejon would indicate an immediate evacuation from Pusan and a regrouping in Japan. MacArthur had already experienced the price a commander paid for evacuations; the Philippines, Bataan and the horrors of Corregidor in 1942 were still fresh in his memory. He was not prepared to take this line; and he believed that General Walker was of a similar mind. He would stay, fight and win in Korea. Fierce ROK resistance at Yongdok convinced him that he could hold a line from this port to Andong on the River Naktong – provided that the five ROK divisions, the 1st, 6th, 8th and Capitol, remained steady in the north and that the 3rd Division in the east could block the enemy drive south to Pohangdong and the key UN airfield at Yonil. In Pyongyang, Kim Il Sung was furious that the offensive was slowing down. He dismissed the senior NKPA commander, General Kim Hwang Hyop, and replaced him with General Kim Mu Chong, instructing him to take Andong and Pohangdong at all costs. Kim Mu Chong ordered the tough and well-equipped 12th NKPA Division to assault Andong; and after a furious battle in which the 12th lost most of its tanks and artillery and its commander killed in action, it managed to occupy the city. It would take the 12th a long time to recover.

General Walker's response was to extend the ROK defence line from just south of Andong to Hamchang and back them up with the US 25th and 1st Cavalry Divisions. However, the 1st Cavalry soon found itself outflanked by the NKPA's familiar tactics and had to retreat from Yongdong; while the 27th Infantry faced an NKPA division committed to the capture of Hwangghan. Here Colonel Michaelis fought the most successful US delaying action since the war began. Equipped with effective anti-tank weapons and able to call on air strikes by F-80 Shooting Stars, Michaelis fought off the enemy for five days, defeated two NKPA battalions attempting their usual enveloping attack, destroyed most of the enemy armour and then successfully withdrew. The 27th had killed or wounded over 3,000 of the enemy and had suffered 325 casualties. General Walker was impressed by Michaelis's achievement but he was not confident he could hold Taegu. On 26 July he asked MacArthur whether it would be prudent to move Eighth Army headquarters to Pusan. Next day a furious MacArthur flew into Taegu and told Walker that he would have to stand and fight. MacArthur, of course, had already assured the Joint Chiefs of Staff that he could do this. Walker's task, his Supreme Commander said, was to restore morale among US troops. There had been too many withdrawals, too much panic, too much talk among the troops about the 'bugout war'. The hardest fight was yet to come: the NKPA 6th Division had reached the south coast of Korea and had taken Mokpo, Poson and Sunchon. Here they were just over 100 miles from Pusan and their commander, General Pang So Hang, was now determined to capture Masan and Chinju. The threat from the 6th Division was very real indeed. It was down to Walker to inspire his men, to instil in them the will to resist.

Walker resorted to Churchillian oratory reminiscent of 1940. He called a conference with the commanders of the US 24th and 25th Divisions, General Church and General Kean, and gave them this message to take to the troops:

> There will be no more retreating, withdrawal or readjustment of the lines or any other term you choose. There is no line behind us to which we can retreat. Every unit must counter-attack to keep the enemy in a state of confusion and off balance. There will be no Dunkirk, there will be no Bataan; a retreat to Pusan would be one of the greatest butcheries in history. We must fight until the end. Capture by these people is worse than death itself. We will fight as a team. If some of us must die, we will die fighting together. Any man who gives ground may be personally responsible for the death of thousands of his comrades . . . I want everybody to understand that we are going to hold this line. We are going to win . . .[1]

But to hold the long perimeter around Pusan required more men and when the 2nd Division arrived it was well understrength. The 5th Regimental Combat Team came in from the United States on 1 August and General Walker sent it to back up the 25th Division. The first 2nd Division troops in action were the men of the 29th Infantry Regiment from Okinawa. Many were half-trained recruits and were rapidly bussed up to Chinju. On 26 July the 3rd Battalion was ordered to occupy Hadong and guard the southern route to Pusan. It followed a tortuous route to Konyang along dirt tracks running through the paddy fields and approached Hadong through a mountain pass. When groups of soldiers appeared the inexperienced Americans were uncertain whether they were friend or foe. Suddenly the crackle of machine-guns and the thud of mortars filled the air. One mortar shell destroyed the battalion radio jeep so there was no means of contacting air support.

Enemy infantry quickly split the battalion into disorganized groups. Some escaped into the hills, others made for the coast and persuaded fishermen to take them to Pusan. Many who fled were captured and murdered by the NKPA. The remainder fought their way back to Chinju.

It was not an auspicious beginning and the NKPA 6th Division now had a golden opportunity to strike at Pusan. Walker had few troops left to guard the south-west though at that moment he was more worried by the advance of the enemy 4th Division towards the Naktong River. But the 6th, suffering from extended supply lines, worn-out armour and artillery, plus ammunition supply problems, decided to occupy all the harbours along the south-west coast rather than begin its advance on Chinju. It resumed its attacks on 29 July and captured Chinju on 31 July. Next day General Walker received 54 M-4 Sherman medium tanks plus more armoured cars; some of these armoured vehicles escorted the 27th and 19th Regiments who were cautiously probing the Chinju road on 2 August. As they drove through a pass known as The Notch they found they had blundered into an NKPA attack. A vicious firefight ensued, with hand-to-hand combats on the mountain sides as well as on the road. But the Americans did not give way and the NKPA troops suddenly withdrew. The Shermans had made all the difference; for the first time in the Korean War the enemy infantry did not enjoy superiority in armour. Walker brought in the 29th Regiment to guard Masan and plug the gap in the south, an enemy attack on Chindong-ni was repelled and the communist offensive stalled. The American and ROK divisions now had a defence line running along the Naktong River, a line that had a chance of being held.

On the evening of 2 August the long-awaited Marines finally arrived at Pusan from their base in the United States. Most were combat veterans of the Pacific War. They assumed that their mission was to undertake the first American offensive of the Korean War and next day they moved out to Changwon to spearhead, as part of the so-called Task Force Kean, a major assault upon Chinju. Their headquarters kept in radio contact with Marine F4U Corsairs on board the patrolling aircraft carriers *Sicily* and *Badoeng Strait*. They also had M-26 Pershing tanks and relieved the 27th Infantry who had held Chindong-ni. Here the Marines fought a major brigade action on the hills around the village on 6/7 July. They pushed the NKPA 6th Division back towards Chinju; few prisoners were taken. The key position was Hill 255. Held by the North Koreans, it controlled the

Chinju-Masan route. The Marines assaulted the hill on 9 August, captured it and then went on to attack Hill 308 to the south of the road. On 9/10 August they resumed their offensive and drove through Paedunu-ni, heading for Kosong until they ran into a machine-gun ambush in Taedabok Pass. The Marines dealt effectively with the machine-gunners but it was the arrival of two Pershing tanks that put the North Koreans to flight.

Under cover of a barrage put down by 105mm guns, and with the aid of F-51 Mustangs and F4U Corsairs strafing the enemy, the Marines advanced into Kosong and moved on towards Sachon. Simultaneously, the 5th Regimental Combat Team advanced along the road to Pansong but had the misfortune to be ambushed at Pongam-ni by swarms of North Korean soldiers backed by tanks and self-propelled guns. They wrecked the American artillery and slaughtered the gunners. When 12 August dawned the Pongam-ni position proved untenable and once more the Marines had to save the situation; but when they expected to resume their advance on Sachon they were called back to Masan. Here the North Koreans were on the move again, with NKPA soldiers at battalion strength actually across the Naktong River during the night of 5 August. They had arrived unobserved, having swum across with their machine-guns and ammunition ferried on rafts. More followed on the second night, hauling their trucks and mortars behind them. Their objective was to take high ground coded Cloverleaf Hill and the commanding Obong-ni Ridge. The positions were significant: the North Koreans had entered the Naktong Bulge, the region where the river curls round 90 degrees so that defenders would be fighting with the river on three sides. As usual the North Koreans targeted the American artillery and swiftly captured the guns of the 34th Infantry and established themselves on both Cloverleaf Hill and Obong-ni Ridge. Attacking them were two battalions of Colonel Hill's 9th Infantry Regiment, swiftly reinforced by his own Regimental Combat Team, the 24th Division's artillery and about 2,100 men from 19th and 34th Regiments. This combined unit was Task Force Hill. Against it was ranged the highly experienced and successful NKPA 4th Division, many of whose soldiers had seen service fighting for Mao Zedong against the Chinese Nationalists.

Complicating matters in the Naktong Bulge were the numerous refugees, many of whom were North Korean soldiers in disguise or communist sympathizers bringing supplies to the NKPA. It was easy for 'refugees' to carry a bandolier of ammunition or a pair of grenades;

while a handcart could carry a couple of T-34 shells or rice rations for a platoon. One 'heavily pregnant' woman was found to be concealing a radio transmitter! As the Americans employed many South Koreans as porters, it was easy for North Koreans to infiltrate American lines without arousing suspicion. This was how information regarding the precise location of American defences was transmitted to the NKPA. And to compound the American problem, the NKPA troops facing them were expert night fighters; when they lost ground to Task Force Hill during the day they recaptured it during the night.

The main American assault was supposed to go in on 14/15 August – the anniversary of the Japanese surrender in 1945 and the date Kim Il Sung had promised his people that he would have captured all of Korea. There was plenty of hand-to-hand fighting but no major American assault. Heavy fog restricted artillery barrages and robbed the Americans of air support. Colonel Hill wanted more men as he feared that the North Korean bridgehead could quadruple in size within a few days. If four NKPA divisions crossed the Naktong, Pusan would be lost. General Walker sent the toughest Battle Group at his disposal – the 1st Marine Brigade.

The brigade had been enjoying R & R (Rest and Recreation) in Miryang and was taken up to the front in Army lorries. On 17 August the Marines were ready to attack the towering ridge of Obong-ni with its numerous peaks and deep, twisting gullies – land formations characteristic of much of Korea. The Marines found the assault exhausting and dangerous and many fell victims to well-placed NKPA machine-guns. Their own artillery and rockets from low-flying Corsair fighter-bombers also hindered their advance and when the day's attack ended the NKPA, oblivious to their own losses, still held Obong-ni Ridge. NKPA tanks, too, had come off worst in encounters with the Marines' M-26s firing their deadly 90mm armour-piercing shells. But the the Battle of Obong-ni Ridge was becoming a protracted affair. While the Marines regrouped they were warned to expect the NKPA 4th Division to counter-attack after dark. Mortars, machine-guns and rifle fire opened up out of the night and robbed the Marines of desperately needed sleep. The infantry attack came at 0230 hours on 18 August and lasted until dawn with the North Koreans again taking heavy casualties. The Marines then launched their own assault with excellent cover from artillery barrage and their Corsair fighter-bombers. Soon the Marines were on the ridge itself, moving towards the highest point, Hill 153. The first squads to arrive found the position wrecked and abandoned. Only a few bodies remained. The artillery barrage had been entirely effective, a lesson the Americans never forgot. Below them they could see the enemy 4th Division in full retreat, presenting easy targets for the roving Corsairs. By the following morning the Marines had secured the entire Obong-ni Ridge and could justly claim to have defeated the 4th Division and prevented an attack on Taegu. Sixty-six marines were dead, 278 wounded but only one man was classified 'Missing in Action.'

Whilst the Marines were winning at Obong-ni Ridge, three North Korean divisions and an independent regiment were preparing to advance down the east coast of South Korea. For some time the ROK 3rd Division had held the NKPA 5th Division in the battles that had raged for the possession of Yongdok. They had plenty of air support and the 8-inch guns of a heavy cruiser, the USS *Toledo*, so useful for bombarding coastal troop concentrations. When the NKPA reoccupied Yongdok on 5 August, UN fighter aircraft swooped over the troops firing guns and rockets and dropping tanks of lethal napalm. The *Toledo* added the power of her armament, enabling the ROK infantry to fight their way back into Yongdok. When the North Koreans retaliated the ROK commander, inappropriately named General Lee, took fright and ran. His replacement was General Kim Suk Wo, charged with holding a key bridge across the Osipchon Estuary. When the North Koreans next attacked a ROK officer ordered the bridge to be blown! General Walker was furious and flew into Yonil airfield to consult with field commanders and the Air Force chief, General Partridge. Yonil, he said, was vital; and promptly created Task Force Bradley to protect it from a North Korean envelopment.

Unfortunately, the ROK forces and their American advisers had lost track of an NKPA division, the elusive 12th. It had abandoned its heavy equipment, crossed the mountain ranges and reappeared as a threat to Pohangdong. On 11 August the 12th captured part of the town and General Partridge had to move his F-51 Mustang close-support aircraft out of Yonil and back to Japan. Matters worsened when the ROK 3rd Division found itself cut off and requiring evacuation by sea! This was successfully accomplished with the aid of two American carriers, the *Philippine Sea* and *Valley Forge*, and four Landing Ship Tanks (LSTs). The LSTs brought off the ROK 3rd Division, the American advisers and a host of refugees. With the NKPA now holding the ground north and south-west of Pohangdong the future for the UN forces looked bleak. But the rapid movement of

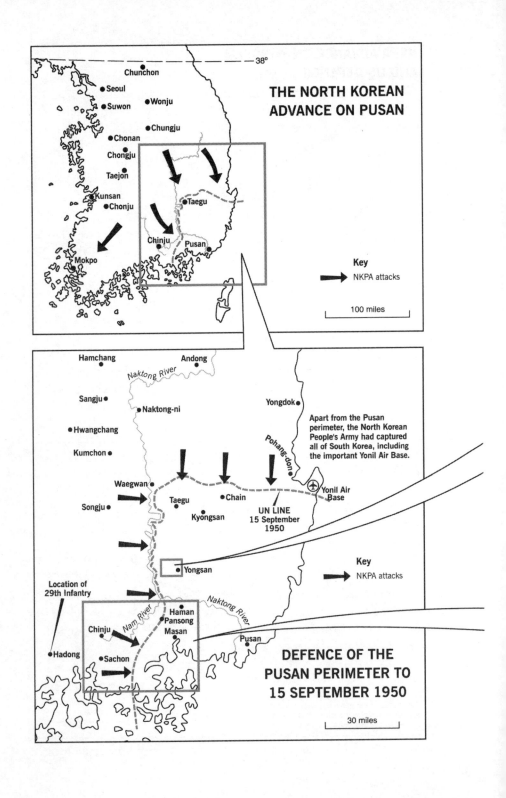

## THE NORTH KOREAN ADVANCE ON PUSAN

Chunchon
Seoul
Suwon
Wonju
Chungju
Chonan
Chongju
Taejon
Kunsan
Chonju
Taegu
Chinju
Pusan
Mokpo

**Key**
NKPA attacks

100 miles

## DEFENCE OF THE PUSAN PERIMETER TO 15 SEPTEMBER 1950

Hamchang
Andong
Naktong River
Sangju
Naktong-ni
Yongdok
Hwangchang
Kumchon
Pohang-don
Waegwan
Taegu
Chain
Yonil Air Base
Songju
Kyongsan
UN LINE 15 September 1950
Yongsan

Apart from the Pusan perimeter, the North Korean People's Army had captured all of South Korea, including the important Yonil Air Base.

Location of 29th Infantry
Chinju
Haman
Pansong
Masan
Hadong
Sachon
Nam River
Naktong River
Pusan

**Key**
NKPA attacks

30 miles

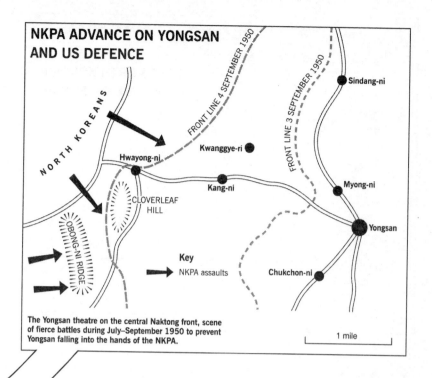

# NKPA ADVANCE ON YONGSAN AND US DEFENCE

Sindang-ni

FRONT LINE 4 SEPTEMBER 1950

FRONT LINE 3 SEPTEMBER 1950

NORTH KOREANS

Kwanggye-ri

Hwayong-ni

Myong-ni

Kang-ni

CLOVERLEAF HILL

Yongsan

OBONG-NI RIDGE

**Key**

NKPA assaults

Chukchon-ni

The Yongsan theatre on the central Naktong front, scene of fierce battles during July–September 1950 to prevent Yongsan falling into the hands of the NKPA.

1 mile

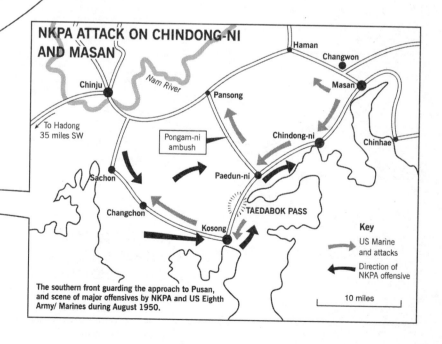

# NKPA ATTACK ON CHINDONG-NI AND MASAN

Haman

Changwon

Chinju

Nam River

Pansong

Masan

To Hadong 35 miles SW

Chindong-ni

Chinhae

Pongam-ni ambush

Sachon

Paedun-ni

Changchon

TAEDABOK PASS

Kosong

**Key**

US Marine and attacks

Direction of NKPA offensive

The southern front guarding the approach to Pusan, and scene of major offensives by NKPA and US Eighth Army/ Marines during August 1950.

10 miles

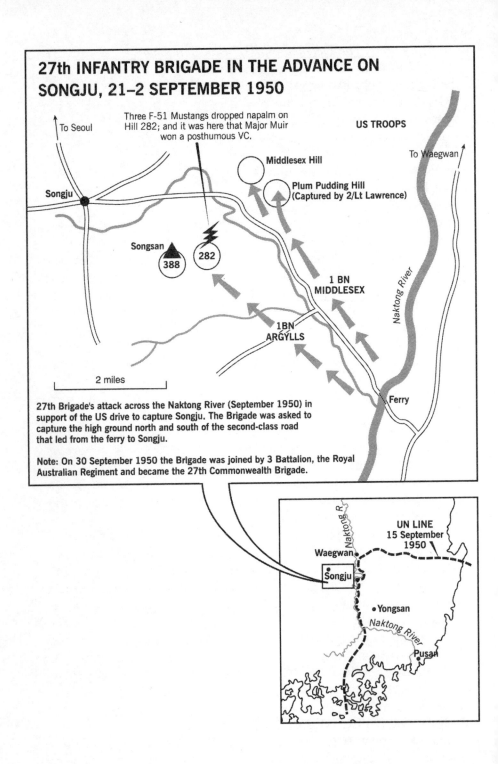

# 27th INFANTRY BRIGADE IN THE ADVANCE ON SONGJU, 21–2 SEPTEMBER 1950

To Seoul

Three F-51 Mustangs dropped napalm on Hill 282; and it was here that Major Muir won a posthumous VC.

US TROOPS

To Waegwan

Middlesex Hill

Plum Pudding Hill
(Captured by 2/Lt Lawrence)

Songju

Songsan

388

282

Naktong River

1 BN
MIDDLESEX

1BN
ARGYLLS

2 miles

Ferry

27th Brigade's attack across the Naktong River (September 1950) in support of the US drive to capture Songju. The Brigade was asked to capture the high ground north and south of the second-class road that led from the ferry to Songju.

Note: On 30 September 1950 the Brigade was joined by 3 Battalion, the Royal Australian Regiment and became the 27th Commonwealth Brigade.

Naktong R.

UN LINE
15 September
1950

Waegwan

Songju

Yongsan

Naktong River

Pusan

the NKPA troops had exposed their lines of communication and two ROK divisions, the Capitol and the 8th, swept behind them and cut off their supply routes. On 17/18 August the NKPA 12th Division began its withdrawal under unrelenting attack from land, sea and air forces. Kim Il Sung managed to send 2,000 replacements south but these were not enough to bring the division up to strength. The North Korean leader's plan had now failed both in the south and in the east. He still had divisions facing the Naktong Bulge and he committed these to another thrust in the centre, across the Naktong River, towards Taegu and Pusan.

Five NKPA divisions began closing on Taegu. Troops could now wade across the Naktong as the river level had dropped three feet during the dry summer season. Soon the enemy divisions were between 10–15 miles from Taegu and by 18 August the city was under NKPA artillery bombardment. The government of South Korea immediately left to seek sanctuary in Pusan. General Walker had the problem of dealing with a city packed with refugees; its panic-stricken population now topped 0.75 million. If they fled they would jam the roads and prevent the arrival of troop reinforcements. He had to save Taegu and sent the US 27th Infantry to hold the road between the high ground – the peaks were almost 3,000 feet high – being contested by the two North Korean armies. The 29th called this stretch of road leading to Sangju and Kunwi 'the Bowling Alley', crucially important to the NKPA if their tanks were to lead the assault on Taegu. NKPA divisions were to make three unsuccessful attacks and the first T-34s clanked down the road on the night of 18/19 August to begin the Battle of the Bowling Alley. Concealed US artillery and bazooka teams shot up the tanks and lorried infantry. The Americans had learnt a few tricks by now and fired captured North Korean flares to lure the NKPA units into ambushes. Cautiously, the Americans moved up the road to occupy new defensive positions under the protection of their artillery, mortar units and Sherman tanks. On 21/22 August the North Koreans began their second round of night attacks and were slaughtered by the Americans; and with total disregard for casualties the NKPA put in a third attack on 24 August. After this third unsuccessful assault, the North Koreans needed time to regroup and secure replacements. They withdrew from the Bowling Alley leaving the ROK and American forces victorious.

The defeat of three NKPA offensives in August 1950 meant that the communist attempts to *pierce* the Pusan Perimeter had failed. However, it did not diminish their capacity or their determination to carry on the fight *around* the perimeter. Incredibly, their supply routes to the Naktong River survived all the air attacks launched by the US Fifth Air Force. A new North Korean field commander, General Kim Chaik, had taken over a reinforced NKPA numbering 100,000 men by the end of August. Stalin was replacing Kim's T-34 tanks and artillery; new automatic weapons were also arriving from the Soviet Union. The South Koreans were also boosting their army. It numbered just over 91,000 men and was being re-equipped by the Americans. Seventy new Patton tanks arrived to bolster American armour in Korea. The four American divisions were up to strength, admittedly by incorporating South Korean soldiers into US units in the so-called 'buddy system'. Equally important was the first sign that another nation was prepared to send ground troops to help the American and ROK forces. On 29 August 1950 a British brigade arrived in Korea.

In Britain, a top secret minute dated 17 August 1950 was sent by the War Office to Prime Minister Attlee. It stated that on 24 July the Defence Committee, mindful of the American request that British help would be needed when the Pusan Perimeter battles had stabilized, recommended that 'a fully balanced force,' ready for battle, should be sent to Korea and placed under American command. The nearest troops were in Hong Kong and some should be sent to Korea but not at the expense of the Hong Kong garrison. The People's Republic of China might interpret such a move as a sign of weakness and occupy the colony. If the 1st Battalion Wiltshire Regiment and a squadron of the 4th Hussars (consisting of armoured cars) were sent to the colony, two infantry battalions could be spared for Korea. Next day, at a Cabinet meeting, the Attlee government agreed to send a Brigade Group to Korea.[2]

The two battalions that were chosen were the 1st Argyll and Sutherland Highlanders, commanded by Lt Col Leslie Neilson, and the 1st Middlesex, led by Lt Col Andrew Man. Over 50 per cent of the Middlesex were British National Servicemen aged eighteen, as were about 20 per cent of the Argylls. As a War Office order prevented 18-year-old soldiers serving in Korea, both battalions were now seriously understrength. The deficiency was made good by Hong Kong-based volunteers from the King's Own Scottish Borderers (KOSB) who joined the 1st Argylls; and from the South Staffordshires, the King's Shropshire Light Infantry (KSLI) and Leicesters who were attached to the 1st Middlesex. They were seen off by General Sir John Harding, Commander-in-Chief Far East Land Forces, who exhorted them to shoot quickly, shoot straight and shoot to kill; and by Malcolm MacDonald,

High Commissioner for South-East Asia, who informed them that the Korean War was part of a Russian attempt to conquer the world. The Argylls then boarded the cruiser HMS *Ceylon* and the Middlesex sailed on the carrier HMS *Unicorn*. Escorted by two Australian destroyers, HMAS *Warramunga* and HMAS *Bataan*, these units, now designated 27 Brigade, under the command of Brigadier Aubrey Coad, arrived in Pusan on 29 August 1950. They were greeted by children waving Union Jacks, a Korean girls' choir and an all-black US military band whose musicians sported chromium-plated steel helmets and a penchant for playing 'Tiger Rag.' The peculiar aroma of Pusan in particular and Korea in general became apparent to all. It was caused by the use of what was delicately called night-soil for fertilizing the fields. They then moved up to their camp near Kyonsang, first by train, on which they consumed American 'C' rations and brewed coffee on small stoves, and then by US 2½ ton lorries driven by American blacks determined to ignore all speed limits. Their arrival at their bivouac area some six miles outside Yongsan coincided with the biggest North Korean offensive of the war and 27 Brigade moved straight into the line along the bank of the Naktong River to the south-west of Taegu.

General Kim Chaik's decision to attack the expanding United Nations' forces on all fronts was perhaps the biggest North Korean blunder of the campaign. He had thirteen divisions at his disposal and yet seemed unaware of the distribution and strength of the United Nations' forces. South Korean agents had less freedom of movement and could provide him with little information; the Americans now opened fire on any civilians caught moving about at night. A *maximum* effort in the east driving south through Pohangdong, or a *concerted* attack on Masan in the south-west might have smashed a hole in the Pusan Perimeter. Instead, Kim Chaik sent all of his divisions against the Pohangdong, Naktong and Haman-Masan-Chinhae sectors of the perimeter. His decision was undoubtedly influenced by Pyonyang; he was under new orders to capture Pusan by 1 September but this was impossible as his plan to begin the final offensives was timed for 2330 hours on 31 August.

He was therefore astonished by events on 27 August. NKPA units on patrol near Kigye in the east encountered a company of the ROK 17th Regiment. The South Koreans immediately retreated, causing the entire regiment to withdraw, taking with it its sister unit the ROK 18th Regiment. Suddenly a part of the perimeter had collapsed. The North Koreans moved into Kigye, the ROK Capital Division gave up more ground and on 6 September the NKPA were in Pohandong. The sudden withdrawal of the ROK 3rd, 7th and Capital Divisions in the face of three North Korean divisions once more threatened the survival of Yonil airfield. American forces from Taegu – three infantry battalions, tanks and armoured cars – rushed to the rescue of Yonil, revitalized the ROK divisions and drove back the NKPA attack. Air strikes and naval bombardments contributed to the UN victory, and the American relief columns returned to Taegu confident that the east was secure and the ROK I Corps could now be relied on to pursue the shattered NKPA divisions.

Simultaneously, the North Koreans attacked the ROK divisions defending the right centre around Hayang and Yongchon. American artillery and ground-attack aircraft supported the ROK 6th Division, helping it wreck the enemy 8th Division heading towards Hayang. ROK units had less success against the NKPA 15th, whose tanks entered Yongchon on 6 September. General Walker was balancing his reserves, dealing with all these crises developing in the first fortnight of September 1950. He ordered his American advisers to reassemble dispersed ROK units and reinforced them with two additional ROK regiments. Between them they blocked the 15th Division's attempt to exploit the capture of Yongchong.

North of Taegu, General Kim Chaik had assembled three NKPA divisions to capture the city. He planned a triple assault and to resist this General Walker could field the US 1st Cavalry and Britain's 27 Brigade, now located in the south-west corner of the Taegu defence line. Responsible for the defence of 18,000 yards along the Naktong front line close to Waegwan, the British were blooded in a series of fighting patrols, each one composed of around a dozen men under a company or platoon commander. On 8 September a Middlesex patrol suffered one fatal casualty. He was Private Reginald Streeter, aged $19\frac{1}{2}$, the first British soldier to die in Korea and a National Service-man. On the same day, an Argyll patrol had an even more bitter experience. During a firefight with North Koreans the patrol commander, Captain Buchanan, and his batman, Private Taylor, were both wounded. On Buchanan's orders, the Argylls reluctantly withdrew. Much later they discovered the bodies of their comrades. Both men had been captured and then murdered.

The 1st Cavalry bore the brunt of the NKPA offensive which had taken to the high ground north of Taegu. American soldiers, faced with clearing the hills, fought a close-quarter infantry battle against the North Koreans who seemed to have infiltrated everywhere around Waegwan. It was clear that they intended to advance on Taegu along the Bowling Alley and, lacking reserves, the 1st Cavalry gradually gave way. An Engineer Combat Battalion was thrown into the fray and ordered to occupy the Korean fortress of Old Kasan (Hill 902) commanding the approach valley to Taegu. Unknown to the Engineers, an NKPA battalion had already taken the hill and a fierce and unequal battle began. It was here that Private First Class Melvin L. Brown held off North Korean attacks with his Browning Automatic Rifle. When his ammunition was expended he used his grenades; and when these were exhausted he used his entrenching tool. His company were pinned down and could not support him and Melvin Brown died fighting alone. For this he was awarded a posthumous Congressional Medal of Honor.[3]

From here the NKPA drove south, facing the tanks of the 1st Cavalry just six miles north of Taegu. General Walker sent in reserves and ordered a full-scale counter-attack against the North Koreans who were holding a key feature, Hill 314, from which they proposed to attack Taegu. There was a heavy exchange of mortar and artillery fire but the deciding factor was the air support that plastered the NKPA positions with napalm. The final assault went in at great cost to the 1st Cavalry. When they reached the crest of the hill they found 200 dead North Koreans. Many wore American uniforms; many had American weapons – had they taken these from murdered GIs? The loss of Hill 314 ruined the NKPA plan and enabled the 1st Cavalry and the ROK 1st Division to advance and, after a lengthy battle, to recover Kasan fortress on 14 September. Their determination to control the hills had frustrated a dangerous North Korean offensive.

Equally threatening was the build-up of the NKPA I Corps in the south-western sector, barely 30 miles from Pusan. General Kim Chaik had ordered an enveloping assault: his 6th Division was to take Haman, Masan and Chinhae; the 7th was to take Naktong and then, with the 6th and the 9th Divisions on its flanks, head straight for Pusan. At 2350 hours on 31 August the North Koreans surprised the suspect 24th Infantry. Two companies fled and lost their mortars, and a 75mm recoilless rifle with which the NKPA destroyed two US tanks! In fact most of the 2nd Battalion had vanished, enabling the NKPA to attack some very surprised US artillery units in the rear and capture Haman.

On the same day an NKPA attack across the Nam River with T-34s and self-propelled guns ran into a minefield sown by ROK engineers.

The US 35th Infantry put up a spirited resistance and held their ground until reinforced by American tanks. Nevertheless, some North Korean units managed to bypass the 35th and pierce the perimeter. Further north, at the confluence of the Nam and Naktong Rivers, the NKPA 9th Division recaptured Cloverleaf Hill and Obong-ni Ridge; and then, with its sister division, the 10th, developed a potentially dangerous salient. Yongsan was now at risk. General Walker sent in the Marines and during 3–5 September their three battalions fought a series of battles to capture key hills, regain Cloverleaf and neutralize the strong North Korean force holding Obong-ni Ridge. They succeeded in all their objectives and, exhausted, moved back to Pusan to prepare for a top-secret assignment.

General Walker's Eighth Army and its ROK allies still faced two more NKPA offensives from the 2nd Division in the north and from the combined attack from the 6th and 7th Divisions in the south-west. So far Walker had blunted North Korean offensives through his quick appreciation of the battle scene, his highly mobile reinforcements and the fighting ability of the UN troops, particularly the 1st Marine Brigade. But it was the thinly defended south-west, where the the 24th Infantry had proved itself unreliable in battle, that the permanent danger existed. Walker was forced to depend on the resilience of the US 35th and 27th Infantry, backing them with as many 105mm howitzers he could spare. When the North Koreans crossed the Naktong River during 31 August-1 September, the Army called down artillery and air strikes, causing heavy losses among the troops and vehicles of the 6th Division. However, the North Koreans pressed on, cut off the 35th Infantry and infiltrated the perimeter. Artillerymen were their prime target and firefights took place in many gun positions. Undoubtedly, one of the aims of this NKPA attack was to capture the American howitzers, but American resistance prevailed. The fully extended North Koreans had fought themselves to a standstill and were compelled to abandon their offensives. On 8 September General MacArthur assured the US Joint Chiefs of Staff that there was not the slightest possibility of Walker's Eighth Army being ousted from the Pusan Perimeter. Apart from patrol activity, the entire perimeter was quiet. A week later the whole nature of the war was changed by an amphibious landing by UN troops at the port of Inchon. Operation 'Chromite', so long in the planning stage, was at last a reality.

# CHAPTER 3

# The Hammer and The Anvil: Inchon and Beyond

General Douglas MacArthur was America's most famous and beloved soldier. Famed for his defence of Bataan and the Manila Bay forts in 1942, and his reluctant departure to Australia by PT boat and B-17 bomber on the explicit orders of President Roosevelt, his dedication was recognized by the award of the Medal of Honor. He had become Supreme Commander of Allied Forces in the South-West Pacific Area and masterminded the campaigns in New Guinea and New Britain. Now the unchallenged master of amphibious warfare, MacArthur went on to command the ground forces at Leyte in the Philippines. He was appointed commander US Ground Forces, Pacific in preparation for an invasion of Japan scheduled for 1945–6 and received the surrender of Japan aboard the battleship USS *Missouri* on 2 September 1945. He was then appointed Supreme Commander Allied Powers in Japan and charged with the reconstruction of post-war Japan. He became Supreme Commander of UN forces in Korea by a United Nations' resolution (8 July 1950) and his Chief of Staff, General Edward Mallory Almond, followed him as the Chief of Staff to the United Nations Command. General MacArthur was now the senior officer in the United States Army.[1]

As the NKPA advance across South Korea rolled on unchecked by ROK resistance, MacArthur called a staff conference on 4 July to consider the possibility of an amphibious counterstroke against the North Koreans. He proposed to land a force either at Kunsan or Inchon, take Seoul, cut the NKPA's supply lines and force their surrender. He coded the attack Operation 'Bluehearts'. Because the situation in Korea was grave, he urged that the landing should take place on 22 July. He would need special amphibious engineers, General Craig's 1st Air-Ground Provisional Marine Brigade and the 1st Cavalry Division. His priority, however, was to have the complete 1st Marine Division to spearhead the amphibious invasion. He was prepared to contribute his one remaining reserve in Japan, the 7th Infantry Division. One other division, the 3rd Infantry, should be allocated to reserve. However, before the Joint Chiefs of Staff were prepared to activate the Infantry and Marines – and the shipping needed to take them to Korea – they required more information about the precise location of the operation and the planning needs it generated. So there was no chance of implementing 'Bluehearts' on 22 July. MacArthur therefore recast his plan and described his new scheme as an amphibious landing at corps strength behind enemy lines, to destroy the NKPA in conjunction with an Eighth Army attack from the south. The capture of Inchon and Seoul would form the anvil; and, faced by a demoralized NKPA, Walker's Eighth Army would become the hammer. Caught between the two, North Korea's military power would be swiftly annihilated. Not entirely convinced, the Joint Chiefs acceded to MacArthur's requests on 25 July. He could have the Marines and some of their air support and they would depart their base in San Diego in mid-August. Meanwhile, General Edward A. Craig would take his Marine brigade to Pusan. The Marines arrived on 3 August and on 7 August were in action near Masan.

MacArthur's request for the 1st Marine Division required the President to reactivate the Marine Corps Reserve and this had been done on 19 July. Reservists appeared at Camp Pendleton on 31 July, to be joined by battalions of the 2nd Marine Division. By 7 August, after scouring embassies, outposts and distant stations all over the world, the strength of the 1st Division stood at 17, 162. Colonel Lewis B. 'Chesty' Puller came out of retirement to recreate his 1st Marine Regiment, the force he had commanded in the Pacific during the Second World War. The commander of the 1st Marine Division was General Oliver P. Smith who did not learn about the invasion plan until 8 August and did not reach MacArthur's headquarters in the Dai-Ichi building in Tokyo until 22 August.

## OPERATION 'CHROMITE'

On 12 August 1950 MacArthur had informed his amphibious operations staff that the landings would definitely be at Inchon, prompting his gunnery officer to utter the famous remark: 'We drew up a list of every natural and geographic handicap – and Inchon had 'em all!'

The operation would be coded 'Chromite' and was to be treated as a matter of urgency. In his usual imperious style, he informed his staff that problems, wherever they existed, must be solved. Admittedly, if one glanced at the map Inchon seemed a good choice. It was only 25 miles from Seoul. Kimpo airfield and the industrial suburb of Yongdungpo were even closer. His staff's overwhelming problem was the sea approach to Inchon: the tidal range involved was some 32 feet and one of the biggest in the world. The tide rushed in and out of twisting sea channels, saltpans and mud flats. The main sea approaches – Flying Fish Channel (leading to the Salee River) and East Channel – were narrow and easy to block; and it would be simple to lay mines. Perhaps some were there already. To make matters even more difficult, Inchon was protected by the mile wide island of Wolmi-do. Once the assault troops had overcome all of these hazards they would have to attack beaches protected by extensive sea walls some of which were 14 feet high. There was also a garrison at Inchon, the NKPA 226th Marine Regiment, and coastal defence batteries equipped with 76mm guns. Seoul was a well-defended city. It was, after all, the headquarters of the NKPA. Its 18th Rifle Division and the local city regiment totalled 13,600 troops. Marine fighter-bombers would have to face the firepower of the 19th Anti-Aircraft Artillery Regiment with its heavy and light AA guns and the deadly 12.7mm machine-guns. Moreover, there was a dedicated commander in charge of defence, Brigadier Wan Yong, who had been trained by the Chinese People's Liberation Army. General Charles Willoughby, MacArthur's intelligence officer, was confident that the coastal defence batteries could be swiftly destroyed so that the invasion fleet would not be subject to heavy calibre gunfire. His major anxiety was the whereabouts of the 105th Tank Division for this could threaten the success of the projected landings. He did not know that this division had regrouped in Kumchon where it was re-equipping with new T-34/85 tanks, SU-76 self-propelled guns and armoured personnel carriers.

MacArthur had also given his team a date: D-Day would be 15

September 1950. This was when high tide in Inchon was at its maximum 33 feet, just enough for the big landing craft to make their run into the beaches. But on that day the morning high tide came just before 0700 hours. If the assault went in then, the invasion fleet would have to make its approach before sunrise; and the evening high tide was just after 1900 hours when it would be dark again. Moreover, the planners were not absolutely sure about their calculations as they depended on somewhat ancient Japanese and American intelligence sources. Fortunately, they found a former warrant officer who had been based on Wolmi-do and had once organized the movement of army boats operating in Inchon harbour. He was Mr W. R. Miller and was living in Yokohama. He said he was keen to come along to use his expertise to help solve the problems that beset the invasion planners. They were also short of recent aerial photographs and the USS *Valley Forge* offered two of its Corsairs equipped for photo-reconnaissance. The pilots had to fly low – 200 feet or less – but they brought back hundreds of photographs. To interpret these several Air Force experts were flown to Japan from the photo-laboratory in Dayton, Ohio. MacArthur was fortunate that he had as his head of amphibious warfare planning Rear Admiral James H. Doyle, a remarkably competent staff officer. He had to cope with the associated problems of weapons, ammunition and specialist assault equipment, and the shipping to transport these matériels. No one could accuse the United States of being ready to fight an amphibious campaign in the summer of 1950! Again, luck smiled upon the planners. During 1945–6 squads of Marines had salvaged everything they could find in the Pacific War theatre. Battered jeeps, amphibian tractors (amtracs), tanks, trucks, amphibious trucks (DUKWs), artillery and personal weapons were all brought back to the United States and restored with loving care at the Marine Corps Supply Depot in Barstow, California. From this Aladdin's cave of military hardware emerged much of the equipment with which the Marines would go to war in 1950.

MacArthur still had to convince the Joint Chiefs that Operation 'Chromite' was viable. General Collins, Admiral Sherman and the Air Force General Edwards came to Tokyo on 20 August. Three days later they discussed 'Chromite' in detail; MacArthur pointed out to Sherman the problems of the sea approach to Inchon. Sherman was confident the Navy could manage that. Then the Joint Chiefs flew back to Washington and on 28 August they approved 'a turning movement' using amphibious forces 'on the west coast of Korea in the vicinity of Inchon in the event that enemy defences at Inchon prove ineffective, or at a favourable beach south of Inchon if one can be located.' So MacArthur finally had their approval – and barely 17 days left before 'Chromite' was to begin.

The plan was beginning to take shape. As Wolmi-do masked Inchon from the attackers, it would have to be captured just after sunrise on the morning flood tide. The usual shipping would be too slow and under-powered to cope with the tidal flow at night. Therefore four high speed vessels escorted by destroyers and rocket ships would carry the 3rd Battalion of the 5th Marines to Wolmi-do to land on Green Beach. They would secure Wolmi-do and then support two Marine battalions tasked with the main Inchon landings on Red and Green Beaches that evening. For this assault at least 47 LSTs would be needed – but the Navy could provide a mere 17. The other 30 would come from those that had been loaned to the Japanese for ferry work between their islands. Ironically, the 5th Marines knew nothing about these plans. At the time they were engaged in a desperate defence of the Pusan Perimeter; as were the 1st Regiment Korean Marine Corps who were scheduled to follow the initial landings and secure Inchon. The 1st Division Marine commander at Inchon was to be Major General Oliver Prince Smith, a veteran of the New Britain and Okinawa campaigns. Daunting objectives faced Smith and his marines: capture Wolmi-do, seize Inchon, secure the beachhead, take Kimpo airfield, cross the Han River, drive the NKPA out of Seoul and finally take up defensive positions east of the city. They could not accomplish this alone. Behind them would come the ROK marines and the US infantry that constituted the rest of X Corps.

The overall planner for 'Chromite' was MacArthur's Chief of Staff, General Almond. During 1945 he had commanded the all-black 92nd Division, an appointment that had not enhanced his military reputa-tion; nor had his refusal to take up the post of military attaché in Moscow during May 1946. He then transferred to Japan where he lived with his family and, at the outbreak of the Korean War, had been with MacArthur when they had witnessed the devastation of Seoul. MacArthur's response to the war left Almond with the task of con-verting the peacetime Eighth Army in Japan into a fighting force for Korea. His four divisions – the 1st Cavalry, the 7th, 24th and 25th Infantry – were at that time seriously understrength and ill-equipped. He was now also Chief of Staff to the United Nations Command and one of the first to learn, as MacArthur's confidante, of the Supreme Commander's intention to invade Inchon. This was why he was so shocked when General Walker suggested that the NKPA summer offensive might force him to shift his HQ from Taegu to Pusan. He knew that MacArthur's plans would be ruined if the NKPA were not contained along the Pusan Perimeter; and promptly advised MacArthur to fly to Taegu to put backbone in the wavering General. It was there that MacArthur, in front of Almond, told Walker that Pusan must never become the Far East Command's Dunkirk.

Almond's remit was to create a unique corps for the attack on Inchon – initially known to the planners as Force X. He swiftly renamed it X Corps, a name well-known in Japan as it had not only conquered Leyte and Mindanao but had occupied Japan until it was deactivated in January 1946. MacArthur remembered it fondly and when Almond asked him the name of the general who would command X Corps at Inchon MacArthur had replied, 'It's you.' X Corps was generously allocated two reinforced divisions: the 1st Marine Division (coded 'Western' and commanded by General Oliver P. Smith); the 7th Infantry (coded 'Bayonet' and under General David G. Barr); the back-up division was 3rd Infantry (coded 'Kaiser' and led by General Robert H. Soule). ROK I Corps had a crucial role: it composed the Capitol and 3rd Divisions plus the 326th Infantry Regiment and 1st ROK Marines (coded 'Rogers' and commanded by General Kim Paik Il). X Corps also had its own air command and a complete artillery group. Its special signal battalion would have direct contact with Tokyo. With its array of medical units and transport battalions it was indeed a 'miniature army', independent of General Walker's Eighth Army.

During 10–12 September 1950 the multinational invasion fleet of 261 ships – including the fast carriers USS *Valley Forge* and *Philippine Sea* of Task Force 77 – all under the command of Admiral Doyle, steamed from many ports into heavy seas, the legacy of typhoons *Jane* and *Kezia*. The 5th Marines had sailed from Pusan, the 1st Marine Division from Kobe, the 7th Infantry from Yokohama. Doyle took his orders at sea from Vice Admiral Arthur D. Struble, so that at this stage of the operation both MacArthur and Almond were in effect temporarily redundant aboard the amphibious command ship *Mount McKinley*. Two facts not generally known to the groups of newspapermen and special correspondents aboard *Mount McKinley* were that Japanese sailors crewed the Marines' LSTs; and that Japanese dock labourers were aboard the transports to help run the docks at Inchon. Ahead of the main fleet seven destroyers were testing the North Korean defences. They ploughed through Flying Fish Channel, skirted a minefield and drew fire from the hidden coastal defences. Once the enemy gun flashes were located the battery sites were destroyed by air attack and shells from escorting cruisers. At the same time Wolmi-do, Seoul and Kimpo were under constant air and sea attack: Corsairs carried double loads of napalm, flying from the decks of two light carriers, the USS *Sicily* and USS *Badoeng Strait*; the new Panther jets lashed every North Korean airfield they could find; aircraft from HMS *Triumph* launched diversionary raids on Kunsan where Royal Marines from 41 Commando landed with a US Special Operations Company to engage the enemy and convince him that Kunsan was the target of the invasion fleet.

The 3rd Battalion, 5th Marines, would spearhead the invasion and they were packed into three specially converted high-speed destroyers, the USS *H A Bass*, *Diachenko* and *Wantuck*. Their tanks and all the specialist equipment for the assault were aboard the Landing Ship Dock *Fort Marion*. Ahead of them were three destroyers – survivors of the earlier dash through Flying Fish Channel which had taken the fire of the North Korean coastal batteries. Bringing up the rear of the assault group were the Landing Ships, Medium (Rocket) 401, 403 and 404. The big cruisers, Admiral Higgins' USS *Toledo* and Admiral Struble's USS *Rochester*, plus Britain's HMS *Jamaica* and HMS *Kenya*, were in the rear to give the Marines fire-support. Just before sunrise on D-Day, 15 September 1950, the invasion force was in position. Landing craft filled with marines circled in Second World War-style less than 2,000 yards offshore, awaiting the order to land. As the first rays of light flickered, Corsairs roared across the water, rocketing and strafing Wolmi-do, followed by the crashing bombardment of the naval guns. At 0615 and under the cover of thousands of 5-inch rockets, the Marines began their run to Green Beach where the first waves landed without opposition at 0633. Backed by M-26 Pershing tanks, flame-throwers and bulldozers, the Marines raised Old Glory at the top of Radio Hill and swept down to secure So Wolmi-do, the island's southernmost point. Enemy fire was slight – very few NKPA troops had survived the devastation poured upon Wolmi-do. By 1115 the 3rd Battalion had captured the island at a cost of 17 wounded. Six hours later the 5th Marines were ready to hit Red and Blue Beaches and take Inchon.

The plan was to seal off all land access to Inchon to prevent NKPA reinforcements from entering it. Task Force 77, expanded by the arrival of the fast carrier USS *Boxer*, used its jets and Skyraiders to harass the the highway into the city. By now the NKPA was recovering

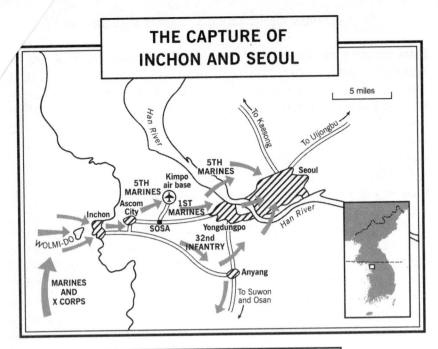

# THE CAPTURE OF INCHON AND SEOUL

Han River

To Kaesong

To Uijongbu

5 miles

5TH MARINES

Seoul

Kimpo air base

5TH MARINES

Ascom City

1ST MARINES

Inchon

SOSA

Han River

WOLMI-DO

Yongdungpo

32nd INFANTRY

MARINES AND X CORPS

Anyang

To Suwon and Osan

# MACARTHUR'S LAST GREAT STRATEGIC VICTORY

NORTH KOREA

SEA OF JAPAN

38°

YELLOW SEA

Amphibious landing at Inchon

Seoul

Inchon

Suwon

Osan

Eighth Army link up with X Corps

Marine landing at Kongsoon beaches and Robb Island on 12/13 September, 2 days before the Inchon landing

Chonan

Taejon

SOUTH KOREA

Taegu

Pusan

Eighth Army break-out from the Pusan perimeter

From Japan

## Key

← Eighth Army advances

--- Pusan perimeter

--- Route taken by Inchon Invasion Force

100 miles

from its surprise, for it had never believed that the UN would approach via the Flying Fish Channel. It was rapidly forming new infantry battalions in Seoul, bringing in the 70th Regiment from its base at Suwon and diverting the well-equipped 18th Division (then assigned to reinforce NKPA units in the Naktong theatre) to Seoul. But they would all be too late to save Inchon for H-hour (the landing) was scheduled for 1730 that afternoon.

On Red Beach a high seawall formed the first obstacle but by using their scaling ladders the marines went over the top and sliced through the first enemy trenches. They immediately headed for Inchon's high ground: Cemetery Hill, Observatory Hill and British Consulate Hill. Enemy squads with grenades and burp guns were everywhere and the fighting was intense. Bunkers and pillboxes had to be stormed and grenaded and the capture of Cemetery Hill cost eight dead marines and a lot of wounded, some hit by friendly fire from the landing ships. Not until midnight did Lt Col Raymond L. Murray's 5th Marines achieve all their objectives. Simultaneously, Col 'Chesty' Puller's 1st Marine Regiment was attacking Blue Beach south of Inchon prior to an advance on Yongdungpo and Seoul. His first three assault waves arrived in amtracs under cover provided by Skyraiders from Task Force 77. They gained the beachhead but the remaining 22 waves, beset by poor visibility caused by mingling rain and smoke plus an unexpected cross-current, suffered from faulty navigation and landed in rather jumbled fashion on the crowded shore. Behind the assault troops came a total of 13,000 troops with all their battle equipment – a triumph of organization.

Between them, the Marine units had achieved all of their tasks on time with minimum casualties: 22 killed and 174 wounded. They had captured Wolmi-do and Inchon and had guaranteed the success of 'Chromite.' MacArthur and his cohort of news correspondents came ashore on 17 September and the Supreme Commander presented Silver Stars to Colonel Puller, Lt Col Murray and General Craig. Kimpo and Seoul were the next targets but before the advance began Almond enjoyed a celebratory dinner with MacArthur aboard *Mount McKinley*. There an exuberant MacArthur rewarded him with the Silver Star for his fearless leadership and the successful execution of Operation 'Chromite.' The medal was America's second highest award for bravery and occasioned a great deal of comment.

## EXPANDING THE BRIDGEHEAD

It was now vital to expand the bridgehead as quickly as possible. The Marines fanned out either side of Inchon's main road leading to Seoul while behind them the 1st ROK Marine Regiment flushed out snipers and hidden machine-gunners. Along this road M-26 tanks encountered the first NKPA infantry-laden T-34s spearheading a series of assaults. Tank after tank 'brewed up' when hit by the Pershings' 90mm shells while the unprotected NKPA infantry were wiped out. Other attempts to penetrate the city were blocked by Marine ambushes and in one of these Corporal Okey Douglas stalked and destroyed two T-34s with his rocket launcher. But resistance would harden now that advance parties of the NKPA 18th Division were fortifying the hills outside Yongdung-po. Nevertheless, the Marine units swept through Ascom City and after a brief firefight captured the 6,000-foot runway at Kimpo. On 18 September they entered Sosa but were badly mortared by the NKPA; and then went on to take the high ground outside Yongdungpo so that they could have their first glimpse of the South Korean capital, Seoul.

Meanwhile, General Almond had become obsessively jealous of the Marines' achievements and as X Corps commander was determined to bring in elements of the Army's 7th Infantry Division. The 32nd Infantry – 57 per cent of whom were South Korean 'buddies' – were the first to come ashore. A distinguished regiment known as 'The Queen's Own', it was followed by the 31st Infantry known as 'The Polar Bears' who in 1942 had surrendered to the Japanese at Bataan. But the Marines remained in the lead and by 19 September were in position to cross the Han River. The first attempt at a river crossing in amtracs was disastrous but the second, early in the morning of 20 September, succeeded and took the 5th Marines and the 2nd ROK Marine Battalion plus their tanks into the outskirts of Seoul. Its capture would not be easy. NKPA units were entrenched in shops, houses, behind barricades and in the hills.

As the 5th Marines crossed the Han River and Colonel Puller's 1st Marines were attacking Yongdungpo, the 32nd Infantry moved south to cut the Seoul-Suwon road. On Almond's orders – he was eager to link up with Walker's Eighth Army – General Barr dispatched a reconnaissance unit which drove through Suwon and set up a road-block to the south. Behind them came the 73rd Tank Battalion and it was this that collided with the NKPA 105th Tank Division that intelligence chief General Willoughby had 'lost.' X Corps had now created a wide fighting front and Almond jeeped along all the newly captured roads to keep in contact with his advance troops. It was unusual for a corps commander to regularly visit front-line positions, and Almond was notorious for interfering with battle tactics at company and even platoon level, but the troops respected his concern for their welfare and disregard for his own safety.

On 21 September MacArthur was satisfied that Almond, who as X Corps commander now had absolute authority over the battlefield, would soon capture Seoul. He confided that he was flying back to Tokyo but would return as soon as Seoul had been taken. There he proposed a ceremony in which he would formally reinstate Syngman Rhee as President of a liberated South Korea. Such an act would have an immense effect upon world opinion. Next day, Almond began the battle for Seoul. By 22 September the NPKA forces in Seoul exceeded 20,000 troops, most of whom were ranged against the 5th Marines east of the Han River. MacArthur had warned Almond not to devastate Seoul as he wanted to preserve as much of the city as possible to lend dignity to the planned ceremony with Syngman Rhee. The North Koreans were less eager to preserve the city environment: there were lots of well-built structures ideal for defence and they happily tore up the roadways to build barricades. It took four days for the Marines to clear the complex bunkers west of the city and involved them in some of the toughest close-quarter fighting of the war. Almond was sure that different tactics would succeed and, to the intense annoyance of Marine General Smith, redrew the command lines of X Corps so that the Army had a greater responsibility for capturing the city. He ordered the 7th Infantry Division to cross the Han River and it successfully created a bridgehead on 25 September and advanced on a hill called South Mountain.

Then came an extraordinary development. X Corps informed Smith's command post that the enemy was fleeing to the north of the city. Smith should therefore take advantage of this new situation and launch a major attack to take Seoul. General Smith was astonished: far from retreating, the NKPA was bitterly contesting every yard of western Seoul. But the order came directly from Almond and Smith had to attack. So he cautiously pushed forward that night but encountered fierce resistance from tanks and several hundred infantrymen; while a 32nd Infantry company in the bridgehead was actually overrun by the enemy. Nevertheless, Almond chose to announce late on 25 September that Seoul had been captured. Next day a delighted MacArthur issued a UN communiqué:

> General Headquarters
> United Nations Command
> Public Information Office
> X Corps Communiqué No. 5    1145 26 September 1950
> *Three months to the day after the North Koreans launched their surprise attack south of the 38th Parallel the combat troops of X Corps recaptured the capital city of Seoul . . . Heavy resistance consisting mainly of intense small arms fire from well prepared positions along the streets and in the buildings slowed the advance of the Marine units but steady progress was made during the day and the high ground west and north of the city was secured.*
>   *The 7th Division crossed the Han River in force against moderate resistance and drove forward to capture the 800 ft hill mass called South Mountain . . . By 1400 hours 25 September the military defences of Seoul were broken and the South Korean troops of the Capitol City Regiment began mopping up strong groups of defeated defenders. Reports . . . indicate that the enemy is fleeing to the north-east . . .*
>   *The coordination of air, tank, artillery and infantry fire power made possible the seizure of the enemy's defences in Seoul with minimum casualties.*

According to the Marines, this was somewhat premature. Marine and Army squads were engaged in bitter street clearance battles, constantly under attack from mortars, machine-guns and grenades. Determined suicide bombers ran under tanks with satchel charges; barricades hid deadly anti-tank guns; snipers seemed everywhere. Many marines died or were wounded in this intense and costly fighting, details of which were not released less they contradicted Almond's statement and MacArthur's communiqué. South of the city, where the 31st Infantry were clearing the vital road link between Osan and Suwon, it took three days of heavy fighting against the T-34s of the NKPA 105th Tank Division before the route was secure.

By 27 September the Marines and 7th Infantry had cleared most of Seoul. 32nd Infantry had skirted the city and reported that enemy units were leaving on the road east; while the 7th Marines were pushing north towards Uijongbu. On 28 September Seoul was finally liberated and Almond was now justified in believing that the anvil was secure. In the south General Walker's Eighth Army, MacArthur's 'hammer', was breaking out across the Naktong River. Walker had ordered General Hobart R. Gay, commanding the 1st Cavalry Division, to create a corridor between Taegu and Suwon along which the Eighth Army's armour and support groups could travel to meet up with X Corps. Gay formed a special unit, Task Force Lynch, to head the breakout. On 25 September three Pershing tanks took the lead and these rushed ahead of the main body, covering over a hundred miles between 1200–2200 hours the following day. Amidst a hail of bullets from GIs who thought they were T-34s they made contact with the 31st Infantry just outside Osan on 26 September, followed by L Troop of the 7th US Cavalry on the 27th. The hammer had arrived.

General Walker now had to convert the Eighth Army from its traditional defensive role into an aggressive fighting force. Deprived of his Marines, Walker divided Eighth Army into two corps, I Corps commanded by General Milburn and IX Corps led by General Coulter. Milburn was to follow the route of Task Force Lynch, Coulter was to clear the south-west of NKPA units and associated guerrilla forces and the ROK divisions were to advance up the east coast. First, the crust of NKPA defenders around the Perimeter had to be broken and this involved Eighth Army in numerous bitter engagements.

Britain's 27 Brigade, together with US 5th Cavalry (1st Cavalry Division), were ordered to cross the 300 yard-wide River Naktong south of Waegwan on 16 September and capture Songju. They were under the overall command of General Church of 24th Division; he had succeeded General Dean, now a prisoner-of-war. 27 Brigade succeeded in crossing under heavy fire and were committed to take the high ground flanking the sides of the road to Songju. A platoon from B Company, 1st Middlesex, led by 2/Lt Christopher Lawrence, attacked Plum Pudding Hill. Using their bayonets, the Middlesex reached the summit of Plum Pudding in a first-class platoon attack for which Lawrence received the Military Cross. D Company then advanced up Middlesex Hill and both features were occupied by the battalion at the end of the day, 22 September. Their position was overlooked by Hills 388, known as Songsan, and 282. A Company Argylls captured 282 and C Company tried an attack on Songsan at dawn on 23 September. It was heavily defended and the Argylls were over-exposed once NKPA units began their usual enveloping tactics

against the battalion. Enemy mortars and artillery now began shelling 282, where B and C Companies were now concentrated, causing
many casualties. Anxious to rescue these, Major Kenneth Muir,
battalion 2 i/c, led a hastily organized party of stretcher bearers.
The situation was becoming serious and, on Muir's advice, Lt Col
Neilson, battalion commander, called for an air strike against Hill
388. Major Muir then organized the defence of 282 against increasing enemy attacks.

Air support in the form of three F-51 Mustangs from the 93rd
Bombardment Wing appeared and ignored the recognition fluorescent
panels prominently displayed on Hill 282. The Mustangs hurtled over,
dropping napalm and machine-gunning the Argylls, in the belief they
were the enemy on top of 388. Jellied petroleum spread over the ridge
and down the hillside, engulfing the defenders and the wounded still
prostrate on their stretchers. Ammunition exploded in the holocaust
and the position was abandoned save for a wounded Private West and
the few survivors of his platoon. Muir determined to regain the hilltop
and rescue his soldiers. Armed with a Stengun, he led the charge to the
summit, ran out of ammunition and resorted to a 2-inch mortar before
dying from wounds. Neilson gave permission for the survivors on 282 to
withdraw: 13 Argylls were dead, including 2/Lt M. D. W. Buchanan,
cousin of the murdered patrol commander, Captain C. N. A. Buchanan;
72 were burned or wounded. The US Air Force was mortified by what
had happened and the 93rd generously subscribed to the families of the
dead and wounded. Major Muir's bravery was recognized by the
posthumous award of the Victoria Cross.

After this disaster 27 Brigade moved up to the Songju-Waegwan area
behind the front line. There had been no attempt by the NKPA to
exploit the Argylls' withdrawal from Hill 282 and on 30 September the
brigade was strengthened by 3rd Battalion, the Royal Australian
Regiment commanded by Lt Col C. H. Green DSO. The Australians
had arrived from Tokyo on the American transport *Aiken Victory* and
had come up to Taegu from Pusan on the usual uncomfortable train. 27
Brigade was now the 27 British Commonwealth Brigade – and,
temporarily, all the Argylls and Australians had to sacrifice for their
new association was their headgear! The Argylls' Balmorals were
replaced by knitted stocking caps and the equally famous slouch hats
of the Australians gave way to US pile caps, though a few devotees
retained their originals. On 5 October the brigade was ordered north
and flew from Taegu airstrip to Kimpo in DC-4 Skymasters and C-119

Flying Boxcars. On 9 October it assembled at Kaesong, just three miles south of the 38 degree Parallel.

Momentous decisions had been made before their arrival at Kaesong. The great issue was whether the United Nations had the moral and constitutional right to advance beyond the 38 degree Parallel. Was its remit simply to re-establish the *status quo* existing before 25 June 1950? Or should it recommend an advance beyond the 38 degree Parallel in pursuit of its abiding aim of creating a unified democratic Korea? It did pass a resolution (376V) as late as 7 October 1950 when it urged that 'all constituent acts' be taken to create a united Korea. This was assumed to be an endorsement by the United Nations General Assembly of a decision, reached by General MacArthur, President Truman and the Joint Chiefs of Staff, that United Nations Forces would cross the 38 degree Parallel early in October 1950.

General MacArthur had arrived at Kimpo airfield on 29 September. He was met by General Almond and President Syngman Rhee and they drove across the Han River through the battered streets of Seoul to the shell-pocked National Assembly hall. Despite the distant sound of shellfire and the crackle of machine-guns Almond created the illusion of an orderly atmosphere for the moment of MacArthur's triumph. The podium was draped with flags; immaculate military police were everywhere. At noon precisely, MacArthur turned to Syngman Rhee and with dramatic solemnity intoned, 'I am happy to restore to you, Mr President, the seat of your government . . .' He then spoke the Lord's Prayer and it was reported that one war correspondent was so emotionally involved in the proceedings that he not only cabled his newspaper with the text of MacArthur's speech but included the the Lord's Prayer as well. That cost his newspaper an extra 15 cents a word![2]

But the military achievement of General MacArthur had been without parallel. In the space of a fortnight he had destroyed the NKPA as a fighting force in South Korea. He had preserved the Republic of South Korea and was now back at the 38 degree Parallel that the North Koreans had crossed in an unjustifiable act of aggression on 25 June 1950. He had, through the remarkable fighting force that was X Corps, more than compensated for the 'bug out' reputation that had once characterized the Eighth Army earlier in the war. History records that the Inchon landings were undoubtedly the most successful amphibious attacks since 1944 and that they reflected great credit upon American skill at mobilizing a mighty fleet and integrating a successful Marine and Army operation in the face of great natural hazards. The Marines had paid the highest price: 422 killed in action, 2,031 wounded and 6 missing. The Army had lost 106 killed, with 411 wounded and 57 missing. The US Navy had suffered 6 dead, 118 wounded and 2 missing. The ROK Marines had 29 killed and 96 wounded while the South Korean 'buddies' in 7th Division suffered 43 dead and 102 wounded. Approximately 14,000 NKPA soldiers had been killed and 7,000 taken prisoner. Indeed, it had been a great victory.

Now MacArthur was planning a further series of military triumphs. Already he had received a dispatch from President Truman, endorsed by the US Chiefs of Staff, in which his prime duty was defined as the destruction of the North Korean armed forces. He was permitted to use airborne, amphibious and ground forces north of the Parallel to achieve that objective. The only conditions contained in the dispatch (dated 27 September) were that: neither Chinese nor Soviet armies had, by the date of the crossing, occupied North Korea or had announced that they would enter North Korea; nor would UN forces cross into Soviet or Chinese territory or engage in air or naval attack upon such territory. Truman's contingency plan in the event of a Russian and Chinese intervention *after* the UN had crossed the Parallel was that MacArthur should continue to fight for as long as UN resistance had a chance of success.

In response to his President's orders, General MacArthur presented a plan for the destruction of the North Korean armed forces. He would order the Eighth Army to advance up the western coast of North Korea; and he would use X Corps in another major amphibious assault at Wonsan on the east coast of North Korea. The Joint Chiefs of Staff approved this plan on 29 September, the same day that MacArthur was restoring Syngman Rhee to power.

Britain was aware of the general picture. At a Cabinet meeting in Downing Street on 26 September Attlee had mentioned that there was 'general agreement' that MacArthur would have to continue military operations north of the 38 degree Parallel. He felt that it would be politic for British forces to be included but that Britain's contribution should be 'as small as possible.' Two days later he heard from Sir Alvery Gascoigne, head of the UK diplomatic mission in Tokyo, that MacArthur certainly intended to cross the Parallel. Both Attlee and Bevin were concerned that the UN should be clear about its objectives when it entered North Korea, an important point with which Dean

Acheson thoroughly approved. Bevin had the backing of the Americans and Indians to 'give teeth' to the United Nations Commission for the Unification and Rehabilitation of Korea (UNCURK) but this was an issue that barely crossed the mind of General MacArthur. On 30 September Zhou Enlai had spoken on the situation in Korea and defined the United States as China's 'most dangerous foe'. He warned the Americans that the continued exclusion of 500 million Chinese from a UN that, under American direction, violated their interests, would certainly lead to 'broken heads' if it were maintained. Zhou Enlai's words received worldwide coverage on 1 October, the day that MacArthur issued an ultimatum to the Commander-in-Chief, North Korean Forces:

> . . . I as the United Nations Commander-in-Chief, call upon you and the forces under your command, in whatever part of Korea situated, forthwith to lay down your arms and cease hostilities under such military supervision as I may direct . . .

By this time patrols of the 3rd Division of ROK I Corps were cautiously probing a few miles *north* of the 38 degree Parallel. On 1 October several battalions crossed the Parallel followed by the Capitol Division on 3 September. The crossing had been authorized by General Walker at Eighth Army headquarters. Thereafter, any attempt to end hostilities or localize the conflict was doomed to failure. A few US forces were across the parallel on 7 October; on 9 October MacArthur made a final broadcast to Kim Il Sung calling on him to cease hostilities. He stated that a failure to respond would mean that he, MacArthur, would be forced to employ military measures to implement the wishes of the United Nations. Next day Kim Il Sung rejected MacArthur's ultimatum. The ground war would now move into North Korea.

# CHAPTER 4

# The Invasion of North Korea

General MacArthur proposed to capture the North Korean capital of Pyongyang with two invading armies forming a giant pincer designed to envelop the NKPA and force its surrender. The Eighth Army would form one arm of this in the western sector by advancing north from Seoul; X Corps would form the other arm by an amphibious landing at Wonsan and arriving in the North Korean capital from the east. Almond agreed with his commander's plan. He had already experienced how North Korean soldiers defended their high ground when the 7th Marines were attacking Hill 550 south of Uijongbu on 2 October. Accurate North Korean anti-tank guns were holding up the Marines' tank support and the infantry advance stalled. A furious Almond ordered the tanks forward but a spent 45mm shell ricocheted close to the general's jeep and he withdrew from the fray. The incident convinced him that whenever possible it would be wise to avoid high ground held by a determined enemy. He knew that Wonsan's hinterland was reasonably flat, good for armour and the rapid movement of infantry. His well-equipped X Corps would effect a surprise landing and swiftly deploy both tanks and infantry units. With these advantages, X Corps could advance in the valley between the menacing mountain peaks rising above 5,000 feet in the Taebaek Range because the ground and rivers would be frozen. Curiously, little consideration was given at this stage of the planning to the possible effects of a Manchurian-style winter on men and matériel.

## X CORPS MOVES TO WONSAN

General Walker was unhappy with MacArthur's plan. He believed that X Corps should be integrated with his Eighth Army and that it would be more sensible to plan a common advance northwards and bring the war in Korea to a rapid end. Valuable time and energy would be expended in transferring the whole of X Corps from its present location to Wonsan; while his Eighth Army would be starved of men and supplies because of the logistical demands of the Wonsan operation. Walker's assessment was correct. Serious transportation problems held up the proposed eastern campaign for well over a week. Inchon harbour had a very limited capacity and this was the proposed embarkation point for X Corps. It could handle the 1st Marine Division, earmarked to spearhead the Wonsan landings; but it could not simultaneously cope with X Corps' own transport and its huge administrative tail. These elements would have to travel by road and rail from Seoul to Pusan and embark from there, an arrangement that clashed with the Eighth Army's normal replacement and reserve units heading north in the opposite direction!

However, the orders could not be changed and once the 31st and 32nd Regiments assembled in Suwon on 3 October the rest of the 7th Division was ready to trek to the south. Ahead were 350 miles of indifferent South Korean roads, 36 hours of difficult driving plus running the gauntlet of attacks from groups of NKPA men still wandering around unchallenged. One battalion from the 32nd ran into an ambush south of Changju on 6 October; another unit was stranded by enemy roadblocks near Mungyong on 9 October; while the next day a convoy ran into NKPA raiders and lost most of its ammunition trucks as a firestorm of rockets and bullets ripped through the soft-skinned vehicles.

Almond relinquished command of the Seoul-Inchon area on 7 October and left his headquarters at Ascom City on 11 October, a week after the move had begun. As he watched the Marines' Sherman and Patton tanks being loaded on the LSTs at Inchon and made ready to sail to Wonsan, the final road convoys struggled into Pusan having delivered the last of the 13,422 soldiers overland. The 7th Division's rear party of 520 flew from Kimpo to Pusan while Almond, on board *Mount McKinley* once more, prepared his final plans for the second great amphibious operation of the Korean War. It was then that totally unexpected news arrived. While he was supervising the complex invasion operations the ROK Capitol and 3rd Divisions had advanced up the east coast of North Korea and occupied Wonsan; while Walker's Eighth Army had moved north on 9 October and broken through the NKPA defences in front of Pyongyang. Almond's journey to Wonsan, it seemed, had been pre-empted.

Nevertheless, MacArthur and Almond persisted with the original invasion plan. Almond decided to fly directly to Wonsan on 13 October. Here he consulted with General Kim Paik Il whose ROK I Corps was chasing the NKPA into Hamhung and the other great east coast port, Hungnam. He heard with dismay that Wonsan harbour was virtually unapproachable for it was reputed that 3,000 Soviet manufactured sea mines had been sown in the main approach channels. These would have to be swept before the invasion force, having sailed from Inchon on 17 October (850 miles away) could discharge its marines and their equipment. Once again, the Americans depended on the Japanese minesweepers of Admiral Takeo Okubo to clear the harbour and after taking several casualties, including the loss of a minesweeper on 19 October, they enabled the 1st Marine Division to land safely on 26 October (see also Chapter 19). They were pleased by the welcome: Bob Hope was waiting there to entertain them! Almond, however, was by now frustrated by the long delay and he changed the final assault plans for the 7th Division by ordering its transports to divert to Iwon. As a result, he had two bases on the east coast of North Korea plus a small sandy beach at Kojo, linked by rail to Wonsan and guarded by the 1st Battalion of the 1st Marines.

## THE EIGHTH ARMY

To the west, General Milburn was deploying the US I Corps north of the Imjin River. He selected General Gay's 1st Cavalry Division, under whose command Britain's 27 Commonwealth Brigade was operating, to attack up the main Seoul-Pyongyang road and rail links. Their left flank was covered by the US 24th Division while 1 ROK Division guarded the right flank. American reconnaissance patrols crossed the 38 degree Parallel on 7 October although General Gay did not authorize the advance into North Korea until two days later. The 1st Middlesex crossed the Parallel on 11 October followed by the Argylls and 3 Royal Australian Regiment (3 RAR). They began the advance on Pyongyang on 17 October. Their first objective was to take Sariwon and en route aboard their 1st Cavalry Sherman tanks they encountered a roadblock formed by an SU-76 self-propelled gun and a group of 70 NKPA soldiers. The Argylls attacked with the bayonet, killed 42 of the enemy and entered Sariwon with no loss to themselves. Roving North Koreans arrived by the truckload and mistook the Argylls for Russians. Unwittingly, they parked next to brigade transport and, after some innocent fraternization during which headgear and cigarettes were exchanged, someone fired a rifle and a gunfight broke out, followed by the rapid departure of dismayed North Koreans. When Colonel Leslie led his reconnaissance party north of the town he passed through NKPA infantry still trudging along the road with the intention of regrouping inside Sariwon! As the NKPA soldiers joined up with the last of their countrymen escaping from Sariwon they ran into 3 RAR. An NKPA officer called out 'Russki?' Someone then fired a burst from his Owen sub-machine-gun and 1,982 North Koreans surrendered immediately.

On 12 October Pyongyang was captured jointly by the 5th Cavalry and the ROK 1st Division. 27 Commonwealth Brigade arrived two days later and once more moved into the spearhead position. General MacArthur had ordered an airborne landing by the 187th Regimental Combat Team (RCT) in the Sukchon-Sudong area some 30 miles north of Pyongyang. The recently arrived Indian Field Ambulance, all parachute-trained and commanded by Lt Col Rangaraj, dropped with 187th RCT. Airborne landings were rarely adopted during the Korean War. One aim in this case was to cut off retreating NKPA units; another was to rescue American POWs reputedly held nearby; a third may have been to prevent the escape of Kim Il Sung and his government although they had long departed. It was important that 27 Commonwealth Brigade linked up with the paratroopers, a mission that led to a sharp infantry battle in and around Yongyu. About a thousand NKPA troops of the 239th Regiment had been ordered to delay the UN advance and many put up a determined resistance against the Argylls whose explosive charges and phosphorus grenades eventually cleared the town. The Australians and the Argylls began the relief of the paratroopers who were pleased to see them as they had run short of ammunition. The arrival of the Middlesex successfully completed the operation. On 23 October they reached the Chongchon River and, battalion by battalion, crossed it during 25/26 October. The brigade was now fighting a rather lonely war, apart from the

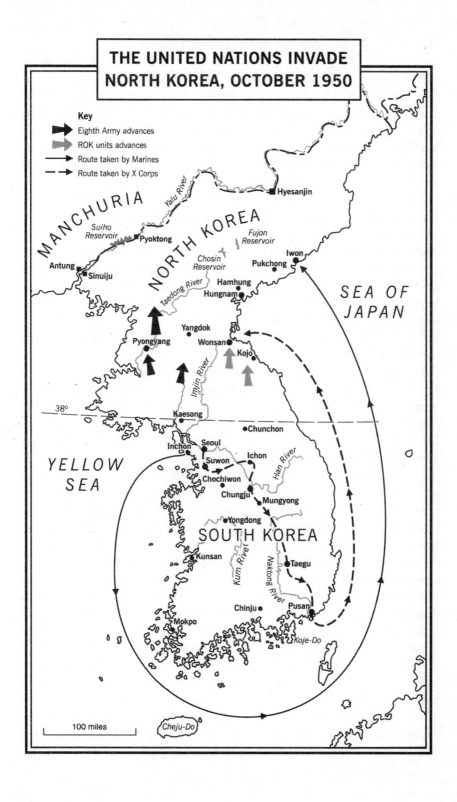

# THE UNITED NATIONS INVADE
# NORTH KOREA, OCTOBER 1950

**Key**

Eighth Army advances

ROK units advances

Route taken by Marines

Route taken by X Corps

MANCHURIA

NORTH KOREA

*Yalu River*

Hyesanjin

*Suiho Reservoir*

Pyoktong

*Fujon Reservoir*

Iwon

*Chosin Reservoir*

Pukchong

Antung

Sinuiju

*Taedong River*

Hamhung

Hungnam

SEA OF JAPAN

Yangdok

Pyongyang

Wonsan

Kojo

*Imjin River*

38°

Kaesong

Chunchon

Inchon

Seoul

Ichon

*Han River*

YELLOW SEA

Suwon

Chochiwon

Chungju

Mungyong

Yongdong

SOUTH KOREA

Kunsan

*Kum River*

*Naktong River*

Taegu

Chinju

Pusan

Mokpo

Koje-Do

100 miles

*Cheju-Do*

faithful tankers of the US 89th Medium Tank Regiment, and meeting sporadic resistance. For example, on 27 October, as C Company Middlesex was advancing up the main road with tanks it came under heavy fire at Kasan near Pakchon; and 8 Platoon, commanded by Lt Leslie Sharpe, was pinned down by a nearby enemy machine-gun that badly wounded two soldiers. Next day they were 4 miles south of Chongju, an important road and rail centre.[1]

It was a very weary brigade that prepared for the attack on Chongju. Apart from a brief relaxation at Kimpo they had been in continuous action since crossing the Naktong. The troops were tired, their equipment was worn and they were ill-equipped to face the icy winds now blowing in from Manchuria. Moreover, the hills around Chongju provided good natural defence and reports from the 'Mosquito' light aircraft spotters located a number of T-34 and SU-76 armoured vehicles. Fortunately, flights of F-80 Shooting Stars and F-51 Mustangs were available to soften up these targets and four of the enemy tanks and one SP gun were destroyed. Under cover of heavy artillery and mortar fire, 3 RAR led the attack but were unable to take all the hills by the end of the day and were twice counter-attacked by NKPA units during the night. The Australians had anticipated this and their artillery lashed the enemy infantry. In the morning, 150 North Koreans lay dead in front of the Australian lines. The Argylls and Middlesex pushed forward and found Chongju deserted. They occupied the town and remained there as the US 21st Regimental Combat Team passed through to take the lead north en route to the Yalu River where elements of the 7th ROK Division were now encamped, close to the town of Chanju.

As dusk fell an enemy armoured vehicle fired from long-range and one of its high-velocity shells exploded outside the tent where the Australian CO, Lt Col Green, was sleeping. Badly wounded by a shell splinter, Colonel Green was rushed to a MASH (Mobile Army Surgical Hospital) at Ansu where he died. Brigadier Coad and 3 RAR were devastated by the loss of an exceptionally brave and skilful commander. However, the capture of Chongju had been a remarkable success, endorsed by General Gay who signalled Brigadier Coad to congratulate him on a 'splendid and sensational' thrust into enemy territory, dealing the NKPA a 'devastating blow'. Next day, 31 October, the Middlesex were ordered north to Taechon in support of the advancing US 24th Division. As they arrived in Taechon the inhabitants presented them with two captured enemy soldiers: one was North Korean, the other Chinese.

After racing through Chongju, the American 21st RCT followed the line of the main coastal road running due west and headed for Namsi-dong, close to the Yalu Estuary. This had been selected as the next objective for the US 24th Division. At the same time the US 1st Cavalry Division had left Pyongyang and was moving north. Its 8th Cavalry Regiment went ahead to assist the 6th ROK which had come off badly in a battle fought outside Unsan against NKPA *and Chinese* forces. The 8th Cavalry disposed its three battalions around Unsan covering the somewhat disorganized withdrawal by several ROK infantry regiments. On 1 November the temperature fell well below zero rendering life inside the foxholes almost unbearable, and freezing the nearby paddy fields so that the enemy had endless opportunities to attack this isolated American force. Unsan was only 45 miles from the Yalu and intelligence reported that enemy forces of indeterminate size were moving ahead of them. By then the ROK forces had managed to reform and reoccupy the battlefield near Onjong. After inspecting the enemy dead, the ROK commander, General Paik Sun Yap, reported that he was certain that some of the corpses were Chinese.

The Chinese offensive against US units began during the evening of 8 November 1950. Chinese assault troops first targeted two battalions of the isolated 8th Cavalry at Unsan while other groups moved swiftly through adjacent paddy fields to cut off any American retreat. They swarmed through the town, tossing grenades into American defences and destroying their arms dumps. The Americans were overwhelmed by the speed and ferocity of the attack; while the cacophony of bugles and gongs used to control Chinese units did nothing to boost American morale. The Cavalry decided to break out using their vehicles under cover of darkness. A full moon thwarted their hopes of a surprise escape and revealed that they were driving into a Chinese ambush. The leading truck, its radiator and windshield shattered by Chinese machine-gun fire, swerved and crashed into a ditch. Behind the truck the driver of a towed howitzer braked, jack-knifed and blocked the entire road. Trapped, the rest of the convoy halted. Soldiers jumped out, returning the enemy fire while a US tank tried to bulldoze the stalled vehicles from the roadway. Amidst flashing tracer and exploding grenades, Chinese soldiers dashed to the tank, wrecked its tracks with a satchel charge and set it on fire. A US half-track armed with quadruple .50 Browning machine-guns mowed down the Chinese until it too exploded in flames when its fuel system was hit.

There was nowhere for the cavalrymen to go except back to Unsan, now burning and partly occupied by Chinese troops. Meanwhile, the 8th Cavalry's 3rd Battalion had no idea of the extent of defeat suffered by the other two battalions until Chinese with fixed bayonets charged among them on 1 November. Satchel charges destroyed the American tanks squatting in the vehicle park; the battalion CO, Major Robert J. Ormond, was fatally wounded. When dawn came the Americans were still resisting, joined by survivors of the 1st and 2nd Battalions. US aircraft appeared and began strafing the Chinese positions, thus enabling the cavalrymen to hold out until 5 November. Then the Americans made a second breakout and this time many were captured by the Chinese. For a time it was feared that the 8th Cavalry Regiment had been obliterated, but over the next few days survivors managed to find a way through enemy lines and stumbled into the forward positions of 27 Commonwealth Brigade. Six hundred cavalrymen were dead or missing; nine tanks, twelve howitzers and almost all the regimental transport had fallen into the hands of the Chinese.

The presence of an aggressive enemy force, assumed to be stiffened by Chinese volunteers, presented a great danger to Eighth Army dispositions. If the enemy marched south he could cut the Main Supply Route at Sinanju and threaten all UN troops south of the Chongchon River. General Walker prudently ordered all United Nations forces to fall back to the Chongchon River. The war had taken a new and dangerous turn.

## THE WAKE ISLAND MEETING

Meanwhile, President Truman and General MacArthur had met on Wake Island in the Pacific Ocean to discuss the progress of the war. Truman had briefly considered a visit to Korea to meet the troops fighting there. As President of the United States, he was by the terms of the US Constitution the Commander-in-Chief of the Armed Forces. It was a long trip for the President in those days before jet travel: he left Washington on 11 October and flew to Pearl Harbor's Hickham Air Base via St Louis and Fairfield in California. After crossing the International Date Line he arrived at Wake Island on Sunday 15 October at 0630 hours local time. Several problems were on his mind. He was concerned about the outcome of the US Congressional elections in November; he was due to speak to the UN General

Assembly later in October; and he, a Democrat President, had never met the Republican General MacArthur who seemed to be running the war in Korea with minimal reference to the UN, the Joint Chiefs of Staff or his President. And although Truman was Commander-in-Chief he did not rate a salute from MacArthur when they met, and this rankled.

The meeting went well though Truman was unaware that one of the secretaries, Vernice Anderson, was taking notes on the proceedings. MacArthur assured Truman that the war would be over by Thanksgiving and that the Eighth Army would be home by Christmas; X Corps would remain in Korea for the time being, at least until democratic elections could be held for the whole of Korea. Truman wondered what would happen if the Chinese or the Russians entered the war; after all, Zhou Enlai had already warned that a UN advance into North Korea would provoke a Chinese response. MacArthur was dismissive of both. Certainly, the Chinese might send in 50–60,000 troops but these could be dealt with primarily by UN air supremacy. Possibly the Russians would send in some aircraft but their pilots would hit language difficulties and they certainly were not as well trained as the United States' aircrews. As for Soviet ground troops, he doubted they would be available for combat before Christmas. He assured the President that his plans for the gradual occupation of North Korea and his respect for the sensitivity of both the Soviet and the Manchurian borders would allay any fears expressed by Stalin and Mao Zedong. He would impose constraints: only ROK troops would be stationed along the Yalu River to act as a buffer between China and the UN Command. The Chinese, surely, would not object to that.

Truman was impressed by MacArthur's reading of the military situation and spoke to the American people from the San Francisco Opera House on Monday 16 October, on the eve of the capture of Pyongyang. He stated that there was 'complete unity' between him and General MacArthur as far as the conduct of foreign policy was concerned. He was generous in his assessment of MacArthur and told Americans how lucky they were to have the right man, in the right place at the right time. This apparent adulation convinced MacArthur that he had a free hand in Korea. He had originally thought that a 'MacArthur Line' should be established at roughly 40 degrees North, linking Chongju, Kunuri and Hamhung. Only ROK troops would have been allowed to operate north of that line. But since the Wake Island Conference and Truman's Opera House speech he felt at liberty to change his orders. On 17 October he pushed the 'MacArthur Line' further north to within 40 miles of the Yalu River. On 24 October he removed all restrictions. He would advance to the Yalu. There was now some confusion among the Joint Chiefs of Staff as to whether his discussions with the President justified such actions. But they let the point pass as everyone believed the war was drawing to an end. In fact, General Walker had already intimated that he no longer needed more supplies of ammunition.

## THE ADVANCE OF X CORPS IN THE EAST

In north-east Korea, Almond was not quite so certain. Several NKPA units were approaching his area. Colonel Cho Il Kwon had formed the remnants of the 5th NKPA Division into a fighting force, supported by soldiers trained in mountain guerrilla warfare, the crack 766th Independent Unit. It was this NKPA force, at roughly regimental strength, that encountered the Marines at Kojo during the night of 27/28 October. The Marines' 1st Battalion was widely dispersed along a range of hills outside Kojo. The enemy achieved total surprise and grenaded and bayoneted many Company B marines asleep in their foxholes. The NKPA soldiers were in small groups and difficult to detect but Sgt Clayton Roberts managed to hold back most with his Browning automatic rifle until he too was killed. The surviving marines regrouped, called down mortar support, and watched as the NKPA disappeared into the darkness. Some NKPA stayed inside Kojo until mid-morning but these were driven out by naval gunfire and air bombardment. In the process the town of Kojo was destroyed.

On Almond's left flank General Kim's ROK I Corps was moving into mountainous country as it attempted to seize North Korea's hydro-electric sites. In the lead was the 26th Regiment of the ROK 3rd Division whose soldiers were mainly raw recruits press-ganged off the streets of Taegu. Not all had military uniform; very few had adequate winter clothing essential for their new environment. Following uncharted mountain paths, they blundered into enemy fire and assumed this was a typical shortlived NKPA rearguard action. The 26th continued their advance near Sudong until they came up against aggressive combat troops supported by T-34 tanks and a battery of mortars. The South Koreans retreated, taking with them 16 prisoners. On interrogation, the prisoners claimed to be members of the 370th

Regiment, 124th Chinese People's Liberation Army (PLA) Division. This occurred on 29 October 1950; and it was only two days later that 1st Middlesex reported they had captured their Chinese soldier at Taechon.

When General Kim telephoned Almond about the experience of the 26th Regiment, the American commander did not want to believe the news. After all, MacArthur had promised that no Chinese troops would intervene. Moreover, his intelligence officer, Lt Col Quinn, thought the prisoners might be reinforcements or replacements rather than members of PLA units based in North Korea. Almond therefore decided to inspect them himself. He was not impressed. He was very rude and called them Chinese laundrymen. Nevertheless, he had to admit that they were Chinese, belonged to a heavy mortar unit, and had been in Korea since mid-October. Reluctantly, he informed MacArthur of the Chinese presence. MacArthur showed little sympathy. He insisted that he wanted the Eighth Army infantry, X Corps plus the South Koreans on the Yalu River as quickly as possible. Only then could the United Nations implement democratic elections and unify Korea into a single state. China would then have no answer.

Accordingly, Almond began his suicidal advance north and fanned out his troops so they would pass more easily through the mountain ranges between X Corps and the Yalu. He received reinforcements: two regiments, the 7th and 15th Infantry of the US Army 3rd Division; plus an understrength regiment, the Puerto Rican 65th. They faced a somewhat disconcerting terrain. Distant mountains rose well over 6,000 feet; many mountain tracks were unsuitable for trucks and armoured fighting vehicles. Pungsan, however, was served by a good road and on 31 October the 17th Infantry (7th Division), commanded by Colonel Powell, left Iwon to join up with the ROK Capitol Division at Pungsan. This would be the base for X Corps' first advance to the frontier, 50 miles away. Powell built a defensive perimeter of linked bunkers but during the night NKPA troops forced their way inside ROK defences and began a withering artillery barrage against the assembled UN forces. Covered by machine-gun fire, the NKPA then rushed the American artillery and forced the gun crews to abandon their howitzers. When the gunners tried to regain their weapons the NKPA put down another barrage. Air power saved the Americans and under a hail of rockets, cannon fire and napalm, the NKPA retreated into the mountains.

With Pungsan relatively secure the ROK Cavalry Regiment used its wheeled transport to advance to Songjin and engage the NKPA outside the town of Kilchu. After heavy fighting they captured the town on 5 November and X Corps had a strong base line from which to thrust further north. Colonel Beauchamp's 34th Infantry now reinforced Pungsan, Colonel Maclean's 31st Infantry advanced into the mountains between the Fujon and Chosin reservoirs while Colonel Litzenberg took his 7th Marines by road towards Sudong. They were to discover that rumours of Chinese PLA divisions marching through North Korea were absolutely true. Scores of Chinese machine-gunners were hidden behind boulders on the high ground on each side of the road. Frontal attacks cost the Marines many casualties while air strikes and artillery barrages failed to blunt the PLA defences on the first day. During the second day the rockets, napalm and phophorous shells plus the superb marksmanship of Marine snipers forced the Chinese to retreat to even stronger positions, notably around the Funchilin Pass en route to the Chosin Reservoir.

Under the watchful eye of Marine pilots flying their Corsairs, the Marines moved up the road abandoned by the Chinese in jeeps loaded with recoilless rifles and rocket launchers. Their battle at Funchilin Pass on 6–7 November revealed the shape of things to come as UN forces assaulted defended hill positions: fierce artillery barrages, unrelenting air attack and then the final assault by infantry in the face of a hail of Chinese 'potato-masher' grenades. While this battle progressed, Almond's 3rd Division was landing at Wonsan to protect the roads in the south, all of which were subject to the attention of NKPA raiders. For example, an isolated black unit (the 96th Field Artillery) guarding Yohung was attacked on 5 November. Though reinforced by the 65th Infantry, the 96th were overrun again the next night by NKPA 'joy-riders' driving captured American trucks and creating mayhem wherever they chose. Brave actions such as that of Lt Paul R. Schultz of the 96th who organized resistance against infiltrators, threw grenades and directed fire against the enemy and won a posthumous Distinguished Service Cross, did little to disguise the lack of preparedness of X Corps for the kind of war that was being fought in North Korea.

Almond hurriedly revised his plans and on the advice of General Kim and Generals Barr and Smith, decided to form a closely defended corps perimeter and preserve his foothold in north-east Korea. Then as suddenly as they appeared the Chinese seemed to have vanished. Perhaps there was a chance that X Corps could reach the Yalu after all. First he tried to establish contact with General Walker's Eighth Army. The original plan was for X Corps to strike westwards and help Walker to capture Pyongyang. But as the North Korean capital had already fallen that part of the plan was redundant. Nevertheless, a battalion of the 65th Infantry left Yonghung on 10 November and headed westwards into the mountains while the 7th Marines advanced from the Funchilin Pass and occupied Koto-ri. Next day Almond ordered X Corps to head for the Yalu even though he had made no effective links with the Eighth Army. A patrol aircraft had spotted ROK soldiers who might have been on the right flank of Walker's army but this was never confirmed. So the Marines moved on, uncertain of the opposition they might encounter. By 14 November they had reached Hagaru-ri on the Chosin Reservoir. Next day Colonel Powell's 17th Infantry struggled across the Ungi River and, unopposed, entered Hyesanjin on the Yalu River on 21 November. A delighted Almond flew in to inspect the frozen Yalu. On the other side of the river Chinese sentries appeared to ignore him. So, having reached the frontier, 120 miles away from his main base at Hungnam, Almond's main problem appeared to be the sustenance of his troops as the main supply routes were ice-bound or filled with snow drifts; or, even worse, subject to ambush by NKPA raiders still roaming the mountains. As for the main enemy force, it had simply disappeared.

## THE EIGHTH ARMY ADVANCE

Even earlier, this had been General Walker's experience in the western sector. While the 8th Cavalry Regiment was trying to escape from Unsan, he prepared to strengthen his flanks by sending the ROK 7th and 8th Divisions to the east and ROK 1st Division to the west. Behind the line, he held the US 2nd and a regiment of the 24th in reserve. At the 'sharp end' the Middlesex were holding Pakchon while the Argylls and 3 RAR were to the west of the Chongchon. Theirs was a confused situation, with large numbers of refugees approaching their positions and frequent small-scale Chinese attacks around the town. But as the remnants of the 8th Cavalry Regiment were withdrawing south the brigade had to hold Pakchon to succour the Americans who were passing through. On 5 November the Chinese were attacking once more and, in an absence of orders from Divisional HQ, 27 Commonwealth Brigade used its initiative and moved to better defensive positions around Pakchon. This unexpected deployment caused more confusion and battalions occasionally fired on one another in error. Fortunately, 77 Squadron RAAF were now based at Pohang and for the first time were able to give direct support to British and Australian soldiers. The Chinese suffered severe losses in this engagement but not sufficient to deter their offensive. Inexplicably, at some time during the night of 5/6 November, the Chinese mysteriously withdrew. During 6 November similar reports came in from Eighth Army's western and central sectors: the enemy had disengaged.

General Walker had no accurate intelligence regarding the strength or purpose of the Chinese forces that had been operating in Korea – the so-called 'dual enigma'. It was assumed that they were either 'volunteers' or regular troops screening other Chinese units still in Manchuria. If there were, as some said, 30–60,000 Chinese troops in North Korea they were still outnumbered by the Eighth Army and its ever-increasing reinforcements. But now they had vanished. Was this the moment to seek a cease-fire and thus bring to an end the war in Korea?

## BRITAIN PROPOSES A BUFFER ZONE

For sometime Britain had hoped that an opportunity such as this would present itself. The British wished to promote the idea of a neutral buffer zone across Korea to separate the belligerents. This was not to be seen as a sign of weakness or vacillation on the part of the British government; nor was it a reduction in the support Britain was giving to American policies. After all, Britain had sponsored the UN resolution of 7 October backing President Truman's decision to cross the 38 degree Parallel, defeat the North Koreans and hold free elections to create a unified Korea. But it was concerned that British troops should not approach the Yalu River frontier and thus clash with either the People's Republic of China or the Soviet Union – or both. The US Chiefs of Staff assured the British that the 27 Commonwealth Brigade would stop 30 miles from the Yalu; and, as we have seen, they advanced no further than Chongju, 40 miles from the river. The battlefield appearance of Chinese forces, though they rapidly drove defeated Eighth Army forces back to the Chongchon, was remarkably brief: from 26

October to the night of 5/6 November, when they vanished into the North Korean mountains.

Britain's Foreign Secretary, Ernest Bevin, was in constant contact with Britain's ambassador Sir Oliver Franks in Washington and by 10 November he was prepared to state in a secret memorandum to the Cabinet that he believed the time was appropriate to complete the UN operations in Korea, withdraw the troops and leave to UNCURK the task of carrying out the 'political and economic rehabilitation' of Korea. To placate the Chinese, Bevin felt that some sort of 'safety belt' should be established along the frontiers. He already had the private support of Sir Keith Officer, the Australian representative at the UN, for a 20-mile wide buffer zone along the Yalu River. Details of this idea had leaked out in the American Press and had drawn caustic observations from General MacArthur in Tokyo that British policy in 1950 was comparable with Chamberlain's appeasement of Germany in 1938! In fact MacArthur was unaware that it was the US Secretary of State, Dean Acheson, who had originally suggested the buffer zone the day before Bevin's Cabinet memorandum. Further progress seemed possible when Sir Oliver Franks cabled the Foreign Office on 11 November to say that the Americans were discussing the idea seriously.

After this and after studying the recommendations of the British Chiefs of Staff on 13 November, Bevin was certainly encouraged to spell out his idea in more detail. On 14 November he told Franks that he had a new scheme to present to the UN Security Council: a demilitarized area, running approximately from Chongju to Hungnam, set upon a temporary basis prior to the unification of Korea. He chose this line as it ran along the narrow 'neck' of Korea. It was some 150 miles long compared with Yalu frontier of 400 miles. The demilitarized zone would be the area north of this line – a huge increase over the idea of buffer zone 20 miles wide. Whether he appreciated that X Corps' 7th Division had already begun landing at Iwon on General Almond's express orders is uncertain. Iwon was 100 miles north-east of the proposed demilitarized line at Hungnam.

Franks gently poured cold water on the scheme. He told Bevin that the Americans were losing interest because they could not fathom the precise intentions of the Chinese. They had no direct contacts with Beijing and, of course, the People's Republic of China had no representation in the General Assembly or in the Security Council. Dean Acheson favoured General MacArthur's next plan to continue an all-out advance to the Yalu as there seemed to be no diplomatic alternative to military action. So while he sympathized with Bevin's ideas for a buffer zone, he had to concede that there were many in the US State Department and in the military who believed that the concept would unnecessarily constrain MacArthur in Korea. The real constraint, of course, was MacArthur's decision to resume the offensive in Korea on 24 November, the day after Thanksgiving. He told Washington on 18 November of his intention to 'probe' north of Chongju. No-one could suggest reasons why this was an unwise policy. Undoubtedly there were Chinese still hidden in the North Korean mountain ranges but their lack of activity since 6 November discounted any view that they were preparing to attack the UN forces. Moreover, it was known (through a leak provided by Katz-Such, the Polish delegate to the UN) that China would only agree to any sort of buffer zone if it were linked to the issue of Taiwan's membership of the Security Council. The United States was certainly not prepared to disown Taiwan or withdraw its Seventh Fleet from the Taiwanese waters. The Americans were by now convinced that China was more interested in driving United Nations forces out of Korea but were unsure as to how far the Chinese would go in backing up their intentions. So the Americans offered talks with the Chinese if they would come to the United Nations Security Council. They agreed to come on 21 November; so Acheson urged Bevin not to raise the issue of a buffer zone until after this date.

So began the extraordinary story of the visit of a Chinese delegation to the United Nations Security Council. As they stopped over in Prague to give an impassioned account of the purpose of their mission they did not arrive in Washington until 24 November – the starting date for MacArthur's new offensive. There were nine delegates, including their leader, Ambassador Wu Xiuquan, all charged with condemning the United States and the United Nations for their actions before and during the Korean War. On 28 November Wu addressed the United Nations precisely when its forces in Korea were suffering new defeats at the hands of the Chinese People's Volunteers. Wu's anti-American resolutions were predictably vetoed by the United States on 30 November and a week later the US persuaded the General Assembly to condemn Chinese aggression in North Korea. The Chinese delegation thereupon walked out of the UN. They would not return until 21 years later.

Events swiftly consigned the idea of a buffer zone to permanent obscurity though the notion of a 'demilitarized zone' would be at the centre of the final armistice agreement. But as that would not occur until July 1953, the failure of the British diplomatic peace effort during October–November 1950 meant that the war would continue and that many thousands, servicemen and civilians alike, would lose their lives in the unhappy peninsula of Korea.

# CHAPTER 5

# China Defeats the United Nations

## THE CHINESE BATTLE PLAN

Hidden in the mountain ranges of North Korea were the Chinese People's Volunteers (CPV), a euphemism for those elements of the People's Liberation Army (PLA) that China had assembled to defeat General MacArthur's United Nations forces. The PLA had been formed by Lin Biao in 1948 and it had campaigned successfully against the Chinese Nationalist forces led by Jiang Jieshi (Chiang Kai-Shek). It had liberated Manchuria during 1948 and captured Beijing in 1949. The Chinese People's 'Volunteers' had secretly arrived in North Korea following a series of decisions reached by General Zhu De, Commander-in-Chief, People's Liberation Army, and his senior generals during a conference in September 1950. There, General Peng Dehuai, Commander-in-Chief of the CPV, had outlined the weaknesses of both the NKPA and the CPV. The NKPA had suffered about 40 per cent losses, equivalent to 50,000 men killed. However, they had been relatively well-equipped by the Soviet Union prior to June 1950. This contrasted with the PLA, operating as it did with matériels captured mainly from the Japanese in 1945 and from the defeated Nationalist armies during 1947–9. Trucks and armoured vehicles were worn out. Most had been cannibalized to keep a few hundred vehicles on the road, artillery was in short supply, radios at company and platoon level were largely non-existent. But the PLA had over five million men under arms capable of fighting under the hostile conditions characteristic of the Korean peninsula. Peng therefore suggested that Chinese intervention in Korea should at first be limited: inflict a quick defeat on the Americans, make them reconsider their policies and force their withdrawal. If this ploy should fail, then launch a full-scale offensive against the United Nations.

Great heed was paid to the words of General Peng Dehuai. He came from a rich peasant family in Hunan, itself a mark of social status in pre-communist China. He had been a brigade commander in the 1920s during Jiang Jieshi's famous Northern Expedition against the warlords through 1923–7 but had switched sides and joined Mao Zedong in 1927. Thereafter, he opposed the Nationalists, fought the Japanese and distinguished himself as one of China's leading military tacticians. Technically, Lin Biao was commander of the CPV but he was in poor health and his judgment was not trusted. Consequently, General Peng acted as the effective commander of the CPV, a position confirmed in the Spring of 1951.

Towards the end of the conference, news arrived that the Americans had landed at Inchon and were advancing on Seoul. Peng agreed that it was time to assemble the CPV, march across the Yalu and then hide in the mountains to await the arrival of the unsuspecting Americans. On 14 October the first elements of the CPV – the 334th Regiment, 112th Division, 38th Field Army – crossed the Yalu at Andong. The crossing site was chosen because of the 3,000-foot rail and vehicle bridges constructed by the Japanese. Both had suffered from US bomber raids and the rail bridge was suspect. Chinese engineers had converted it into a second vehicle bridge and eventually three Field Armies (38th, 39th, 40th) would cross here, together with three supporting divisions from the 41st Field Army. Together, these formations composed the Thirteenth Army Group commanded by General Li Tianyu. His task was the oppose the US Eighth Army. Further east, troops of the 42nd Field Army slogged into North Korea via the 1,400-foot rail bridge at Manpojin. Their mission was to hold Kanggye, the temporary seat of Kim Il Sung's government, and to act as a stop to ROK troops advancing up the east coast. The Chinese were aware of the American plan to land X Corps somewhere along the east coast and wished to protect the vital hydro-electric stations fed by the Suiho Reservoir. They were preparing two more Field Armies, the 50th and 66th, to advance from Sukchon; while the 20th, 26th and 27th, reinforced by divisions from the 30th Field Army, would cross in November using the entry points at Manpojin and Singalpajin. These new forces composed the Ninth Army Group commanded by General Song Shilun. Even though Chinese formations were smaller than their British or American equivalents, the total Chinese commitment in North Korea during October–November 1950 amounted to 380,000 men.

Once in North Korea the Chinese took to the mountains, moving cross-country at night, hiding by day on the hillsides in skilfully camouflaged tents or tucked away in innocent-looking villages. Their brown uniforms matched the prevailing colour of the Korean environment – brown hills, brown villages – and this made the troops difficult to detect. US reconnaissance aircraft rarely concentrated their cameras on the high ground. Their main interest was always the roads and the Chinese avoided these wherever possible. Moreover, the Chinese soldiers were unimpeded by heavy equipment such as field artillery. Rocket launchers and mortars were their mainstay, though compared with the Americans they had relatively few of these. Manchurian coolies carried the ammunition and food. Approximately 500,000 of these followed the Chinese Field Armies. The greatest strength of the Chinese lay in their tactics: concealment and surprise. From their hiding places they could emerge at will, deliver a telling blow and then vanish. Peng Dehuai was confident that the Americans knew nothing of his army's disposition. His headquarters had carefully monitored US radio traffic and found no signs of reaction to the Chinese moves. This was proved by the totally unexpected appearance of the 39th Field Army at Unsan and the Chongchon River early in November and the shattering effect it had upon American forces there. Unsan had been an unqualified disaster for the Americans and a great victory for the Chinese. At the Chongchon River the US 19th Infantry Regiment had swiftly 'bugged out', though the resistance put up by 27 Commonwealth Brigade and its doughty US 61st Field Artillery Battalion had in turn surprised the Chinese. When the battle ended – and the 3rd Royal Australian Regiment (3 RAR) had held their ground against the Chinese – the enemy simply vanished into the mountains and the United Nations forces were left wondering precisely what sort of foe was facing them. The tactics so far adopted by the enemy were inexplicable. There was no attempt to hold the ground he had captured during the conflict; and as there was no tangible 'front line' it was impossible to gauge his strength and whereabouts.

## MACARTHUR'S EIGHTH ARMY
## OCTOBER–NOVEMBER 1950

General MacArthur was not much concerned. He agreed that Chinese supporters of the NKPA had unexpectedly confronted his advance forces. He agreed their appearance had been a surprise. But now they had vanished, having failed to follow up their local victories. On the advice of Willoughby, his senior intelligence officer, he was inclined to the view that 180,000 Chinese 'volunteers' might be operating inside North Korea. He had little regard for their fighting qualities and was ignorant of General Peng Dehuai's distinguished military career. He was confident that his own expanding military forces would be victorious. In fact, he was prepared to say that the troops would be 'home for Christmas.'

MacArthur certainly had some impressive reinforcements. Eighth Army's 2nd and 24th Divisions had plenty of replacements and updated equipment. There were three ROK divisions on the central front. In the east, X Corps' 1st Marine Division and the Army's 7th Division had made excellent headway and more men and matériel were arriving daily at Wonsan and Hungnam. Other members of the United Nations were sending help. Thailand provided an infantry battalion on 7 September; 12 days later an infantry battalion arrived from the Philippines. A Turkish brigade, commanded by Brig. General Tahsin Yazici, reached Korea on 17 October and comprised a Brigade Headquarters and a full Regimental Combat Team that operated as a single fighting unit. General Yazici was an advocate of the armoured fighting vehicle but in Korea his brigade would become renowned for its extraordinary infantry skills. A Dutch infantry battalion was scheduled to arrive on 23 November; a French infantry battalion composed of veteran soldiers was promised for 29 November. South Africa provided a fighter squadron, the famous 'Flying Cheetahs'. They piloted American F-51 Mustangs and these became operational on 5 November. Then in November Britain's long-promised 29 Brigade arrived at Pusan.

The brigade was equipped as Brig. Aubrey Coad's 27 Brigade had never been. Brig. Tom Brodie, brigade commander, brought with him three infantry battalions: the 1st Battalion The Royal Northumberland Fusiliers commanded by Lt Col K.O.N. Foster, the 1st Battalion The Gloucestershire Regiment led by Lt Col J.P. Carne and the 1st Battalion The Royal Ulster Rifles under the command of Lt Col R.J.H. Carson. Their armour support was provided by the 64 Centurion and 6 Cromwell tanks of the 8th King's Royal Irish Hussars commanded by Lt Col J.W. Phillips. C Squadron 7th Royal Tank Regiment, commanded by Major A.J.D. Pettingell, had two Churchill Command tanks, 2 Churchill Recovery tanks and 16 Churchill Crocodile (Flame-thrower) tanks. The 45 Field Regiment, Royal Artillery, brought its 24 25-pounder field guns and six Cromwell Observation Post tanks and the 170th Independent Mortar Battery came with their 18 4.2-inch mortars. There was a Signal Squadron, a counter-mortar radar Troop and an Independent Field Squadron of the Royal Engineers. 29 Brigade also boasted 57 Company, Royal Army Service Corps; 26 Field Ambulance, Royal Army Medical Corps; a Royal Electrical and Mechanical Engineers Light Aid Detachment and Heavy Workshop, plus 104 Photographic Interpretation Section; 73 Forward Base Pay Office (Royal Army Pay Corps) and 249 Provost Company of the Royal Military Police. Last but not least came the dentists, the Casualty Reception Station and the all-important NAAFI.

It had not been easy to assemble 29 Brigade. All three infantry regiments were under strength and widely scattered over the UK. The Royal Northumberland Fusiliers were at the School of Infantry, Warminster, serving as the demonstration battalion, while the Royal Ulster Rifles were based in Colchester and the 8th Hussars in Tidworth. The Gloucester Regiment had just returned from a tour in Jamaica. Reservists had to be called up, often protesting that they had done their bit in the last war or that present commitments prevented their return to khaki. One celebrated returnee to the Ulsters, Rifleman 'Red' Martin, produced documentary evidence that as he was a paid-up member of the Communist Party he was ineligible to serve in Korea. Lt Col Robert Carson smiled weakly at the interview and said that was all right: Martin could always come along for the ride. Nevertheless, the War Office was still short of men and advertised for veteran soldiers to re-enlist voluntarily. In this way K-Force was formed and, together with the reservists, provided a wealth of military experience for 29 Brigade. It sailed early in October 1950: the Royal Ulster Rifles on the *Empire Pride*; the Royal Northumberland Fusiliers on the *Empire Halladale*; the 8th Hussars on the *Empire Fowey*; and the Gloucester Regiment on the *Empire Windrush*, a vessel that had already entered British social history by bringing Jamaican immigrants to Britain in 1948. They disembarked at Pusan to the usual reception committee in early November 1950.

## MACARTHUR'S 'GENERAL ASSAULT', 24 NOVEMBER 1950

On 20 November General MacArthur published his orders from General Headquarters in Tokyo. He still believed that his widespread forces in North Korea would be able to crush the enemy in a massive pincer movement. General Walker's Eighth Army would begin the offensive in the west on 24 November. He flew to the front to watch the advance begin and that night published Communiqué No. 12:

> This morning the western sector of the pincer moves forward in general assault in an effort to complete the compression and close the vice.
> There was no expectation that the offensive would encounter strong resistance or that it would be fated to fight a great battle along the Chongchon River.

Reconnaissance patrols from three American divisions (24th, 2nd and 25th) formed the spearhead and initially encountered little resistance as they set out on 24 November. The US 24th captured a few Chinese soldiers outside Chongju but there was no sign of a major enemy force. The US 2nd and 25th Divisions moved off their start lines around the Chongchon River and headed north to the Yalu. On their right the ROK II Corps would give the Americans vital flank support. Suddenly the advancing United Nations troops found themselves swamped by thousands of infiltrating Chinese soldiers, attacking units piecemeal and causing confusion and consternation wherever they appeared. The Chinese offensive of November 1950 was quite different in style from the original NKPA invasion across the 38 degree Parallel the previous June. There were no artillery bombardments to herald their advance, no strafing aircraft appeared and the menacing rumble of T-34 tanks was absent. American platoons and companies on hilltops were enfiladed by Chinese grenadiers and machine-gunners. Some units resisted and were overrun; others 'bugged out;' a few went on the offensive themselves but were cut off by apparently endless columns of Chinese coming over the hills. Withdrawal meant escape to unit transport and soon the roads leading south were crammed with American vehicles of all descriptions. Three Chinese Field Armies forced the 24th Division to about turn and retreat towards Pakchon. Three more hammered the ROK II Corps which collapsed under sheer weight of numbers. This particular crisis presented an immediate threat to the 2nd and 25th Divisions, whose commanders, lacking information about the size and purpose of enemy forces, were unable to gauge the best form of resistance to meet this surprise assault.

The 2nd Infantry Division, who would suffer the heaviest casualties, were below strength with only some 12,000 troops available – 3,000 men short. Its three rifle regiments, each composed of three battalions and a company of support tanks, were located in offensive positions to the east of the village of Kunu-ri. They were under orders to begin an attack on Huichon the next morning (26 November) and then advance to the Yalu. Because they were preparing an attack, their defences were minimal; only one regiment, the 23rd Infantry, had constructed a defensive perimeter. The other two regiments, the 9th and the 38th, were widely dispersed, easy to infiltrate and surround. This was why they took heavy casualties when the Chinese appeared among them and why the Chinese could move south so quickly through ill-connected defences.

## THE ESSENCE OF CHINESE STRATEGY

The Chinese plan was simple: they had already decided that the key to their operation was Kunu-ri from which two roads, essential for an American roadbound retreat, headed south. One road ran along the Chongchon River to Anju before heading south; the other, which led directly south, wound its way through the mountain passes. The Chinese plan was to cross the Chongchon, get behind the Americans and cut the mountain road so that their transport would be trapped in the steep-sided valleys. Accordingly, seven columns from the Chinese 40th Field Army would wade across the Chongchon where it was relatively shallow – it still had not frozen over – and attack the US 2nd Division across the hills at points where American tanks and artillery would be at a disadvantage. These were tactics reminiscent of German stormtroopers in 1918 and Japanese assault troops in the famous 'Ichi-go' offensive in eastern China during 1944; highly mobile, well-equipped soldiers tasked with attacking targets of opportunity with the intention of not only destroying the enemy's will to resist but to force him into a situation where surrender was inevitable.

Although MacArthur would not at first concede that a superior Chinese force was engaging the Eighth Army, General Walker realized that the ROK collapse on his right exposed his entire flank to attack and the threat of encirclement. Accordingly, he sent the 1st Cavalry to form a defensive line below the Taedong River where it could reform the remnants of the four ROK divisions into a useful fighting force. To assist the ROK units, the Turkish Brigade was ordered north while 27 Commonwealth Brigade was sent to check out the vital pass at Kunu-ri. Even further north, where its three regiments were being overrun, the US 2nd Division was still holding the road between Kujang-dong and Kunu-ri. The US 25th had forded the Chongchon and was already heading towards Anju. Clearly, the whole of the Eighth Army was in retreat and even MacArthur had to recognize the gravity of these new developments. He issued another public communiqué on 28 November:

> A major segment of the Chinese Continental Forces in Army, Corps and Divisional organization of an aggregate strength of over 200,000 men is now arrayed against the United Nations in North Korea. Consequently we face an entirely new war.

The 2nd Battalion of the Chinese 40th Field Army had the crucial mission. It had been in the van of the attack and the soldiers were exhausted after their advance over the hills and mountains of North Korea. To take an objective located three miles from one's position on the map meant a forced march through passes and up and down mountain roads – possibly an actual distance of nine or ten miles on the ground. And now the Chinese had reasonably accurate maps – all captured from the Americans! Their task was to block the exit from Kunu-ri at a crucial pass by midnight 29/30 November and the best way to do this was to trap US trucks, destroy them and create an insurmountable barrier. They could hear the sound of engines, heralding an American convoy. A Quad-50 – a half-track mounting four .50 calibre Browning machine-guns – led a convoy in the direction of Kunu-ri. Behind the Quad came some huge trucks, four tanks and another Quad. The Chinese let these pass and waited for the main convoy stream of soft-skinned supply trucks.

Once the main convoy entered the trap, Chinese mortars, machine-guns and burp-gun automatics riddled the unsuspecting American vehicles until about 20 had stalled, caught fire and blocked the pass. Whilst this was happening the US 2nd Division was moving into Kunu-ri. General Keiser, its commander, was unsure about the condition of his escape road. There was no word from a relief convoy coming north with the Turks; and no news from a squad of Military

Policemen who had been scouting the route. These had already been ambushed in and around the pass at Kunu-ri. As a precaution he sent ROK soldiers to scour the ridges on either side of the road to Sunchon and ordered air strikes to burn any Chinese they found off the hills with napalm. He had high hopes that the last stages of his retreat would be covered by 27 Commonwealth Brigade at a position code-named 'Nottingham.' General Keiser selected the survivors of the 9th Infantry Regiment to lead the breakout from Kunu-ri, and on 30 November its 2nd Battalion Sherman tanks, covered with heavily-armed infantry, set off towards Sunchon. They had travelled three miles south, blasting away at every ridge that might hide a Chinese soldier, when the lead tank encountered the first of the abandoned American vehicles. From the surrounding hills came a withering hail of Chinese machine-gun fire, salvoes of mortar bombs, Chinese 'potatomasher' grenades and well-aimed rifle volleys. The 2nd Division convoy was going to drive into a trap from which there was no apparent escape. The Americans soon had their own names for the place – 'the Gauntlet' and 'the Pass'.

The lead tanks bulldozed the previously shot-up convoy out of the road. Soldiers riding the Shermans could see the Turkish insignia on some of the vehicles. They fired incessantly at the enemy positions, broke through the wreckage of The Pass and went on to the Taedong River to reach 'Nottingham'. They were safe. The soft-skinned vehicles behind them were not. The 3rd Battalion made its run with eleven jeeps and five were knocked out by the Chinese even before they entered the Gauntlet. The battalion commander, Lt Col Harold V. Maixner, ordered nearby tanks to eliminate the nearest machine-gunners with high-explosive shells; while Air Force jets finished off the enemy with rockets and the deadly napalm. Maixner acquired a tank to act as a bulldozer and led his surviving jeeps, now piled high with wounded, into the Gauntlet. He rammed a stalled jeep ahead, accidentally injuring a badly wounded black soldier, and used the heavy machine-gun on the tank to keep up a constant rain of bullets sweeping across the Chinese. This slackened the enemy fire and the jeeps raced on to reach 'Nottingham.' He had lost 18 of his 63 soldiers who had begun the run. Samuel Lyman Atwood Marshall, the outstanding American military historian, had this to say about Maixner's experience:

> In this small incident were all of the elements of the greater drama at 'the Pass' which shortly followed. The Chinese had

at last clamped on the heights in their bid to seal the gauntlet at its end by concentrated automatic fire. Within the Pass itself, the column was becoming evermore slowed and choked by the weight of its own ruined metal and human débris.[1]

Behind the 9th and 23rd Infantry came the bulk of 2nd Division's transport. By the afternoon of 30 November a dreadful carnage had begun in the Pass. Trucks slewed off the road, tanks burst into flames. American, Turkish and ROK soldiers, dead, wounded and unscathed men alike, were either strewn under vehicles or were littering the gullies on each side of that bullet-torn highway. Today it is difficult to imagine the intensity of fire brought down by the Chinese division now installed on the ridges or to underestimate the courage of the men who ran the Gauntlet and survived the Pass. General Keiser had a charmed life. He managed to enter the Pass in his jeep and walked its entire length to assess the possibility of escape. Behind him came General J. Sladen Bradley, his aide-de-camp, and these two senior officers created small units of resistance among the tired, exhausted men of the 2nd Division. Last to come through the Gauntlet were the surviving divisional heavy howitzers. The artillerymen reached salvation just as the Taedong River was rising and beginning to freeze. Probably 3,000 men of the 2nd Division were dead or missing in the Battle of the Chongchon – sometimes referred to as the Battle of Kunu-ri Pass, America's worst defeat in the Korean War.

27 Commonwealth Brigade had played a relatively modest part in the battle. It had been ordered to move south to Chasan but orders changed and the Middlesex went north to guard the southern end of Kunu-ri Pass and facilitate 2nd Division's retreat. They encountered a few Chinese, were briefly in action and met the first tanks from the 9th Infantry and some survivors of the Turkish Brigade. From a distance, beyond the range of their rifles and Bren guns, the Middlesex could watch the tragedy unfold at the end of Kunu-ri Pass. The Argylls were ordered to Sunchon and marched all the way – the cynical Jocks called it the 'Death March from Kunu-ri' – but discovered that the retreat south would go on even longer. By early December the Argylls were still on the flank of the 1st Cavalry just outside Unsan while the Australians and Middlesex were just south of Suchon at Chasan. For them the critical point was the bridge being built at Yopa-ri, another vital escape route. The Chinese had occupied a hill some two miles from the American bridge builders. 3 RAR attacked the hill under a

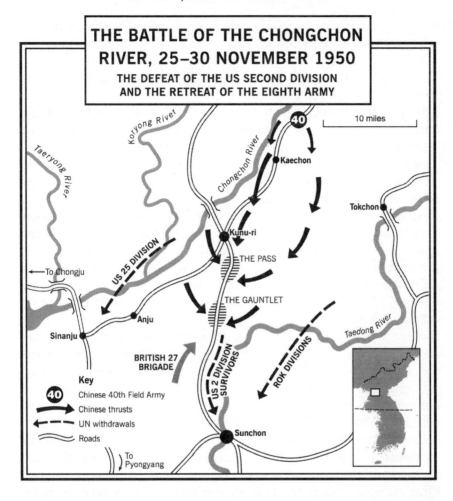

THE BATTLE OF THE CHONGCHON
RIVER, 25–30 NOVEMBER 1950
THE DEFEAT OF THE US SECOND DIVISION
AND THE RETREAT OF THE EIGHTH ARMY

devastating artillery barrage from US howitzers, drove off the Chinese and then withdrew across the completed bridge. To their dismay they were then ordered to retreat to Hayu-ri, 94 miles further south. The weather was now distinctly wintry and the Australians were lucky to find some abandoned US trucks (the victims of a guerrilla attack) from which they liberated some useful winter clothing. On they went, the Argylls enjoying the company of an attached American unit, Charlie Company, 3rd Chemical Mortar Battalion.

To the north of Pyongyang, on 4 December, they encountered the forward elements of the newly-arrived British 29 Brigade. For a short period, the 29 were covering the evacuation of Eighth Army through the North Korean capital. As the Royal Northumberland Fusiliers,

Glosters and Royal Ulster Rifles prepared to defend the city they were amazed to be facing thousands of American and ROK soldiers coming south as fast as possible. The Americans discarded everything that hampered their departure and the British joyfully acquired more winter clothing. This was tempered by their astonishment that so many troops, tanks and artillery units should be racing away from the enemy and that the Taedong River, relatively easy to defend, should be abandoned to distant Chinese soldiers without a fight. President Truman and his advisers were appalled by the extent of 'bug-out fever' and appreciated that it was a reflection of inadequacy in the chain of command at battalion, regimental and divisional level right through to Eighth Army headquarters. The Tokyo-based planners appeared to have no concept of the war being fought by the infantry-man. Solutions to these problems were not yet to hand and the US government had to accept that the Eighth Army was withdrawing to the Imjin River Line in the hope of saving Seoul, Taegu and Pusan. Truman and the Joint Chiefs of Staff had already wired MacArthur on 2 December informing him that the safety of US troops was now the 'primary consideration' and that they would concur in the creation of appropriate evacuation beachheads if the worst came to the worst.[2]

As the last American units, mainly 187th Airborne, left Pyongyang via specially constructed pontoon bridges, US engineers exploded ammunition dumps, military buildings and stores that could not be evacuated. The Argylls and the Australians had found an unhappy Indian Field Ambulance stranded in the Pyongyang rail sidings, unable to move their six months' supply of medical stores already loaded into three railway wagons. A locomotive was swiftly found, a head of steam was fired up and the train chugged across the last of Pyon-gyang's battered bridges at 0400 hours. At 0500 hours the engineers blew the railbridge and then the pontoon bridges. Above them screamed American jets, bombing and strafing the first Chinese troops moving into the North Korean capital. They probed the outskirts on 5 December and their patrols rowed across the Taedong to establish a Chinese bridgehead south of the river. Kim Il Sung arrived to make a speech that ended with the exhortation to 'march south'. General Peng also drove into Pyongyang. He had acquired a captured American jeep as well as a brand-new Molotov command car. In conference with the commander of the lead 50th Field Army, General Zeng Zesheng. Peng asked how soon he could reach the 38 degree Parallel. Zeng estimated a month. Peng retorted that it must be achieved in a matter of days and he ordered the 50th to begin an offensive immediately. In his heart, Peng must have realized that he was making very heavy demands on his troops. Food and ammunition shortages, plus the worsening weather, meant that Chinese penetration across the 38 degree Parallel was initially slight. In fact, it was North Korean guerrillas who first occupied the South Korean towns of Haeju and Kaesong.

By 5 December the retreating Eighth Army had lost contact with the Chinese Field Armies. Firefights with guerrilla forces were common behind the line that had been stabilized roughly along the 38 degree parallel. It had few natural defensive features but at least it was not currently being contested by the Chinese. Thus the Eighth Army had this unexpected opportunity to reform and replenish its forces and by mid-December a reorganized army was in position. From the Turkish Brigade in the west to the ROK Army in the east a new line of resistance had been created. There was even time for congratulation. On 23 December 27 Commonwealth Brigade's contribution since the Naktong breakout was to be recognized by the award of Syngman Rhee's Presidential Citation. General Walker would arrive to present the citation. On the way his brightly polished jeep crashed into a truck and then hit a telegraph pole. 'Johnnie' Walker was not wearing his helmet and suffered fatal injuries. General Milburn presented the citation. Eighth Army's new commander was General Matthew Bunker Ridgway, then based in Washington. A distinguished airborne general, Ridgway had dropped with his troops on D-Day (6 June 1944) and commanded XVIII Airborne Corps (82nd and 101st Airborne) during the Arnhem operation and in the Battle of the Ardennes 1944–5. He arrived in Tokyo on Christmas Day and met MacArthur on 26 December. He heard the bad news about the Eighth Army's retreat. MacArthur asked him take command of that Army together with X Corps whose campaign experience in north-east Korea had led to defeat and enforced evacuation.

## THE CHINESE VICTORY IN NORTH-EAST KOREA:
## WEST OF THE CHOSIN RESERVOIR

The events that had befallen the Eighth Army had very little impact on the X Corps campaign fought in north-east Korea. Both forces had separate command structures; moreover, they were separated by a towering mountain mass that had made physical contact and radio communication between them well-nigh impossible. MacArthur's plan for the reunification of Korea had depended on an advance across a broad front so that UN forces could take up positions along the south bank of the Yalu River. He had therefore allocated to X Corps a fighting front of about 500 miles, not knowing that three Chinese Field Armies would contest this unsafe deployment of American and ROK manpower. Even more worrying was MacArthur's interest in Kanggye, Kim Il Sung's temporary seat of government and an assembly point for Chinese Field Armies. If X Corps could cut across the mountains to Mupyongni and hold the approaches to Kanggye, this would, in MacArthur's opinion, help shorten the war. MacArthur readily convinced General Almond that this was the proper strategy. General Smith, however, was loathe to commit his Marines to such a plan involving as it did a winter campaign in almost inaccessible country as far as supply and casualty evacuation routes were concerned. General Almond was not impressed with this attitude. He had the Marines, 7th Infantry Division, ROK I Corps and, since 21 November, the 3rd Division as well. The ROK divisions were still advancing north and by 25 November the Capital Division reached Nanam, 50 miles from the Soviet frontier. Almond had no idea that the 27th Chinese Field Army (79th, 80th, 81st and 90th Divisions) and the 20th Field Army (58th, 59th, 60th and 89th Divisions) had been transferred to north-east Korea between late October and 10 November. Behind them came the 26th Field Army (76th, 77th, 78th and 88th Divisions). All three were élite PLA armies, well-versed in amphibious warfare, guerrilla search and destroy tactics and mountain warfare. Almond's calculations were based on the assumption that he was facing the 42nd Field Army whose three divisions, the 124th, 125th and 126th, had already been badly mauled by the Marines. He assumed that he enjoyed numerical superiority but in fact the divisions of the three fresh Chinese Field Armies totalled 160,000 front-line troops, rather more than the 114,000 that X Corps could mobilize.

On 25 November the Marines entered Yudam-ni, to the south-west of the Chosin Reservoir. It was an important village as its road junction led to Mupyong-ni from which X Corps expected to march to the Yalu. The 7th Infantry Division was to advance on the east of the reservoir, ROK I Corps would continue to move up the coast and the 3rd Division would protect the western flank in support of the Marines. On 27 November the Marines attacked Chinese hill positions but despite air support and howitzer fire they could not break through the

Chinese defences. Once night fell, the Chinese launched their own offensive and infiltrated the Marines' hilltop defences at Yudam-ni. As the Chinese 79th and 89th engaged the Marines in hand-to-hand fighting, the 59th circled to the south of the village to cut the main supply route to Hagaru-ri. The road was guarded by two Marine companies, Company C under Captain John F. Morris and Company F led by Captain William E. Barber who realized that they must retain control of the Toktong Pass, a three mile defile ideal for ambushes.

Freezing conditions prevailed throughout north-east Korea as the defenders of Toktong Pass huddled in their foxholes for warmth while the Marines at Yudam-ni gradually reduced their defence perimeter. C-119 Flying Boxcars parachuted food, ammunition and medical supplies to the beleagured Marines but it was obvious that they could not hold out indefinitely against these unrelenting Chinese attacks. They therefore decided to break out and escape to Hagaru-ri. Led by the legendary M-26 Pershing tank D-23, commanded by Sgt Russell A. Mansell, the Marines moved out on 1 December. D-23's 90mm gun knocked out enemy machine-gun and anti-tank nests. The slow-moving column, with its flanking riflemen struggling through waist-high snow drifts, reached Captain Barber's Company C, defenders of the Toktong Pass for nearly a week. Barber had 82 able-bodied men left out of his original 220. The rearguard battalion was constantly in action against Chinese soldiers dressed in captured marine uniforms and parkas. One squad leader, Sgt James E. Johnson, resisted all attacks and, despite his wounds, was last seen throwing grenades at the Chinese. His efforts won the posthumous award of the Medal of Honor.

## THE 41 (INDEPENDENT) COMMANDO ROYAL MARINES

The British 41 Independent Commando Royal Marines played an important role in the battles around Chosin Reservoir. Commanded by Lt Col D. B. Drysdale, it had been formed on 16 August 1950 from 200 volunteers. Kitted out in American-supplied civilian suits, many of 41 Commando flew to Japan, arriving on 5 September 1950. Here they were issued with American uniforms and weapons, wearing their green berets to distinguish themselves from their American colleagues. They trained at Camp McGill prior to their three raids on the North Korean railway system between Chongjin and Hungnam in October, described below. Since then, UN advances northwards had made coastal raids redundant and the US 1st Marine Division asked for 41 Commando as a specialist reconnaissance company. They arrived in Hungnam in mid-November to join the Marine regiments near the Chosin Reservoir. 41 Commando left Hungnam on 28 November but after covering 40 miles it faced a Chinese roadblock outside Koto-ri and immediately reinforced the perimeter defence around the town and stood-to in sub-zero temperatures.

Next day, Lt Col Drysdale formed a 900-strong 'Task Force Drysdale', composed of his own unit, plus Company G, 1st Marines, and soldiers from Company B, 31st Infantry. Their task was to make contact with the divisional base at Hagaru-ri, a short journey of about ten miles. Led by 17 American tanks, the Task Force successfully negotiated the potentially dangerous Funchilin Pass after which they ran into a Chinese roadblock. Drysdale received orders from Marine General Smith to fight his way through to Hagaru-ri. The American tanks decided to press on as an armoured spearhead, though Drysdale had wished them to remain scattered along the column. Seventeen tanks at the head of the column left the soft-skinned trucks vulnerable to flank attacks as well as reducing its firepower. Harrassing fire slowed down the convoy and then, quite unexpectedly, troops from three Chinese regiments ambushed the convoy in a deep ravine named 'Hell Fire Valley' and split it into three segments. The rear vehicles reversed and wound their way back to Koto-ri while the rest sat stalled in the middle of the valley, the troops firing their recoilless rifles and light machine-guns against the Chinese who were lobbing mortar bombs into their midst. There appeared to be little chance of survival.

Next morning, 29 November, the Chinese called for a cease-fire, promising to give medical aid to the wounded if the rest would surrender. For a time, the survivors were willing to fight on while some 400 men, including some of 41 Commando, made their escape in Marine and Army trucks heading to Hagaru-ri and back to Koto-ri. Most who remained were made prisoner and, true to their word, the Chinese looked after the wounded and gave them food. Next morning the Chinese had vanished and many of the prisoners found themselves free. Some of the truck drivers who had already abandoned their vehicles followed Lt Alfred J. Catania, of the 377th Transportation Truck Company, in a desperate attempt to take cover. He had spotted Chinese troops advancing along the narrow gauge railway on the right of the road from Koto-ri. On the left was a stream dividing the road from the mountains 400 yards away. He was already wounded:

I was hit once in the back by a shell fragment, and in the shoulder by a calibre .45 slug that broke my collar bone and lodged in my neck. The pain was great. I thought I had been hit in the neck and an infantryman even bandaged me there. He also gave me a shot of morphine to ease the pain. I had my head propped up on my helmet and continued to give what little control was possible in the situation.[3]

He decided to make for the mountains and with other truckers and infantrymen waded across the stream. This meant that his feet would rapidly freeze. Catania cut through his frozen bootlaces and tried to take off his socks. These were frozen to his boots so he discarded the lot and made temporary snow shoes from his pile-liner cap and strips of blanket. He rejoined the road and hobbled in the direction of Koto-ri. The Chinese troops positioned either side of the road let his little party through. He had lost three of his truckers killed; seven were wounded and there were eight missing. Catania was flown out from Koto-ri back to Hamhung and then by C-54 to Japan. His wounds were severe and he was later flown to the United States.

Meanwhile, the survivors of 41 Commando were determined to reach Hagaru-ri and by the time they arrived they had suffered 79 casualties: 13 killed, 39 wounded and 27 missing. Nineteen marines were stricken by pneumonia, exposure or frostbite. Some of the missing managed to find their way back to Hagaru-ri. Task Force Drysdale had suffered over 300 casualties and had lost most of its trucks. For a week, as the hard-pressed 5th and 7th Marines were fighting their way through from Yudam-ni, Drysdale and his Royal Marines helped defend the perimeter around Hagaru-ri. Throughout, they were succoured by the US Air Force who flew in supplies and over 500 marine replacements, and evacuated 4,312 casualties.

### THE CHINESE VICTORY IN NORTH-EAST KOREA: EAST OF THE CHOSIN RESERVOIR

It fell to the 31st Infantry, commanded by Col MacLean, to advance up the eastern side of the reservoir: two battalions, the 1st led by Lt Col Don C. Faith, and the 3rd under Lt Col R. Reilly. Every fourth man in the 31st Infantry was a 'buddy' or KATUSA (Korean Augmentation to United States Army) soldier who rarely spoke English.

Both battalions came under heavy Chinese attacks, though the main road, challenged by a T-34 and an SU-76, was held by Corporal James H. Godfrey who dispatched both with his 75mm recoilless rifle. However, roadblocks had cut them off and all attempts to send tanks north to relieve them failed. Faith's battalion, isolated at Pungnyu-ri inlet had no option but to retreat south and join up with the survivors of the 3rd. Now known as 'Task Force Faith,' it loaded its 500 wounded into trucks. They had little firepower as their Quads were out of action and there was barely any ammunition left.

As they set off, Marine Corsairs gave them as much cover as they could. Tragically, one Corsair dropped its tanks short and dowsed the leading element with napalm. They had to drive round the wrecked bridge at Paegam-ni Creek and then encountered a major roadblock composed of logs piled round two destroyed American tanks. Now there was no escape. Bullets were everywhere and many wounded, prostrate on litters in the backs of soft-skinned trucks, were killed here. Lt Col Faith died after being seriously wounded at the log trap where the column was virtually wiped out by incessant fire from the Chinese 80th Division. Not a single vehicle escaped. A few survivors crossed over the ice covering Chosin Reservoir and made it to Hagaru-ri. When the 31st Infantry paraded, only 385 men were left. They were merged with 500 other troops inside the Marine perimeter and formed a new makeshift battalion.


## X CORPS RETREATS TO THE SEA

General Almond had decided to recall all his forces in north-east Korea and conduct an ordered evacuation by sea. In the far north were General Kim's ROK I Corps, code-name 'Rogers,' and the valiant 17th Infantry still based at Hyesanjin on the Yalu River. The rest of General Barr's battered 7th 'Bayonet' Division had already suffered 40 per cent casualties. The Rogers' retreat was contested by reorganized NKPA units, while Bayonet managed to withdraw in its own vehicles. The 3rd Infantry Division, code-named 'Kaiser', had to contend with the occasional ambush with segments of its convoys trapped with usual Chinese skill. Air support was vital for the Marine withdrawal from Hagaru-ri as enemy MiG-15 jet fighters were beginning to challenge the Corsairs, A-26s and Skyraiders as they swooped low over the mountains to attack Chinese troops.

The Marines departed Hagaru-ri on 6 December in an 11-mile convoy flanked by marching troops. Five hundred yards ahead of the lead tanks, the Corsairs and Skyraiders plastered every suspect ridge with napalm, rockets and machine-gun fire. Beyond Koto-ri, a vital bridge had been partially wrecked by guerrillas and the 58th Engineer Treadway Bridge Company came up with a brilliant solution. If replacement steel spans could be dropped by parachute they could repair the bridge. This was a unique operation in the Korean War and it fell to the C-119 Flying Boxcars to accomplish it successfully. The engineers repaired the bridge and the lead Marines pressed on through Koto-ri, where they found some of 41 Commando Royal Marines. Snowstorms hindered their advance and reduced air support on 8 December when the convoy came to Funchilin Pass. Many Marines suffered from frostbite and it was policy to airlift the worst cases to hospital rather than allow them to slow down the pace of the column. To ensure the safety of the Marines, the 3rd Infantry Division formed 'Task Force Dog' and equipped it with specialist engineer and artillery units. It moved north to the Funchilin Pass and linked up with the advance units at Majon-dong on 7 December. During 8–9 December the advance guard was approaching Hamhung in company with 41 Commando Royal Marines. They had shared the horrors of the march to the sea when night temperatures were minus 15°F and there was little food and no sleep for 72 hours. They would ultimately share, with the 1st Marine Division and its attached units, the award of a United States Presidential Unit Citation.[4]

As was his custom, General Almond reconnoitred, covering the terrain north of the Hungnam-Yonpo-Hamhung perimeter in a light aircraft on 10 December. He flew north as far as Koto-ri, abandoned by the Marine rearguard that afternoon. Fighting continued as Chinese troops shadowed the Marine rearguard. They seemed to have no regard for the slaughter inflicted on them by Quad gunfire, tank shells and, most deadly of all, the 40mm anti-aircraft guns firing low trajectory air bursts. On the same day, Almond inspected Hungnam's port facilities and calculated that he could evacuate X Corps plus its 17,500 vehicles by 22 December. To protect that evacuation he had ringed his perimeter with artillery and strongpoints and could call upon immense air power flying in from patrolling carriers and Japan. His own patrols, mainly 7th Infantry Division men, probed some 10 miles north of the perimeter but reported no contacts with the enemy. In the port area, the 7th Marines took a well-deserved position at the

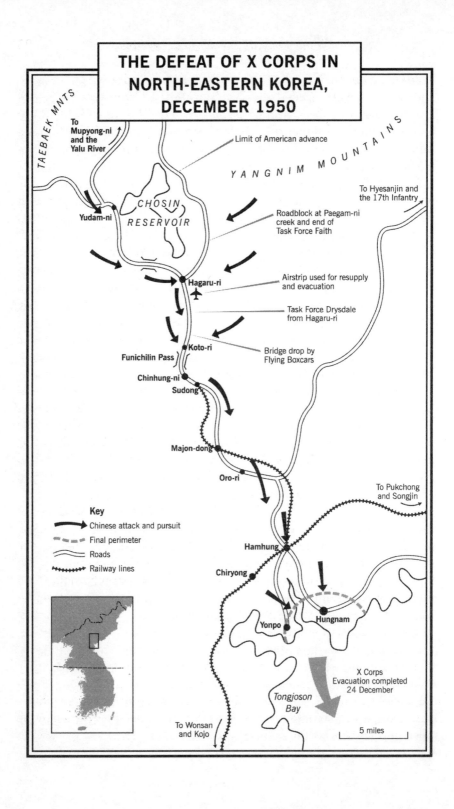

# THE DEFEAT OF X CORPS IN NORTH-EASTERN KOREA, DECEMBER 1950

*TAEBAEK MNTS*

To
Mupyong-ni
and the
Yalu River

*YANGNIM MOUNTAINS*

Limit of American advance

To Hyesanjin and
the 17th Infantry

*CHOSIN RESERVOIR*

Yudam-ni

Roadblock at Paegam-ni
creek and end of
Task Force Faith

Hagaru-ri

Airstrip used for resupply
and evacuation

Task Force Drysdale
from Hagaru-ri

Koto-ri

Funichilin Pass

Bridge drop by
Flying Boxcars

Chinhung-ni

Sudong

Majon-dong

Oro-ri

To Pukchong
and Songjin

## Key

➤ Chinese attack and pursuit
〰️ Final perimeter
══ Roads
✛✛✛ Railway lines

Hamhung

Chiryong

Yonpo

Hungnam

X Corps
Evacuation completed
24 December

*Tongjoson
Bay*

To Wonsan
and Kojo

5 miles

head of the queue. No other formation had achieved so much in Korea and if proof were needed the 7th Marines had won ten Medals of Honor. They were followed by the heroes of the 7th Infantry Division. Covering the final stages of the evacuation were the troops of the 3rd Infantry Division, notably the Puerto Rican 65th Infantry plus several black infantry, tank and artillery units.

On 18/19 December a few NKPA soldiers penetrated part of the wire perimeter, but major assaults were inhibited by the ease with which Almond could call down heavy naval shelling and air attack to stop infantry charging across the open terrain. By 21 December NKPA troops were attacking the black soldiers holding the eastern end of the perimeter and Almond decided to withdraw the last of his troops and defend the perimeter with naval gunfire. Most stores had been destroyed by engineer units but some remained on the quayside and the beach. Again, naval shelling destroyed these, though the frugal Almond insisted that refugees who wanted a ride on the evacuation fleet should first tow barrels of fuel behind their rowing boats and deliver them to the waiting ships!

The evacuation was a triumph of organization and a tribute to the US Navy. X Corps needed 103 troop transports and 89 LSTs to move 90,000 soldiers from Hungnam. Just over 16,500 ROK soldiers came out at Songjin and the ROK Marines sailed from Wonsan. Almost as many refugees accompanied the soldiers. X Corps' last ships sailed away at 1400 hrs on 24 December 1950 and the force returned to South Korea to be placed under the command of the Eighth Army's new commander, General Ridgway. Despite the hysterical headlines of the day, it was no Dunkirk. Though the strategy of General MacArthur may have been mistaken and the tactics of General Almond unwise, the performance of the fighting men had been truly of the highest order. To initate a war in mountainous country with the paraphernalia of a modern army equipped with the latest technology of the day is never an easy task, especially when it is roadbound. But to do this at the height of the Manchurian winter was asking too much. The frost and the ice, the searing winds and the sheer difficulty of functioning in heavy clothes with a frostbitten nose and freezing feet and fingers taxes any soldier. Apart from this, at 15°F tank and truck radiators freeze, as did the 1950 issue anti-freeze! M-1 rifles, carbines and Browning machine-guns froze up and would not fire on automatic while shells stored in the open gun limbers would solidify and even crack. These factors do not excuse defeat but they go some way to explain it.

The Chinese would not argue with the cold. They lacked the creature comforts – the Hershey bars and the turkey on Thanksgiving Day. In fact they often lacked food entirely and were dependent on abandoned American rations. They also had problems with their weapons, though the burp guns rarely jammed and the 'potato-masher' grenades usually exploded satisfactorily. But the troops still froze to death. Horrific examples were plentiful in Korea during 1950 as the Chinese infiltrators and their porters trudged across the mountain ranges. These were the unfortunate 'snowmen' of the Korean battlefield and one Chinese soldier was shocked to encounter them that December:

> Whole platoons appeared to have perished, squatting in squad order, rifles on shoulders, kitbags on backs, all snow-sheathed, terrible. Gangs of coolies had frozen to death, pressed down by their heavy A-frames, and there were smatterings of North Korean refugees, women and children mostly, heaped hopelessly together in search of warmth. A few old men in tall Korean hats had chosen to meet their end sitting bolt upright, hands folded in laps, like Buddhas frosted by the snow.[5]

Chinese soldiers had endured the cold and American firepower at the cost of enormous casualties. The three Field Armies who had fought X Corps in the great battles around Chosin Reservoir now had to be withdrawn from battle. Deaths amounted to 40,000; frostbite victims and wounded soldiers numbered even more. General Peng was incensed by this waste of his best forces and told Mao Zedong that the Chinese Volunteers were ill-equipped for further campaigning in South Korea when they would be 400 miles away from their supply bases. What was the Chairman of the People's Republic of China going to do about this? Chairman Mao informed him that he was buying the best arms that the Soviet Union could produce. There would be better infantry weapons, a massive increase in artillery, ammunition supplies would vastly increase and a new Chinese Air Force flying the latest Soviet jets would challenge America's domination of the air. Already, UN bombers had been surprised by the appearance of the new Russian-supplied jet aircraft, the MiG-15s, then superior to anything the Americans were flying in Korea. Much was on its way – certainly enough to support a new offensive against the United Nations in early 1951. Peng was pleased and returned to his headquarters to lay plans for the conquest of South Korea.

## AMERICA'S REACTION TO THE CHINESE INTERVENTION

The United States delegate to the United Nations was Warren Mitchell. He was concerned to demonstrate to the United Nations Security Council that the attacks initially launched by the UN forces had been designed to finish their 'assigned task' of repelling the aggressor (North Korea) and ensure that peace and security reigned in Korea. That attack, he explained to the Council on 28 November 1950, had been broken by Chinese Communist forces engaged in North Korea. He estimated that some 200,000 Chinese troops were involved and, in his opinion, the war in Korea could not now be finished quickly. He condemned the Chinese as aggressors and reviewed the historical circumstances leading up to that aggression for the benefit of the Chinese representative present at the Security Council meeting for the first time.

Mitchell noted that the United States had been aware for some time that Mao Zedong had previously refrained from open support of Kim Il Sung's government in Pyongyang. But Mao had given Kim a great deal of moral encouragement and provided a massive military arsenal for the North Korean forces. It had transferred from the Chinese Army some 140,000 combat troops of Korean origin. These were now serving in North Korea as were thousands of other Koreans who had been recruited from the substantial population living in Manchuria. Mitchell said all these things had been done covertly but now 'the Beijing regime openly sends its fighting units in large numbers across the border from Manchuria to join battle with the United Nations. These forces immediately attacked the United Nations forces . . . Their supply bases and reinforcement depots were protected by the Manchurian frontier, a frontier which the United Nations forces respected despite the serious disabilities which this practice laid upon their operations.'[6]

Mitchell went on to explain why the President had ordered the Seventh Fleet to prevent any attack upon Taiwan (Formosa). Truman had also ordered the Nationalists on Taiwan to cease air/sea attacks on mainland China – and promised to enforce that order using the Seventh Fleet. America had no territorial ambitions in the Far East and certainly none in Taiwan. He was dismayed that Communist China should claim the contrary, especially after all those years of American aid to China and the Sino-American friendship that that had engendered. He questioned the Chinese representative about the status of the Chinese People's Volunteers serving in Korea. Could he assure the US that these forces were entirely volunteers? Were the jets that attacked from Manchurian bases 'volunteered' in some way? How could private citizens come to possess jet aircraft? What were his government's interests relative to Korea? Mitchell went on to note that Taiwan had never considered itself subject to US aggression and quoted Nationalist China's statement to the Security Council on 25 August 1950:

> I need only one minute to make a statement, and that statement is contained in one sentence. There has been no United States aggression against the island of Taiwan.

What the UN Security Council needed, said Warren Mitchell, is 'an assurance of the peaceful intentions of the regime at Beijing. More important than that assurance, it seeks deeds which will demonstrate that its intentions are genuine. Only if these deeds are forthcoming can China's neighbours, and the people of the world, feel assured that peace and security will be restored to the Far East.' In this way the United States presented its case to the UN. Two days later, Dean Acheson broadcast his foreign affairs address to the American people. He described the advent of the Chinese People's Volunteers as an 'act of brazen aggression . . . the second such act in five months.' He warned his listeners that 'this is not merely another phase of the Korean campaign. This is a fresh and unprovoked aggressive act, even more immoral than the first.' These were powerful words, designed to prepare the American people for a hard struggle ahead, a struggle that would eventually be resolved by superior American military capacity. However, his message made far less impact than did the President's remarks the same day.


## TRUMAN, ATTLEE AND THE ATOM BOMB

At a press conference on 30 November 1950 President Truman had assured reporters that the United States would do whatever was necessary to resolve the military problems now surfacing in Korea. One reporter asked him if that included the atom bomb. The President then emphasized in his off the cuff response that all military weapons were under consideration. After this exchange, the President's Press secretary issued a public statement to clarify the Presidential position. He outlined the US constitutional position: that only the President may authorize the use of the atom bomb but therafter the field commanders would have the power to use the 'tactical delivery' of the atom bomb. Unfortunately, the political damage had been done and the media of the day chose to interpret the President's words as a threat to use nuclear weapons in Korea.[7]

There was uproar in the British House of Commons and 100 Labour MPs signed a letter to Prime Minister Attlee to show their hostility to the use of nuclear weapons in Korea. Parliament debated the issue and there was general agreement that Korea must not become the springboard into a Third World War. At the close of the debate Clement Attlee informed the House that he would fly to America to speak with President Truman. Before he left for Washington, Attlee had discussions with Foreign Secretary Bevin, French Foreign Minister R. Pleven, and Commonwealth Ministers. Pleven stated that France was 'disquieted' with reports that atomic weapons might be used in Korea; Attlee confirmed that this was also the British attitude. Loose talk about their use was highly dangerous. Ahead of the Prime Minister's arrival in Washington on 4 December (when the military situation in Korea was in crisis) Bevin sent a cable labelled 'Secret-Emergency' to Sir Oliver Franks stating that the British government's preferred choice was for the UN to hold bridgeheads in Korea rather than drift into 'a futile war with China.'[8]

Attlee began a series of meetings with the President, starting that evening. The text of these meetings is astonishing for the range of subjects covered and for the frank speaking between the leaders of the United States and the United Kingdom. Attlee was clearly impressed by the sheer power of the United States and forced to accept by implication the logic of its leadership both in Europe and in Asia. It was clear that the United States would not recognize the People's Republic of China; that it would defend the Chinese Nationalist claim to Taiwan; and would use the Seventh Fleet as a powerful deterrent in the Far East. So there was little sympathy for the British position which favoured a positive, constructive approach to Chairman Mao Zedong – in the interests of world peace. As far as Korea was

concerned, the Americans saw in British proposals for an uncondi-
tional ceasefire all the weaknesses of appeasement that had marked
the Chamberlain government in 1938. Yet, as Truman noted in his
diary, Attlee seemed ready to support everything the United States did
in Korea.

The first time the atom bomb was mentioned was during the fifth
meeting on 7 December, though President Truman gives the date as
the 8th in his own memoirs. In a meeting when the two leaders and
Ambassador Franks were alone, Truman promised Attlee that he
would never use the bomb without consulting the British Prime
Minister. Later, this was literally interpreted as applying to Attlee,
not his successors. Attlee then flew to the United Nations in New York
and then to Ottawa where the Canadians quizzed him on his atom
bomb agreement with Truman. Whatever its weaknesses, the gentle-
man's agreement between Truman and Attlee over the use of nuclear
weapons was sustained. Admittedly, the matter did emerge later in
American politics after General Eisenhower became President two
years later. However, at the Washington talks of December 1950 the
British accepted US policies with regard to Taiwan and the Seventh
Fleet; and promised to give political and military support to the US
campaigns in Korea. They kept their word and the Americans were
always grateful for this. For all sorts of reasons, it became fashionable
to deride the 'special relationship' between the USA and Britain, but
though it may no longer be between equals it still exists. NATO's
intervention in Serbia during 1999 demonstrated this to a marked
degree. Perhaps the most tangible feature to emerge from Attlee's
flight to Washington was that thereafter the United States usually
sought and respected British opinion.

CHAPTER 6

# The Chinese Winter Offensives and the UN Response, January–April 1951

## AMERICAN DECISIONS

After Clement Attlee had returned to London to assure his Cabinet that America would not employ atomic weapons in Korea without prior consultation with himself, President Truman and his advisers evolved policies that would encourage the UN General Assembly not only to condemn China as an aggressor but to support the United States' continuation of the war in Korea. Most significant, it was agreed that America would embark on a massive, long-term policy of rearmament that would itself have a lasting effect upon world history. First, Truman had to persuade a doubting – and ignorant – American public of the crucial importance of the war in Korea and to protect his key adviser, Secretary of State Dean Acheson, from the attacks of some Republican Senators and Congressmen who favoured extending America's military commitments and involving the forces of Nationalist China on Taiwan. This was a move that General MacArthur pointedly repeated in his cables to the Pentagon. On Friday 15 December Truman made a telling nationwide radio broadcast to the American people, warning them of the dangers they faced. He defined the forces of Chinese and Soviet Communism as a threat to the future of civilization:

> I am talking to you tonight about what our country is up against and what we are going to do about it. Our homes, our Nation, all the things we believe in are in great danger

> . . . we will continue to uphold, and if necessary, defend
> with arms, the principles of the United Nations . . . to work
> with other free nations to strengthen our combined defences
> . . . (and) . . . build up our own Army, Navy and Air Force,
> and make more weapons for ourselves and our allies.[1]

Next day he declared a national emergency and on 19 December held a Press conference to underline the importance of Dean Acheson to his administration. The significance of this was that Acheson had, in the eyes of the Republican Party, lost the nation's confidence and should be dismissed. It was a measure of how unpopular the war was becoming in America. To compound his political difficulties, Truman's proposal for a UN condemnation of the People's Republic of China as an 'aggressor state' met initial opposition from Britain, the Commonwealth and individual UN members. There was still a belief that a cease-fire was possible, that China would agree to withdraw the People's Volunteers, without making a settlement of the crucial questions surrounding the future of Taiwan and Korea a pre-condition of withdrawal. Much diplomatic energy was expended during December 1950-January 1951 in an effort to secure peace on the basis of 'Five Principles': a cease-fire; foreign troop withdrawals from Korea; UN supervizion of Korea prior to unification; a national Korean government; and a General Assembly body to seek the peaceful settlement of issues that bedevilled the Far East. Zhou Enlai showed interest in some aspects of the Five Principles but it was clear from events on the ground in Korea that neither side intended to stop fighting. Accordingly, on 30 January 1951 the General Assembly formally condemned China as an aggressor state.

## THE THIRD-PHASE CHINESE OFFENSIVE, JANUARY 1950

Chinese troops had entered Chinhung-ni on 28 December 1950 where the commanders of the Chinese Field Armies discussed the problems that would face them when their New Year offensive began. There was a shortage of infantry weapons and ammunition – partially due to the terrible losses sustained by their porters during the winter. The soldiers too were suffering not just as battle casualties but from the frostbite that was killing more troops than American bullets. Moreover, there was still a lack of artillery support though a few batteries were now available for the attack on Seoul, the next major objective for the Chinese Field Armies. To their amazement the offensive on 1 January 1951 met little resistance. ROK forces collapsed in the face of determined squads of Chinese grenadiers; American troops bundled into their vehicles and headed south. The most appalled witness of the American 'bug-out' was none other than General Matthew Ridgway who had driven north of Seoul to assess the extent of the Chinese advance. He personally intervened to halt the 'bug-out' but failed to stop the frenzied escape south. All he could do was to order US Military Policemen to establish roadblocks and organize some form of resistance.

Seoul could not now be defended and the government established by MacArthur after the Inchon landings fled. Behind them were Syngman Rhee's execution squads, rounding up critics of the President's conduct and shooting them in public without compunction. Shocked UN troops and their commanding officers deplored this but the circumstances of the moment permitted only occasional intervention on humanitarian grounds. Ridgway had to arrange matters so that the Eighth Army could make an orderly withdrawal, as far as possible, across the remaining Han bridges, the original Japanese railbridge and three pontoon bridges capable of bearing the weight of carefully driven tanks.

Much had depended on the British and Commonwealth brigades. For two days 27 Commonwealth Brigade guarded the approaches and exits to Seoul while elements of the US I Corps and IX Corps plus 29 Brigade passed through. 29 Brigade had been in action on the Kaesong-Seoul road near the mountain mass of Nogo San in company with the US 35th Infantry Regiment; while 27 Commonwealth Brigade had fought the Chinese on the Chorwal-Seoul highway. 29 Brigade had support from a scratch unit of tanks, the 8th King's Royal Irish Hussars, whose Cromwells and the OP tanks of 45 Field Regiment Royal Artillery formed 'Cooperforce' under the command of Captain Dudley Aston-Cooper. The Centurion tanks at 50 tons apiece were too heavy for the now flimsy Han bridges, and had been stationed south of the river. Here at Yongdungpo they fired their guns in anger on 11 February 1951 supporting US patrols along the Han River and managed to score their first tank kill. Ironically, the enemy tank was a Cromwell captured by the Chinese. Commanded by Captain George Strachan MC, the Centurion Mark 3 known as *Caughoo* (named after a famous race-horse), together with another

Centurion, engaged the Cromwell and destroyed it with its second shell – at the amazing range of 3,000 yards.

When the Chinese attack came on 3 January, 29 Brigade's advance positions were overrun and Chinese infantry appeared on the hills facing the little village of Chaegunghyon (also spelt Chunghungdong on other units' maps), after which the following battle on 3 January 1950 is named. Cooperforce blasted the enemy high ground as did the Field Artillery's 25 pounders, the 4.2 mortars and the Ulster Rifles' own 3-inch mortars. Air strikes came in to help and four F-80 Shooting Stars whistled over to napalm and rocket the enemy troops. The Royal Northumberland Fusiliers had been equally successful in stemming a Chinese assault further east. They held three hilltop positions just to the north of the village of Chaegunghyon. At more than battalion strength the Chinese scrambled up the steep hill in the face of concentrated Bren and rifle fire. Well-placed mortar bombs and superb fire control decimated the Chinese who fell back, no match for Northumberland's 'Fighting Fifth'. On this occasion the Chinese had avoided the Glosters located in the centre of a five-mile front. At the Battle of Chaegunghyon the Chinese had been beaten and forced to retreat. Why was it then, asked 29 Brigade, that the Americans and ROKs had been unwilling to stand and fight? They had no time to discover the answer for the brigade was ordered to reform south of the Han.

On 4 January The Royal Ulster Rifles (1 RUR) had the hardest withdrawal to the south. Passing through a long narrow valley at night, their column was inadvertently illuminated by flares dropped from US aircraft. This gave the Chinese machine-gunners a perfect target and they created confusion in the centre of the column. From the rear of the column the Cooperforce Cromwells were in action with their 75mm guns and Besa machine-guns. A close-quarter combat raked by artillery and automatic fire developed in and around the stalled column where several trucks had caught fire. Some Chinese actually ran to the vehicles and pulled the drivers from their cabs. Gallant Cooperforce was attacked by extraordinarily brave Chinese infantry carrying satchel charges and most of the Cromwells were burnt. After taking – and inflicting – heavy casualties, 1 RUR extricated itself and reached Suwon. Next day the Ulsters mounted the 8th Hussars' Centurion tanks and rode 40 miles south to Pyong-taek. They had learned the hard way about the qualities of the Chinese fighting man, his ability to survive on minimum rations, his skill at fieldcraft, his mobility and his prediliction for night attacks. 27 Commonwealth Brigade left Seoul on 4 January. An angry General Ridgway pulled out at the same time roaring past the infantry in his siren-fitted jeep. His set face and the two grenades taped to his field coat symbolized his determination to take the offensive as soon as possible. The Argylls had the distinction of being the last across the Han. To the 14th Engineer Combat Battalion fell the task of dismantling the pontoon bridges, one of which had to be blown using TNT and Bangalore torpedoes. Several spans of the rail bridge were then destroyed. In this manner, Seoul was finally abandoned to the Chinese. So was a great deal more of South Korea. Along the entire front, Chinese divisions were advancing south heading for Suwon, Osan, Ichon and Wonju. By 13 January the 120th Division leading the 40th Field Army was within striking distance of Wonju though still struggling through the snowdrifts and bowed under the constant hammering delivered by the American guns. The US 2nd Infantry Division had withdrawn across the road bridge over the Wonju River where the 3rd Platoon of Company C, the 2nd Engineer Combat Battalion, devised the most complicated destruction imaginable. Its task was to blow two substantial bridges, one road and one rail, 16 boxcars filled with high explosives and ammunition and the valuable airstrip facilities nearby. Nothing could be left for the Chinese. There were enemy troops – probably NKPA soldiers still en route for North Korea – who fired at the engineers as they worked. Vast quantities of Composition C3 explosive were fitted round the piers, log cribbings and concrete supports that held up the two bridges. Fuses were set and everything exploded when the 3rd Platoon was six miles away. For several minutes night turned into day and Wonju was left as a barren shell for the Chinese 120th Division to occupy.

When the Chinese arrived the Americans fought back and did not bug out. The war was not over after all, as the Chinese generals had hinted it might be once Wonju had fallen. The Americans had merely retreated to ridges less than four miles away, showering the Chinese troops with air bursts that killed hundreds of infantry surging into the ruined town. The US 2nd Division halted the Chinese attack outside Wonju. Ichon had fallen but there was no food for the assault troops. The coolies were dying from cold, and the Chinese had no hope of capturing Wonchon in mid-January for the snowdrifts were too deep for a banzai-style charge and the American artillery pulverized infantrymen caught in the open. For the first time the Chinese halted and then retreated. Just as the NKPA had fought themselves to a standstill on the Naktong the previous year, so the Chinese had reached the point when they too could go no further. At Pyongtaek the story was the same. A confident 38th Field Army had advanced through Osan and sent their patrols into Pyongtaek. American machine-gunners drove them back and the Chinese began a modest but general withdrawal through Suwon and further north. On 15 January Ridgway sent his first offensive patrols up the western highway to Suwon. They met no resistance and he felt confident enough to plan a major counter-offensive against the numerically superior but inadequately equipped Chinese Field Armies.

## RIDGWAY AND THE 'MEATGRINDER'

The Eighth Army's new commander had very specific plans for dealing with the Chinese. It was crucial that his army believed that they could stop and defeat the Chinese tactics of demoralizing night attacks, infiltration and envelopment. It was partly a matter of morale and partly a matter of better leadership. One way of impressing the ordinary infantryman was to increase the sheer hitting power of the big guns, the 155mm howitzers (many of these fitted on self-propelled M-40 tracked vehicles) and the deadly 8-inch guns known as 'Persuaders'. Artillery was to become – as it had become in the First World War – the key weapon for the destruction of enemy manpower. Ridgway had to show that the Chinese could be stopped with firepower, accurate air support plus a resolute infantry spirit both in offensive and defensive actions. Once this had been demonstrated, the killing of the Chinese could go on unabated until even Mao Zedong would have to call a halt. As one British officer observed, Ridgway's strategy was not so much geographical as homicidal. So effective was his idea that, when he implemented the killing machine, it became known as the 'meatgrinder', a phrase that pleased the troops but worried some sections of the American and British public.

The United Nations Command now enjoyed a relative abundance of troops. Several nations made good their promises and despatched their battalions to serve with the Eighth Army. The French battalion, all veterans, arrived in November 1950 under the command of Lt Col Raoul Montclar (a former general in the French Foreign Legion). A Netherlands battalion reached Korea the same month. The Greek infantry landed during 8/9 December and at the end of the month the New Zealand Field Artillery plus supporting units provided a welcome Commonwealth addition to the hard-pressed British gunners. The first of a substantial Canadian Army contribution sailed on board the US troopship *Private Joe P Martinez* and reached Pusan on 18 December 1950. This was the 2nd Battalion Princess Patricia's Canadian Light Infantry, usually abbreviated as 2 PPCLI and universally known as the 'Princess Pats' or 'the Patricias'. The Belgian battalion was on its way and would arrive at the end of January 1951.

The apparent disappearance of the Chinese, backed by reports from his 1st Cavalry Division's reconnaissance patrols, gave Ridgway sufficient confidence to launch his own offensive on 25 January 1951 with the aim of destroying the enemy south and west of the Han River. Codenamed Operation 'Roundup,' his was a cautious advance. Every few miles he planned a 'Line of Resistance' capable of being held should the Chinese resume their attacks. The 24th Reconnaissance Company of the US 24th Division penetrated Yoju on the Han River; the 5th Regiment of the 24th Division occupied Ichon. Both reported that the Chinese had gone. Whenever sightings of Chinese soldiers in local villages were reported by civilians, the ground troops called up the Shooting Stars and the Australian Mustangs to destroy their hideouts. The 1st Cavalry kept the lead, supported by the newly-arrived Greek battalion. As the Greeks were regular soldiers, most with long experience of mountain warfare, they skilfully defended each hill position they occupied. The Chinese contested Hill 381 just to the west of Ichon and the Greeks ably defeated three assaults by 3,000 Chinese soldiers on their position. They set the tone for the advance: never bypass the enemy, hold the high ground, avoid the roads and call down air support, artillery and mortars whenever needed. It was a slow and dangerous business always culminating in the courage and skill of the infantryman who had to go in at close-quarters with rifle and bayonet – just as the Greeks did at Hill 381.

As the UN forces gradually eliminated the enemy west of the 'bend' in the River Han so the Chinese decided to launch a major assault in the east. Its momentum was rather different from previous offensives. Its precise purpose was obscure and Ridgway moved IX Corps, including 27 Commonwealth Brigade, north-eastwards to contain the likely line of enemy advance. Consequently, 27 Commonwealth Brigade found itself at Yoju, a Han River crossing, while to the north-east of their position the 23rd Infantry Regiment of the US 2nd

Division and Lt Col Monclar's French battalion held Chipyong-ni on the other side of the river. Australian patrols maintained contact between the two positions and found little evidence of enemy activity. However, patrols from the UN base at Chipyong-ni reported that the Chinese were moving from Wonju to threaten this latest UN line of communication. Suddenly, a new kind of battle developed and its outcome in many ways was the turning point of the Korean War. It has gone down in history as the siege of Chipyong-ni.

## THE SIEGE OF CHIPYONG-NI, 13–15 FEBRUARY 1950

The 23rd Infantry Regiment at Chipyong-ni was equipped as a Regimental Combat Team and commanded by Colonel Paul Freeman. They were all veterans, tried and tested at Taegu, the Battle of the Chongchon and Kunu-ri. They had come to the town of Chipyong-ni on 3 February 1951 via Wonju and a location that Freeman's troops called 'Twin Tunnels'. They had with them 2,100 riflemen, 18 105mm howitzers, the 82nd Anti-Aircraft Battalion's M-16 and M-19 tracked vehicles, 14 Sherman tanks, some combat engineers and a Ranger Company trained in guerrilla fighting – about 4,000 men in all. It was not until they reached Twin Tunnels that they encountered the enemy – an entire division! There was a brief battle in which many surprised Chinese were killed. The Americans then advanced into Chipyong-ni whose sole importance was that it bestrode a vital crossroad and commanded a railway line linking Wonju with Seoul. Freeman posted his 4,000 men in sound defensive positions in and around the town and was pleased to welcome the thousand French troops led by Lt Col Monclar on 4 February.

## THE FOURTH CHINESE OFFENSIVE

Hidden in and around the town of Hoengsong, some 15 miles north-east of Chipyong-ni, was the so-called 'Phantom Army', the 4th Field Army that had occupied Seoul. It had moved away and US air reconnaissance had failed to locate it. It comprised 18 regular PLA divisions and included the remnants of numerous NKPA divisions that had escaped General Walker's great drive north from the Naktong in 1950. Thus it was a substantial force, numbering in excess of 200,000 soldiers. It was not well-equipped by American standards but in Korea most 4th Army troops carried either US Thompson sub-machine-guns (captured from Chinese Nationalists during 1945–9) or the efficient Soviet 7.6mm PPSh 41 burp gun. They were well-supplied with hand grenades and Russian 82mm and 120mm mortars. They also had some portable 75mm mountain howitzers. Fortunately, General Ridgway became aware of this huge threat to his advance just before he ordered his troops to begin 'Roundup.' Reports from reconnaissance aircraft were rushed to him, listing enemy troop movements fanning out across country and stretching over distances that would defy any air attack. They had spotted the beginning of General Peng's Fourth Offensive. Its aim, said Mao Zedong and Kim Il Sung, was to cause chaos among Ridgway's troops and force yet another bug-out. Chinese and NKPA forces would sweep south, kill 30,000 Americans and ROKs and thereby win the war. Little attention was paid to the quality of the new American commander, General Ridgway, or the extent to which he was revitalizing the morale of his Eighth Army.

The 4th Field Army's divisions were employing the usual, effective *Hachi-shiki* open V-formation designed to penetrate enemy defences and then envelop them when the tips of the V slammed shut. Ridgway decided to halt his own northward advance and diverted the ROK III Corps to a position outside Hoengsong with the 38th Regiment, US 2nd Division, the Netherlands Battalion and batteries of 105mm howitzers in support. His aim was to stop a Chinese penetration. General Almond, commanding X Corps, advised a retreat to a more easily-defended line and abandon Chipyong-ni but Ridgway disagreed. Col Freeman would have to hold Chipyong-ni until the situation had been contained and a relief force could be mobilized. This was easy to order but difficult for Freeman to implement. Chipyong-ni was located in a long valley and he had only 5,000 troops, too few to defend an extensive terrain. He therefore decided to ring Chipyong-ni with a solid defence system. Defence of this 'box' and the high ground and paddy fields around the town absorbed all of his rifle battalions so he formed his Rangers and the combat engineers into a fighting reserve.

The 4th Field Army assault had begun on 11 February, heading first for the 8th Division of the ROK III Corps. It was a masterly attack, enveloping the 8th ROK Division, inflicting thousands of casualties and forcing the survivors to flee. Its swift demise exposed their supporting gunners and they too became victims of the Chinese attack.

# LIMITS OF ADVANCE AND LINES OF RESISTANCE: THE 'MOBILE WAR' IN KOREA, 1950–1

**Key**

- — — British proposal for a buffer zone 1950
- ▷▷▷➤ Limits of UN advance 1950
- ▨▨▨ South Korean territory captured by the Chinese 1951
- •••••• No Name Line
- — — Line Kansas
- ••••••• Line Wyoming

Chongjin

Yalu River

Hyesanjin

Kanggye

Chosan

Chosin Reservoir

Fujon Reservoir

Kunu-ri
Koto-ri
Sudong
Hagaru-ni
Chinhung-ni
Iwon

Chonju

Chongchon River

Taedong River

Hungnam

SEA OF JAPAN

Pyongyang

NORTH KOREA

Imjin River

IRON TRIANGLE
Pyonggang
Kumhwa
Chorwon
Kansong
Taepori

38°

Munsan

Hoengsong
Kangnung

YELLOW SEA

Chipyong-ni

Seoul
Suwon
Wonju
Samchok

Osan

Han River

Ansong
Pyongtaek

SOUTH KOREA

Kum River

Naktong River

Masan
Pusan

100 miles

Cheju-Do

During 12/13 February the 38th and the Netherlands battalion managed to extricate themselves from the *Hachi-shiki* trap. Sadly, the Dutch commander, Lt Col M.P.A. Den Ouden, was killed when enemy troops dressed in US uniforms and carrying US weapons surprised them and brought down heavy Chinese mortar fire on the unsuspecting battalion. Thus the overall effect of the 4th Field Army offensive was to threaten all the UN forces in central Korea.

In the opening stages of their offensive the Chinese had bypassed Freeman's position but at 2200 hours on 13 February 4th Field Army focussed on capturing Chipyong-ni with two divisions allocated to each side of Freeman's square-shaped defence perimeter. Montclar's soldiers were the first to be hit but they responded with a bayonet charge that broke the Chinese assault. Preceded by heavy Chinese artillery and mortar fire, more attacks on the perimeter at battalion strength came early next morning. Enemy squads broke through the perimeter wire and minefields with the intention of wiping out the forward foxholes and destroying the machine-guns that were killing so many Chinese in their crossfire. But the foxholes held, the machine-guns cut down the attackers and as the first rays of sun appeared the Chinese once more withdrew. Colonel Freeman was himself wounded by mortar fragments but he was still mobile and maintained patrols outside the perimeter all day. Air support was singularly absent – Ridgway had committed all ground-attack aircraft to deal with Chinese advances in the centre. However, C-119s from 314th Troop Carrier Group were available and they parachuted 87 loads of supplies into Chipyong-ni on 14 February, while the 3rd Air Rescue Squadron came with its H-5 helicopters to bring medical aid and evacuate the seriously wounded. One helicopter brought in General Ridgway himself. He told Freeman he would have to hold for another 24 hours. Ridgway promised to have the base illuminated by parachute flares that night and to send a relief force from the 1st Cavalry and the British and Commonwealth Brigades.

When night fell, the defenders heard the usual Chinese bugles heralding another assault. Fresh Chinese divisions were sending in specially trained troops equipped with explosives fitted to long poles designed to destroy foxholes. The destruction of these suicide squads was an horrific process. They were mown down by American 155mm shells exploding in their midst. Even worse was the killing of the hundreds that followed in their bloodstained footsteps, all illuminated by the blue-white parachute flares dropped by US aircraft high above the carnage. On the south of the position the decreasing numbers of soldiers dug-in at the perimeter gave all they could but the sheer weight of Chinese numbers gradually overwhelmed them. Entire platoons were killed in these savage moments. Freeman despatched a portion of his fighting reserve – a Ranger company and a solitary tank – to help hold the embattled south side where the situation was approaching a crisis. Had the Chinese exploited this weak spot at divisional strength it is likely that Chipyong-ni would have fallen within an hour or two. But they preferred to hammer the entire perimeter rather than break through at one point. To meet Chinese infiltration during the darkness, Freeman committed his entire reserve and sent it in to defend the embattled south. As dawn approached the Chinese attacks subsided. Hundreds of Chinese walked slowly towards the French line. They were carrying burning torches high above their heads as they searched for their wounded among the piles of dead. For once that dreadful night the French did not open fire.[2]

By dawn on 15 February only the southern perimeter was still under direct Chinese attack. Before long, American fighter-bombers arrived, working under the direction of 'Mosquito' spotter aircraft. They hit the Chinese withdrawing from the other three sectors with napalm and rockets. Freeman's counter-attacks on the south side of the perimeter made little headway; while the defenders managed to hold the Chinese thrusts. For a time it was stalemate though it seemed unlikely that Chipyong-ni could survive yet another night, especially when, despite his protests, the wounded Freeman was evacuated by helicopter. Command of the besieged base now passed to Lt Col James Edwards of the 2nd Battalion 23rd Infantry Regiment. He knew that his old friend Colonel Marcel Crombez of the US 5th Cavalry Regiment was leading a relief force. But would it come in time? The Chinese in the north and west were temporarily out of artillery range and regrouping for the final blow.

The 27 Commonwealth Brigade then played a vital role in this complex operation. It defeated a Chinese attempt to capture a key ridge in an action at Chuam-ni. On 14 February 1 Middlesex led the brigade from its base at Yoju just across the Han River, towards a hill some six miles distant and supposedly held by a US reconnaissance company. On arrival, the Middlesex found that the Americans had been driven off the hill by Chinese infantry. Surveying the situation, A Company of the Middlesex discovered that beyond the hill was a commanding ridge some 800 yards long and flanked by precipitous ravines. A Company advanced and took the ridge to the astonishment of the Chinese who counter-attacked in the early hours of the following morning under cover of mortars and machine-gun fire. A Company soon ran dangerously low on ammunition and one rifle section was overrun as the Chinese kept coming regardless of casualties. New Zealand gunners helped save the day: in a brilliant shoot their 25 pounders caused terrible carnage among the Chinese assault troops and the Middlesex finished off the survivors with the bayonet. The rifle section that had been overrun managed to return to A Company and the Chinese abandoned their attack and withdrew. In front of A Company lay 48 dead Chinese; seven Middlesex men had been killed. This hard-fought action at Chuam-ni guaranteed the right flank for the American relief force en route for Chipyong-ni the same day.

'Task Force Crombez' had set out on 14 February with a company of M-46 Patton tanks, two platoons of Shermans, some self-propelled howitzers and numerous armed jeeps and tracked support vehicles. It was confined to a narrow road and was for a time held up by a destroyed bridge. Aware of the urgency, Crombez decided to speed up the relief by forming Task Force Crombez composed of tanks with heavily armed infantry riding on board. It ran a constant gauntlet of fire as it drove north. More brave Chinese soldiers died as they dashed out with satchel charges and bangalore torpedoes in a vain attempt to stop the charging tank column. They enjoyed one success in a ravine where they knocked out two Pattons but the main force of tanks defied the hail of rockets and bullets fired by Chinese infantry and gradually broke out of the ravine onto higher ground. As the tanks approached the crossroads they could see the battle raging on the south of the Chipyong-ni perimeter. The Chinese were actually in front of them and Crombez ordered his tanks to charge through the enemy lines. Astonished Chinese soldiers abandoned their foxholes and fled from this unexpected attack from their rear. The Crombez Task Force crashed through the Chinese lines and entered Chipyong-ni a few minutes before sunset. Of the 165 infantrymen who had ridden on the Pattons, protecting the tanks from flank attack, only 23 had survived that harrowing journey.

The arrival of Crombez Force signalled a general retreat by the Chinese 4th Army which began to depart towards the north-west. Edwards ordered his artillery to bombard them until they were out of range. The siege of Chipyong-ni was over. Interestingly, the tanks of

Task Force Crombez had been painted in the most bizarre manner. Frontal armour and gun turrets bore images of dragons and tigers in the belief that superstitious Chinese would be terrified by the sight of animal devils. There is no evidence that this form of psychological warfare had any effect on the enemy, but it certainly boosted the morale of the American tank crews. They spent the night at Chipyong-ni to ensure that the relief was effective and then departed in the morning to escort the resupply column still driving up from Yonju. The siege had proved the capacity of United Nations forces, outnumbered by 18 to 1, to defeat a Chinese Field Army and to hold a position of crucial strategic importance. The victory at Chipyong-ni, one of the most significant defensive battles fought in the Korean War, would symbolize the fighting spirit of United Nations' forces thereafter. The Chinese had deployed 90,000 men at Chipyong-ni and suffered well over 10,000 casualties – the final statistics have yet to be released – in their first major defeat. Chipyong-ni was a bonus for both President Truman and Prime Minister Attlee. They now judged that the war in Korea could be contained without danger of the conflagration spreading into the Soviet Union and the Far East. For the politicians, if not for the fighting men, Korea had become a 'limited war'.

## OPERATION 'KILLER' 21 FEBRUARY

Ridgway decided that it was vital to pursue the Chinese, to keep up the pressure and exploit their temporary disarray. Operation 'Killer' therefore began on 21 February with the aim of inflicting maximum casualties on the enemy via air strikes, artillery bombardment and massed armoured fighting vehicle gunfire. Climatic conditions ruined his original plan: to imitate the Chinese on a vast scale and use IX Corps and X Corps to envelop the retreating enemy. Heavy rain caused swollen rivers and turned the roads to mudslides. On the hills and mountains the snow still filled the gullies and ravines but the ridges turned to ice at night and remained dangerously slippery all day. This meant that troops could advance carrying minimum gear; all their heavy equipment had to be borne by Korean porters who manhandled mortars, ammunition and water to the firing points on top of every hill.

2 PPCLI had joined 27 Commonwealth Brigade on 19 February and

in company with the Argylls, Middlesex and 3 RAR fought their way towards the country around Chipyong-ni hill by hill, ridge by ridge. Chinese forces were still dug-in on many of the surrounding heights, and typical of the fighting was the Australian and Canadian assault on Hill 614 during Operation 'Killer' on 24 February. Air strikes softened up the crest with the usual napalm; artillery and mortars swept the ridges in the hope of hitting the Chinese weapon pits. Steep sided slopes covered in waist-high scrub made the infantry attack difficult – and dangerous when the Chinese began rolling hand grenades down the hill. Corporal Len Opie, with Lance Corporal Thorburn and Private Hughes (all from 3 RAR) reached the enemy positions and later Hughes recalled the situation:

> Everything started to happen at once. A Chink threw three hand grenades and Len Opie threw one back at him. Then a Chink appeared out of the ground behind me, but Lance Corporal Charlie Thorburn ran him through as he was taking aim. Opie snatched up a blood-stained carbine from a Chinese he had killed and used that. As fast as he ran out of ammunition he picked up another weapon. Then, looking down from a peak, he saw a cluster of Chinese on a knoll nearby. With me shooting a Bren from the hip we went after them. Suddenly I heard Len yell out, 'Grenade! Grenade!' A grenade landed near me and stunned me but five minutes later I'd recovered sufficiently to join the others in finishing off the job.[3]

All units in the Eighth Army were similarly engaged, killing Chinese every day and pushing onwards to the Han River. By the end of February, when Operation 'Killer' had effectively ended, the Chinese had retreated behind the Han and Ridgway called a brief halt to rest his troops. Then on 6 March the offensive renewed under the codename Operation 'Ripper'. It took the UN forces across the Han and into Seoul once more. Still the Chinese retreated and Ridgway devised a plan to capture thousands. The 187th Airborne Regimental Combat Team was dropped on 23 March 1951 to form a roadblock along the Seoul-Kaesong road while an advancing tank commmn coming from Seoul would take the Chinese in the rear. Chinese and North Korean divisions evaded the trap but the Eighth Army continued north virtually uncontested. On 27 March Ridgway called a conference of corps commanders to evaluate the strengths and weaknesses of Operation 'Ripper' and to propose a response to plans by the Chinese to launch a Spring offensive. He proposed Operation 'Rugged' to place the UN forces on 'Line Kansas' (Imjin-Chunchon-Chosan); followed by Operation 'Dauntless' to carry US I and IX Corps to 'Line Utah' and then to 'Line Wyoming.' For the British 29 Brigade it meant advancing to Uijongbu beyond which American units (65th Infantry and 7th Infantry) were clearing enemy hilltop positions. They passed through Uijongbu, relieved the 65th, and with the Belgian battalion, took up their positions on the 'Kansas Line.'

29 Brigade was now under the command of the US 3rd Division and was given responsibility for some 14 miles of the front line. This meant that the rifle companies were spread rather thinly: the Glosters on the left facing the Imjin River and backed by Centurious of 6 Squadron 8th Hussars and C Troop, 170 battery with its 4.2-inch mortars; in the centre were the Royal Northumberland Fusiliers; on the right were the Royal Ulster Rifles; while the Belgian battalion was in reserve. 29 Brigade was ready for action, but where were the Chinese? On 13 April a Fighting Fifth patrol commanded by Lt M.D. Young brought in a Chinese prisoner; on 14 October D Company RUR was briefly attacked by the Chinese. For the next six days the brigade conducted sweeps across the Imjin where mines proved to be the biggest danger. The most dramatic development was that the Eighth Army was to have General James Alward Van Fleet as its new commander as a consequence of President Truman's dismissal of General MacArthur and Ridgway's move to become Supreme Commander, Allied Powers, Japan.

## A CHANGE IN COMMAND

On 11 April 1951 President Truman wired General MacArthur expressing regret that he had to relieve America's popular five-star general of his post as Supreme Commander Allied Powers and all associated commands. Unfortunately, as a result of a press conference held in Washington at 0100 hours, US radio stations broadcast the news before Truman's wire reached MacArthur. Consequently, the Commander-in-Chief of the United Nations Command in Korea heard it second-hand from one of his aides, Colonel Sidney Huff, who telephoned MacArthur's wife, Jeannie, who told her husband who was lunching with two guests. It was hardly a fitting conclusion to the military career of America's most famous general, spanning, as it did, 52 years of service to the nation.

In fact, Truman had been faced with a serious constitutional issue and had no option but to dismiss MacArthur. The general was convinced that his mission was to destroy the enemy, Chinese as well as North Korean: cross the 38 degree Parallel, advance once more to the Yalu and reunite North and South Korea. If this required taking out Chinese air bases in Manchuria, or bombing power stations on the other side of that river, or bringing in Chinese Nationalist troops from Taiwan to fight against the communists, so be it. He frequently spoke of his major difficulty in conducting a war against the Chinese: their possession of Manchuria on the other side of the Yalu. Here their soldiers could mobilize and their supplies could be assembled. Their aircraft were based in Manchuria and were free to fly across the Yalu and engage aircraft operating under the UN command. Yet he was forbidden to attack this 'privileged sanctuary'. Perhaps it did not occur to him that his bases in Japan afforded him precisely the same privilege in the limited war that his President, Commander-in-Chief of the US Armed Forces, required him to fight.

Consistently, MacArthur had shown Truman remarkably little respect. For some time, the President had resented MacArthur's acts of insubordination ranging from the dispatch of three squadrons of US jets to Taiwan at the beginning of the war without reference to the Pentagon, to his failure to salute his President when they met at Wake Island. It had become more serious in 1951 when General MacArthur was clearly misreading the international situation. He did not feel that Ridgway's 'meatgrinder tactics' were likely to compel the communist armies in North Korea to surrender; and he certainly did not agree that Ridgway should consolidate the UN position at 'Line Wyoming.' As he said in correspondence with Congressman Joe Martin, the Republican Minority Leader, other tactics and other weapons must be used including Nationalist troops from Taiwan; and as he put it on 20 March: 'There is no substitute for victory.' Truman and Acheson were both content with Ridgway's push to the 38 degree Parallel for this gave them some hope of opening negotiations with the Chinese. On 24 March MacArthur proposed hostile action against mainland China and the advantages inherent in a personal meeting between himself and the Chinese command in Korea. Generals in conference, he thought, could work out some mutually acceptable conclusion to the war. He, MacArthur, was prepared to act where, it seemed, neither the United Nations nor the United States seemed capable of resolving the impasse in Korea. These views appeared in a communiqué received in Washington and led to an emergency meeting between Acheson, Dean Rusk and the Deputy Secretary of Defense, Robert Lovett.

Lovett was appalled by MacArthur's suggestions. Here was an officer of the United States Army undertaking executive decisions that were the constitutional and democratic rights and privileges of the US President. Lovett recommended that MacArthur be instantly dismissed. Next day the three men met Truman who, when he heard of MacArthur's insubordination, was enraged. The President's controlled response was to send MacArthur a curt reminder that all public statements must first be checked out with the Joint Chiefs of Staff as instructed by a Presidential Order of 6 December 1950. The crisis came on 5 April 1951 when Congressman Joe Martin read out MacArthur's letter of 20 March on the floor of the House. When they heard of this both Lovett and Acheson agreed that MacArthur had to go. The Chiefs of Staff favoured recalling MacArthur for consultation but both Acheson and Lovett wanted to secure the maximum political advantage accruing from MacArthur's dismissal. Acheson's way through was to strip MacArthur of all military status and responsibility *in the field*. MacArthur would therefore return to the United States as a private citizen. It was then agreed that General Matthew Ridgway should replace MacArthur; and that General Van Fleet should take command of the Eighth Army in Korea. This message was conveyed by General George Marshall to the Joint Chiefs of Staff who promptly approved the appointments. Ridgway was invited to carry on with his Eighth Army command for the time being but he preferred to hand over immediately to General Van Fleet.

Acheson believed that MacArthur had presented the United States with the most serious constitutional crisis in its history. However, the American people had never seen MacArthur's leadership in the Far East as a problem and so his return to the United States on 17 April occasioned a display of public emotion unprecedented since the end of the Civil War. His appearance at the joint session of Congress on 19 April was so dramatic and so moving that Congressmen and Senators wept. His sonorous words remembering his youth and the ballad 'Old soldiers never die, they simply fade away' were broadcast to the world and captured on records and wire recorders everywhere: 'And like that

Chinese postage stamp commemorating the 1950 Treaty between Stalin and Mao Zedong. Korea may be discerned just to the right of Chairman Mao

Snatch squad, Duke of Wellington's Regiment

A Marine Corsair is flying through smoke after dropping napalm on an enemy position outside Hagaru-ri in December 1950.

US Infantry firing a 75mm Recoilless rifle in Korea

Centurion tank *Artist's Proof*, 4 Troop, A Squadron, Royal Inniskilling Dragoo
Guards. 'Little Gibraltar' looms in the background with the Chinese-held Hill 22
('John') on the far left, November 1952

Captured Chinese field gun, now the property of 45 Field Regiment, Royal Artiller

Sikorsky helicopter brings in a patient for surgery at NORMASH 1953

oy Williams with his well-known NAAFI van near the Imjin River. As he later said,
'ravelling along routes trying to find different units of the Commonwealth Division
as a bit hair-raising. Near the Hook was the worst where the Scots were holding . . .'

Members of Company L, 7th US Infantry. Exhausted after holding Hill 717 against an all-night Chinese assault, they illustrate the vacant expression that was often called the 'thousand-yard stare'

eed by Chinese Combat Troops: Richard Drozdowski of 2 Recon. 2nd Infantry
ivision was wounded and captured by the Chinese. He was then released and is here
seen being helped by Australian solder, Roy Ingle

*HMAS Sydney* launches a Firefly during a patrol off the Korean coast. *Sydney* had borrowed the Sikorsky helicopter from the US Navy in order to rescue aircrew in the event of a take-off/landing mishap

*USS Missouri* bombards a North Korean target, 1950

old soldier of that ballad, I now close my military career and just fade away, an old soldier who tried to do his duty as God gave him the light to see that duty. Goodbye.' Truman's reaction to such high drama was unprintable.

# CHAPTER 7

# The Chinese Offensives, April–May 1951

## PROBLEMS OF INTERPRETATION

Lt General Van Fleet had commanded Patton's Third Army in France and Germany and played a significant role in the Battle of the Bulge 1944–5 before leading the First Army's III Corps in its breakout from Remagen into central Germany. President Truman had appointed him to lead the Military Advisory Mission to Greece and Turkey during the troubled years 1947–9 and he remained in the region until called to lead the Eighth Army in Korea on 11 April 1951. Now he had inherited Ridgway's achievements and the limitations – and he would find these irksome – imposed on his tactical freedom by the President, the Joint Chiefs of Staff and General Ridgway. There was no time for him to oversee the consolidation of his forces and to ensure that they were capable of adequately resisting the anticipated Chinese counter-offensive. His only ploy in the face of determined Chinese attacks was to retreat from 'Wyoming', 'Utah' and 'Kansas Lines' and move south of the 38 degree Parallel to prepared positions – the so-called 'No-Name Line'. He also had to consider the prospect of a stalemate if negotiations for a peace settlement actually began. He had respect for his adversary, General Peng. Both Walker and Ridgway had found it difficult to fathom the intentions of the Chinese Command, though in a sense this was balanced by the mistaken beliefs the Chinese entertained about their Anglo-American enemies. However, on the day of his appointment Van Fleet was unaware of the dimensions of the offensive Peng was about to launch against the UN Command.

Chinese interpretations of western moves towards a possible peaceful settlement were flawed by their own unshakeable beliefs in Marxist principles. Their enemies were capitalist imperialists; therefore their offers for an armistice or a peaceful settlement must be automatically suspect. Mao Zedong was positive that an ultimate Chinese victory would emerge. Thus there would be no need for peace talks. The prerequisites of victory were more trained and skillful fighting men, better supply and distribution systems especially for food and ammunition and, above all, better weapons. General Peng had long complained of such weaknesses and Mao was prepared to endorse his requests for all-round improvement. Three new Army Groups 3, 9 and 10, plus new engineer and artillery forces, would be available for a Spring offensive. For Peng the weakness in his planning was the erroneous assumption that the United Nations forces in Korea would be reinforced by Chinese Nationalist armies from Taiwan and the entire 11th Airborne Division from the United States. When he discussed his plans with Chinese commanders at Sanyang-ni on 6 April he dwelt on the quality of the new weapons received from Russia, especially the automatic weapons for the infantry, and the artillery and anti-aircraft guns that would perhaps prevent a repeat of the disaster at Chipyong-ni. A novel idea was the inception of deep reconnaissance units whose task was to cause mayhem in the enemy rear and, at the same time, pass back relevant information to the parent armies. But as Peng feared a possible amphibious landing in his rear, time was the essence. He urged his commanders to be ready for his 'First Step, Fifth Phase Offensive' on 22 April 1951.

Four days before H-Hour Peng issued specific orders. The main attacks in the west and central sectors would be directed against the British 27 Commonwealth Brigade, 29 Independent Infantry Brigade, the Turkish Brigade, the US 3rd Division and the 1st and 6th ROK Divisions. Once these had been eliminated the next blow would fall on the US 24th and 25th Divisions. The road to the south would then be open, Seoul would be recaptured and the western imperialists would be driven into the sea. Simultaneously, two more Field Armies together with reformed NKPA divisions would fall on the enemy spread across the east central and eastern sectors. It was expected that these would quickly succumb to mass infiltration and allow a rapid advance beyond Seoul and towards Chungju and Taegu. Logistical problems, particularly the supply of food and ammunition, would be the main limiting factor. Speed was of the essence and so to confirm intelligence assessments of UN troop dispositions preliminary reconnaissance must begin two days ahead of H-Hour.

Later interrogation of Chinese and NKPA prisoners added flesh to these bones. Most of the Chinese troops used in Peng's offensive came from China via Manchuria by rail. Many were replacements and merged immediately into units already in the field. Substantial numbers were 'political troops,' communist party members whose task was to maintain morale and deal with the increasing problem of desertion to UN troops. The spearhead force, 65th Chinese Field Army, was seen as a 'shock army' whose task was to penetrate as far south as possible. In a sense, they were Panzer troops without the Panzers. Very few soldiers from the 65th deserted.

Descriptions of Chinese tactics provided by the prisoners fitted in well with the UN experience. Their basic fighting unit was the regiment composed of three battalions. One battalion launched the initial attack, mostly at night, using a company as the assault force with two companies kept in reserve. Each platoon in a company probed for weak spots and on finding one immediately infiltrated the enemy position to permit the attack to build up to regimental level. Communication between units and individual soldiers was by bugle and trumpet, whistles, hissing or by tapping rifle butts. If the assault failed, one or two more similar attacks went in before dawn at which time the survivors withdrew and dispersed. Movement was aided by horse-drawn carts; ruined buildings sheltered soldiers for rest and recovery.

Chinese troops who opened the assault in April were in good physical shape and dressed in winter uniforms, often with summer uniforms underneath. They had extra underwear, a pair of leather shoes or fur-trimmed boots as well as the usual rubber-soled canvas shoes. They all had combat rations issued: mainly rice and baked wheat cakes, sufficient to last a week of combat. In the line, two and sometimes three meals a day were provided though the NKPA prisoners said they received less. Fitness of all soldiers in Korea depended on preventative medicine and the Chinese soldiers had all been immunized against cholera, typhoid, typhus and tetanus. Malaria was a problem that atabrine tablets did not cure and dysentery was common once combat began. Strong troops were often exhausted by the style of their advance – a jogtrot of 10–15 miles before an attack. All soldiers complain, but the Chinese bemoaned the fact that letters from home took a month or more to arrive. They were highly critical of poor maps and inadequate supplies of ammunition – in action they carried a hundred rounds per rifle and only 150 rounds per burp gun – but they appreciated the quality of their new Soviet-made weapons. Their main complaints, however, focused on the lack of food and the difficulty of replacing battle-worn clothing. Why had they deserted? UN air attack, devastating artillery fire and downright exhaustion.

## THE BATTLE OF THE IMJIN

General Van Fleet was confident that the road and rail links to Uijongbu and Seoul were adequately defended by the 3rd US Infantry Division, commanded by General Robert H. Soule. Most of its units were well north, close to 'Line Utah' and under orders to withdraw to 'Line Kansas' in the event of an overwhelming Chinese attack. Further south the British brigades, 12 ROK Division, the Belgian Battalion and the Turkish Brigade were spread along 'Line Kansas' west of the Imjin and Hantan Rivers. Beyond Route 33 leading to Seoul was the US 25th Division. In front of the 29 Brigade sector reconnaissance aircraft brought reports of enemy activity: smoke screens to mask daylight troop movements and filled-in anti-tank ditches to facilitate the movement of supplies. But there was nothing specific to report. On 20 April, after ten days of relative inactivity, the Royal Ulster Rifles were brought back from their isolated position north of the Imjin and placed in reserve with 26 Field Ambulance. Lt Col Crahay's Belgian battalion now took the hinge position in their place. All of 29 Brigade was now well-established on hills rising, apart from the heights of Kamak-san, to less than 2,000 feet. In front of them was the Imjin, flowing east to west with fords at Gloster Crossing and Ulster Crossing, the latter leading to the Belgians. All the brigade could do was to send out patrols and wait.

Late on 21 April one of the Gloster's listening posts on the river bank, manned by Corporal Cook, Drummer Eagles and Private Hunter spotted fourteen figures on the opposite bank. Corporal Cook had a telephone link with Battalion HQ. He reported the presence of Chinese to his adjutant, Captain Anthony Farrar-Hockley, who asked the Gunners for flares to illuminate the enemy. The adjutant then advised Cook to open fire. Signaller control in 29 Brigade was superb: all units were netted in on a radio link supervized by the ultra-efficient 45 Field Regiment Royal Artillery. There was soon news from the US

24th Division that the enemy was approaching in very large numbers. Suddenly Chinese soldiers began crossing in front of the Glosters where 2/Lt G.F.B. Temple and his No. 7 Platoon ambushed scores of Chinese wading across the Imjin in bright moonlight. Others appeared in front of the Royal Northumberland Fusiliers (RNF), suggesting that the brigade area was being probed so that the Chinese could define their targets. Brigadier Brodie ordered an RUR Battle Patrol – 130 riflemen plus mortars and machine-guns – to mount Oxford carriers to guard Ulster Crossing. Commanded by Lt Hedley Craig, the patrol drove into smallarms fire and a hail of grenades and two of its carriers caught fire. Craig and his riflemen covered the withdrawal and were then captured by the Chinese. Beyond the crossing the Belgians were surrounded and fighting desperately. Elements of three Chinese divisions – the 187th, 188th and 189th – were determined to destroy 29 Brigade, and by daylight were actually holding the centre of the British positions. A thousand Chinese were attacking the Glosters; two of the RNF rifle companies were gradually being infiltrated.

Brigadier Brodie was in need of urgent assistance and he contacted General Soule who sent American tanks and infantry to bolster the Belgians. The 1st Battalion 7th Infantry would attempt to reoccupy the centre and the 65th Infantry would move back to 'Line Kansas' But the sheer press of the Chinese meant that the solution of one crisis was jeopardized by the next. All three companies of the Royal Northumberland Fusiliers had to carry out a partial withdrawal during the morning of 23 April but managed to cling to the high ground in the west. With a company of the RUR straddling Route 11, the gun line well-established below them and the news that the Belgians had managed to escape, all did not seem lost. Signallers were ordered to withdraw and Norman 'Taff' Davies packed the section Bren with plenty of spare magazines. He later wrote;

> The unmistakeable sound of the 4.2 mortars made everybody's head turn in that direction. We did not know at the time but it meant that the enemy had encircled the Glosters and were getting between us and the infantry, bringing them in range of the mortars. These were the reserve troops of 170 Mortar Battery and were sited to the left of the Tactical Headquarters position. Also, in the distance, we could hear the 25 pounders of the 45th Field Regiment barking out what seemed a continuous roar. Later analysis of the battle

showed that the guns fired more rounds per gun – the average was a thousand rounds – than had been fired at El Alamein in World War II.[1]

The Glosters' A Company – this company and the Belgian battalion were the only brigade elements that had been located north of 'Line Kansas' – endured the first mass attack by waves of Chinese infantry who killed or wounded half the company strength. Chinese machine-gunners then forced their way on to the crest of 'Castle Site' separated from the defenders by 40 yards of open ground. This machine-gun nest dominated two Gloster companies. In an act of selfless heroism Lt Philip Curtis, already badly wounded, ordered his platoon to remain under cover while he went forward to grenade the machine-gun nest. He died as the grenade exploded, killing the Chinese and destroying the gun. For this he was awarded a posthumous Victoria Cross. However, Castle Site was lost to the enemy but Lt Colonel Carne, the battalion commander, ordered the A Company survivors to defend their positions at all costs. On the right, D Company was being similarly hammered and Carne then decided to withdraw all survivors from both companies, together with C Troop 170 Light (Mortar) Battalion, Royal Artillery, into the Battalion HQ on Hill 235, thereafter known as Gloster Hill. B and C Companies were the next to receive mass Chinese attacks and Carne withdrew the entire battalion to Gloster Hill in order to concentrate his defences and give his men a chance of survival. C Company came in swiftly whilst the Chinese were regrouping but B Company was given no respite. Pursued by teh Chinese, it made a dash to reach Gloster Hill, covered by, among others, Corporal Walker firing a Bren gun from the hip. B Company survivors, Major Harding, CSM Morton and 13 men came in with their weapons but they were out of ammunition and grenades.

Carne now held a defence perimeter of 600 yards and prayed for relief, though his position was now four miles away from the nearest friendly unit. Filipino light tanks plus the 8th Hussars' Centurions were blocked by Chinese fire; Belgian and Puerto Rican infantry were pinned down as they moved towards Gloster Hill; an American column tried to break through to Gloster Hill but they too were frustrated. The Glosters, now isolated and lacking air and artillery support, were there to buy time and save Seoul. Three hundred men were left to fight through the night of 24/25 April. A Company had no officers; Carne himself was carrying a rifle and bayonet. Captain Farrar-Hockley took over A Company and led it on a charge that

## THE BATTLE OF THE IMJIN RIVER, 22–5 APRIL 1951

Sokchangsang-ni
65
Charumul
63
BELGIANS
Chongong-ni
Ulster crossing
LINE KANSAS
Tunjan
64
Imjin River
Gloster crossing
RNF
RUR (from reserves)
Choksong
Solma-ri
LINE KANSAS
HILL 235 Gloster Hill
Main Break-out route
Kwangsuwon
45 RA Gun Line 25 April
ROUTE 11
ROUTE 33
25 April
ROUTE 57
RNF
RUR
Tokchong
To Uijongbu and Seoul

**Key**
〰 Roads/ tracks
**RNF** Royal Northumberland Fusiliers
**RUR** Royal Ulster Rifles
63 Chinese Field Armies
➤ Chinese thrusts
⇨ UN withdrawals
▲ UN hill positions

5 miles

regained its original position. He then famously ordered Drum Major Philip Buss to sound bugle calls – his Chinese counterparts were using gongs, whistles and trumpets to control their infantry attacks. Though morale among the Glosters remained high as men cheered on their Drum Major, Carne knew that the remnants of his battalion could fight no longer. The spirit was willing but the ammunition was spent. Brodie appreciated this and over the failing radio gave Carne permission to use his discretion. Carne decided that all those able and willing to break out should do so shortly after 0930 hours on 25 April; the wounded had to be left behind in the care of Captain Bob Hickey, Battalion Medical Officer.

Carne's duty as an officer was to evade capture and he was on the run for just under 48 hours before being caught by the Chinese. Two years later, after terrible privations as a POW, he would be awarded the Victoria Cross for his conspicuous bravery and powers of leadership rarely equalled in the history of the British Army. Captain Farrar-Hockley led a party of survivors from A, B and C Companies until surrounded by Chinese machine-gunners who, on this occasion, did not open fire. He ordered his men to stop fighting and surrendered. D Company decided to move north and work round the Chinese rear. Ninety-two Glosters set out. Unaware that they were marching into a pitched battle between the enemy and a I ROK battalion backed by US tanks, they soon ran into Chinese machine-gunners and lost half their men. The survivors pressed on and were spotted by a Mosquito pilot who showed them the route to follow. Emerging from ditches at the side of a paddy field, they encountered three US tanks. The Americans assumed they were Chinese and opened fire, hitting six Glosters. Desperate wing-waggling by the Mosquito spotter aircraft persuaded the Americans to cease firing. Five officers and 41 men had survived out of the 622 Glosters who had originally gone into action on 22 April.

On the ridges and across the valley roadway west of the Glosters the Royal Northumberland Fusiliers endured similar attacks throughout the day and night of 24/25 April. Both the Belgian battalion and the Ulster Rifles had been badly mauled and were withdrawing, leaving 1 RNF in a dangerously vulnerable situation. Z Company was the first to be hit but 2/Lt William Shepherd and the company commander, Major John Winn, held the key positions all night. The RNF famed for their control of accurate firepower killed over 500 Chinese that night. They were helped by 11 (Sphinx) Light Anti-Aircraft Battery whose six 40mm Bofors guns fired over open sights and slaughtered the enemy. Corporal John Martin, a K-Force volunteer (see Chapter 14), had just arrived in Korea and on 24 April was part of a resupply convoy of three Oxford carriers bringing up mortar bombs, Mark 36 and Mark 66 grenades plus Bren, Sten, Vickers and rifle ammunition. As he later recalled, 'The column raced through the entrance to the valley and the first thing I saw, outlined against their own muzzle flashes, was the battery of Bofors in a paddyfield on our right, with barrels horizontal, obviously firing over open sights across the track in front of us. Not a good start to the day . . .'[2]

He went on to help the wounded Fusiliers, as did a squad of young replacements from the East Yorkshire Regiment flown in from Japan to become instant Fusiliers. Martin was shocked to see the condition of Z Company. 'The first men I saw were in a pretty bad way, battledress ragged and bloodstained, hands and face blackened by continuous gunfire, their eyes reddened and staring through strain and lack of sleep, staggering down the rocks bearing a stretcher on which lay a Fusilier with field dressings bound round both his legs . . . We moved up the hill amid the crackle of small-arms fire where we met Major Winn . . . bandages round his head, walking-stick in hand, staggering down the hill. I had often wondered why British officers affected walking sticks, now I knew . . . we set off in the general direction of the Ulsters.'[3] Last to leave the Fusiliers' shattered hillsides was their commanding officer, Colonel Kingsley Foster. As his jeep drove away a Chinese mortar bomb scored a direct hit and he and his orderly were killed instantly.

The Royal Ulster Rifles, still seriously under strength due to earlier battles, defended high ground on the right of the brigade and, crucially, B Company kept open Route 11. The 25 pounder gun line was already under attack and the great danger was that the 189th and 188th Chinese Divisions would encircle 29 Brigade's three surviving battalions. Brigadier Brodie therefore decided on a general withdrawal down Route 11 which followed a valley whose western slopes were already occupied by Chinese infantry. The Ulsters were disappointed in that they felt they could hold their present positions though events were to show that had they remained the sheer weight of Chinese numbers would have overwhelmed them. The Fusiliers passed through the Ulster's B Company holding position followed by the rest of the RUR. Heavy fire came from the western slopes and the Ulsters moved into the foothills. The Hussars' Centurions, two of which had already been lost, were crowded with troops as they set off to run the gauntlet. RUR's regimental historian noted that:

the road for a mile and a half south of Hwangbang-ni was seething with Chinese; every bank, ditch and house was filled with them and, though many were crushed under the tracks of the Centurions, the unprotected infantry riding on the outside came under a continuous hail of small arms fire, grenades and mortar bombs. Many were killed on the tanks and many, wounded, lost their grip on the wildly pitching hulls and fell to the ground. Two tanks were knocked out by pole charges, but the remainder, with their load of dead and living, broke through to the comparative safety of the Brigade Headquarters valley.[4]

A long column of weary riflemen, accompanied by Fusiliers, American troops and Belgians reached the crossroads at Tokchong where the survivors of 29 Brigade received orders to dig in and await the arrival of the US 15th Regimental Combat Team before proceeding to Yongdungpo, south of the Han River. From here the Battle of the Imjin may be said to be over for the men of 29 Brigade. On their broad backs three of General Peng's divisions had been broken, suffering well over 10,000 casualties. For three days 30,000 Chinese soldiers had thrown themselves at four battalions of infantry, the Gunners and the Hussars. Brigadier Brodie had lost the Glosters and many more of his men, dead or captured, totalling well over one thousand casualties. During those vital three days the entire I Corps had successfully withdrawn to secure the line of the Han River and, the greatest political prize of all, the city of Seoul, capital of South Korea. The men who had won this crucial respite were rested and refitted at Yongdongpo during 26/27 and on 28 April moved back into the Kimpo area. The Glosters, numerically enlarged by the arrival of replacements, had won international acclaim as the 'Glorious Gloucesters'. Together with 170 Light (Mortar) Battery, Royal Artillery, the 1st Battalion The Gloucestershire Regiment were awarded the United States Presidential Citation in recognition of their gallantry:

> Their sustained brilliance in battle, their resoluteness and extraordinary heroism are in keeping with the finest traditions of the renowned military forces of the British Commonwealth, and reflect unsurpassed credit on these courageous soldiers and their homeland.

This was a proper recognition; but it is equally important to record that all the battalions and their supporting arms who fought at the Battle of the Imjin River acquitted themselves with distinction.

## THE BATTLE OF KAPYONG, 23–24 APRIL 1951

To the east of the Imjin River battle, 27 Commonwealth Brigade had been fighting to clear the road that ran alongside the Kapyong River, a tributary of the Pukhan River. In company with 6th ROK Division, the US 1st Cavalry and a US Marine Regiment, the brigade reached 'Line Kansas' by 8 April and then took part in Operation 'Dauntless'. This required the capture of a series of hills rejoicing in the code-names 'Cod', 'Sole', 'Kipper', 'Dab', 'Salmon', 'Turbot' and 'Sardine'. They involved some short, sharp actions with the Middlesex, Patricias and 3 RAR all suffering casualties. Chinese resistance was undoubtedly stiffening as the Middlesex discovered when, after capturing 'Cod', they made two assaults on the 2,500 foot 'Sardine'. It was a tough assignment in that the Middlesex first had to descend into a forested gully and then rush the steep slopes of the hill. They were helped by air strikes and tank gunners, but not by American artillery whose shells landed on the Middlesex positions. The mission was then passed to the Australians and two of A Company's platoons, led by Lt Harold Mulry and Sgt George Harris, which carried out a neat flanking assault on the Chinese, 30 of whom were killed in the final charge. The Australians took eight casualties, mainly the result of fragmentation grenades. Next day Captain Reg Saunders led C Company in an assault on 'Salmon' and took the hill without firing a single round. The only Chinese reaction was to employ some of their mountain howitzers to shell their vacated positions. In this manner 27 Commonwealth Brigade reached their objectives on the 'Utah Line' where they dug in until relieved by 6th ROK Division.

On 17 April 1951 the 27 Commonwealth Brigade was put into reserve and based in and around the Kapyong Valley, a traditional route for northern invaders moving south. It was a time for celebration as the 1st Battalion The Argyll and Sutherland Highlanders and the 1st Battalion The Middlesex Regiment were due to leave Korea. Movement orders for the Argylls were complete and the battalion left for Inchon at 1100 hours on 24 April. Their journey was memorable in that their American mortar friend, Charlie Snow, company commander of the US Chemical Mortar Battalion, which had been attached to the battalion since December, stood at a road junction to salute them as they drove past. They then had a brief meeting with their relieving battalion, the 1st Battalion The King's Own Scottish Borderers (1KOSB).

It was at 1600 hours on 24 April that General Sir Horace Robertson, Commander-in-Chief British Commonwealth Forces in Korea and Japan, came on board the Borderer's troopship, the USS *Montrose*. He brought serious news: the Chinese had begun a major offensive against both British brigades and 27 Commonwealth Brigade was desperately fighting to hold the road in the Kapyong Valley. It was vital that Lt Col J.F.M. Macdonald, battalion commander, take 1 KOSB into battle as quickly as possible. He and his advance party reached the Kapyong Valley on 24 April when the battle was at its height. General Peng had instructed the three armies of 9 Army Group to 'quickly wipe out the British 27th Brigade . . .' and 10,000 Chinese soldiers of the 60th Infantry Division began their attack just before midnight on 22 April. Their first target was the unfortunate 6th ROK Division who had so recently been positioned at 'the sharp end'. Behind the ROK soldiers were two batteries of the 16 Field Regiment, Royal New Zealand Artillery, plus a battery of US 105mm howitzers.

By 0300 hours on 23 April the gunners heard smallarms fire approaching their positions and withdrew side by side with the 6th ROK just over two miles north of Kapyong. General Van Fleet was concerned to limit the Chinese advance and ordered 27 Commonwealth Brigade to block them. 1 Battalion Middlesex had expected to follow in the footsteps of the departing Argylls and put the hills of Korea far behind them. But they were not so lucky. There was one more battle to fight before they left that war-torn peninsula. The Middlesex, 3 RAR and the Patricias were ordered to set up a defensive position in the valley of the Kapyong north of its confluence with the Pukhan. The valley floor was about 1 1/2 miles wide, narrowing as it twisted northwards. Two hills, 677 and 504, overlooked the valley and all the high ground was characterized by spurs and re-entrants, making access to and from the heights easier than usual. To the northwest was the great mass of Sudok San towering well over 2,500 feet.

It was a complex area to defend and the brigade was deployed on both sides of the Kapyong. Brigadier Brian Arthur Burke, now commanding 27 Commonwealth Brigade since the sudden departure of Brigadier Coad to Hong Kong (on compassionate grounds) was forced to extend his battalions across a wide front. Thus he ran the risk of that most dangerous hallmark of Chinese attacks: infiltration. Brigadier Burke had lost the Argylls, and the Borderers' battalions were still en route to Inchon. However, he had the 2 PPCLI, the Middlesex and 3 RAR. The Australians were positioned on the right on Hill 504 with a company of US 72nd Tank Battalion Shermans in support, and they began to dig-in during the morning of 23 April. One officer noted that it was a wonderful sunny day and that the war seemed a long way off. It was actually about six miles distant, where 6th ROK Division was trying to reform in the face of overwhelming numbers of Chinese troops. Burke was anxious that the South Koreans would give way and moved up the New Zealand guns – and the Middlesex who were to protect the Kiwis. This meant that a gap of about 1 1/2 miles separated the Australians and the Canadians who were manning a defence perimeter on Hill 677.

By 1900 hours streams of refugees (with Chinese soldiers in civilian garb intermixed) were choking the road south. With them came the ROK soldiers, the New Zealand guns and the Middlesex. The Sherman tanks gathered around the tiny village of Chuktun-ni and were the first of the Kapyong defenders to go into action. An enemy force at about company strength appeared at 1930 hours and there was a brief gun battle after which the Chinese withdrew. Within a few minutes Chinese troops had infiltrated as far as the New Zealand gun line, forcing the Kiwis to move south of the Middlesex. 3 RAR had been outflanked and the Sherman tanks fell back rather than risk destruction at the hands of Chinese equipped with rocket launchers. Around midnight 23/24 April, the Chinese began assaulting the hills, concentrating on the Australians and showering them with apparently limitless supplies of hand grenades. Much of the fighting centred around the Battalion HQ where it is possible that the commander, Colonel Ian Ferguson, was stunned either by a Chinese grenade or mortar blast.

Certainly for a period Ferguson was 'out of action' and D Company 1 Middlesex, was brought in to assist the embattled Australians. Their task was to capture a ridge and thus prevent a Chinese encirclement of 3 RAR's HQ. It was pitch dark as D Company 1 Middlesex came under heavy fire and was immediately threatened by encirclement. 2/ Lt Barry Austin Reed was the assault platoon commander. On the ridge, several of his platoon were wounded and one section was in danger of being overrun. Reed rallied his section, repelled another attack and forced the Chinese to flee, a fearless act in the best tradition of the 'Die-Hards.' For this he was awarded the Military Cross.

After this, the Middlesex withdrew with their wounded. Brigadier Burke's assessment of the situation was that the Australians could not hold as their hills were now nearly three miles behind the Chinese advance units infiltrating between the battalions. The Australians' A Company endured half a dozen separate attacks while a rain of mortar bombs made half the force casualties. B Company was withdrawn, a controversial decision as it was clear that the Chinese were determined to take Chuktun-ni and advance along the valley floor. Yet this was still held by the 14 American tanks (two were still in action despite being hit by rockets) and covered by the New Zealand and American guns. There was also news that a 5th Cavalry Regimental Combat Team (in strength roughly equivalent to three British battalions) would arrive to reinforce 27 Commonwealth Brigade. B Company was ordered back to its original position, seemingly without regard to the fact that it was now held by Chinese who could fire on any movement in the valley. B Company troops filed up the valley floor, encountered unexpected resistance from an old defensive position known as 'the Honeycomb' and fell back. It was eventually taken but the value of reoccupying the original B Company site was in doubt. Moreover, Hill 504 was facing assaults from literally hundreds of Chinese grenadiers and burp gunners; and, to add to the Australians' suffering, two Marine Corsairs misjudged their napalm drop, hit D Company's defence perimeter, covered two Australians with burning petroleum jelly and injured several more. Invaluable stocks of weapons were burning and ammunition exploded among D Company defences. Many of the wounded were later carried out by Chinese POWs. Withdrawal was now vital and the departure from 3 RAR's advanced positions was accomplished smoothly as a fighting retreat. Their eventual arrival among the relatively secure lines held by 1 Middlesex marked the end of 3 RAR's participation in the Battle of Kapyong.

Part of their success was due to the constant protection afforded by Company A of the US 72nd Tank Battalion during 3 RAR's withdrawal. Their expenditure of ammunition was phenomenal and their commander, Lt Koch, was awarded the British Military Cross and the American Distinguished Service Cross for his outstanding leadership and courage. His tanks had fought the Chinese to a standstill and carried numerous wounded out of battle. They had won the respect of friend and foe alike and it is a matter of record that the Chinese refrained from firing on Lt Koch's tanks when they bore wounded or the flag of the Red Cross. There were occasions when stretcher cases were hit by mortar fire but Chinese commanders now tended to allow the unimpeded evacuation of wounded.

The Patricias bore the second stage of the Chinese attack. They had been left alone during the Chinese assault on the Middlesex and 3 RAR's hill positions (24 April) and had assiduously laboured to strengthen their own perimeter. They had the advantage that the approach to their defences on Hill 677 was very steep and disheartening even to the fittest infantry; but steep slopes inhibit platoon and section crossfire and render artillery support less effective. B Company was the first to be attacked at 2130 hours. With help of mortars and controlled rifle and machine-gun fire the Canadians drove off the enemy with little difficulty. More Chinese tried to take the defenders in the rear by infiltrating D Company and again the attackers were repelled. Small squads of Chinese persisted for most of the night with no success whatsoever and when dawn came on 25 April the Chinese contented themselves with encircling Hill 677. Lt Col Stone feared that his troops would exhaust their food and ammunition if subjected to a siege and requested an air drop. Reliable as ever, American C-119 Flying Boxcars parachuted his supplies into the perimeter while helicopters evacuated wounded with their usual efficiency. By early afternoon the Middlesex reported that the road into the Canadians on Hill 677 was clear of Chinese infantry.

2 PPCLI's determined resistance had cost them ten killed and 23 wounded, a sacrifice that resulted not only in the retention of a vital hill but also in the award of a US Presidential Citation, shared with 3 RAR and A Company of the US 72nd Tank Battalion. The Patricias found themselves members of a new brigade. It came into being at midnight on 25/26 April, when 27 Commonwealth Brigade's operational tour formally ended in Korea. The 1st Battalion King's Own Scottish Borderers had seen no action in the Battle of Kapyong but was now fully operational in this new brigade. 3 Royal Australian Regiment formed the third battalion; the 1st Battalion The King's Shropshire Light Infantry (1 KSLI), en route from Hong Kong on 11 May, would form the fourth. Brigadier Burke handed over command to Brigadier George Taylor as 28 Commonwealth Infantry Brigade was born in the midst of battle. The Middlesex were still there, anxiously awaiting the arrival of 1 KSLI. They busied themselves in a sector of 'No Name Line' preparing a highly sophisticated line of defence involving elaborate minefields, barbed wire, numerous artillery and mortar positions plus scores of heavy machine-gun nests. This was was a mark of General Van Fleet's determination that the Chinese would advance no further. It was also the first time in the history of the

US Eighth Army in Korea that a fortified defence had been so meticulously undertaken. During the evening of 13 May 1 KSLI arrived in the 28 Commonwealth Brigade area and the Middlesex swiftly bundled into the the same trucks and drove off to Inchon. 'The Die-Hards' departed Korea aboard the USS *Montrose* on 14 May.

Further Commonwealth reinforcements were on their way. A large Canadian force had assembled and trained from November 1950 onwards at Fort Lewis, Washington State, an American training ground. The infantry force comprised the second battalions of three regular Canadian regiments: the Royal Canadian Regiment, The Royal 22e (Vingt-Deuxiéme) Régiment and the Princess Patricia's Canadian Light Infantry. When 2 PPCLI departed for Korea, the battalion's place was taken by 3 PPCLI. Supporting units were generously included: the 2nd Field Regiment Royal Canadian Horse Artillery, A Squadron 1/2 Armoured Regiment, engineers, signallers, transport and a Field Ambulance of the Army Medical Corps. Most sailed from Seattle aboard three US troopships, the *President Jackson*, *General Patrick* and *Marine Adder*. The units disembarked at Pusan and at Kure, Japan, during 4–6 May and the armoured force, now termed C Squadron, Lord Strathcona's Horse, took over US Sherman tanks in lieu of its self-propelled guns. Such was the structure of the 25th Canadian Infantry Brigade and it would fire its first shots in anger on 17 May 1951.

## UNITED STATES ARMY RESISTANCE

ROK and US divisions facing the great Chinese offensive in the east central and eastern sectors carried out an orderly withdrawal towards the fortified 'No-Name Line' north of Seoul. They were surrendering about ten miles of previously occupied North Korean territory each day. This concept of the fighting retreat to prepared defensive positions was new to the Chinese and they were unable to exploit such an unexpected manoeuvre. Even so, the sheer speed of the initial Chinese attacks did trap some of the American units, in particular the 7th Infantry Regiment of the 3rd US Division in the central sector of the 'Kansas Line'. It had received the same orders dispatched by Van Fleet to all units: move to the fortified 'No Name Line' north of Seoul.

However, two of the 7th Infantry Regiment's battalions were under direct Chinese attack on 22/23 April and faced the usual threat of encirclement. An order was issued – not always understood in the chain of command – for two battalions to withdraw though the 3rd Battalion. The key to a safe withdrawal was the defence of Hill 283 and a nearby grassy knoll, two crucial firepoints. The Chinese swarmed up Hill 283, targeting the 3rd Platoon commanded by Lt Middlemas. Convinced that the enemy numbered thousands, the forward troops were understandably inclined to depart their foxholes. Middlemas prevented his squads from running away and covered five men occupying the knoll. They held this dangerous position despite the bullet swarm coming from Hill 283 and the Chinese soldiers who wormed their way close to throw grenades. They were brave men but all were killed by the Americans. Other squads, inspired by these actions, brought up the light and heavy machine-guns and within minutes were containing the Chinese attack. Morale escalated. The 3rd Battalion then began its withdrawal under a precise artillery barrage that annihilated the pursuing Chinese and then put down smoke so the last men could escape. The Americans filed away, the artillery ceased and air strikes held back the Chinese. The last men in the column kept firing at Chinese at the top of the hill and the 7th Infantry Regiment disengaged successfully.

## THE CHINESE REACTION

General Peng now had to accept that his 'First Step, Fifth Offensive' had stalled and that his armies were overextended. Consequently, though his troops reached the north-eastern outskirts of Seoul on 29 April, they did not have the resources to attack the strongly-defended capital of South Korea. He may have been reminded of those German troops in 1941 who reached the outskirts of Moscow but had no capacity to advance. Peng's soldiers had suffered severe losses. He acknowledged that these were due largely to the Glosters' and 29 Brigade's holding actions on the Imjin and at Kapyong and the intense artillery and air bombardment now available to the UN Command. That two Army Groups had actually crossed the 38 degree Parallel gave him little comfort. He had maintained some pressure on the UN forces in the extreme west but an amphibious landing across the Han River at Kimpo on 28/29 April failed. During the same night, gunfire from the heavy cruiser USS *Toledo* had wrecked an attempt by the Chinese 65th Army and an NKPA division to enter Seoul. On 29/30

April, when the Chinese 60th Army attacked south of Uijongbu, naval guns and artillery barrages forced the enemy to withdraw. Peng therefore decided to regroup and attempt an offensive at a weaker point in the UN lines while launching diversionary attacks along the rest of the front. This was his 'Second Step, Fifth Phase Offensive,' 16–21 May 1951. Peng could call on 21 divisions together with nine re-equppied NKPA divisions stationed in the east.

For the first time the Chinese encountered intense resistance along the entire line. When they moved against the high ground in the Hangye area between the Hongchon and Soyang Rivers the US 2nd Division grimly held on to Hill 800, called 'Bunker Hill' by the troops. It was over ten miles away from its Main Supply Route and the infantry depended on their Korean porters to manhandle their food and ammunition up the mountain sides. On 17 May the Chinese launched a full offensive in this area in an attempt to swamp both the 2nd Division and the forces based on its flanks – the ROK divisions and the Netherlands and French battalions. General Van Fleet skil-fully moved his reserves from 'No-Name Line' to block every Chinese attempt to create a major salient in the UN lines. When the 1st US Marine Division moved across to support the 2nd, he transferred elements of the 3rd Division to block any infiltration.

The UN forces were confident as they had never been before and were supported in the most rugged terrain by dedicated Medical Companies. For example, when the 7th Infantry moved from Seoul to block the Chinese in the steep mountains of Soksa-ri the surgical team followed close behind its three battalions as they went into the attack. Because of fast-flowing streams and steep mountain tracks it was impossible to bring the litter jeeps and the aid station to the battle area. On 21 May the battalion surgeon, Captain Gilbert S. Campbell, actually gave medical aid to casualties on the front line. Bearers gently took the wounded men to the jeep evacuation point from which they went to the advanced clearing station and, if necessary, went to base hospital by helicopter. It was a fierce battle and casualties were high. But the 7th Infantry held as did all the units fighting with their backs to the 'No-Name Line'. Peng had no answer to the new-style American resistance and between 19–21 May 1951 there was a general Chinese retreat northwards.

General Van Fleet interpreted Peng's retreat as a chance to under-take a general advance, though he still devoted some of his resources to strengthen his defence lines. Once again UN troops headed towards

Uijongbu, Kapyong, the Taebaek Mountains and the east coast town of Kansong. Van Fleet halted them when intelligence reports indicated a build-up of enemy soldiers in the east-central and eastern sectors. Peng was actually transferring Chinese and North Korean divisions eastwards across country to divide and block ROK units. He anticipated they would rapidly disintegrate into a rabble. His ploy was initially successful as his infantry thrusts shattered III ROK Corps, exposing General Almond's X Corps and threatening the US 2nd Division. Van Fleet quickly reinforced X Corps with artillery and summoned air support from the Marines and the Far East Air Force. Apart from the right flank of X Corps, most of the communist advance was contained. Van Fleet entertained hopes that a counter-offensive would entrap thousands of Chinese but in the event the Chinese withdrawal moved quicker than the UN troops and the Field Armies retreated well away from the 38 degree Parallel. General Ridgway decided to consolidate the Eighth Army on 'Line Kansas' with a tentative push to 'Line Wyoming' and the capture of key towns of Kumhwa and Chorwon at the base of the Iron Triangle, centre of road and rail communications in North Korea. After a bitter battle, his troops also captured the heavily fortified enemy base at the 'Punchbowl' which would prove something of a liability in the months to come. He was content with this arrangement. Unquestionably, Ridgway had defeated Peng's Fifth Offensive and had bought time for the politicians and Joint Chiefs of Staff to re-evaluate the situation in Korea.

# CHAPTER 8

# Talking and Fighting,
# May–November 1951

## A CHANCE FOR PEACE

On 2 May 1951 the UN Security Council had spent the day discussing the Palestine problem. Korea was not on its list of priorities. At the end of the afternoon two US delegates were looking for a ride into Manhattan and the Soviet delegate, Jakob Malik – famed for his long absence from the Council – gave them a lift. On the way Malik was receptive to a suggestion that it was time for a settlement of the Korean War and intimated that it might be profitable for the USA and the Soviet Union to hold talks. The Americans reported this to the State Department who took the matter seriously. There followed a certain amount of cloak and dagger activity involving, among others, the career diplomat and historian George Kennan, who was much respected by the USSR. On 31 May he and Malik met and considered the idea that the war might be conveniently ended at the current front line. A second meeting was held on 5 June and Malik discussed the prospect of a cease-fire. For the Americans, the problem was to make contact with the Chinese. During May a US diplomat, Charles Burton Marshall, visited Hong Kong and there met an individual whose name is still, at the time of writing, classified material. Kennan made it clear that the USA was seeking to end the war on the basis of *status quo ante bellum* rather than attempt to win an outright military victory. This discussion, sadly, did not lead to direct talks between the Americans and the People's Republic of China; but at least by mid-June there had been a one small step in the direction of peace. China was aware of the aims of the United States and presumably the Soviet Union had conveyed its point of view to Mao Zedong.

Surprisingly, Malik now agreed to broadcast to the American people and on 22 June he recorded a statement hinting at the need for a cease-fire and the withdrawal of armies from either side of the 38 degree Parallel. His broadcast was heard by the American people on the evening of 23 June. They interpreted it as a genuine wish by the Soviet Union to support discussions between the warring parties in Korea and a move towards an armistice. This was followed by General Ridgway's broadcast to Pyongyang suggesting that, if the communists desired an armistice, they should meet the Americans aboard the Danish hospital ship *Jutlandia* in Wonsan harbour. The response was positive though the communists proposed a venue at Kaesong, just to the south of the 38 degree Parallel. Ridgway proposed a preliminary meeting on 8 July with full negotiations opening on 10 July. The communists agreed. The talking had begun.

There were enormous complications. Some sort of Armistice Commission was needed, with powers to visit all parts of Korea; both sides must agree on a demilitarized zone; and there must be an exchange of prisoners. Perhaps the major complication was the fact that the senior negotiators would not be trained diplomats but serving officers of the opposing armies uttering words that had first to be cleared by their respective governments. The governments, of course, made proposals that would be to their own advantage, a process that made constant dispute inevitable. Such arrangements aroused little enthusiasm in Syngman Rhee who was fundamentally hostile to the prospect of a cease-fire. His political record was marred by corruption, assassination, mass murder and a perpetual demand for the USA to expand South Korea's armed forces so that they could march to the Yalu and reunite Korea. This was a policy that no longer had either American or United Nations' approval. Consequently, the United States tended to override the expressed interests of the leader of the very country on whose behalf America had gone to war in 1950. Similarly, the Chinese were at times embarrassed by Kim Il Sung, who was equally opposed to an armistice and wanted more military aid from Stalin and Mao Zedong so he could defeat the UN and unite Korea under communist rule.

It was clear that the communist delegates would contest US proposals every inch of the way and drain every drop of propaganda value from the exercise. China's appointment of NKPA General Nam

Il, rather than one of their own senior commanders as their Chief Delegate, was in itself a skilful propaganda move. It was not long before the Americans, led by Vice Admiral C. Turner Joy, USN, came to realize that they were not facing the communists as military men but as westerners meeting a culture whose values they could not comprehend. Americans soon discovered that the delegates seated opposite them interpreted a concession as a weakness, a situation that made compromise on any matter both difficult and unlikely. The negotiations, clearly, were going to last a very long time. For as long as the negotiators parleyed, and for one reason or another their talks frequently stalled over the next two years, men were killed in battles that were driven by political objectives rather than by a determination to punish the aggressor or to secure an ultimate victory. Consequently, after the defeat of General Peng's Fifth Offensive in May 1951, the media of the day tended to lose interest thus contributing to a feeling among veterans that the Korean conflict had become 'The Forgotten War'.

## THE FORMATION OF THE COMMONWEALTH DIVISION

British loyalty towards United Nations policies in Korea remained undiminished even though it was having an unexpected impact on domestic politics. Maintaining relatively large numbers of warships and rotating infantry battalions and their support units between Korea, Hong Kong and the UK meant that increased defence spending forced up taxes. On 22 April 1951 Aneurin Bevan and Harold Wilson resigned from Attlee's government, technically as a protest against increased health charges. This 'Bevanite revolt' split the Labour Party and led to a General Election on 25 November after which Winston Churchill formed a Conservative government with an overall majority of 17. Such political turbulence did not inhibit the formation of the 1st Commonwealth Division on 28 July 1951 under the command of Maj. General A. J. H. Cassels. His precise orders are interesting in that they reflect the reduced ambitions of the UN: 'The role of the force under your command is, as an integral part of the United Nations forces, to act in operations in Korea, designed to restore international peace and security in the area.'[1] 1st Commonwealth Division comprised three brigades: 28 Commonwealth Brigade, 29 Independent Infantry Brigade and the 25th Canadian Brigade. It held the line in

Korea in company with seven US divisions and ten ROK divisions. The division lost the Belgian Battalion, now transferred to an American command.

General Cassels divisional operational centre was west of the Imjin River and flanked by 1st ROK on the left and the 1st US Cavalry on the right. His first move was to consolidate patrol positions beyond the Imjin. This was Operation 'Minden' which began when 3 RAR took control of 'Teal' ford and 1 KOSB secured the 'Pintail' crossing. Engineers then built bridges here and at 'Widgeon' on the left flank. Cassels promptly moved the division across the Imjin and began fortifying new defence positions and patrolling up to the line known as 'Jamestown' in No Man's Land. Beyond Jamestown the Chinese were building even more elaborate fortifications to conceal new artillery batteries, tanks and the troops of the 191st Infantry Division. They had the advantage of overlooking not only the new bridges crossing the Imjin and the Commonwealth Division's defences but also the front held by the rest of the US I Corps. General Van Fleet deemed it wise to occupy the entire area up to and including Jamestown and he allocated five divisions – 1st ROK, US 1st Cavalry, 3rd Infantry and 25th Division, plus the Commonwealth Division – to undertake Operation 'Commando'. Chinese resistance would be intense and a major battle was anticipated. In the history of the British and Commonwealth Armies, Operation 'Commando' would witness the last offensive carried out by an infantry division.


## OPERATION 'COMMANDO'


General Cassels decided not to commit his entire force to the operation and kept some of 29 Brigade in reserve. 28 Commowealth Brigade plus the Northumberland Fusiliers and the 8th Hussars were ordered to capture the mountain mass of Kowang-san, Hill 355, on D-Day, 3 October 1951; while the 25th Canadian Brigade and the Ulsters would assault the hills along the Sami-chon valley on D+1. On D-Day Commonwealth gunfire swamped the Chinese positions as the 1st King's Shropshire Light Infantry (1 KSLI) opened the attack. The Shropshires marched some five miles towards Kowang-san to hold ridges crucial to the final attack. On 4 October 1 KSLI occupied Hill 227 and held it in the face of a series of Chinese counter-attacks. The 1st King's Own Scottish Borderers (1 KOSB) advanced to their attack position; while 3 RAR progressed with their usual flair, and killed, captured or put to flight a Chinese platoon. On 4 October the main assault on Kowang-san went in with with 1 KOSB and 3 RAR unwittingly achieving a classic pincer attack that forced the Chinese defence battalion to evacuate. Kowang-san had fallen at the cost of seven Borderers killed. Meanwhile, the Canadians advanced in line abreast and succeeded in holding the paddy fields on both sides of the Samichon River.

The first stage of the divisional offensive was completed when the last Chinese were driven off Hills 227 and 355. The next, directed against the complex hill mass of Maryang-san (Hill 317), would engage the division in furious combat with a courageous enemy ensconced in sophisticated defences. Even a cursory examination of Maryang-san would indicate that its capture would be well beyond the capacity of a single infantry battalion. There was evidence that the Chinese had extensive fortifications on the reverse slope, including numerous artillery batteries, and that they were bringing in contingents of fresh troops and large quantities of ammunition, grenades and shells. They would not surrender Maryang-san easily. The Commonwealth Division was fortunate that it now had at its disposal the Auster AOP 6 light aircraft of RAF 1913 and 1903 Light Liason Flights whose pilots could direct artillery shoots and relay details of enemy troop dispositions.

The Northumberland Fusiliers and 3 RAR planned a co-ordinated attack following the tactics that had proved so successful at Kowang-san. When dawn broke on 5 October it was very misty and the assault companies were hampered on their march by this and by uncertain map-reading and temperamental radios. The Fusiliers' objective was Hill 217 on the left; the Australians were to come up on the right via a series of features labelled 'Victor', 'Whisky', 'Uniform', 'Tango', 'Sierra' and Hill 317, Maryang-san. Ferocious firepower from the Chinese positions on 217 and from other sites further north inflicted heavy casualties on the Fusiliers who had to withdraw. The Australians carried out their own pincer movement, lost the aerial on their radio due to enemy fire and waved fluorescent aircraft recognition panels to show their line of advance. Supporting fire from the New Zealand guns and the Australians' mortars and several Centurion tanks proved invaluable and D Company carried out a successful bayonet charge that killed 68 Chinese and persuaded 30 to surrender. Their charge, led by Lt Jim Young, was terrifyingly effective for their weapon was the First World War Lee-Enfield at the end of which was the lethal 18 inch sword bayonet.

While 3 RAR was fighting the Chinese on the eastern approaches to Maryang-san, its A Company was moving from the south to draw some of the enemy fire. The images of war recalled are striking in their diversity. Private Pat Knowles remembered how A Company began their advance:

> We made our way up towards 317 until we reached the first line of trenches, where we were held up by a Centurion tank of the 8th King's Irish Hussars and a Chinaman with a bazooka having a quiet little duel. The shells from the tank were exploding about 14 feet from us; the rockets from the bazooka were scoring direct hits on the tank but to no effect. We called out to the tank commander to cease fire so we could flush out the Chinaman but he probably couldn't hear us and rightfully attended to his own front. After about five minutes the Chinaman ran out of ammunition, dropped his bazooka, came out of his hide and took off down the track – for about six paces, anyway. Later, after we took our part of the hill, one of the boys spoke to the sergeant tank commander and asked what damage the bazooka had done to the Centurion. The sergeant replied, 'No damage. The Chinaman saved us the trouble of scraping off the mud'.[1]

The other three RAR companies made the final assault and C Company led by Major Gerke rushed the crest. Lt Pembroke commanded the assault platoon:

> In the attack on 317 the Chinese were 'beaten for pace' – we were moving too fast for them. I shall never forget the sight of wild, red-eyed, blackened Jim Young (of D Company) giving us some quick information as we moved through the tremendous bombardment of 317 as we advanced: small groups of dazed Chinese moving down past us. Strangely, we ignored each other – they were intent on avoiding our murderous shelling; we were conscious of our own orders not to let anything hold us up. We finally scrambled up the last precipitous few yards and 317 was ours.[2]

One more objective remained: Hill 217 that so far had frustrated all the Fusiliers' attacks. Their commander, Lt Col Speer, was asked to move to higher ground and mount a dawn attack on 6 October, but the sheer difficulty of moving swiftly in the deep gullies and ravines characteristic of their sector prevented this. Once more there was a misty start to the day. The Fusiliers moved forward, the mist cleared and Chinese mortar and artillery fire caught the troops in the open. During the afternoon the Chinese infantry began a counter-attack and the Fusiliers had to withdraw. They had suffered heavy casualties: ten dead and 85 wounded. They had also been in action too long. 1 RNF was the last of the original 29 Brigade battalions to remain 'at the sharp end' in Korea and was due for relief.

Air strikes by No. 77 RAAF Mustangs and artillery took up the attacks on 217, supplemented by further Australian advances over the mountain mass east of Maryang-san. On 9 October B Company of 1 KOSB relieved the battle-weary Australians on Maryang-san and observed that the Chinese seemed to have abandoned Hill 217. The Borderers sent in D Company to investigate and they occupied Hill 217. They encountered no Chinese opposition. Operation 'Commando' had been successfully concluded. General John W. O'Daniel, commander of US I Corps, was delighted and commended the Commonwealth Division on the professional skill and courage displayed by its officers and men and on the speed of its deployment, achieving all its objectives. The end of 'Commando' gave the Commonwealth Division a chance to reorganize. It was time for the Royal Ulster Rifles to depart Korea. Their front-line position was undertaken by the Canadian Royal Vingt-Deuxiéme Regiment. To replace the Ulsters came the 1st Battalion The Royal Norfolk Regiment, commanded by by Lt Col J. H. R. Orlebar. The battle-hardened Fusiliers also left Korea in October and were replaced by the 1st Battalion The Royal Leicestershire Regiment commanded by Lt Col G. E. P. Hutchins.

## JAMESTOWN: THE NEW DEFENCE LINE

Throughout the late summer ROK and US divisions had made substantial progress towards capturing and holding terrain, especially in the region around the Punchbowl, that denied enemy access to good observation points. West of the Punchbowl lay hills dominated by

Taeu-san (Hill 1179). One group, especially well-fortified by the Chinese, has become known to history as 'Bloody Ridge' because of the intensity of fighting that took place there. Success there required the further capture of ridges north of the Punchbowl, notably 'Heartbreak Ridge' to which the communists had withdrawn. It was during Operation 'Commando' that the US 2nd Division began Operation 'Touchdown' and finally captured Heartbreak Ridge on 13 October. The final stages of 'Touchdown' witnessed the now familiar storming of a crest by determined infantry soldiers, this time the men of the US 1st Battalion 23rd Infantry and Lt Col Montclar's French battalion. Next day, the Netherlands Battalion captured another crucial ridge while the American 3rd Battalion completed Operation 'Touchdown' on 15 October. The Americans now had a sound defensive line across central Korea, largely the achievement of the 2nd Division which had been in action for 103 days. Its relief was the US 7th Division, backed by the US 3rd Division and the 1st US Cavalry.

The new defence line, 'Jamestown', was now well in advance of the original 'Kansas' and 'Wyoming Lines' and, in the main, ran across North Korean territory. It placed the UN Command in a good position to exert pressure on the communist negotiators whose progress in the peace talks at Kaesong had been, at best, desultory. For much of the time the talks had been discontinued and then eventually reopened at Panmunjom on 25 October 1951. It seems likely that the reappearance of the communist negotiators was related to their various defeats on the hill positions along 'Line Jamestown.' Their presence did not hamper the Chinese field commanders in their determination wherever possible to win back the ground lost during the period August-October 1951. During November there were heavy communist attacks on the front line held by the United States I Corps.

The King's Own Scottish Borderers now occupied the hills captured by the Australians during Operation 'Commando.' C Company held the forward position on the ridge called the 'Hinge'. B Company defended the wasteland on top of Hill 217; C Company was dug in on Maryang-san, Hill 317 and on 280, known as the 'Knoll'. All could be surveyed from Chinese observation posts on the hill called 'Baldy'. Each day 1 KOSB worked hard to create a wire barrier some 30 yards from the trenches; each day the Chinese mortared every move they made. Weapon pits, store pits, water pits and ammunition pits were all carefully sited and sandbagged and dug into ridges and hillsides, a process adopted by all the UK battalions along the line. The Shropshires on 227 were continually in action. Each day the Centurions drove up to a convenient spur on 227 to fire their deadly accurate 20 pounders at the Chinese bunkers; and when evening came they withdrew in case they were overrun by Chinese infiltrators.

On the night of 3 November the Borderers on the Knoll could hear the sound of Chinese troops digging furously and at daybreak they could see a long trench dug from Baldy towards the Hinge. Air strikes on Baldy were summoned and four Sea Furies drenched the hill in napalm. This had absolutely no effect on the Chinese gunners who swamped 217 with high explosive and then bombarded the Knoll and Hill 317. It was calculated that shells fell on 1 KOSB at the rate of 6,000 per hour from artillery supplemented by self-propelled guns and rockets. When the Chinese appeared they walked unconcernedly through their own and the Commonwealth barrages to lay explosive Bangalore torpedoes in the Borderers' wire. B Company on Hill 217 was involved in hand-to-hand combat with Chinese grenadiers and burp-gunners and it was during this desperate struggle that Private Bill Speakman carried out his personal counter-offensive against the Chinese. Collecting handfuls of grenades, he led six other men in no less than ten grenade charges against the enemy, forcing each wave of Chinese to retreat once they had reached the crest of his hill. He was wounded in the leg, had a field dressing applied and then returned to the battle. He fought for hours and then made one last charge, long enough for his company to withdraw. There were many awards to B Company soldiers in recognition of their heroic defence of Hill 217. Private William Speakman received the Victoria Cross.[3]

The Knoll was defended by two platoons and under imminent threat of being overrun. Two young officers were in command and one, 2/Lt Henderson, was already wounded. The burden of command fell upon 2/Lt William Purves, a National Service officer. Although wounded, he held his unit together for five hours, threw grenades at the Chinese and ensured that his wounded men were secure. In the early hours of the next morning he managed to contact Lt Col Tadman, the new commander of 1 KOSB. Tadman ordered Purves to withdraw and this the young officer did under mild protest as he believed he could hold his position. Purves brought out his men, all the wounded and all the equipment. He became the first and only National Service officer to be awarded the Distinguished Service Order.

Despite these brave efforts, ground had been lost and The Royal

Leicestershire Regiment entered the fray. Two companies were to advance on Hill 127 (named 'United'); two more would move along a ridge to occupy Hinge and Knoll en route to the enemy on Hill 317. Supporting firepower came from 1 Leicester guns and mortars at their base coded 'Crete' and the 20 pounder tank guns from the Centurions operated by the 8th King's Royal Irish Hussars. As the rifle companies of 1 Leicester left their start lines on 5 November they came under heavy and sustained Chinese bombardment which they had to endure for some three hours. For inexperienced young soldiers this was a testing time but they did not falter when two platoons, led by 2/Lt G.A. Havillands and 2/Lt W.K. Roberts, were ordered to take 127. This they did but immediately encountered determined Chinese grenadiers and burp-gunners. They held until darkness came and then withdrew. It had been a well-conceived plan and courageously executed by 1 Leicester in the face of superior firepower and manpower. The Battalion had lost nine men killed and five officers and 74 men were wounded. A dozen were unaccounted for, including 2/Lt Roberts.

The same day, 5 November, the Shropshires on Hill 227 were hammered by a battalion of the Chinese 569th Regiment. Captured papers indicated that the Chinese troops had orders to annihilate the opposition and recapture lost hills so as to place the communist negotiators at Panmunmjom in a 'favourable situation'. Similarly, the Chinese tried their luck against the Patricias holding Hill 159. Every Chinese assault failed but their initial victories, the recapture of Maryang-san and its associated hills, could not be denied. Despite the firepower of the Centurion tanks and the divisional artillery, even fresh units such as the Royal Leicesters were unable to make much headway. Hill 227 remained for several days the focus of Chinese interest. Intense Chinese shelling persisted during 15–17 November, heralding an enemy assault. The Shropshire had to abandon their positions to the Chinese who then came under divisional bombardment. The Mortar Platoon alone fired 40 tons of bombs at the Chinese! Next day, 18 November, the Shropshires returned to Hill 227 to find the Chinese had gone, only to have them reappear in the evening. So the exchanges of real estate went on with men dying on a bare and devastated hill in Korea. Twenty-one Shropshires died, 64 were wounded and 6 men were reported missing though two returned. Released by the Chinese, one man actually walked back to the Shropshire's lines; another wounded man was carried to the Patricias' defensive wire by the Chinese.

The achievement of these three battalions, 1 KOSB, the Royal Leicesters and the Shropshires, may be gauged from a special order of the day issued by Major D.H. Tadman OBE, commander of 1 KOSB, on 11 November. It was read to all soldiers in the battalion:

> From the interrogation of recently captured prisoners and from other intelligence sources, it is apparent that on 4 November 1951 the Battalion was attacked by virtually a complete enemy Division supported by another holding the line. The means that some 5,000 enemy were committed against us, supported by a great weight of artillery, mortars and self-propelled guns.
>
> It is estimated that the enemy suffered well over 1,000 casualties as a result of your courage, skill and determination, together with that of our supporting arms.
>
> That the Battalion withstood and stopped this colossal onslaught, making only limited adjustments of Company positions, is tribute to everyone of you. I thank and commend you all from the bottom of my heart for your magnificent efforts, and this applies equally to those of you, not immediately in the front line, who gave and are giving such excellent and efficient support and service.
>
> The Corps Commander and the Divisional Commander have requested me to convey to you their heartfelt thanks and congratulations, and I do this with great pride.
>
> In this recent action, your courage and tenacity and refusal to accept defeat in the face of innumerable odds will, I am sure, become an epic in the history of our great Regiment and of the British forces in Korea.[4]

Modest front-line changes occurred during November 1951. On 22 November the Commonwealth Division transferred the right-hand sector held by 28 Brigade to the US 3rd Division. 29 Brigade took over from 1st ROK on the west of the Samichon and the Canadians moved forward to hold some four miles of line extending north-east from the Samichon. 2 PPCLI had been relieved by its sister battalion 1 PPCLI and this held the Canadian centre, flanked by 1 RCR on the left and the Royal 22e on the right. Hill 355, where so much blood had been spilt, was now in the care of the 7th US Infantry Regiment. Hill 227 had been abandoned by both sides. Defences seemed to be firm and the worst the infantry faced was the cold rain that at night turned into snow and progressed, especially on the supply roads, to thick mud. When the Chinese resumed their shelling during 22/23 November the Canadians were taken by surprise.

Chinese shellfire was in fact covering a serious attack upon Hills 355 and 227. Enemy infantry swarmed up 227 and 355 and both hills changed hands over the next 24 hours. The potential loss of 355 was a threat to the entire Eighth Army defence system: 'Line Jamestown' hinged on it and the Chinese were risking their best troops from two divisions, the 190th and the 192nd. The US 7th Infantry, reinforced by the 15th Regiment to which the Belgian battalion had been attached, won back 355 and the Chinese gave up the struggle after seven infantry assaults. Over 600 Chinese lay dead and as many other fatalities must have been carried away. It is conservatively estimated that this November action against the Canadians, the US 3rd Division and the 1st Cavalry must have cost the Chinese in excess of 2,000 casualties.

Many of these casualties were the result of flame-throwers used by the 1st Cavalry. They were difficult to use and heavy to carry in the steep hillsides along the 'Jamestown Line'. Nevertheless, 1st Cavalry mounted 97 flame-thrower operations during 'Commando'. Ninety actually attacked Chinese positions but most of the weapons were either lost or abandoned during an attack. Flame-throwers were also invaluable in repelling Chinese at night as well as having the side benefit of illuminating the battlefield for three or four minutes. 1st Cavalry also developed the refinement, adopted by Commonwealth troops, of placing drums of napalm in front of their own defences. Fitted with explosives and with electric fusing they would have created mayhem. They were never used, largely because artillery barrages destroyed the fusing wires running from the UN defences to the napalm drums.

This style of warfare and the huge casualties inflicted on the Chinese soldiers must have had a bearing on the peace talks, for on 27 November the communist delegation agreed to the concept of a military demarcation line based on the current battlefield situation rather than the 38 degree Parallel to which General Nam Il had been previously wedded.

## THE SIGNIFICANCE OF 27 NOVEMBER

On 26 July the delegates had originally agreed on a five-part agenda on which to base their discussions. This agenda was basically:

1. The adoption of an agenda for future discussions.
2. The creation of a military demarcation and a demilitarized zone.
3. Cease-fire and armistice arrangements and an appropriate organization to oversee such arrangements.
4. Settlement of prisoner-of-war repatriation problems.
5. Recommendations and advice to the respective national governments.

When the peace talks reconvened at Panmunjom on 25 October – there had been a gap of over two months – the Americans accepted that the communists could claim the former site at Kaesong as part of their sovereign territory. They adopted the communist definition of an armistice line so that by mid-November the delegates appeared to be working together more closely and the North Koreans were less rude in their mode of address to the Americans. On 27 November, after much drawing of lines on battlefield maps, it seemed that both sides could agree on an armistice line *provided all the other issues on the agenda could be settled in the space of 30 days.*

This news was interpreted by General Van Fleet without reference to his Supreme Commander, General Ridgway. Van Fleet had immediately issued orders to his divisional commanders to initiate operations only if they were needed to maintain 'present positions'. There must be no further offensive moves except when it was vital to recapture terrain lost to enemy action in the future. Ridgway was livid: Van Fleet had virtually announced a cease-fire, thus freeing the communist armies from the threat of attack and giving them time to rebuild and improve their defence systems. The international Press gave prominence to Van Fleet's orders; Washington vainly denied that there was a cease-fire. As the usual vile Korean winter approached, troops on both sides of what was now termed the 'Main Line of Resistance' settled down in static lines of defence awaiting a decision that could either send them home or condemn them to years of unproductive confrontation.

CHAPTER 9

# Life and Death on the Line, 1951–2

## THE TWO DEFENCE SYSTEMS
## ON 'THE MAIN LINE OF RESISTANCE'

The Chinese took full advantage of the 30 days' grace negotiated at Panmunjom on 27 November. It represented a virtual cease-fire and so they were confident that General Ridgway would not authorize a major offensive against them before 27 December. Using their huge manpower resources – 850,000 troops and the local North Korean population – they set about creating a defence system in depth that skilfully exploited the hills and mountains fronting their battle area. Each hill was tunnelled so that communication was possible between the front and reverse slope and between troop accommodation areas, artillery sites, mortar positions and infantry foxholes. The effort involved was prodiguous for some of the mountains exceeded 5,000 feet; yet within these a warren of intercommunication tunnels and unlimited storage facilities came into being. Chinese gunners could wheel a 76mm field gun to the lip of a tunnel, fire a round at the UN positions and then withdraw the gun into absolute safety within the tunnel. So deep did the Chinese engineers dig that their inner fortifications were safe from any kind of artillery or air attack. General Maxwell Taylor, who had fought against the Westwall and Siegfried Line during 1944–5 and who would ultimately succeed General Van Fleet, rated the Chinese defences as more formidable than their German counterparts. They would probably have survived a nuclear strike.

Equally impressive was the Chinese belief in the *permanence* of their fortifications. Behind their 'Main Line of Resistance' they constructed a system of defence in-depth that rivalled First World War installations on the Western Front. It stretched between 10 and 25 miles and featured minefields, strongpoints and military roads. Critics of Chinese strategy during 1951–2 have pointed to the weakness of tying up infantry and artillery support in a mountain fastness and thus removing from field commanders any chance of offensive warfare. However, the Chinese had been re-equipped by Stalin with large numbers of improved T-34 tanks and SU-76 self-propelled guns. This gave them firepower mobility. Stalin's dispatch of personnel carriers and more powerful trucks offered them the chance to transport their assault troops and artillery support into new battle areas should the need arise.

The third major achievement of the Chinese and North Koreans during 1951–2 was the improvement in their supply systems between Manchuria and the 'Main Line of Resistance'. Most credit for this must go the North Koreans who conscripted labourers to repair roads bombed by the UN during the day. At night, when the craters had been filled and the bridges strengthened, the communist convoys would move southwards. Russian-built trucks were always hidden during the day – the Chinese were past masters at the art of camouflage – and the supply convoys made their run down to the Chinese lines under cover of darkness. Off-loading stores at the 'Main Line of Resistance' was also shielded by secure cover and the Chinese and the NKPA were able to build up massive reserves of ammunition, particularly artillery shells and mortar bombs. The one weakness of the truck convoys was the speed in which they gulped down the precious diesel fuel, supplies of which had to come from China.

In contrast, the railways ran on coal and this was the one fuel that was plentiful in North Korea. Unfortunately for the communists there was no rail link leading directly to the 'Main Line of Resistance' but they struggled to keep open the routes between Manchuria and Pyongyang and Sariwon. Heavy UN bombing caused constant damage but the same energy and imagination devoted to road repairs was expended on the railways. The daunting mountain ranges meant that North Korea was already well-endowed with tunnels that were difficult to block by air attack and wonderful places to conceal ammunition trains during daylight hours.

In stark contrast with the elaborate Chinese defences was the UN 'Main Line of Resistance'. Theoretically, it stretched across the 155 miles of central Korea to form an unbroken network of fortified defences. In fact, the American and South Korean positions were built on an entirely different principle. Construction went on during the winter of 1951–2 and became more sophisticated during 1952–3. A trench line between 5 and 7 feet deep was cut across the forward slopes of hill crests and ridges, spotted with deep firepoints and bunkers designed to provide mutual support and protection. US Marine units tended not to dig as deep as their Army colleagues, preferring to raise high sandbagged structures covered in earth. During 1952 their engineers devised a 'prefabricated bunker' made of timber that could slot into a ready-dug pit. They suggested to the Marines on the hills that a safe depth was 7 feet but it was rare that a marine bunker went that deep.

In front of the trench line were scores of fortified positions or outposts, usually located on hill crests. Outposts featured solidly-built bunkers housing command posts, artillery observation posts and weapon posts, each reinforced by timber supports and covered with sandbags and earth and designed to make the defenders immune to mortar and artillery bombardment. Further down the hill were troops in trenches and outguard positions whose role was to spot enemy movement and give the alarm. The outguards linked with the trenches and these in turn linked with the bunkers on the crest. Ringing each outpost were wire entanglements and minefields to inhibit rapid enemy infiltration. An infantry or marine platoon equipped with rocket launchers, light and heavy machine-guns, vast stocks of ammunition and case upon case of grenades manned each outpost. Food and ammunition supplies came up by personnel carriers or by Korean porters, usually in daylight when the Chinese were less inclined to wheel out their artillery and fire on UN positions.

Platoon commanders were in direct telephone link with their companies and battalions and could call down 'Flash Fire' on their positions. The guns would be previously ranged on each outpost to provide a semi-circular curtain of fire aimed to take out an enemy attack and protect the defending platoon. The strategy behind this somewhat dangerous form of defence was simple: an outpost defended by such a small group of men invited attack. When Chinese soldiers emerged from their underground galleries, American artillery would slaughter them. The fate of the soldiers manning these outposts was at best uncertain and this risky tour of duty meant that outpost platoons were usually relieved every 4 to 5 days.

The Commonwealth Division adopted different methods along its relatively short front line although some Canadian units did imitate the American outpost system. It regarded each battalion on the front line as a 'defence island' with its forward companies rotating regularly. Initially, its accommodation was even cruder than that devised by the Americans with little or no overhead protection in slit trenches. It was not long before matters were put right for the winter was upon them. The first snow fell during the night of 23/24 November 1951, followed by 16 degrees of frost the next night and a heavy snowfall throughout the day. How the Commonwealth forces reacted is described below. There were modest changes in the order of battle as on 22 November 1951.

## THE 1st COMMONWEALTH DIVISION

The 29th British Infantry Brigade located west of the Samichon River:

> 1st Battalion The Royal Norfolk Regiment
> 1st Battalion The Royal Leicestershire Regiment
> 1st Battalion The Welch Regiment

The 25th Canadian Infantry Brigade located east of the Samichon up to the US 3rd Division:

> 2nd Battalion The Royal Canadian Regiment
> 1st Battalion Princess Patricia's Canadian Light Infantry
> 2nd Battalion Royal Vingt-Deuxiéme Regiment

The 28th Commonwealth Infantry Brigade in reserve:

> 1st Battalion The King's Own Scottish Borderers
> 1st Battalion The Shropshire Light Infantry
> 3rd Battalion Royal Australian Regiment

On 6 December the 5th Inniskilling Dragoon Guards, commanded by Lt Col A. Carr, had arrived in Korea to relieve the 8th Hussars.

## WINTER CONDITIONS

By the nature of their operations, the personnel of both naval and air units fighting in the Korean winter were exposed to its worst excesses. Yet on most days, in the warmth of naval messes or in well-heated aircrew and ground crew accommodation, it was possible for most individuals to find some moments of relief from the bitter cold. For the fighting men facing the enemy from their static defences, the Korean winter seemed to be the worst in the world and had to be endured for months at a stretch. From November to March, the climate is essentially damp and cold yet subject to wide variations of temperature. Consequently, it can freeze overnight, thaw in the morning and freeze in the afternoon. Because of the high humidity in central Korea and the strong winds coming off the mountains the 'wind chill' factor is pronounced and it often seemed colder to the troops on the ground than the thermometers actually showed. These conditions could have detrimental effects on morale, as could the view from the sandbagged bunkers. Korea's hills can be very beautiful in the summer, with lots of fresh green undergrowth and, later on, carpets of colourful azaleas. In the winter they become barren, brown monsters, their spurs and re-entrants and knife-edge ridges all capable of hiding a dangerous and well-camouflaged enemy.

The Americans were relatively well-equipped with snug winter clothing, superb food and well-designed battle accommodation. They knew that frostbite and trenchfoot casualties usually arose through ignorance and neglect and had set up a training programme in the Eighth Army led by William F. Pounder, a civilian observer employed by the US Quartermaster General. These programmes were translated into Korean, Turkish, Spanish and French to serve the needs of the different nationalities fighting in the UN Command. Eventually every company had its own cold-injury prevention team with an emphasis upon regular sock exchange. Due partly to this work, US weather casualties dropped to 4 per cent of total casualties, comparing favourably with Second World War European combat figures of 8 per cent. However, the battle training environment was highly significant. Marines who had trained in Greenland, the 2nd Infantry Division who had undergone battle courses in US mountain areas and the 7th Infantry who had worked up for Korea in northern Japan did not have a single wet-cold or dry-cold injury.

British and Commonwealth battalions together with their support units had to learn wet-cold/dry-cold wisdom the hard way. When the Middlesex and Argylls had arrived from Hong Kong in 1950 they were better served for a tour in the tropics rather than the Moscow-style winter with which they soon had to contend. Too long, British soldiers had been condemned throughout two World Wars to stand in the rain in ammunition boots and a poncho, yet the boots and the ponchos were still issued to recruits in the UK training camps during 1950–5. When 29 Brigade arrived from the UK they were a little better off. They wore battle-dress and greatcoats, gloves and string vests. Windcheaters had been issued and some had ski boots. All blessed the War Office's secret weapon: the long johns. In Korea the first thing they wanted was an American parka and access to that most wonderful and lethal invention of the Korean War, the drip-feed petrol stove or 'chuffer'. They could be found everywhere: in rear echelon among the signal and supply trucks, in the mortar platoon bunkers on the reverse slopes and, most of all, in the 'hoochies' (sometimes 'hooch,' 'hutch' or 'hutchie') built to house the troops at the 'sharp end'.

The hoochies or living quarters were ideally cut into the reverse slope of a hill among trees and placed out of the prevailing wind. Those attached to the fighting bunkers had perforce to face the wire, the minefields, the incoming Chinese mortar bombs and artillery shells during the daily 'stonk'. Hoochies had to be deep enough – at least 4 feet to be below the frost line – and strongly revetted to shore up the crumbly Korean soil. Thick top cover gave protection against artillery bursts. Plentiful use of sandbags, hurdles, 6-inch balks of timber and waterproof tarpaper was advised and the soldiers, as ever, scrounged that which the Royal Engineers could not supply. Double walls helped to insulate the living bunker, which had to have a slightly sloping floor for drainage. As the troops dug their own bunkers, there was some variety between battalions but all had to observe the basic rules of camouflage and ventilation for their own survival. Where troops were in individual foxholes, water had to be baled out and a wooden 3-inch base built over the soil so the soldier could stand clear of water. Those lucky enough to acquire Tilley lamps had light and a useful source of heat, but most made do with candles in a 50-cigarette tin (the sentry's friend) and with red-hot chuffer stoves whose exhaust disappeared up a pipe (often a chimney made of empty shellcases) through the bunker roof. Because of accidents the use of petrol was later banned and chuffers used diesel fuel instead. Troops complained that diesel spoilt the taste of their food – usually American C7 rations and bully beef or stew cooked in mess tins. Bedding was a problem as it was unwise to wrap oneself in a cosy sleeping bag. Too many had died there, bayoneted by infiltrating Chinese soldiers. Blankets had to suffice, preferably on some sort of camp bed to keep oneself off the floor. Everything was helped by the evening tot of rum though the medical orderlies warned that alcohol aided the rapid loss of body heat. It was a risk most were prepared to take.

The winter reached its peak during January–February 1952 when all men learned to wear the string vest next to their skin; then a singlet vest, army issue shirt, green pullover plus a winter pullover on top of this. Under-trousers and the windproof combat trousers plus the new hooded anorak were vital but best of all was the green parka. Puttees returned as they proved much more efficient than the webbing gaiters issued to all during 1950–3. A sweat-rag was useful to seal the neck. But it was attention to detail that saved men from the cold. The two most common injuries were frostbite occurring when the temperature fell below 20°F; and trenchfoot, caused by the cold and wet at about freezing level. Men were urged to have plenty of spare socks, to carry extra pairs on duty and to change them daily as far as possible. Washing and shaving were compulsory daily chores and normal standards of hygiene were never relaxed. Norman Davies summed it all up: 'The cold was the constant enemy. It required every atom of willpower to try and push it from one's mind and concentrate on the job in hand. Yet no-one, to my knowledge, shirked his duty. We all depended on each other. We had to, if we wanted to survive.'[1]

Weapons and equipment also suffered from the cold. Ice-cold barrels and triggers caused injury to the unwise who handled them without gloves: and the issued leather gauntlet mittens had attached an unlined trigger finger. Thick oil froze automatic weapons and caused stoppages while thin oil of the standard 'Oil Low Cold Test No. 2' type could not be used below 0°F. Troops had to use oil mixed with kerosene to keep weapons effective. Dirt and cold together caused carbine and machine-gun stoppages – often the cause of unnecessary loss of life. When a soldier retired to his warm hoochie, condensation immediately formed on weapons. These had to be thoroughly cleaned and the correct oil mixtures sparingly applied. In the mortar platoons the troops had to ensure that the base plates were kept warm with rice sheaves or thick grass to prevent their freezing to the ground. Anti-freeze was a misnomer as it frequently froze, and drivers tended to run their engines for long periods to avoid a cold engine and thus prejudice a quick getaway in the event of a sudden Chinese breakthrough. Tanks and carriers had to be moved backwards and forwards to free their tracks of ice; and once the engines started – everything depended on first-class batteries – it was sometimes difficult to change up from first gear if the box was frozen.

## REST AND RECOVERY AND CARE OF THE TROOPS

Divisional commanders were highly conscious of the need to maintain the fighting man's morale and combat troops were regularly rotated from the 'sharp end' into reserve. In the Commonwealth lines alcohol was readily available and the basic fare in what were delicately termed 'watering holes' was Japanese Asahi beer. Whisky, rum and gin were good for trade with nearby Americans and there was plenty of opportunity for jovial fraternization behind the 'Main Line of Resistance.' American GIs usually headed for the Tokyo PX building – still there, but part of a Japanese department store – as American aircraft operated regular flights to leave centres in Japan. Most soldiers managed a week away from their units during their tour in Korea. There was the Commonwealth Division Rest Centre in Inchon for those who had leave for a day or two. Here Hilda Wood Women's Voluntary Service (WVS) and Patricia Whittal WVS sold WVS wares and organized trips to Seoul. Most soldiers on R & R took a Globemaster or Skymaster to Tokyo where there was accommodation available to Commonwealth troops in the Ebisu Hotel. Short tours were arranged by other members of the WVS and most visited Hiroshima where the effects of the first atomic attack were still visible, etching themselves forever on every soldier's mind.

Quality entertainment was a welcome feature of life on the line. American radio and film personalities visited Korea and the famous PX (Post Exchange) enabled the typical GI to spend his money on relative luxuries. Less well-endowed financially, the British soldier had the NAAFI (Navy, Army and Air Force Institute) shops and canteens such as Roy Williams' famous 'Ned Kelly' NAAFI canteen that was a welcome sight to all in 1953. Most battalions operated rest camps with stages, and cinemas sometimes fitted with tiered seats made out of ammunition boxes. British screen and radio personalities came out to Korea during 1951–2. Brian Reece and Jack Warner arrived in

1951; Ted Ray came in 1952 and gave shows with Helen Ward and Julie Shelley. In the same year Frankie Howerd brought a concert party to Korea, Japan and Hong Kong. Frankie and singers Eve Boswell and Vera Jessop and Eddie Arnold, the impressionist, performed to enthusiastic audiences.

Perhaps the most popular star among the British troops was Carole Carr who in 1952 was singing in the BBC variety show 'Calling All Forces'. The War Office invited her to tour Korea, Hong Kong, Japan and Malaya and she spent three weeks in Korea, the only female in the Commonwealth sector apart from the nurses in the Norwegian Mobile Army Surgical Hospital. Carole Carr also did one show for the Americans at I Corps and visited army hospitals. She relates several stories in the British Official History: 'one of my most vivid memories is the show I did for the Welch Regiment in a rain storm. They were getting soaked, so I asked them if they wanted me to carry on. They yelled YES, but they had the last laugh. Suddenly the canvas roof over the stage caved in and I was drenched . . . to a wave of cheers and whistles. Afterwards the CO said my stock had gone up 100 per cent, whether because I had 'carried on singing' or because my dress had clung in a most revealing way, your guess is as good as mine!' In that strictly male environment she was not surprised when she asked the Royal Inniskilling Dragoon Guards for song requests and a voice called out, 'Don't sing, just stand there!' Performers usually had the use of a Humber staff car, a three tonner to carry the stage 'props' with a separate truck for changing and an caravan for sleeping. They regarded their time in Korea as a great privilege; for the troops it was well-earned relief.[2]


## HOSPITAL CARE

Soldiers wounded in battle were given immediate treatment by Royal Army Medical Corps personnel (Commonwealth Division) and by enlisted medics in the US Army. They were skilled in the use of tourniquets, bandages and were qualified to give sedatives. Medical officers in the field could of course give plasma and blood. Casualties were then evacuated by ambulance, litter jeeps or helicopters to forward aid stations and Mobile Army Surgical Hospitals (MASH). The role of the MASH was to provide emergency surgery and to make the patient sufficiently stable so that he could be transported to rear medical installations or to Japan or to his home country. Most of the American MASH were originally 60-bed hospitals but the demands of the battlefield soon required them to grow into 200-bed hospitals, one to each US division. They had to be mobile and the 8075th MASH, for example, had most elaborate arrangements to ensure that half the hospital facilities moved while the other half offered full surgical facilities plus the necessary sterilizing units. Careful attention was paid to temperature by operating Far East Air Force hot air heaters, to effective and emergency surgical lighting and to sprinkler systems to keep down the dust. The 1st MASH which had arrived at Iwon in 1950 served first the US 7th Division and then transferred to X Corps where it expanded its resources to accommodate 200 beds.

In the Commonwealth Sector, casualties were tended by 26th Field Ambulance, Royal Army Medical Corps; 25th Canadian Field Ambulance, Royal Canadian Medical Corps; and by the Norwegian MASH (NORMASH) which rendered sterling service throughout 1951–4. NORMASH was born in 1951 through negotiations between the Norwegian government, the Norwegian Red Cross, the US State Department and the United Nations. Norway would supply the medical teams and purchase the necessary supplies from US depots in Japan and Korea. During April-May 1951 the first contingent of hospital personnel flew to Korea and began work on 19 July 1951. It would remain in Korea after the war until 10 November 1954, by which time it had treated over 90,000 patients. Some 622 medical personnel served with NORMASH, including 111 female nurses. None was killed in action although NORMASH was located close to the front line. NORMASH surgeons performed 9,600 operations and for a military hospital had a remarkably small death rate of 1.2 per cent.

Colin Ross was a medical corporal in Korea after the front had stabilized. 26th Field Ambulance was at Commonwealth Divisional HQ and a mere two miles from the sharp end. He and his colleagues were terrified of the shelling – they never got used to it – and were always anxious about the 'old tales of 1951, of how the hordes would sweep down on us.' The Field Ambulance received every type of injury from the front. '. . . shell and mortar being the commonest. Many suffered out of the line, and after the armistice, from VD, typhus, water-borne diseases and psychological problems. We also received many North Korean prisoners, often with extensive burns from napalm, filthy stuff. They all seemed to believe they would be shot

and could not understand they were being cared for and not tortured!'
He was not much impressed by the level of medical equipment. 'Ideas
were hangovers from World War II. We had paratroop field surgical
teams who had in their standard panniers Nelson Inhalers, pots in
which menthol was added to boiling water for stuffed noses! Terrible
old-fashioned Thomas splints. Agonizing old-fashioned tourniquets.
Even smelling salts! Plastic drip feeds were not yet available and vast
amounts of saline had to be produced and transported in glass
containers. Sterilization of dressings and instruments was still in
old-fashioned field autoclaves. Field dentistry was a real horror.
The dental officers still used treadle mill drills – in the open air.
Screams of patients would have made good propaganda!'[3] Despite the
problems, nursing care was of a high standard.

The British also operated a specialist medical hospital, the Britcom
Communication Zone Medical Unit. Usually abbreviated to Britcom
Z Medical Unit, this small hospital was formed in Seoul in 1952
having evolved from the British Commonwealth General Hospital at
Kure, Japan. In 1953 nursing sisters, including three 'QAs' (Queen
Alexandra's Royal Army Nursing Corps), two Australians and two
Canadians, were allowed to serve there. One was Jill MacNair neé
Hall. She wrote numerous letters home, describing her experiences
working in a converted school-house that had no running water: '. . .
there is no running water available, so that every drop that is needed
has to be carried up in cans, which at times can be a little inconvenient.
On the other hand, it is really amazing how quickly one adapts to a
tapless situation and consequently manages very well.' Seoul suffered
from several air raids, usually delivered by aged but skilfully flown
Russian biplanes known as 'Bedcheck Charlies.' Jill Hall could hear
the gunfire from the 'sharp end' as well as the bombs, and knew the
details of British soldiers killed and wounded during the hill battles
and the fighting patrols: 'You see there really is a war going on out
here and it seems a pity that people at home do not take much interest
in what's going on . . .'[4]

There was also the famous HM Hospital Ship *Maine*, a 7,500 ton
vessel on station in Hong Kong when the Korean war began. Her task
initially was to ferry American casualties between Pusan and Osaka,
Japan, where the 5th United States General Hospital was based. In
describing her work on board the *Maine*, Sister Ruth Stone mentioned
the verdict of the First Sea Lord, Lord Fraser of North Cape: 'One of
Britain's most useful contributions to the United Nations' effort in the

Korean War has been Her Majesty's Hospital Ship *Maine*.' Ruth Stone was a member of the Queen Alexandra's Royal Naval Nursing Service aboard the *Maine* in 1950 when it was the solitary hospital ship in Korean waters. The sisters and Sick Berth Attendants cared for the first American casualties and the severely burned Argyll and Sutherland victims of that terrible napalm error. Every soldier suffering from wounds or burns was treated with penicillin twice a day: 'In those days this life-saving drug was prepared in a suspension of beeswax; quite diabolical to draw up speedily into a syringe but here our Dental Officer and his assistant came to the rescue. They toiled from bed to bed from one end of the ship to the other and each evening they began all over again. This they somehow achieved in addition to attending to intricate jaw and facial reconstructions which presented themselves on each trip.'[5] The Danes provided a comparable vessel, the *Jutlandia*. Initially she offered 356 beds but this was expanded to 500. After her first tour, *Jutlandia* took home 200 casualties, so badly wounded that they could not safely travel by air. On her return to Korea she was fitted with a helicopter pad so that wounded could be flown directly from Forward Aid Stations to the ship, for surgery at the hands of highly skilled professionals. Surgical operations were customarily carried out while the ship was at sea. *Maine* was later replaced in the war zone by *Haven*, *Repose* and *Consolation*. These were the much bigger American hospital ships displacing 15,000 tons and staffed by 15 doctors, 40 nurses and 90 sick berth orderlies.

## IN RESERVE, PATROLLING AND FIGHTING, 1951–2

Men continued to patrol and fight throughout the peace talks. The 1st Battalion The Welch Regiment, commanded by Lt Col H.H. Deane, joined 29 Brigade in November 1951. After a brief spell in reserve it went into the line on 24 November, the day before the US 7th Regimental Combat Team recaptured Kowang-san which would soon become home to the Royal Welch. The King's Own Scottish Borderers replaced the Royal Welch in reserve so that, apart from one platoon of C Company detached to the Royal Norfolks on Yong Dong Hill, they were out of enemy artillery range. Remembering their earlier experiences, the Borderers began building defence systems and planned and rehearsed counter-attacks in case the Chinese ever infiltrated 'Jamestown.' Before long they took part in Operation 'Skunkhunt', the search for communist guerrillas and enemy agents operating within the Commonwealth Divisional area. This was in response to a lorry ambush carried out by enemy forces behind the Commonwealth lines on 10 December. For this the battalion wore the new armoured vests known generally as 'flak jackets' and tested new infra-red telescopic sights on their sniper rifles. It was the first of many 'Skunkhunts' conducted by the division as other ambushes occurred on 5/6 and 15/ 16 January 1952 and 12/13 February 1952 during which several soldiers died.

In reserve troops could enjoy the benefits of mobile bath-houses and spend their pay at the NAAFI. The Borderers were luckier than most as regimental friends in the UK had subscribed funds for this purpose. Moreover, the Borderers received special food and clothing from the San Francisco Group of the English Speaking Union who had 'adopted' the battalion. An unusual duty was to relieve four companies of the 25th Canadian Brigade, and this fell to B Company of 1 KOSB who carried out the four reliefs at 0400 hours each morning! The purpose was to enable the Canadians to enjoy their Christmas dinner in peace! That Christmas was memorable for another reason: the Chinese sent Christmas cards to the Commonwealth Division either by pinning them on the wire or despatching small boys – one was actually caught – across No Man's Land with a sack of cards bearing goodwill from the Chinese People's Volunteers and the North Korean People's Army!

1 KOSB was back in the line on 18 January 1952 when it relieved the Royal Canadian Regiment. There had been little activity apart from patrols. The Royal Welch had captured their first prisoner; the Royal Canadian Regiment apprehended another; and there had been a company raid on Hill 227 carried out by the Patricias on 10/11 December coincidental with an RAR fighting patrol on Hill 166. Both raids suffered losses but claimed to have reached their targets and inflicted casualties. The Borderers' new position was in full view of Chinese observers and though there were no battles for the next two months there was an all-pervading tension. After all, the Chinese were but a thousand yards away and 75 per cent of the battalion stood-to every night. The Borderers were providing 5–7 standing patrols each night and a fighting patrol at least once every week.

There were different kinds of patrols; most were self-explanatory. A fighting patrol usually numbered 15 men in this period and included a scouting group, a command group and two fighting groups. Later, these were sometimes refined into smaller 'snatch squads' specifically designed to capture prisoners. Standing patrols went forward to observe enemy movements and to give warning of their approach. These patrols were an integral part of the battalion defence system and operated directly under the control of the battalion commander. Standing patrols usually had three or four 'hides' in No Man's Land and used a different one each night. Lie-up patrols went out for two or three days and operated behind the enemy lines. Reconnaissance patrols and minefield patrols were a daily occurrence. In the event of trouble, battalions maintained a Flying Squad to go to the assistance of a patrol in No Man's Land and, if necessary, help evacuate any wounded.

## OPERATIONS ALONG
## 'THE MAIN LINE OF RESISTANCE', 1951–2

There were changes in the order of battle of the US Eighth Army. America's famous 1st Cavalry Division departed for Japan on 12 January 1952, replaced by the 40th Division which joined IX Corps. On 23 February the 25th Division relieved the 7th Division, now in reserve. Eight Chinese armies, flanked by three NKPA Corps and one brigade faced the American and ROK divisions and several went into action after 27 December 1951. All the campaigns were localized and centred on hills of doubtful tactical significance. For example, on X Corps front Hill 104 and 'No Name Hill' were lost to the Chinese but regained after lively ROK attacks early in January 1952. Hill 104 was disputed on I US Corps front and again ROK forces counter-attacked with verve. They claimed a victory and counted 1,611 Chinese dead for the loss of 129 of their own number.

At first glance, it seems difficult to justify such bloodthirsty fire-fights except in terms of bargaining counters at the peace talks, assuming they were even in session at the time. But as General Sir Anthony Farrar-Hockley (whom we last encountered as a Gloster captain at the Imjin) has noted in his Official History, military commanders fail to discharge their duty if they do not encourage the 'offensive spirit' among their soldiers. Had the UN policy been simply to defend the 'Main Line of Resistance' and not counter Chinese build-up and local attacks, then the men at the 'sharp end' would suffer a drop in morale and be inclined to abandon defensive positions in the face of a previously unchallenged and determined enemy. When survival becomes a soldier's primary concern, perhaps induced by factors such as imminent leave or the prospect of unit relief, a demoralizing *defensive* policy may reduce his value as a fighting man.

However, few battalion commanders enthused about one extra-ordinary operation, codenamed 'Snare', involving all of Eighth Army during 10–16 February 1952. Orders from Van Fleet required front-line units to cease firing unless enemy troops attacked. If that occurred UN reaction would be limited to the firing of smallarms. Additionally, all patrolling would be stopped. Apparently the aim was to mystify the enemy and encourage him to send out large exploratory patrols to establish whether UN forces had withdrawn from 'Jamestown'. When these curious Chinese appeared, UN artillery would kill them in large numbers and, as a bonus, UN patrols would take some prisoners. General Cassels protested strongly at the dangers implicit in 'Snare' and expressed no confidence in its outcome. Certainly, the Chinese were mystified by this bout of UN stupidity. Their patrols came forward, quickly established that the UN forces were still in position, retired a short distance and then began extending their defence system into No Man's Land without any interference from the Eighth Army! When 'Snare' ended, nothing had changed except that the Chinese were in even better fortified bunkers and a little closer to the UN positions! When the 5th Dragoon Guards sent out their Centurions to investigate the situation one hit a mine. It had proved to be an unproductive week.

During the last five days of February 1952 the Chinese tested the defences of 1 KOSB and the Royal Leicesters but made little impression. The Welch Regiment were now dug in on the Hook and had a platoon based on Umdalmal, a spur jutting out into the Samichon valley. Every night they had expected a major Chinese attack but it did not materialize. They were relieved in March 1952 by the Princess Pats who made a great impression on the Welch Platoon Sergeant, E R 'Jigger' Lee:

> Almost every one seemed to be carrying a Browning ma-chine-gun with belts of ammunition around their necks . . .
> I took the Platoon Sergeant to the Company HQ position
> . . . and then proceeded to put him in the picture, explaining positions of own troops, prominent features, arcs of fire . . .

He stopped me, holding his head with both hands. He said, 'Never mind that, just show me where they are and you can go.' Apparently he was suffering from an almighty hangover from his last night in reserve.[6]

Once the Princess Patricias had taken over the Hook, the Chinese showed much more interest and sent a company against a single platoon. The Canadians were located on a curiously-shaped spur some 1,200 yards to the west of the Samichon. Chinese infantry attacked through a minefield and surrounded the platoon. It fought back and forced the enemy to withdraw. 1 PPCLI had lost four men killed and ten wounded. Their success was largely due to the leadership and fire control of the Platoon Sergeant, R.G. Buxton, who was awarded the Distinguished Conduct Medal. This was the first action on a Korean hill whose name 'the Hook' would be writ large in the battle histories of many regiments. On the occasion of this, the first fight on the Hook during the night of 26/27 March 1952, the Chinese had hoped to drive the Canadians off the spur and the nearby Hill 163 held by the Royal Canadian Regiment. Having failed to shift the Canadians the Chinese probed the Borderers' A Company defences on 6/7 April. They were driven off by divisional artillery which fired over 7,000 rounds that night.

## THE BATTLES OF 'OLD BALDY' AND 'BUNKER HILL', JULY–AUGUST 1952

During the spring and early summer of 1952 the atmosphere along the 'Main Line of Resistance' was reminiscent of *All Quiet on the Western Front*. Fights would flare up in different corps or divisional sectors, sometimes during a period when one division was relieving another. This was true in mid-July when strong Chinese attacks concentrated on a hill called 'Old Baldy' just as the US 23rd Infantry (2nd US Division) was relieving the 45th Division (1/18 July 1952). The 23rd lost the crest and then regained it at the cost of 39 dead and 84 missing. Torrential rainstorms discouraged the fighting until the end of July when the Americans attacked and seized the ridge, defying every Chinese counter-attack and fortifying their position with masses of barbed wire and trip-mines. The Chinese gave up attacking Old Baldy for the rest of August and the 'Main Line of Resistance' (MLR) remained intact.

Further west and holding the left flank of the 'Jamestown Line' was the 1st Marine Division, reinforced by the excellent ROK 1st Marine Regiment. Facing them were numerous battalions of the Chinese People's Volunteers, drawn mainly from the 119th and 194th Divisions. There had been several small-scale firefights in this delicate area which included the truce talks site at Panmunjom. On 25 July 1952 Colonel Walter F. Layer became commander of the 1st Marine Regiment and on 27 July disposed his three battalions along the MLR. A key feature was Hill 229 or 'Paekhak Hill' overlooking the road to Panmunjom, and Colonel Layer appreciated the psychological effect it would have if the Chinese managed to capture this height. Facing him, the Chinese 352nd Regiment had dug into Hill 122 to which the Marines gave the name 'Bunker Hill.' Behind Bunker Hill was a mountain known as Taedok-san, the key observation point of this sector of the MLR.

The Marines had established outposts about a mile beyond the 'Main Line of Resistance' and one squad from the 2nd Battalion was holding outpost 'Siberia'. Determined Chinese rushed this position just after midnight on 9 August 1952 and pushed the Americans out of their bunkers. A Marine platoon came forward but was frustrated by intense Chinese shelling. The Marines called up an air strike and four Marine Panthers straddled 'Siberia' with napalm and bombs, followed by F-80 Shooting Stars that hit the position with 1,000lb bombs. Following this up with heavy artillery fire, the Marines retook 'Siberia' the same day only to face Chinese counter-attacks which inflicted heavy casualties along the 1st Marine Regiment's positions. Once more 'Siberia' was lost – as was another outpost known as 'Samoa' east of Siberia.

The Americans now decided to play the Chinese at their own game and put in a silent night attack without the preliminary artillery bombardment. Captain Casimir C. Kyscewski led the assault, surprised the Chinese and occupied the crest of 'Siberia' in a ten-minute rush. When the Chinese recovered, they contested the heights for the next four hours and because of casualties, caused mainly by Chinese mortar and artillery fire, Kyscewski had to withdraw. Clearly, this increase in Chinese firepower was causing problems and Colonel Layer was convinced that the Chinese gun sites on Bunker Hill had to be neutralized before any more Marines were killed. Accordingly, a major attack would be launched against Bunker Hill backed by flame-throwing M-4A3E8 tanks and the deadly Marine M-46 Patton tanks with their 90mm guns equipped with new battlefield support lighting systems. Once more air strikes tried to soften up the Chinese redoubts and scores of napalm, bombing and machine-gunning sorties churned up these barren but tactically important targets.

The attack went in just before midnight on 11 August and the Marines fought with bayonets and carbines against equally determined Chinese defenders. By dawn on 12 August one of Captain Sereno S. Scranton's platoons won a vicious hand grenade battle with the Chinese and forced them to retire. Marine casualties numbered one killed and 22 wounded – a small but remarkable victory. At 0135 hours on 13 August the Chinese sent in a battalion against Bunker Hill. Most were killed or wounded in a crescendo of Marine artillery fire: 4.5-inch rockets, multi-tubed mortars and 155mm howitzers were now dominating the battlefield and annihilating Chinese soldiers as never before. Captain John G. Demass of Company H was now master of Bunker Hill and he successfully resisted Chinese attacks on 14–15 August. Relief came in the shape of Captain Scranton's Company B and his Marines held Bunker Hill throughout 16–17 August until he too was relieved by Company C. Such was the price paid for a commanding position along the MLR. For eight days the Marines had fought complex night actions to win a single hill. They had lost 48 Marines killed and 313 badly wounded. Chinese losses could only be estimated; 3,200 killed and wounded was the Marine figure.

## THE BATTLE OF 'WHITE HORSE HILL', 6–15 OCTOBER 1952

Though the early Autumn had been deceptively quiet along the IX Corps Sector, interrogation of a prisoner on 3 October revealed that a major Chinese attack upon Hill 395 to the north-west of Chorwon was imminent. Known as 'White Horse Hill,' this feature was important in that it controlled the approach to Chorwon. It was held by units of the 9th ROK Division and the skill of these soldiers in defence reflected the high quality of training, leadership and morale that characterized the new ROK Army, burying forever its old reputation for unreliability during the early battles of the Korean War. US intelligence supported the prisoner's story and provided 9th ROK, commanded by General Kim Jong Oh, with armour and artillery reinforcements. General Kim stationed two battalions of his 30th

Regiment on White Horse Hill and held his 28th Regiment in reserve. Around his flanks he assembled tanks and the deadly Quad-50s while behind the hill were scores of US 8-inch Persuaders and 4.2-inch mortar teams. He had the promise of full support from the Fifth US Air Force. His division was well-prepared for the enemy attack.

First the Chinese opened the floodgates of a reservoir at Pongnae in the hope of flooding the Yokkok-chon River separating the US 2nd Division and the ROK 9th. Their plan was to create a water barrier and prevent mutual reinforcement. It failed, as did the Chinese diversionary attack (6 October) upon the nearby 'Arrow-head Hill' held by the French battalion. Simultaneously, two Chinese battalions swarmed across the low ground to assault White Horse Hill but were repulsed after three attacks. Now the Chinese sent in infantrymen at regimental strength and the crest of White Horse Hill changed hands several times before the 28th Regiment, led by Colonel Lee Chu Il, forced the Chinese to retreat, though not for long. It was as though the Chinese were prepared to commit infinite numbers of men to the attack and on 8 October the seesaw battles, usually involving hand-to-hand fighting amidst murderous shell and mortar fire, continued without respite. For seven more days the Chinese took horrendous losses, prepared to expend the lives of most of the 25,000 soldiers involved in the battle. In all, they made 27 attacks upon the ROK division before abandoning their offensive and surrendering White Horse Hill. They have never published their casualty figures for this protracted battle but the ROK Army esti-mated that these exceeded 10,000 dead. The ROK division had lost 3,500 men but had demonstrated as never before the quality of its defensive skills.

The fighting around White Horse Hill and Arrowhead Hill was replicated in all the ROK and US sectors but not always as success-fully. General Van Fleet took the initiative in Operation 'Showdown' during 14 October–24 November. He proposed to capture three small hills, 'Pike's Peak', 'Sandy Ridge' and 'Jane Russell Hill' – collectively known as 'Triangle Hill' – and a nearby feature known as 'Sniper Ridge'. All of these positions were tunnelled and fortified with usual Chinese throroughness and in general the American attacks met only local and temporary success. ROK units took part in the unrewarding outpost battles on Sniper Ridge, again with only partial success. Operation 'Showdown' was a complete failure, and underlined the difficulty of any attempts by UN forces to penetrate the Chinese defence system using conventional infantry tactics supported by extravagant firepower. Under the existing circumstances, expansion of the Korean War in the search for a decisive victory would remain an unfulfilled hope in the mind of General Van Fleet.

## CHANGES IN THE COMMONWEALTH DIVISION

There had been further changes to the Order of Battle in the 1st Commonwealth Division. Fresh infantry battalions arrived as a result of the rotation programme that ensured a battalion would spend only one winter in Korea. The advance party of the Black Watch (Lt Col D. C. Rose DSO) arrived on 8 June 1952, the 1st Battalion The Royal Fusiliers commanded by Lt Col G. R. Stevens relieved 1 KOSB (4 August 1952); the 1st Battalion The Durham Light Infantry (DLI) commanded by Lt. Col P. J. Jeffreys relieved 1 KSLI (11 September 1952); and the 1st Battalion The King's Liverpool Regiment commanded by Lf. Col. A. J. Snodgrass relieved 1st Norfolks (21 September 1952). The 1st Battalion The Duke of Wellington's Regiment, commanded by Lt Col F. R. Bunbury DSO, arrived in the Divisional sector on 31 October 1952.

## 1ST COMMONWEALTH DIVISION, November 1952

### Major-General M. M. West DSO

25th Canadian Infantry Brigade (Brigadier M. P. Bogert DSO):

> 1st Battalion The Royal Canadian Regiment
> 3rd Battalion Princess Patricia's Light Infantry
> (had replaced the 1st Battalion on 3 November)
> 1st Battalion Royal 22e Régiment

28th Commonwealth Infantry Brigade (Brigadier T. J. Daly DSO):

> 1st Battalion The Royal Fusiliers
> 1st Battalion The Durham Light Infantry
> 1st Battalion Royal Australian Regiment
> 3rd Battalion Royal Australian Regiment

29th British Infantry Brigade (Brigadier A.H.G. Richetts DSO)

1st Battalion The King's Regiment (Liverpool)
1st Battalion The Duke of Wellington's Regiment
1st Battalion The Black Watch

Maj. General Cassels had been posted to a NATO command and his successor, Maj. General West, continued his quest for prisoners by means of fighting patrols. There had also been changes in the Chinese divisions, most of which were now drawn from the Chinese 39th and 40th Field Armies. Apart from their usual advantages – tunnelling skills and an abundance of mortars – their artillery firepower now rivalled that of the United Nations. Consequently, artillery would dominate the battlefield over the next few months. However, in the summer and early autumn of 1952 artillery exchanges in the western sectors, apart from the American experience at the Battle of Bunker Hill, remained desultory. There were also local exceptions. The 1st Royal Canadian Regiment, whose main bunkers on Hill 355 ('Little Gibraltar') featured a series of outposts, did receive unwelcome shell-fire on 1 October during which the Chinese guns totally destroyed Outpost 'Vancouver' and knocked out a tank from the Lord Strath-cona Horse. On 23 October the Chinese brought in heavy artillery and self-propelled guns that wreaked destruction among the fighting and communication trenches of both A and B Companies. Chinese in-fantry overran the wreckage. Calling down artillery fire on their own abandoned positions, the Canadians regrouped and counter-attacked, with a company of the Royal Fusiliers in reserve. It was difficult to assess the exact intentions of the Chinese infantry as their survivors eventually withdrew and the Canadians quickly restored their posi-tions. They had lost 18 killed, 43 wounded and 14 men missing, believed captured by the enemy. Chinese losses were hard to gauge, but later RCR patrols discovered bodies that the enemy had failed to recover. They were located in trenches and bunkers used by the Chinese to form up their assault troops and Canadian pioneers promptly blew up these positions so that they could not be a danger in the future.

As for Chinese prisoners, between 1 July and 31 October the Commonwealth Division had managed to capture a mere 12 despite the heavy emphasis on raids and patrols and the use of specially trained and equipped 'snatch squads'. Battalion commanders were inclined to put a bounty on the capture of a prisoner who sometimes rated a bottle of whisky or even five days R & R. The Durham Light Infantry had little luck; a potential prisoner who had let rip with a round from his burp gun was shot by an irate Light Infantryman. During their tour the 1st Norfolks had captured three slightly wounded prisoners but these had all curled up and died. The Leicesters and the Welch had scored one each; the Australians preferred to kill the enemy and proved forgetful when required to take prisoners. Canadians seemed to produce the best results. Lt H. R. Gardner led a six-man patrol on 24 September from the RCR lines towards a known enemy bunker. After establishing a nearby 'firm base', Lt Gardiner and Corporal K. E. Fowler went forward to the bunker but found it deserted. They did find a telephone wire in the enemy kitchen area. They cut the wire and awaited results. A Chinese signaller arrived to repair the line and was promptly snatched. Three Chinese infantrymen appeared and were dealt with by fire from the firm base. Lt Gardner brought back his patrol and his prisoner safely.

Of course, 'snatch squads' were not confined to the UN for the Chinese proved equally adept. For example, on 4 November a Black Watch patrol operating in front of the Hook was enveloped by a large Chinese fighting patrol. Six of the Black Watch were killed, six were wounded and two were missing. Three soldiers escaped. Chinese probes of this nature were continually testing for weak spots in the defence, and their commanders were always interested in acquiring tactically important hills to help influence the peace talks or to bring them defensive advantages if the peace talks failed. For these reasons, the Chinese began shelling the Hook on 16 November. They had already made an attempt to capture this feature when the 7th US Marines Regiment were in occupation during October. On 26/27 October the Chinese captured the Hook and were then driven off it by the Marines. It was a crucially important feature: whoever controlled it dominated the Samichon valley and the route to Seoul. The US Marines handed over the Hook to the Black Watch on 14 November and the battalion, with the aid of Korean labourers and the Royal Engineers, worked feverishly to repair the shell-blasted bunkers and fighting trenches.

Now the Chinese launched a battalion attack against the Black Watch during the night of 18/19 November. They surrounded a Black Watch patrol and then put in a company assault on the Black Watch positions. The Chinese came in under their own artillery and mortar fire and scores were killed in the process. Four Centurion tanks of 4 Troop B Squadron Royal Inniskilling Dragoon Guards were dug-in along the Hook with a fifth located on a nearby feature known as Yong-dong. Great respect was shown by the Chinese towards the British Centurions: rumour had it they had offered one million pounds for the capture of a Centurion in good working condition! Their 20 pounders and co-axial Besa machine-guns slaughtered scores of Chinese. When the Chinese pushed A Company Black Watch out of their fighting trenches, the Scots retreated into their main bunkers and called down defensive artillery fire on their new position. The guns from the rear plus the Centurions' firepower held the enemy back for three hours and though the Black Watch were initially forced off the Hook they recaptured it next morning.

The tanks played a crucial part in this battle because of their ability to illuminate the scene with their new American searchlights. Moreover, unlike most American tanks, the Centurions could climb steep slopes and could position themselves in a tactical position where they could bring their searchlights and accurate 20 pounders to bear on enemy bunkers. Their powerful illuminators required the Centurions' engines to work at full throttle and the scream of engines was a macabre accompaniment to the noise of this and other battles fought in the vicinity of the Hook. Naturally, the searchlights were targeted by Chinese artillery and the Centurions frequently suffered damage to hulls and turrets. Most vital to the tank crews were the extractor fans, for these removed the cordite fumes filling the turret whenever the 20-pounder gun was fired. Battle damage would force a Centurion to leave its heavily reinforced revetment and retire for repairs and to replenish its main gun and Besa ammunition. It is worth mentioning the role of the bulldozer tanks – the Centaur dozers – whose task was to scoop out the soil so that the Centurion could nestle in behind a protective earthen rampart topped by sandbags. Another important tank was the Armoured Recovery Vehicle (ARV) that could pull a damaged Centurion out of its revetment. Initially British Churchill ARV Mark 2s were operated in Korea but it was soon obvious that a heavier, more powerful ARV was needed. Centurion ARV Mark 1s replaced the Churchills and were fitted with a protective gun cupola and a dummy gun so that Chinese observers would be misled.

## OPERATION 'PIMLICO'

Patrols and raids could also prove costly for the Commonwealth units as they moved into No Man's Land in search of prisoners. Every effort was made to minimize losses as battalion commanders came to place more reliance on the performance of their subalterns. Patrol members were well-prepared for their mission. They trained on cross-country runs behind the MLR, they rehearsed their attacks, their radio procedures and their techniques for calling down defensive fire from their own artillery batteries and mortar platoons. They were briefed as well as current battalion intelligence permitted on the aims, objectives and mode of completion of each patrol. Security was crucial but it was sometimes broken, perhaps by a Korean porter crossing the lines. The story of Operation 'Pimlico' November 1952, provides an example of a well-planned raid that went awry.

During the night of 22/23 November 1952 D Company of the 1st Royal Fusiliers was ordered to raid a feature code-named 'Mark'. This was one of four barren hill features collectively known as 'the Apostles'. They rose some 400 feet above the paddy fields and Mark was just over 3,000 yards from the Royal Fusiliers' bunkers. In between was a minefield, a stream, a wooded ridge called Kigong-ni and a large Mound. The aim of the patrol was primarily to capture a prisoner; additionally, it was ordered to kill Chinese troops and demolish enemy bunker defences. D Company, about 70 per cent National Servicemen, carefully rehearsed the operation until each man knew his role precisely. Fusiliers were allocated specific tasks: snatch squad, bunker demolition party, casualty evacuation group. Maps, models and air photographs were all studied. Good cover and support would be available, including tanks, the divisional artillery, masses of mortars and machine-guns. 12 Platoon would make the actual assault after A and C Companies were in position to cover the flanks and 10 Platoon had achieved the firm base on the Mound. The initial attack would be in silence and would last the entire operation if the operation proved successful.

All was ready for the raid to go in on the night of 22/23 November. In fact 10 Platoon had reached the Mound and Company HQ was actually treading its way through the minefield gap when the operation was cancelled. Intelligence reported that the enemy might have secured details of the raid; certainly, there was some evidence that the

Chinese were on stand-to and ready for action. 'Pimlico' was therefore put back two days until 24/25 November. The original plan remained unaltered and D Company moved off in high spirits, festooned with Stens, Brens and bunker charges, each man carrying six grenades and spare magazines. All wore armoured vests. Officers carried a wireless set and 2/Lt Hoare and 10 Platoon once more led the way towards the minefield gap.

10 Platoon was on Kigong-ni ridge by 1800 hours and as they began their sweep they could hear noises in the valley below. This, thought 2/ Lt Hoare, was his chance to seize a prisoner. He had already planned for this contingency: No.2 Section with Platoon Sergeant Nash would provide cover while Hoare and the rest of the platoon moved in to investigate. Almost immediately a burp gunner appeared in front of Nash who shot him with his Sten at point blank range. Wounded, the Chinaman fell to the ground, while another rose and ran for his life. Hoare removed his armoured vest and attempted to bring in the wounded Chinaman. He brought him back within the platoon's defensive perimeter but the Chinaman promptly died. More China-men could be heard chattering in the valley and Hoare decided to call down fire on them while he made for the Mound. By 2000 hours he had occupied the feature and set up his section defences under sporadic Chinese mortar and machine-gun fire. Clearly, the Chinese knew something of Plan 'Pimlico'.

By midnight D Company was established on the ridge and 2/Lt de Roeper and his 12 Platoon passed through at 0100 hours with the message, 'Am leaving HEARTACHE [the ridge].' They crossed the stream and walked straight into an ambush made up of 50–60 burp gunners firing at them from a range of about 12 yards. 12 Platoon fired back until most were stunned by a shower of concussion grenades. De Roeper called for his platoon to form a defensive perimeter but by then Chinese infantrymen were amongst them and de Roeper was concerned to withdraw in the hope of saving his wounded. In fact, the Chinese were on the ridge, moving in and out of the trees, firing their burp guns and generally harrassing the aid post and stretcher parties assembled there by CSM Manson. Several Fusiliers later remarked that the Chinamen seemed to be enjoying themselves as they frequently burst into peals of laughter.

The operation was now in a state of chaos with men from D Company dribbling back to relative safety within the Fusiliers' mine-field while the Mound defended by 10 Platoon came under direct

Chinese fire. Every 15 minutes Chinese grenadiers crept up the hill and lobbed in concussion grenades followed by bursts of burp gun fire. 10 Platoon responded with automatic fire and its own grenades plus frequent use of the bayonet. 2/Lt Hoare was an example to his men and conducted a remarkable defence under hopeless conditions while his signaller, Fusilier Hodkinson, relayed details of the battle back to battalion. Hoare was then fatally wounded; all NCOs were now dead or wounded. Fusilier Hodkinson, himself wounded, remained on top of the Mound and took over direction of the battle. He called down artillery and mortar fire on the Chinese edging ever closer to the top of the Mound. When he was hit in the face he refused a field dressing as he said it would hinder his transmissions. The Kiwi gunners received all of Hodkinson's messages including those that praised the accuracy of the 25 pounders that were keeping the enemy away. But not for long. At 0420 hours the enemy were rushing the Mound. Hodkinson's voice came over clearly: 'We shall be over run. Nothing can stop them. We are being overrun . . .' Of the 21 men making up 10 Platoon, seven wounded remained awaiting their fate.

Chinese burial parties moved around the Mound and those Fusiliers who could played dead. One was Fusilier Newell who opened his eyes to see a Chinaman gazing at him. Newell shot him and the sound of his shot brought another fusillade of gunfire and grenades on the heads of the wounded. Next day the Kiwis fired smoke as search parties went out to seek the wounded. Four Fusiliers, including Newell, made it back to the battalion. Search and rescue patrols went on for a week and more casualties occurred. In all 'Pimlico' cost 22 killed or missing and 19 wounded. Fusilier Hodkinson received the Distinguished Conduct Medal; Fusilier Newell was mentioned in despatches.

Papers found on enemy dead were said to be helpful to the battalion. Possibly 'Pimlico' had blundered into a full-scale enemy attack on the battalion's bunkers. Little was certain. What was certain were men's memories of patrolling that damp November in wet paddy fields, in the dark, unsure where the enemy might be. As Fusilier Peter N. Farrar later commented,

> It was not so much an ever-present sense of danger out there but the uncertainty of what would happen in the next few seconds that was so breathtaking. You could be crouched in the paddy, with the hand of the man behind you on your shoulder, tapping out a warning. You could hear rustling

movements near you, perhaps three or four yards away. Were they the Chinese? But there was nothing there. So you moved on, clutching your sten, your feet wet and cold, hoping the sten would work – they weren't always reliable – and whether you had fused your grenades properly. The worst part I remember was out in the paddy one night, the last but one in a patrol and a new chap behind me. We stayed out for two hours. On the way back, I looked over my shoulder. I was the last in the line. I never saw him again.[7]

Patrols and raids continued along the MLR. It was growing colder and the first heavy snowfalls had begun. By mid-December the line was quiet and the Chinese began an unusual propaganda campaign against the UN forces. Enemy broadcasts began calling for troops to lay down their arms and end the war. This was different from their usual style which was to welcome a new battalion to the line, somewhat disconcerting for fresh young soldiers to discover that the enemy knew exactly who they were! Christmas 1952 saw the Chinese garlanding the wire in front of UN positions with cards expressing best wishes from the Chinese People's Volunteers and the North Korean People's Army. Invitations to tea abounded, with little packs of tea attached, and sometimes a small white China dove – much prized by the troops who wore these in their balaclavas to prove they had served in the sharp end. Banners proclaimed that the British were unwittingly serving American industrialists, waxing fat on the profits from the munitions industry; others bore pictures of girls anxiously awaiting the return of their loved ones from Korea, only to be heartbroken when they heard they were dead. This material, highly prized as souvenirs, made no impact on the morale of UN troops as they settled down to await their future in 1953, the third year of the Korean War.

# CHAPTER 10

# Naval and Air Operations in the Korean Theatre, 1950–1

## INITIAL NAVAL OPERATIONS

At the outbreak of the Korean War, the Commander-in-Chief of the US Pacific Fleet, Admiral A. W. Radford, was based at Pearl Harbor. He commanded two major units. The first was Admiral Struble's US Seventh Fleet composed of Task Force 77's fast carriers under Rear Admiral J. M. Hoskins and a flotilla of eight destroyers under Captain C. W. Parker. The second was the command structure in Japan headed by Admiral Joy, Commander Naval Forces Far East, and in effect the United Nations commander in Korean waters. Admiral Joy was directly responsible to General MacArthur in the Dai-Ichi building in Tokyo and, after 29 June 1950, decided on the best way of using the Royal Navy and Commonwealth vessels placed under his command. Joy's aim was to mount a total blockade of the North Korean coastline and to use his sea and air firepower to harass the invading North Korean armies and their supply routes. Accordingly, he decided that Rear Admiral W. G. Andrewes, commanding Royal Navy vessels, together with Commonwealth and Allied warships, should form the West Korean Support Group while the American forces would form the East Korean Support Group. Apart from the specially convened invasion fleets for the two major amphibious operations at Inchon and Wonsan during September and October/November 1950, this division worked smoothly over the next three years although there was a constant interchange of individual warships. The United States Navy, capable of drawing on its fleets of large warships, including the 57,000 ton battleship *Missouri*, reactivated from its role as a training ship, together with her sister ships, would bear the main responsibility for the prosecution of the war in Korean waters and for the interdiction of enemy forces and their means of supply on land.

Royal Navy vessels, including *Belfast*, *Jamaica*, *Black Swan*, *Consort* and *Triumph*, then sailed to Okinawa to join the US Seventh Fleet whose centrepiece was the aircraft carrier *Valley Forge*. This was an 'Essex' class vessel, the mainstay of America's Second World War Pacific Fleet and the basis of her 'blue water' strike force in the post-war world. *Valley Forge* displaced 35,000 tons fully laden, bristled with anti-aircraft weapons and carried over 90 aircraft. She had been reconstructed so that her decks could handle the new jet aircraft. As the light fleet carrier HMS *Triumph* (18,300 tons) steamed into Okinawa on 1 July 1950 the ship's company marvelled at the Panther jets, the Corsairs and the burly Skyraiders ranged along *Valley Forge*'s impressively long flight deck. Although this was at a very early stage of the war the sheer size and firepower of the UN naval forces dwarfed the tiny North Korean vessels, most of which were converted merchantmen, torpedo boats, gunboats, junks or sampans.

Early UN naval operations were interesting in that they exposed several fundamental problems. On 2 July Task Force 77's *Valley Forge* and the big American cruiser *Rochester* sailed for the west coast and the Yellow Sea. *Rochester* was a 'Baltimore' class cruiser and was only three years old. She had nine 8-inch guns, displaced 17,000 tons and carried a crew of 2,000, a most formidable vessel. She would soon be joined by her two sister ships, *Toledo* and *Helena*, and the big 'light' cruiser the *Worcester*, that boasted 12 6-inch guns. HMS *Triumph*, one of the 'Colossus' class of light fleet carriers, was four years old and carried Supermarine Seafires and Fairey Fireflies. The UN Navy was worried that they closely resembled North Korean Yak-9 fighters so they sported the famous 1944-style black and white 'D-day stripes' to aid the notoriously weak American skill of aircraft recognition. The issue arose during a bomb run by 22nd Group B-29 Superfortresses on Seoul's marshalling yards on 28 July. Four Seafire FR47s from HMS *Triumph* appeared out of cloud just aft of the tail-turret of a B-29 gunner who blazed away, convinced he had been jumped by four Yaks. As the central fire-control system of a B-29 could disintegrate a close-flying fighter, one Seafire rapidly burst into flames. The pilot baled out and was rescued. Consequently, 'invasion stripes' became mandatory to prevent confusion happening again.

*Triumph* was joined by *Belfast*, built by Harland & Woolf and still preserved in the Pool of London, a rakish 15,000 ton warship whose 12 6-inch guns made her comparable with the American *Worcester*. *Belfast* was escorted by the destroyers *Cossack* and *Consort*, both launched in 1944, displacing 2,500 tons and capable of 37 knots. *Juneau*, the smallest type of US cruiser, flew the flag of Rear Admiral Higgins USN and was joined by the Royal Navy's *Jamaica*, a somewhat venerable 11,000 ton cruiser, and the frigate *Black Swan*. This group sailed for operations off the east coast of Korea and at dawn on 2 July participated in the first naval action between warships in the Korean War. Six North Korean torpedo boats attacked. Five were destroyed and the sixth escaped, badly damaged. Later that day the fleet began the first naval bombardment of the war, edging ever closer to the shore for maximum accuracy and effect. Six days later, *Jamaica* was engaged in a similar action when a skilfully camouflaged shore battery responded, hit *Jamaica* and killed a British sailor.

*Valley Forge*'s first mission was to destroy enemy aircraft and its Corsairs strafed eight North Korean aircraft on the ground at Heiju air base, just outside Pyongyang. They shot down two more in an air battle that lasted barely a minute. One Corsair had to ditch but the pilot was swiftly rescued. This success was not shared by the British who went into action without preliminary reconnaissance. Twelve Seafires and nine Fireflies flew approximately 120/130 nautical miles to Kaishu air base outside Haeju. This was as far as a fully loaded Firefly could safely fly so it was disappointing to find the airfield devoid of Yak fighters and Ilyushin bombers.

By then the British Commonwealth warships assembled in Korean waters had swollen to an impressive fleet. Eleven more warships arrived: the British destroyers *Cockade* and *Comus*; Australia's frigate *Shoalhaven* and the destroyer *Bataan*; Canada's destroyers *Cayuga*, *Athabaskan* and *Sioux*; and two New Zealand frigates *Pukaki* and *Tutira*. Some 7,000 sailors were now serving in Korean waters, undertaking tasks that were demanding, often uncomfortable and frequently boring. Blockading warships had to maintain patrols up and down the same part of the coast in all weathers. Navigation was difficult because the current charts, many of pre-1940 Japanese origin, were usually inaccurate. Floating mines were a constant threat and newly-sown minefields, expertly laid by North Koreans from shallow-draught, motorized sampans and junks, needed constant sweeping. Enemy forces sometimes sheltered up inlets and behind the islands;

unwary approaches ran the risk of an enemy artillery barrage. *Cossack*'s log showed that between 24 June and 16 August she steamed 14,424 miles, averaging 272 miles a day. This was the blockade duty that would last for the entire Korean War, enlivened by moments of tension and high success. During the defence of the Pusan Perimeter, for example, *Belfast* fired 380 shells at enemy positions within Yongdok. At the end of the shoot it was reported that Yongdok had ceased to exist.

After the successful Inchon landings and the recapture of Seoul, the UN navies liberated several islands and sometimes found themselves involved in humanitarian work instead of battle. When Australia's *Warramunga* approached one tiny island, its crew at action stations, all they found was a crowd of starving South Koreans to whom the crew gave sacks of rice. *Ceylon* had a similar experience at the island of Chayaku-ko where the sole inhabitants were a matron and a score of undernourished, sickly children. The ship's chaplain broadcast an appeal over the Tannoy, the sailors donated warm clothing and cut timber for firewood. In one particularly difficult night operation during the early Chinese offensives, five Commonwealth destroyers (*Cayuga, Warramunga, Sioux, Bataan, Athabaskan*) plus the American *Forest Royal*, gave gunfire support to ships evacuating refugees and soldiers from the docks east of Chinnampo. Over 7,000 people were saved.

## THE UNITED STATES FAR EAST AIR FORCE (FEAF)

General Stratemeyer commanded FEAF as from April 1949. An Air Force general with considerable experience of the air war in the Far East 1943–5, he headed two major air forces. The first was the Fifth Air Force, commanded by General Earle E. Partridge. His role was the defence of Japan for which he had the 8th Fighter Bomber Wing flying F-80C Shooting Star jets and the 68th Fighter All-Weather Squadron equipped with F-82 Twin Mustangs, based at Itazuke on Kyushu, Japan. On Honshu he had the 49th Fighter Bomber Wing flying F-80s out of Misawa Air Base. At Yokota Air Base in central Japan he stationed F-80s and F-82s plus the RF-80 photo-reconnaissance aircraft.

From Johnson Air Base flew the twin-engined B-26 light bombers, formerly known as Douglas Invaders. Stratemeyer's second power source was the Okinawa-based Twentieth Air Force led by General Ralph E. Stearley (after 31 July 1950) at Kadena. His F-80Cs and F-82s were supplemented by photo-reconnaissance versions of the B-29 Superfortress that had dropped the atomic weapons on Hiroshima and Nagasaki in 1945. Standard B-29 Superfortress bombers of the 19th Bombardment Wing were based at Guam in the Marianas.

Additionally, Stratemeyer had the services of No. 77 Squadron Royal Australian Air Force based in Japan and flying the F-51D Mustang, the finest fighter of the Second World War. In Korea 77 Squadron proved to be the most highly trained unit in ground-attack and rocket firing techniques. No. 77 Squadron was to be of inestimable importance in the early days of the war when it achieved results out of all proportion to its relatively small number of aircraft – 24 front-line Mustangs and 14 held in reserve. No Royal Air Force fighter squadrons served in Korea but RAF pilots were attached to US and Australian units. However, three Short Sunderland flying boat squadrons were based in Japan and proved invaluable. The Far East Flying Boat Wing incorporating 88, 205 and 209 Squadrons had been based at Seletar, Singapore, but on the orders of Air Marshal Bonham Carter it was ordered to move to Iwakuni, Japan. Here its main patrol line was the Tsushima Straits between Korea and Japan. Its main role was to seek enemy blockade runners and spot targets for the UN navies and air forces.

Against these aircraft the North Korean Air Force (NKAF) could assemble about 180 serviceable aeroplanes, all of Soviet vintage apart from a few former Japanese transports and trainers dating from the Second World War. Most dangerous were the 62 armoured Ilyushin 1–10 Sturmovik ground-attack aircraft and the 70 Yak-3, Yak-7 and Yak-9 fighters. There were a few Polikarpov Po-2 biplane trainers, destined to become the legendary 'Bed Check Charlies'. The Yaks, especially the Yak-9P, matched the Mustang and proved very dangerous. The Yak-9P was an improved post-1945 design with a 1650 hp engine and two 12.7mm machine-guns and a 23mm cannon all located in the engine cowling, compared with the six .50 calibre machine-guns fitted in the wings of the Mustang.


AIR OPERATIONS, JUNE–DECEMBER 1950

The overwhelming need of the ground troops falling back under NKPA pressure was constant and accurate support from the air. F-

51 Mustangs, some newly-supplied to the ROK Air Force and to the Australians, were on call for strikes against tanks, infantry, truck convoys and bridges. They suffered heavy casualties due to ground fire and the difficulties of flying in a hazardous terrain all exacerbated by the vulnerable radiator and cooling system characteristics of the Mustang's Packard-Merlin in-line engine. Replacement F-51s were not a problem (there were over 1,550 available in the United States) and the first of these arrived via the USS *Boxer*. What was needed was an effective air-ground control system such as the one that had existed between the Typhoon squadrons and their ground controllers in Europe during 1944–5.

To remedy this, three Stinson L5-G light aircraft and, on 10 July, a T-6 Texan (the Harvard in the RAF), were stationed in the Pusan Perimeter to fly Forward Air Control (FAC) missions. Thus was born the Fifth Air Force's 6147th Tactical Control Squadron (TCS). It was probably the most international of all the military units that went to war in Korea. Pilots and observers were all volunteers. The T-6, a noisy but rugged aeroplane, became their favoured aircraft known as a 'Mosquito', a name that had no connection with the RAF's 'Wooden Wonder' of the Second World War. Their early call signs were always prefixed with 'Mosquito' – 'Mosquito Able', 'Mosquito Baker' – and the ubiquitous T-6 Texans were known as Mosquitos from 15 July 1950 onwards. Their first T-6 mission was flown on 10 July and as their FAC techniques developed, the pilots and observers of the 6147th were able to call down fire from jet as well as piston-engined aircraft.

Edward R. Murrow broadcast his admiration of the indispensable and courageous 6147th TCS after it had been awarded the following Presidential Unit Citation:

> The 6147th Tactical Control Squadron is cited for heroic, unique and valorous action in Korea during the period 5 July to 25 November 1950. This unit distinguished itself while carrying out its primary mission, the reconnoitering of potential enemy targets and their subsequent destruction through air-to-air direction of friendly tactical aircraft . . . During this period . . . (it) . . . flew 4,902 combat sorties while directing and controlling tactical aircraft attacks which resulted in the following damage and destruction to the enemy: 436 tanks, 785 trucks, 1,547 miscellaneous

vehicles, 598 artillery and anti-aircraft guns, 1,045 villages housing enemy troops and equipment, 1,302 troop concentrations, 29 bridges, 101 railroad cars, 8 locomotives, 228 supply dumps, 27 ammunition dumps and 98 fuel dumps . . .

Ed Murrow's broadcast on 6 February 1951 expanded on 6147th's achievement:

It is my inclination and duty to raise a voice in salute to some unusual 'mosquitoes.' The 6147th TCS in Korea has received a Presidential Citation. That's the Mosquito outfit, and it is, I think, without parallel in the whole history of aerial warfare. A Mosquito plane is a T-6 without guns, without an inch of armour plate. It's an old advanced training plane, single-engined, dual controls, with room for a pilot and observer. It was never built to do the job it's doing in Korea . . . These Mosquito pilots can only be compared to scouts in the days of Indian fighting on the western plains. They literally track tanks across a river, up a valley and under the trees. Much of the time they work at an altitude of a hundred feet or less . . . They are a gallant crew of aerial scouts, with uncanny ability to penetrate enemy camouflage. Their low-flying and spotting have not been equalled since men began to use flying machines to make war.

Eventually the Mosquitos received three US Distinguished Unit Citations.

The success of the Mosquitos came with a cost in casualties. Fifty men were killed. Sixteen were reported missing and are presumed dead. Thirty-one became prisoners-of-war, 12 of whom died or were killed in prison. Approximately one-third of the Mosquito casualties were Tactical Control Air Party (TCAP) members. Most of these occurred immediately after the Chinese intervention and during the battles of the Chosin Reservoir and the Chongchon River.[1]

TCAP units were drawn from the United States Air Force and formed the unique 6150th Tactical Control Squadron. A TACP team leader was usually a pilot experienced in Mosquito operations and competent to act as a Forward Air Controller (FAC). Two communications experts functioned as radio operator and radio mechanic. Each team had an AN/ARC-1 radio jeep plus one other jeep to serve as a personnel carrier. Their VHF radios required line-of-sight with the aircraft they were seeking to control. When divisional command ordered the destruction of an enemy position, the target detail would be radioed to the TCAP radio jeep. The FOC attempted a visual identification – a very dangerous role during the mobile war. He then passed precise details to the patrolling Mosquito who would in turn control the ground-attack Mustangs, Shooting Stars and, later on, the specialist F-86 Sabres. Radio jeep personnel served with the Eighth Army and the US Marines and one radio operator, George Hanrahan, was with the Marines at Suchon and during the Hungnam evacuation. Tactical Air Control Parties were the unsung heroes of the Korean War and the contribution of the 6150th Tactical Control Squadron's TCAPs was crucial to the destruction of communist targets throughout the conflict.

## THE POWER OF THE F-51

On 4 August 1950 the South African government promised to despatch to Korea No. 2 Squadron of the South African Air Force. Known as the 'Flying Cheetahs' from their squadron insignia, No. 2 Squadron had a distinguished history in Africa and Italy during the Second World War. Led by Wing Commander J. S. van B. Theron DSO DFC AFC, the squadron embarked on the SS *Tjisadane* at Durban and arrived at Yokohama on 4 November 1950. At Johnson Air Base they converted to F-51 Mustangs purchased by South Africa from the United States government and became operational from K9 air base on 19 November 1950. It formed an integral part of Fifth Air Force's 18th Fighter-Bomber Wing and specialized, as did the Australians of the 77th, in close-support and ground-attack operations. All Mustang squadrons used the napalm-filled bombs manufactured in Japan. This deadly weapon, contained in a streamlined plastic tank that cost a mere $40, was capable of neutralizing tanks, artillery and enemy troops in horrific fashion.

Mustangs occasionally engaged in air-to-air combat during the early stages of the war when their opponents were flying Soviet-built

Yaks. Captain Robert Thresher, a Second World War P-47 Thunderbolt pilot, fought a Yak-3 on 1 November 1950. He served with 67th Squadron, 18th Fighter-Bomber Group, then based at Pyongyang, and left this graphic account of a battle of wills that led to his first 'kill':

> It was 0700 and bitter cold. There was a fresh layer of snow on the ground. The cold Mustang started on the first try and the instrument needles settled exactly where they should . . . A good sign! My wingman was Captain A. R. 'Dad' Flake. Minutes later I was lined up on Flake's wing ready for take-off. The lead element was already halfway down the snow-covered runway. We were armed for close-support with .50 calibre rounds, six .5-inch rockets and two large tanks of napalm. This close-support role just did not sit right with most of us old World War II fighter pilots, but we did what we had to do.
>
> When we reached our assigned area, we picked up the Mosquito [T-6 Forward Air Controller] who had already lined up a strike for us against a roadblock. We lined up, blasting the target . . . All of a sudden, big orange balls were snapping across my left wing. I yelled 'flak' and broke right . . . a blurred shape flew past me and I knew that my problem was not what I had thought, but an enemy fighter!
>
> Being an old P-47 pilot, out of instinct I initiated evasive action and rolled into a left turn . . . Squinting into the sun, I knew he was still up there and I did not want him to have another clean shot at me. Suddenly the Mosquito pilot yelled, 'Look out No. 4, he's right on your tail.' I snapped my head around and saw the yellow winking lights of a Yak's two 12.7mm machine-guns and 20mm cannon. He had been sitting there all this time in the sun and now he had the advantage over me. I went into a sharp turn . . . At 7,000lb max gross weight, the Russian-built fighter had the turning edge over any Mustang.
>
> I rolled out to see that the enemy pilot had gone across the top of my Mustang and, taking advantage of his speed, he had pulled up into a tight loop . . . Now the pattern had been established . . . I was flying a tight circle on the horizontal; he elected to fly his sparring circle on the

vertical, snapping at me as we passed each other. We held our turns, I looked for a break and as he picked up speed I saw we were getting closer each time we closed on the south side of my circle . . . I was able to snap a shot at him each time now . . . The North Korean pilot saw this. He knew that after another pass, I would be coming in behind him as he began his climb . . . I wrapped up my '51 and began firing. I saw the tracers converge and pour on his wings. Then a puff of blue smoke spouted from his wing. He wobbled and fell out of his turn. Slowly, he rolled over and went into a long glide. I watched him go down. A Yak-3. A left-over from the last war, just as my Mustang and I were! But this kill meant a lot to me as I knew I still had what it took to be a fighter pilot . . .[2]

Helicopter evacuation of the seriously wounded began early on in the Korean War, arising out of the Army's call for help in moving their wounded out of difficult terrain. Initially, the helicopters serving in Korea were part of the 3rd Air Rescue Squadron specializing in saving aircrew who had been shot down. On 22 July Sikorsky H-5 helicopters arrived at Taegu specifically to evacuate battlefield casualties to rear hospitals, and these were soon supplemented by USAF H-5s transferred to Korea and by USMC HO-3 helicopters operating as battlefield support in the Changwon region. On 4 September Captain Robert E. Wayne had the distinction of being the first pilot to be rescued by helicopter from behind the enemy lines. His F-80 was hit north of the 38 degree Parallel and he baled out close to North Korean troops. F-80s from his 35th Fighter Bomber Squadron maintained a watchful orbit overhead while an H-5 piloted by Lt Paul W. Van Boven carried out an impeccable rescue.

Helicopters suffered from severe operating limitations. Normally, they did not fly at night or during gales and snowstorms. They needed flat terrain for landings and take-offs and they were at the mercy of enemy ground fire. Those equipped with pods for casualty transportation often had pipes feeding warm air from the engine to the patient during flight. Although patients in the pods could not receive medical attention there were devices fitted to administer plasma. During the Battle of Chipyong-ni operating rules had to be broken. The defenders urgently needed medical supplies and had many wounded awaiting evacuation. Six Sikorsky H-5s from the 3rd Air Rescue Squadron flew in medical supplies on 21 February 1951 and brought out the wounded – 180 men. Next day they flew through snowstorms gusting at 40 knots and evacuated another 22 injured men, a remarkable achievement at the height of the Korean winter in the most dangerous of battle conditions.

Air support was an asset that could be called on almost continuously throughout the Korean War. Early morning mist deterred even the bravest Corsair, Thunderjet and Mustang pilot though it tended to clear quickly. They were dedicated to air support, taken to its limits by the Marine Air Units based at Yonpo during the saga of 'Task Force Faith'. Captain Edward P. Stamford was the Marine air-ground controller with Lt Col Faith's shattered force, so desperate for ammunition. From his little radio jeep Ed Stamford called down literally scores of air strikes and without these Task Force Faith would have been overrun. At Yonpo the Marine engineers came up with a scheme to mount parachute containers filled with ammunition on Corsair bomb racks. Two aircraft were needed to test out the idea over Faith's position. Major Ed Montagne and Captain Tom Mulvihill agreed to carry out a test run and arrived over Task Force Faith just before dusk. They flew across the Chosin Reservoir and, directed by Ed Stamford, came down the road at 20 feet, dodging the tracer criss-crossing in front of them. They could see their aiming point and, pulling up hard, began their final run at low speed from the rear of Task Force Faith. It was a perfect ammunition drop and the two pilots roared into a climb to join the 'cab rank' of Corsairs pummelling the Chinese with rockets, bombs, napalm and machine-gun fire.

Equally demanding were the strategic bombing operations. Six B-29 Superfortress bomb groups were available and their first major raid was on 30 July when 47 B-29s raided Hungnam. Their target was a monazite processing plant believed to produce the radioactive thorium used by the Soviet Union in its research into nuclear weapons. This was one of a long list of strategic targets drawn up by the US Joint Chiefs of Staff and was based on somewhat scanty data. Maps, mostly of Japanese origin, used a variety of spellings that often caused confusion. General MacArthur supported B-29 bomb strikes but urged General Stratemeyer not to neglect ground interdiction raids, especially towns housing enemy soldiers, tank concentrations and bridges. Eventually, there was a satisfactory compromise between the need to destroy the enemy's transport/industrial infrastructure and the urgency of bringing air support to troops fighting on the ground.

Apart from the Shooting Stars and Thunderjets, the Fifth Air Force had the very useful B-26 Douglas Invader, a twin-engined attack bomber that had seen service in Europe during 1945. It was a very sturdy aeroplane and could be fitted with 14 forward-firing .50 calibre machine-guns. It had the distinction of carrying out the first and last air strikes of the Korean War. The devastating firepower of the B-26 is well-illustrated just for the period 7–9 July 1950; 197 trucks and 44 tanks destroyed for the loss of one aircraft.

One important target that emerged was the North Korean hydro-electric system. This had been built by the Japanese and the great Suiho complex on the Yalu River was the fourth biggest hydro-electric power-plant in the world. In 1950 North Korea exported 150,000 kilowatts to power China's industries in Manchuria. Russian factories in Siberia also bought electricity generated at Suiho. For the time being this target was ignored and the B-29s concentrated on chemical plants. Between 30 July and 3 August they attacked the Chosen Nitrogen Explosives Factory and the Bogun Chemical Plant at Hungnam so effectively that General Stratemeyer reported that the largest chemical complex in Asia had been rendered ineffective. On 21 September FEAF recommended that hydro-electric plants be on the strategic target list and the first strike against the Fusen Plant went in on 26 September. In view of the forthcoming advance into North Korea it was decided to terminate the strategic bombing raids at this point. New targets for the B-29s were troop-training and assembly centres and soon the B-29s were destroying these at Pyongyang, Hamhung and Nanam.

Throughout this period attacks along the Yalu were formally vetoed by President Truman even though a build-up of enemy aircraft appeared at Antung and Sinuiju. Clearly, communist pilots were prepared to intervene in the air war. Three Yak fighters based at Sinuiju attacked a B-26 and a Mosquito on the morning of 1 November. That afternoon another Mosquito with four F-51 Mustangs were fired on by six swept-wing aircraft over Namsidong. The aeroplanes were Russian-built MiG-15s. Designed by Artem Mikoyan and Michael I. Gurevich, the MiG-15 was fitted with a jet-engine based on the British Rolls-Royce Nene exported to the Soviet Union by a somewhat naive Attlee government. With a speed in excess of 600 mph, the MiG-15 had a service ceiling of 40,000 feet and excellent climb and manoeuvrability characteristics. Powerfully armed with two 22mm cannon and one 37mm cannon, it was undoubtedly a dangerous air-superiority fighter. Ably flown, it could threaten FEAF's entire strategic and air interdiction bombing campaign. On 9 November Staff Sgt Harry J. LaVene, tailgunner of a flak-damaged reconnaissance B-29, claimed to have scored the first MiG 'kill' when two MiG-15s attacked. The second MiG inflicted more damage on the B-29 and the huge aircraft crash-landed at Johnson Air Base, killing five of the crew. LaVene's score is not supported by Soviet battle records.

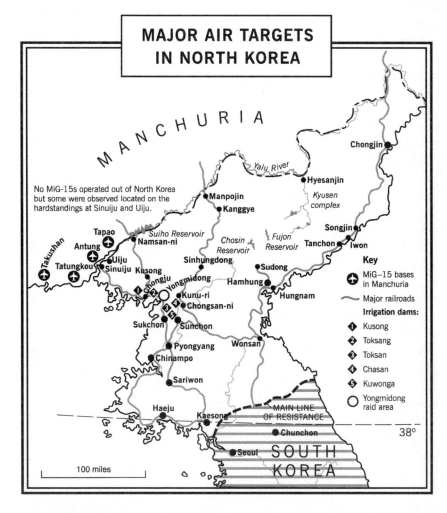

**MAJOR AIR TARGETS IN NORTH KOREA**

MANCHURIA

Yalu River

No MiG-15s operated out of North Korea but some were observed located on the hardstandings at Sinuiju and Uiju.

Chongjin

Hyesanjin

Manpojin
Kanggye

Kyusen complex

Tapao
Antung
Takushan
Tatungkou
Uiju
Sinuiju
Kusong
Chongju
Yongmidong
Kunu-ri
Chongsan-ni

Suiho Reservoir
Namsan-ni

Chosin Reservoir
Fujon Reservoir

Sinhungdong

Songjin
Tanchon
Iwon

Sudong
Hamhung
Hungnam

Sukchon
Sunchon
Pyongyang
Chinampo
Sariwon

Wonsan

Haeju
Kaesong

MAIN LINE OF RESISTANCE

Chunchon

38°

Seoul

SOUTH KOREA

100 miles

**Key**

⊕ MiG–15 bases in Manchuria

〜 Major railroads

Irrigation dams:

❶ Kusong
❷ Toksang
❸ Toksan
❹ Chasan
❺ Kuwonga
◯ Yongmidong raid area

On 10 November the US Navy entered the stakes when F9F-2 Panthers were escorting AD-4 Skyraiders attacking Sinuiju. Lt Commander William T. Amen was given a lucky shot when a MiG-15, closing on a Skyraider, flew into his gunsight. Amen immediately shot it down. It was a surprising victory in that the MiG pilot, Kapitan M. F. Grachev, was an experienced Second World War aviator. His Russian wingman claimed a Panther but there is no evidence that one was lost on 10 November. Two other Panther pilots, flying from USS *Valley Forge* claimed another confirmed MiG 'kill' that day. The first confirmed MiG 'kill' on 10 November was when Major Kharkovskiy (28th Interceptor Air Division) shot down a 307th Bomb Group Superfortress. The arrival of the swept-wing Russian jet fighters represented a serious threat. Clearly, a new aeroplane was needed in Korea to recover UN air superiority.

FEAF therefore asked the 4th Fighter Interception Wing (FIW) to bring its North American F-86 Sabre jets to Korea. Its role in the USA was to protect the eastern coastline against possible Soviet attack. Based at New Castle County Airport in Delaware, its three squadrons had the first F-86A model Sabres armed with six .50 calibre machine-guns. There was not much to chose between the performance of the American and Russian swept-wing jets; the outcome of their clash in what was to be known as 'MiG-Alley' south of the Yalu would depend on the quality of their pilots. Two leading pilots of the 4th FIW were Lt Col John C. Meyer and Lt Col Glen Eagleston, both outstanding Second World War Mustang aces when based in the UK. Others of their calibre would soon appear in Korea and it seemed that the Americans might have the edge as far as piloting skill was concerned.

Suspicions expressed during 1950–3 that many of the MiG-15 pilots were regular Soviet Air Force officers were of course well-founded, though their presence remained a closely-guarded secret until 1991. Since the collapse of the Soviet Union, from 1991 onwards Russian archives have released considerable data regarding the personnel who actually flew MiGs in combat over Korea. Former Soviet pilots have testified on Moscow Radio and in Russian newspapers and confirmed that they flew in Chinese flight suits and had to learn basic radio procedures – some 200 words sufficed – in both Chinese and Korean. Lt Chizhmade made the first combat claim in a MiG when he said he shot down a Mustang on 1 November. Ultimately the Russians would claim in excess of 1,000 victories over UN aircraft and these numbers excluded the claims submitted by Chinese and North Korean pilots. In all, 27 Soviet Air Force Aviation Regiments were rotated through the combat bases in Manchuria. This enabled the maximum number of pilots to have combat experience against enemy jets though none remained long enough to build up a fund of sound practice upon which their successors could draw.

Russia's most successful pilots were Kapitan Nikolai V. Sutyagin (21 victories, including 15 F-86 Sabres) and Yegenni Georgievich Pepelyaev, commander of the 196th Aviation Regiment (20 victories, including 14 Sabres). Three other aces were Major Lev Kirillovich (15 victories, 5 Sabres) who was himself shot down three times; Alexandr Pavlovich Smorchkov, 2 i/c of the 523rd Aviation Regiment (15 victories, details unknown) and Major Serafim Pavlovich Subbotin who secured one 'kill' by ramming his opponent (12–15 victories, 3 Sabres). In combat it was never possible to differentiate between the nationalities of the communist pilots. Some MiGs were unmarked but most carried the insignias of the North Korean or Chinese Air Forces.

Tactics depended on certain limiting factors: the height superiority of the MiG-15s, the limited combat range of the Sabres, the escape route enjoyed by the MiGs who could flee to Manchuria whenever they wished; and the fact that all UN aircraft were forbidden to violate Chinese or Soviet air space. The first major all-jet air battle on 8 November was uncharacteristic of future combats. A B-29 mission against Sinuiju was preceded by flights of Mustangs and Shooting Stars whose task was to suppress Triple-A fire (Automatic Anti-Aircraft fire). Top cover was provided by F-80s from the 51st FIW. MiG-15s under the command of Colonel A.V. Alelyukhin took off from Antung Air Base, climbed above the American F-80s and then dived to attack. As one MiG finished his pass he unwisely dived away. Lt Russell J. Brown, flying a much heavier F-80, followed him down, closed up and destroyed the MiG in a five-second burst. Although Chinese guns put up a terrific barrage they failed to deter the B-29s whose incendiary clusters dropped from 16,000 feet burnt out most of central Sinuiju. Disconsolate Russian pilots returned to Antung where Lt Shchegolev claimed a Mustang, a victory not borne out by USAF records.

17 December 1950 saw the first air-to-air combat between MiGs and the Sabres of the 4th FIW. Lt Col Bruce N. Hinton's 336th Squadron Sabres were flying below the contrail level when he spotted four MiGs some 6,000 feet below. He dived on the enemy and destroyed one before it reached the sanctuary of Manchuria. Both sides learned from this incident. MiG pilots now patrolled well above 30,000 feet and dived on their enemy. Sabre pilots tended to enter MiG Alley at much higher speeds in four-ship flights, phased at five

minute intervals at different heights. Thus the typical Sabre patrol was 16 aircraft in the combat zone for about 20 minutes. This was the famous 'jet-stream' applied on 22 December when Lt Col John C. Meyer, commanding 4th FIW, engaged his Sabres in a 20-minute dogfight in which one Sabre was lost and six MiGs were destroyed. By the end of the month the Sabres had restored UN air superiority in the Korean War, at least for the time being.

The shifting ground war and the Chinese advance into South Korea meant that the precious Sabres were transferred to Japan and were thus unable to patrol MiG Alley. Thunderjets with their slightly longer range took over flak suppression duties when B-29s attacked Pyongyang on 23 January 1951. They encountered some 30 MiG-15s that rose from Antung and managed to destroy four during a brief combat fought below 20,000 feet. But until Eighth Army recaptured the ground lost to the Chinese, General Partridge of Fifth Air Force was adamant: he would not risk his Sabres in Korea. Tremendous damage to Suwon, Kimpo and Seoul airfields had occurred during the ground war and the repair of runways and dispersals received top priority. Eventually, the 334th Sabre Squadron returned to a slushy, waterlogged Suwon and the 336th operated out of Taegu. The 4th FIW was back in business.

It needed to be, for the B-29 Superfortresses were required to soldier on in Korea. They were now near-obsolete aircraft, relatively slow but with a very good computer-controlled centralized fire control system. They had never been designed as air interdiction bombers in the battle conditions of North Korea. Inherent weaknesses in combining slow and fast aircraft were illustrated on 1 March 1951 when the 98th Bomb Group's mission was to destroy a bridge at Kogunyong. The F-80s arrived at the rendezvous on time but the B-29s were delayed by a headwind. Consequently, they began their bomb run without an escort. Bounced by nine MiGs, three B-29s were badly damaged and had to make emergency landings in South Korea. On 23 March the B-29s returned to Kogunyong under F-86 Sabre cover and the mission went well. Similar strikes against key bridges at Chongsonjin, Manpojin and Namsan-ni on 30 March were also successful because the Sabres could deny the MiGs access to the Superfortress squadrons. So it was not long before the MiGs tried different tactics: they dived from 35,000 feet through the Sabre screen, hit the bombers and then climbed back to 35,000 feet while their comrades repeated the manoeuvre, soon to be known as the 'yo-yo'. Such was the experience of three Bomb Groups on 12 April 1951 when they attacked that most obdurate of targets, the bridges at Sinuiju. Three B-29s were lost, more were badly damaged and attacks on Sinuiju were abandoned until 9 May.

By then Sinuiju airfield was probably the best defended target in North Korea. Ringed by radar-controlled Triple A fire, it was the target for 312 F-51s, Shooting Stars and Marine Corsairs. Protected by Sabres, Panthers and Thunderjets, the attack squadron went in low to accomplish a highly successful mission. No UN aircraft was lost and the MiGs were unusually shy. This was not due to a lack of offensive spirit. Rather, it was because of the reorganization of the Chinese Air Force, the construction of new jet airfields and the expansion of MiG units, many equipped with the up-rated MiG-15*bis* fitted with an improved VK-1 engine. By June 1951 the Chinese could boast some 400 MiG-15s, contrasting with the Americans' 44 F-86 Sabres, now being replaced by the improved F-86Es. As a stop-gap measure, the new FEAF commander, General Otto P. Weyland, increased the number of Thunderjet aircraft and looked for help, specifically from his British ally.

The British government remained unwilling to commit the Royal Air Force to battle in Korea, though it permitted many RAF pilots to be attached to American fighter squadrons. As a gesture, it shipped out 15 Meteor F8 twin-jet fighters on board the carrier HMS *Warrior* to replace the Mustangs flown by the 77th Squadron, Royal Australian Air Force. Not all the Australian pilots welcomed the change as they had become attached to their Mustangs. Air tests showed that the Meteor would be able to cope with the MiG-15 in battle, although the large metal fairing on the back of the canopy seriously restricted the pilot's rear view. On 30 July the Meteors began their first sweeps in company with Sabres but combat eluded them until 25 August when one Meteor flight chased some enemy jets. Sadly, two Meteors collided, killing the pilots. Then on 29 August, while escorting B-29 Superfortresses, one Meteor was badly damaged by MiG cannon-fire and another was lost near Chongju, reinforcing fears that it was outclassed by the communist jets. During September–October 1951 the air superiority battles intensified over North Korea in which the Meteor could not play the crucial role. Victory in the air war over Korea would be won by the F-86 and on 16 October the outnumbered Sabres fought a furious air battle reminiscent of those fought between the USAAF and the Luftwaffe during 1944–5. Nine MiG-15s were destroyed that day.[3]

FEAF's new concern was the number of enemy airfields mushrooming in North Korea. Its new commander was General Joe W. Kelly, who was determined to use his B-29s in a more effective manner. Kelly decided to use the Superfortresses as night-bombers, putting his faith in a new radar guidance system known as SHORAN. Two ground beacons sent target range data to a B-29 fitted with a SHORAN transceiver. All depended on the accuracy of operational maps for North Korea and these were always suspect. Saamcham airfield was the first SHORAN target (13 and 14 October) but the B-29s met with little success. Kelly therefore reverted to daylight raids and nine Superfortresses managed to crater the runway at Saamcham. B-29s of the 98th Group then made three attempts to neutralize Taechon's runway. The first two missions were diverted to secondary targets but the third, on 22 October 1951, was successful. As the B-29s turned for home, MiG-15s dived through their formation and forced one Superfortress to lose height. It reached the coast where the crew baled out and were safely rescued.

MiG-15 pilots now put up a direct challenge to the B-29 formations. On 23 October, during a raid on Mamsi airfield, the communists' superior numbers enabled them to engage the Sabre top cover while others concentrated on the B-29s and their Thunderjet escorts. Each of the three B-29 flights lost an aircraft and most of the survivors had dead or wounded crewmen on board. Next day eight B-29s targeted a bridge at Suchon and one Superfortress went down in Wonsan harbour. Four more were damaged in a raid on 27 October when they attempted to destroy a bridge at Sinanju. Ninety-five MiGs outnumbered the escort of 16 Meteors and 32 Thunderjets. This was undoubtedly a 'Black Week' for the Superfortresses during which they lost five B-29s and 55 crewmen, dead or missing. Clearly, they could not afford this rate of attrition. The MiG-15s had won a great victory and the Russians and Chinese were preparing to send fighter and bomber aircraft to airfields south of the Yalu. Namsi, Saamchan and Taechon airfields, so long the targets for B-29 bombers, were all operational again, though not for MiG-15s whose bases were always in Manchuria. During December 1951 the MiG pilots could flaunt their supremacy with high speed flights at 35,000+ feet south of Seoul.

More Sabres seemed to be the answer and 75 were loaded on the US escort carriers *Cape Esperance* and *Sitkoh Bay* bound for Korea.

Sabres of the 4th FIW engaged the MiG-15s in a series of air battles that climaxed on 13 December 1951 when the Sabres encountered 145 MiGs and shot down thirteen. Had the Americans so wished they could have committed even more Sabres and some of their faster high-flying jet bombers to Korea. However, the demands of the Cold War were such that the Joint Chiefs of Staff steadfastly refused to reduce the air forces allocated to the defence of the continental United States and Western Europe in favour of Korea. In that sense, even the air war was fought as a limited war by the Americans. It forced the B-29s to revert to night missions in November and December 1951 leading to battle situations that were reminiscent of RAF Bomber Command experiences over Germany between 1943–5. Uiji airfield, for example, had more than 50 searchlights and well-sited radar-controlled flak batteries. B-29 crews found themselves coned by searchlights and then attacked by specially-equipped MiG-15 night-fighters. Many B-29s suffered battle damage but all managed to regain their bases.

Though it became a truism that any kind of UN air operation over North Korea required an escort, it did not mean that the communists ruled the skies. This was well-illustrated on 6 November when 12 TU-2 bombers raided Taehwa-do. Several off-shore islands in the Yellow Sea had been the scene of conflict between ROK troops and NKPA amphibious units. Sixteen LA-9 fighters gave the bombers close escort while 16 MiGs provided top cover. Thirty-one Sabres led by Colonel Benjamin S. Preston intercepted the bombers. Eight TU-2s were shot down as were three LA-9s and one MiG.

Somewhat belatedly, the success of the Mosquito force convinced the British of the wisdom of creating their own units of observation aircraft. No. 1913 Light Liaison Flight formed at Middle Wallop, UK in June 1951 equipped with Auster Air Observation Post aircraft. They were shipped out to Korea and operated along the Commonwealth Division's 'Main Line of Resistance.' A second unit, No. 1903 Independent Air Observation Post Flight, became operational in October and also flew Austers. Both Flights were part of the Royal Air Force and represented the only RAF contingents operating from Korean soil during the war. All the pilots and most of the dedicated band of mechanics were Army personnel. Unusually, 1913 Flight had a solitary Cessna L-19 Bird Dog on charge. Apparently, the Flight acquired the Cessna after General Cassels had suffered an unpleasant landing experience in an Auster. He vowed he would never fly in an Auster again and a sympathetic

American unit lent 1913 Flight the Bird Dog – reputedly in exchange for a case of Scotch.

Captain Downward, commander of 1913 Flight (later Maj. General P. A. Downward CB DSO DFC) was ordered by General Cassels to take the Bird Dog on charge to be used solely for flying Very Important People around Korea, but never over the front line. It received a new call-sign, Army 754, and the US white stars were delicately replaced by the RAF's red, white and blue roundels. General Downward later recounted the problems arising from the acquisition of Army 754. The Air Officer Commanding Hong Kong wanted to know who had signed for the aircraft, who would pay for the fuel and who would pay compensation if it crashed. As a distinguished naval officer would later remark, it seemed that the bureaucrats failed to appreciate that there was a war going on in Korea. The Bird Dog saga pursued the General into the 1960s when he was asked if he had actually signed for it, as a tired old American L-19 displaying RAF roundels was coming to the end of its life and nobody could account for its origin when it was time to strike it off strength.


## NAVAL OPERATIONS TO THE END OF 1951

In some respects the US and Commonwealth Navies had been the salvation of the ground forces in Korea during 1950. From the flight decks of the American carriers *Valley Forge, Philippine Sea, Sicily* and *Badoeng Strait*, sortie after sortie took off to challenge the advance of the NKPA. Undoubtedly, as General MacArthur later said, constant attacks from carrier aircraft helped to save the Pusan Perimeter from a communist breakthrough. They were 'the vital factor.' HMS *Triumph*, in company with Australia's *Warramunga* and *Bataan* and Canada's *Athabaskan*, relieved the Seventh Fleet carriers on the east coast of Korea. Here *Triumph*'s Fireflies came into their own, their rockets proving lethal to North Korean rolling-stock. After the Inchon landings, *Triumph* departed Korea, to be succeeded by HMS *Theseus*, commanded by Captain A. S. Bolt DSO DSC. *Theseus* patrolled from 29 September 1950 to 23 April 1951, a period devoted to interdiction and close air support.

Perhaps the most remarkable operation that took place during that period was the evacuation of X Corps from Wonsan and Hungnam during December 1950. It was an operation that demonstrated the enormous firepower that could be assembled by the United States Navy. As the first forces departed Wonsan (3–7 December 1950), constant gunfire from the 8-inch gun cruiser *St Paul* and its two escort destroyers frustrated all NKPA and Chinese efforts to intervene. No less than seven aircraft carriers provided close air support: the fast carriers *Valley Forge, Leyte, Princeton* and *Philippine Sea* and the escort carriers *Bataan, Badoeng Strait* and *Sicily*. Supplementing this awesome display of American naval power were the battleship *Missouri*, the *St Paul* and *Rochester*, three rocket ships and seven destroyers. Their combined barrage could and did fire up to ten miles inland but as the last forces waited to leave the beaches that gunfire concentrated on a coastline barely 2,500 yards wide and to a depth of some 3,000 yards. No enemy dared penetrate this barrage and more than 105,000 servicemen, over 90,000 refugees, 17,500 vehicles and 350,000 tons of stores were safely evacuated.

Of course, as Churchill had remarked some ten years earlier in the context of Dunkirk, 'Wars are not won by evacuations.' The UN Navies returned to their blockade duties and coastal patrols. Snowstorms, iced-up flight decks and gale-force winds hampered the carriers over New Year, 1951. West coast harbours and inlets were frozen and enemy activity behind the front line slackened. *Theseus* took the opportunity to give direct battlefield support to the US 25th Division and the British 29 Commonwealth Brigade. A Mosquito pilot directed the Sea Furies and Fireflies to specific targets and was impressed by the accuracy of the Fleet Air Arm crews who destroyed a command post and troop positions just ahead of the 25th Division. These attacks on 5 January 1951 set a pattern for which *Theseus* became renowned.

April 1951 saw a change in command when Rear Admiral A. K. Scott-Moncrieff replaced Rear Admiral Andrewes. It was also a month of varied naval activity. HMS *Cockade* sighted a junk bearing a black cloth inscribed, 'Have American on board.' An unkempt, bearded figure was hauled aboard – they had rescued an American pilot. In the midst of this operation, *Cockade* was ordered to rescue the crew of a ditched aeroplane 25 miles away but there was only one survivor and he had been taken aboard an American rescue amphibian. On the same day, 7 April 1951, 250 Royal Marines from the 41 Independent Commando landed from the Landing Ship Dock *Fort Marion* south of Songjin and blew up a section of the coastal railroad, leaving a crater 16-feet deep. They were ashore seven hours and throughout had US air cover and gunfire support from USS *St Paul*. This was their first operation since the Chosin Reservoir battles in December 1950 after which they had recovered and re-equipped in Japan.

During April, the UN Navies were alerted to the urgency of acquiring an example of a ditched MiG-15. One had been shot down over Sinmi-do in the Yalu Gulf. As the crash site was barely 40 miles from Antung air base, the fleet was at some risk. HMS *Kenya* took charge of the salvage operation on 12 April while the Fifth Air Force provided air cover. *Warramunga*, *Nootka* and *Amethyst* began the search, but after four days, during which *Amethyst* found a body, the warships abandoned their quest for a MiG-15. HMS *Glory* replaced *Theseus* on 23 April and was also involved in the search for a MiG-15. On 11 July a MiG tailplane was spotted rising from a mud flat near Hanchon and arrangements were made to recover the entire aircraft. Success came on 20 July and at last the Americans had a MiG-15 to evaluate. *Glory* was also involved in a rare event on 28 July when one of her destroyer escorts had an Asdic contact and depth-charged a suspected enemy submarine. It was known that the Russians had given North Korea two submarines. A few oil patches surfaced but there was no other evidence of an enemy submarine. Nevertheless, all escorts ensured that their anti-submarine patrol tactics were well-rehearsed and that their Asdic equipment was totally reliable.

*Glory*'s patrols in the Yellow Sea lasted until 30 September 1951 when she was relieved by His Majesty's Australian Ship *Sydney*. This marked the first occasion in which a Dominion aircraft-carrier was on active service. In less than a fortnight *Sydney* had the distinction of serving on both the west and east coasts of Korea. Initially she relieved the US carrier *Rendova* but after two days of patrolling in which she launched 94 air sorties, she was ordered to join *Belfast* and five destroyers and take part in an attack on Kojo, south of Wonsan on the east coast. Here *Sydney*'s aircraft spotted for the big guns of the battleship USS *New Jersey*. Unusually, she carried three squadrons of aircraft and therefore needed 24 Fury pilots and 14 Firefly pilots. During October 1951 she had to ride out one of the hazards of Korean waters, Typhoon 'Ruth.' It reached its peak during the night of 14–15 October when wind speeds topped 100 knots. Those aircraft that could not be stowed below deck were lashed as securely as possible. Nevertheless, the fury of the typhoon tore one aircraft from its lashings and when its undercarriage collapsed it slithered over the side. Three more followed in quick succession, their long-range fuel tanks splitting open and spilling avaition spirit as they too disappeared overboard. Other aircraft suffered damage to wings, rudders and tailplanes.

This was but a prelude to a harsh winter in which snowstorms and low cloud restricted flying operations. Just as the soldiers on the bitterly cold 'Main Line of Resistance' had to devise methods of combating the cold, so the Australian crew of *Sydney* had to cope with engines that would not start, propellers that were iced up and coolant lines that were frozen solid. Deck crews in heavy parkas and thick mittens found that simple tasks took three times as long to carry out in these sub-zero conditions. Pilots and observers had to wear uncomfortable rubber immersion suits that might give them a chance of survival if they were shot down into the sea. Despite these hazards, *Sydney* put up a creditable performance. By the time her patrol tour ended on 27 January 1952 she had inflicted over 3,000 casualties on the enemy, destroyed 66 bridges, 7 tunnels, 495 junks and sampans and inflicted great damage on locomotives, boxcars and railroads. Very rarely was a camouflaged enemy junk – usually a minelayer – ever captured until the Canadian Tribal destroyer HMCS *Huron* achieved this in May 1951 and brought back the crew as prisoners.

## AN EVALUATION OF THE INTERDICTION PROGRAMME

By means of the sea and air operations during 1950–1 the UN Command was able to inflict immense damage on the movement and supply of troops from China. For example, in a fortnight of uninhibited train-wrecking during May 1951, the frigate HMS *Morecambe Bay* fired 1,000 rounds of 4-inch ammunition. Her gunnery, it was said, was deadly by day and night, when she illuminated her targets with starshell. She destroyed two steam locomotives, a diesel locomotive and a North Korean mobile repair unit. Her shells tore up hundreds of yards of railroad. When one damaged locomotive reversed into a tunnel, *Morecambe Bay* promptly blocked the entrance. Similar stories could be told of many ships and many air squadrons. But the magnitude of permanent damage is difficult to quantify precisely though the words uttered by the North Korean General Nam Il, the senior NKPA delegate at Panmunjom, do sum up the strategic significance of UN interdiction policies:

Without the support of the indiscriminate bombing and
bombardment by your air and naval forces your ground
forces would have long ago been driven out of the Korean
Peninsula.

The interdiction programme had concentrated on the destruction of
bridges and tunnels, road and rail links and, wherever possible,
locomotives and boxcars. Its aim was to isolate the Chinese soldiers
in the battle lines from their means of supply in Manchuria. By the end
of 1951 the Americans had hoped to bomb the North Korean railroad
system south of Pyongyang into a state of dereliction.

Clearly this had not happened. By the end of 1951, when the 'static
war' was in place, estimates of the daily needs of Chinese soldiers were
3,000 tons, carried mainly by rail. However, air and naval interdiction
had accounted for less than half of this. There were no supplies by sea
– the blockade saw to that. So by the end of 1951 it was obvious that
while the proximity of the east coast railroad made it vulnerable to air
and naval attack the same could not be said for the routes in the west.
They retained the capacity to supply the front-line Chinese soldiers.
Certain statistics were known: it took a direct hit by a 500lb bomb to
cut a railroad line though this could be repaired overnight by a gang of
coolies; 16 Skyraiders and 32 × 2,000lb bombs or 60 shells from a US
battleship's 16-inch guns would wreck a bridge, again readily repaired, often by using removeable temporary spans.

This was hard for the military mind to accept. FEAF therefore
devised Operation 'Strangle' in May 1951. One hundred B-26 bombers would act as night intruders and the entire Thunderjet fighter-
bomber force would focus on the destruction of the North Korean
railroad system. During October-November 1951 'Strangle' had
modest success. But north of the Chongchon River the MiGs were
the masters of the Thunderjets and south of the river the Chinese sited
hundreds of mobile Triple A guns. Every weapon the Americans
employed – delayed-action bombs, anti-personnel bombs (similar to
the German 'butterfly' bomb) – did not halt the repair work. At great
risk to aircrews, desperate attacks went in day and night against
communication targets. Yet the Chinese were never thwarted. They
were ready to take any casualties while the frustrated Fifth Air Force
was forced to count the cost. Between August and November 1951 it
lost 115 fighter-bombers while another 750 sustained battle damage.
In early December 1951 Fifth Air Force photographic interpretation

experts discovered the 'badly damaged' railroad between Pyongyang and Sariwon was in active use; and by the end of the month they were forced to conclude that the Chinese and North Korean repair gangs had reopened all the key railroads and in particular those fanning out from Pyongyang. Tactics would have change in 1952.

# CHAPTER 11

# Prisoners-of-War

## THE KOJE-DO PRISON RIOTS

When General Mark Clark took over the United Nations Command his immediate problem was the riots among communist prisoners on Koje-do, a 150 square-mile island off the south coast of Korea. Some 150,000 North Korean and Chinese prisoners were held there, many of them 'hard-line' communists. Almost all had been captured during the 'mobile war' of 1950–1. Nearby were several large compounds housing 100,000 refugees and political internees. It was a complex organization to administer and a succession of commandants had failed to deal with prisoner unrest. This indiscipline was heightened by the captured political commissars, led by the North Korean activist Pak Sang-hyon, who reacted to instructions fed to him via North Korean intelligence sources. One perpetual source of disorder was the 'screening' process to which the Americans subjected the prisoners and the civilians in the other compounds. Their object was to discover a prisoner's political background and to establish whether he wished to be repatriated to North Korea or China. American policy was based on their experience at the end of the Second World War when they and their western allies had been persuaded by the Red Army that all East European displaced persons and Russian citizens should be returned to the Soviet Union irrespective of an individual's personal wishes. It was known at the time that many were being sent to certain death. This had been appropriately known as Operation 'Keelhaul' and the Americans were determined that this should not happen to the Chinese and North Korean prisoners in their care. Humanitarian principles must prevail in the matter of prisoner repatriation. The screening process provided communist delegates at Panmunjom with opportunity for vitriolic argument with their UN opposite numbers; and was one cause of the disorder inside the prison compounds on Koje-do.

Trouble at Koje-do went back to the summer of 1951. There had been killings by prisoners in June and August. These were followed by 'no-go' areas inside the camp and the ROK and US Army guards dared not penetrate the communist compounds. More military reinforcements poured into the island but these failed to stop the murders of non-communist prisoners by the communist hard-liners. Throughout, the communists refused to be screened. To enforce the screening, guards drawn from the 3rd Battalion, 27th US Infantry Regiment, moved into the compounds on 13 February 1952 and there fought a pitched battle with the communist resistance groups. Seventy-seven prisoners died; one US soldier was killed. On both sides, many were wounded. A month later, ROK guards opened fire on hard-liners throwing stones at a non-communist fatigue party and ten more prisoners died. Screening continued except in the hard-liners' compounds and General Ridgway decided that these particular prisoners were all eligible for repatriation. Then came an event that bordered on the ludicrous were it not so significant.

On 7 May 1952 hard-line prisoners captured Brigadier-General Francis T. Dodd, commandant of the island. Dodd had responded to a request to meet representatives of Compound 76 at the compound gate so that prisoners' complaints and requests could be forwarded to higher authority. For a time Dodd listened to the prisoners and then terminated the discussion. He turned to leave whereupon he was rushed by the prisoners and dragged inside the compound. Prisoners then took part in defiant demonstrations against the 11,000 American and ROK troops on the island. More American troops arrived on Koje, together with a battalion of tanks, and Brigadier-General Charles F. Colson, US I Corps Chief of Staff, took command. Colson assembled an impressive array of firepower around the compounds: prominently placed machine-guns, M-46 Patton tanks and even flamethrowers. Colson promised no more compulsory screening and after considerable discussion with the prisoners, including telephone calls to their captive Dodd, Colson signed a conciliatory document. General Dodd was released on 10 May. Next day General Ridgway handed over supreme command to Mark Clark who soon discovered evidence that UN intelligence sources had warned Dodd in April that there was a communist plot being hatched in the compounds to make him prisoner and hold him hostage. That he should have deliberately risked capture in the light of these warnings is inexplicable. Both Dodd and Colson were later demoted.

The affair sparked off intense media interest and only then was it revealed to the world that there had been major anti-UN demonstrations and open conflict between communist and anti-communist prisoners in the previous year. Gradually, the Americans came to understand that the Chinese and North Korean High Command regarded the prisoners at Koje-do as combatant soldiers still under communist discipline, controlled by political commissars within the compounds. These commissars were initially members of a special unit training agents in camp leadership techniques. They had *deliberately* surrendered to UN troops. Women agents had infiltrated South Korea as refugees and sought employment in POW hospitals and refugee camps and helped relay information back to North Korea. Through this underground intelligence system the camp commissars received instructions designed to benefit the communist negotiations at the Panmunjom peace talks at crucial moments in the discussions.

Prisoner-of-war issues, especially screening and repatriation, would dominate the peace talks for two years, and the communists, through their control of Koje-do, believed they would always hold a trump card. Rock-throwing was common while 'kangaroo courts' instituted by the commissars dealt out summary justice to those prisoners who denied the 'truths' of communism and refused to be re-educated. Because of prisoner hostility towards the Americans it was decided to replace many of the ROK and US guards. First to arrive was the Netherlands battalion followed by a company from the Greek Battalion. Then B Company of the King's Shropshire Light Infantry and Baker Company of the Royal Canadian Regiment entered the camp in May 1952 and restored order over the next six weeks.

Such events involving prisoners-of-war were beyond the experience of the the western captors. The use of prisoners for propaganda activities seemed in conflict with the Geneva Convention and the much publicised 1949 Convention on Prisoners-of-War. Of course, neither the Peoples' Republic of China nor the North Korea Democratic Republic were signatories of either agreement. Consequently, their treatment of western prisoners, the first ever captured by a communist regime, is of unique importance in understanding the aims and objectives of their Chinese and North Korean captors and the effect these had upon the protracted peace talks at Panmunjom.


## BECOMING A PRISONER OF THE COMMUNISTS

To be captured in battle, when one is disorientated by gunfire and enemy movement, is in itself a traumatic experience, effecting each man differently. Then to suffer pain, indignity, intense cold and near-starvation during the march towards captivity in an alien culture is a demoralizing and weakening process over which only the most heroic and determined spirits may rise and triumph. Every man's story, every woman's story – for some women were captured in Korea – is different but always characterized by physical hardship or mental suffering, or both. This had been the experience of all who had been captured by the Japanese during 1941–5 when values and attitudes displayed by Asian captors were foreign to western beliefs. But the harshness and brutality of Japanese POW camps had never involved a persistent propaganda element; and it was this that became the dominant factor in the lives of all POWs during 1950–3. Of course, when captured, the POW had no inkling that this would be the case. He would have rather more on his mind, as had George Hobson, a Bren-gunner in C Company, 1 Battalion The Royal Ulster Rifles. He was involved in the Ulsters' fighting retreat after the Glosters had been surrounded at the Battle of the Imjin River in 1951:

> The Chinese continually fired on us from the hillsides. I was hit with a burst from a machine-gun. Luckily for me I was only wounded by one bullet and that was in my abdomen. Some passed through my trousers and one passed through a pocket bible, my wallet and hit a nail file that was in it. These were in my left shirt pocket. I could hardly walk or stand so I crawled to the cover of a ditch hoping not to be seen and maybe get out under cover of darkness; but a short time later I was taken prisoner and my wound was dressed with my own wound dressing. I was then taken to their own HQ which was near a ditched Centurion tank. It was dark then and I stayed out all night with them. I thought I was the only POW.
>
> At first light I noticed there were a few Korean houses

close by and to my surprise out came about 200 other POWs, mostly Glosters. I asked the Chinese (some could speak English) why I wasn't put with them. They said they didn't think I would last the night! We were all put on a small hill in the open so that we could be seen by US planes and so protect the Chinese. When night came we were all marched north. I don't know how far but it took all night. I am sorry to say I could hardly walk. I received no help from other prisoners.

On arriving at a small village the wounded were put under cover in a house, about 15 or 20 of us. During this time we received no food or medical treatment, only drinking water . . . Eventually we received our first food, rice and mule meat . . . We were marched by haphazard routes for many days and the only time we had a stop was to change guards and sort out where we had to go next. One bit of luck was that the villagers would hit and shout abuse at us but at the same time put small balls of rice and beans in our hands without the guards knowing.[1]

Bob Guess was a member of the Royal Norfolks Assault Pioneer Platoon, attached to the Royal Welch Regiment when he was captured during a night patrol on 28 May 1952.

The enemy was very close and, it appeared to me, above and around us in an arc. I was firing in a kneeling position when two grenades exploded close to me, followed by a third, the blast knocking me over and concussing me . . . I regained my feet and blundered into Bill Chapman, who was wounded in the leg . . . I told him to stay put and I'd find John Wells, our radio operator, to request support and stretcher bearers. In the pitch black, this proved to be impossible, the fireworks were still in full spate as I resumed a firing position, when suddenly my right leg collapsed under me. I had copped a bullet through the femur, just above the knee . . . Brian bent down to make me more comfortable . . . and . . . he told me since that another grenade had exploded nearby. That must be where the iron in my back came from . . . Eventually some Chinese soldiers emerged from a trench in front of me and came over to where I lay. They picked me up in the 'chair' position with their hands under my knees and arms. I shouted in pain and one of them administered an anaesthetic – a clout under the chin with a rifle butt![2]

Bob Guess was operated on by Chinese surgeons in an aid station located in bunkers on the side of a hill. Much of the equipment used, including the anti-gas gangrene injections, had been captured from the Americans. After his 32 wounds had been dressed, Bob Guess travelled north on a wheeled stretcher pushed by Chinese. Later he transferred to a truck and was finally ferried across the Yalu River to a camp near Pyoktong for sick and wounded POWs, mainly Americans. He later moved to POW Camp 3 Annexe for 'difficult' prisoners at Sonsadong.

## LIFE AND DEATH IN THE PRISON CAMPS

There was general agreement that it was preferable for UN soldiers and aircrew who became prisoners to fall into Chinese hands rather than North Korean. Korean prison guards had enjoyed an unhappy reputation during the Second World War and their North Korean successors were in most cases equally cruel. Communist guards treated all POWs as criminals guilty of political and imperialist crimes for which they could expect the death sentence. Captured civilians were not excepted. Journalist Philip Deane was captured in 1950 and published his experiences in 1953, describing his interrogations and maltreatment, an early western experience of 'brain-washing'. Prisoners could 'expiate' their 'sins' by conversion through a process of political education, the objects of which was to adopt the aims and objectives of the peace-loving Chinese and North Korean peoples. Philip Deane was invited to broadcast over the North Korean radio and condemn the United States for its indiscriminate air attacks upon civilians. The implication was that the 'successful', co-operative POW would join the communists in their cause and decry the capitalist imperialists who governed Britain and the United States. As far as the prisoners were concerned, their attitude towards communist political correctness was governed by the need to survive, avoid pain and acquire food. Maltreatment was more likely to be suffered at the hands of the North Koreans who took a direct physical approach towards the extraction of 'confessions' from prisoners rather than the slightly more subtle 'brainwashing' techniques favoured by the Chinese Peoples' Volunteers.

This was the so-called 'Lenient Policy' based upon Peoples' Liberation Army policies towards Nationalist soldiers during the Chinese Civil War, when it had successfully converted large numbers of Nationalist troops to the communist cause. During the static war in Korea (when very few UN troops were captured by the communists) UN soldiers became quite familiar with the Lenient Policy as Chinese mortars bombarded UN positions with packs of propaganda leaflets explaining their ideas in the vain hope of encouraging UN troops to surrender. Each leaflet explained how to pronounce 'I surrender' in Chinese and North Korean and promised any soldier four guarantees if he surrendered:

1. He would be promised survival of the war in a Chinese prison camp
2. He would be allowed to keep all his personal belongings.
3. He would be protected against any ill-treatment or abuse.
4. He would enjoy proper medical care if he were wounded or taken ill.

However, it was not until POWs actually reached the camps that they discovered some of the sanctions employed by the Chinese. The communists required all POWs to become friends with their captors and drop the hostile attitudes encouraged by their former imperialist commanders. They were required to study, to make specific progress in their understanding of Marxist-Leninism and learn to admire the achievements of Josef Stalin and Mao Zedong. With a proper attitude displayed throughout, the 'progressive' prisoner would be re-educated and rendered fit to return to his home at the end of the war. This was the Lenient Policy and there was no way that a POW could change it. A progressive would be rewarded with food, leisure and the opportunity to write to and receive mail from his family. Unco-operative prisoners would not be tolerated. Any form of opposition meant immediate punishment and this included many sophisticated varieties of torture. As the Chinese observed, 'the Lenient Policy has its limitations as regards our enemies.'

This led to levels of brutality that resulted in the deaths of many thousands of prisoners, particularly among those Americans who had been captured early on in the war. Ultimately, this state of affairs would embarrass the Chinese who gradually appreciated that most of these deaths occurred under North Korean supervision. As the Chinese were inclined to boast about the number of UN prisoners captured, it was difficult to explain why there were relatively small numbers (12,000 remaining from the 60,000 originally quoted) when possible repatriation figures were discussed at the Panmunjom Peace talks. Possibly it was this awareness that eventually reduced the torture and unspeakable punishments inflicted on UN POWs.

Captain Farrar-Hockley DSO MC, the Glosters' adjutant, was forced to endure diabolical water torture for attempting to escape and assisting in the escape of others. He was led to a torture chamber, kicked and beaten. Tied to a chair, he was then doused in ice-cold water and a towel placed over his face to cover his nose and lips. His torturers poured water on to the towel. To breathe, Captain Farrar-Hockley was forced to inhale water which starved his lungs of oxygen. He was slowly being drowned. At just the right moment the torture ceased and a North Korean officer then applied a lighted cigarette to his back. For nearly a week he endured these horrors until, on the sixth day, his torturers promised him relief through execution. Later he was told that he would be shot if he ever again tried to escape. This did not deter Captain Farrar-Hockley who continued to plan and organize escapes until his repatriation from that 'uneasy leisure', as he later described his time as a POW.

Captain Farrar-Hockley encountered a 'remarkable young soldier', Fusilier Derek Kinne, 1 Battalion Royal Northumberland Fusiliers. Kinne became a legend for his implacable hostility towards communism throughout his captivity and a distinct problem for his captors. He had been captured on the last day of the Battle of the Imjin River, 25 April 1951. He managed to escape almost immediately but was then recaptured. He suffered prolonged interrogation during July 1952 when he hit a Chinese officer. His punishment was to stand on tiptoe to prevent a noose round his neck from throttling him. He escaped again and was confined for 81 days in handcuffs during which he was tortured and beaten up by his guards. During one beating with the butt of a sub-machine-gun the weapon accdentally fired and killed the guard commander. For this 'crime' Kinne was punished and denied all medical attention. He was eventually transferred to a penal battalion but remained defiant until his release at the end of the war. For his courage and example Fusilier Kinne was awarded the George Cross.

Lt Terence Edward Waters was a young officer who received a posthumous George Cross for a different but equally courageous act of self-sacrifice during which he maintained, to the dismay of his captors, the honour and prestige of his regiment and the principles for which the United Nations were fighting. His commission was with The West Yorkshire Regiment (The Prince of Wales's Own) but he was temporarily attached to the Glosters. At the Imjin he suffered two serious wounds and was marched to the notorious Camp 12 near Pyongyang, known as 'the Caves' at Kangdong. This was a series of tunnels located in the side of a hill and was permanently cold and damp due to the presence of fast flowing streams in the tunnel floors. There were many South Korean, American and British prisoners crowded into The Caves, lice-infested, deprived of medical attention and all suffering from malnutrition. The weekly death-rate was appalling and Lt Waters was told that if he wished to save himself and his men they should all volunteer to join the 'Peace Fighters'. This was a 'progressive' group of POWs who in return for medical attention, clean clothes and good food were prepared to lend themselves (superficially, at least) to the communist propaganda programme. Lt Waters then ordered his men to volunteer for the Peace Fighters based at Camp 12 and save their lives. He refused to accompany them, unwilling to compromise his prestige and authority as a British officer. This frustrated the North Koreans who pleaded with him to join his men. Shortly afterwards, Lt Waters died.

Captain Acton H. G. Gibbon, Royal Regiment of Artillery, also suffered at the hands of the North Koreans. He was held captive in the infamous 'Pak's Death House' or 'Pak's Palace', located north of Pyongyang. He infuriated Major Pak, the Camp Commandant, by assisting in the escape of three POWs. Pak strung Captain Gibbon from a tree, suspended by his wrists tied behind his back. Here he was systematically kicked and beaten for many hours until Major Pak became convinced that no-one could endure this punishment without confessing. Clearly, Captain Gibbon did not know the direction in which the prisoners had gone! For his determination and endurance Captain Gibbon received the George Medal.

Twenty-nine Australian soldiers and pilots were made prisoners-of-war but their resistance to communism was out of all proportion to their numbers. Four, Privates T. H. J. Hollis, R. Parker, Keith R.

Gwyther and Corp. D. P. Buck were inveterate escapers. Private H. W. Madden was the sole Australian POW to die in captivity. He was too ill to march, having endured beatings because of a constant defiance towards his captors. His cheerfulness and humanity provided an example and a comfort to all even when he was forced to lie on a cart filled with sick and dying prisoners en route to the Yalu River. Three men in the cart died on the journey and the survivors, including Madden, were taken to hospital for modest treatment and better food. It was too late. All the sick men on the cart died. Last of all was the defiant, unco-operative Madden who died in 1951. For his courage and inspiration Private Madden was awarded a posthumous George Cross. By then all UN prisoners apart from South Koreans were removed from North Korean control and placed in camps run by the Chinese People's Volunteers. Torture diminished and food and medical conditions generally improved.

British and Commonwealth prisoners were sent to Camp 1 at Chongshon on the Yalu River where the death-rate especially among the long-serving American prisoners remained high. On arrival all prisoners were required to complete an autobiographical registration form which elicited details of parents, home, school, political affiliations plus of course their service record. Few refused to give their name and number as the penalty was solitary confinement for an unspecified period. Some POWs retained a sense of humour and if the intake were large the communist interpreters were unable to translate readily all the comments made in, usually, rather poor handwriting. Few dared to emulate the British soldier who gave his number as 123456 and his name as Joseph Stalin residing at 1 Kremlin Terrace, Moscow. But most made up false details regarding their background and units though in view of later interrogations those details had to be well remembered!

Until the late summer of 1951 (some 1,600 UN POWs were reported as having died that year) food supplies and medical aid still depended on co-operation. Camp life was governed entirely by the process of re-education and much of the day was devoted to lectures followed by group discussions. It was a requirement that all discussions should end in an agreement that won the approval of the senior squad leader (often a very junior soldier) and the communist supervisors. Disagreement meant that the discussion would be prolonged until that agreement was reached. It was a perfectly understandable reaction when soldiers – not all noted for their literary and academic talents – would succumb in order to have something to eat and go to bed. Their progress in re-education was constantly monitored by Chinese interpreters who set regular questionnaires; and by their willingness to co-operate in the production of propaganda material.

Media techniques were useful in the re-education process, for the communists controlled all news broadcasts and access to the printed word. Periodicals were mostly from communist sources and gradually appeared in camp libraries during 1952–3. The London *Daily Worker* was the most prominent English language newspaper – popular because it always carried the cricket scores and no Chinese interpreter was capable of fabricating these! A camp-produced newspaper *Towards Truth and Peace* was widely circulated among POWs. Perhaps the most influential newspaper was the skillfully produced *Daily News Release* published by a news agency in Beijing. Radio Beijing provided English language broadcasts and occasional music programmes in which Beethoven and Tchaikovsky were the staple fare.

At first library books and pamphlets were exclusively economic/political texts such as Stalin's *The Foundation of Leninism*, Karl Marx's *The Class Struggles in France 1848–50* and Franz Engels' *The Family, Private Property and the State*. These were supplemented by texts such as Edgar Snow's *Red Star over China* and I. Ehrenburg's *The Storm*. Highly popular were literary classics such as George Eliot's *Silas Marner*, Charles Dickens' *David Copperfield* and Alexandre Dumas' *The Man in the Iron Mask* – all approved by the communists. Singsongs and church services were rigorously controlled, as were plays, sports and any form of prisoner leisure. Four military chaplains had been taken prisoner but they were often forbidden to hold church services and never allowed to visit the sick and dying during 1950–1. The three American chaplains were all dead by the summer of 1951 but the Glosters' chaplain, the Rev. Sam J. Davies, survived 'through the mercy of God.' In Camp 2 he was allowed to conduct religious services during October 1951-February 1952 but thereafter the Chinese became less tolerant, defining choir practice and religious instruction as 'reactionary political activity.'

## VISITORS TO NORTH KOREA

Equal hostility was shown towards the International Red Cross and one Chinese interrogator described it as 'a capitalist spy organization.'

Very few foreign visitors were permitted to visit North Korea and those who did arrive were hand-picked 'fellow travellers'. During the 'germ warfare'. controversy, groups of left-wing scientists (The International Scientific Commission) and lawyers (The International Association of Democratic Lawyers) visited North Korea to examine the evidence. Most prominent was Joseph Needham, a distinguished historian specializing in Chinese affairs, a fluent linguist and a former British attaché in China who claimed to have seen evidence of the Japanese use of germ warfare during the Second World War. In February-March 1952 the communists had accused the United States of engaging in biological warfare. Charges that infected flies, fleas and spiders carrying anthrax, cholera and encephalitis had been dropped in 'germ bombs' were supported by confessions extracted from American aircrew POWs. All evidence presented – apart from the confessions – was inconclusive and the photographs of 'germ bombs' proved to be typical US or Chinese propaganda pamphlet carriers. Naturally, the United States denied that it had engaged in what would have been universally called a war crime and the issue was swiftly dropped after it had made worldwide headlines.

Other visitors included two journalists who wrote for the *Daily Worker*, Alan Winnington and Michael Shapiro. They were permitted to visit the POW camps. Winnington had made numerous reports to the *Daily Worker* and was responsible for much of the publicity surrounding the germ warfare charges. He always sent glowing accounts of life in communist POW camps, contrasting these with the misery experienced, in his view, by communist prisoners held by the UN. He interviewed selected progressive prisoners and gave numerous lectures in the camps particularly on the progress of the Panmunjom Peace Talks. Michael Shapiro visited POWs held under appalling conditions during early 1951 and made many promises that he would personally ensure that supplies of DDT, cigarettes and reading materials would arrive. Very little materialized. He was violently anti-American and was not above threatening US POWs with instant execution.

Another far from popular visitor was the Australian William Burchett, a journalist who had worked for *Ce Soir* and *L'Humanité*. Possibly he had the greatest influence of all westerners with the Chinese POW Administration Command and could easily have persuaded them to inform POW relatives that their loved ones were prisoners. He could also have improved the mail service between

Korea and the western world. POW morale would have rocketed had regular letters been received and written home. Of course, it was not in Chinese interests to improve prisoner morale and they permitted improved mail services solely for those POWs who became progressives. Burchett once met Fusilier Kinne and told him that he, Burchett, could have him shot if he persisted in his defiant attitude.

Two British communists went out to North Korea. One was Jack Gaster, a London solicitor, who helped examine the germ warfare evidence. He brought back stories of the idyllic lives led by POWs in Korea compared with the poor British people who had to exist on rationed foodstuffs! The other was Monica Felton, chair of the British National Assembly of Women, a communist front organization. After her first visit in May 1951 she reported on an array of UN 'atrocities' in Korea and brought home mail from British POWs. She returned to North Korea in 1952, having been awarded a Stalin Peace Prize in Moscow, and visited Camp 5. She met more progressives, joined them in a meal, collected more mail and recorded a talk on the need for world peace and the dangers of US imperialist aggression. The talk was relayed over the camp Tannoy system. It may have been because of these activities that Monica Felton lost her job with Stevenage Development Corporation.

## THE CHANCES OF ESCAPE

It was the duty of all officers to attempt to escape from the enemy, a duty gladly adopted by many private soldiers, enlisted men and non-commissioned officers. However, escape was especially difficult in North Korea filled as it was with Chinese and North Korean troops and a generally hostile North Korean population. Geographical and climatic conditions were against the escaper for whom there were no organized 'safe houses' or underground escape channels such as had characterized Occupied Europe during the Second World War. Moreover, a soldier at the time of capture carried few personal possessions – compasses, watches, pens, maps were usually confiscated by his captors. In the camps his tattered uniform was replaced with Chinese prison garb and he had no access to civilian clothing. There were no Red Cross parcels so that he had no means of bribing guards or the local population. Thus he had few resources with which to plan and execute an escape and even if he did manage to slip out of camp his height and appearance as a Caucasian stood out clearly in an alien Oriental population. The Australians Corporal Buck and Privates Parker, Gwyther and Hollis (whom we met earlier) took part in many escapes for which they were relatively lucky to be punished by long spells in a small cell known as the 'sweat box'. All four took part in a major 24-man break-out led by Corporal Buck but were promptly betrayed by an American prisoner. They displayed an indomitable spirit throughout their captivity but despite their efforts they failed to escape. All were later Mentioned in Despatches.

One prisoner group was especially well-prepared mentally, physically and in terms of resources to effect an escape: American aircrew. Large numbers of US Air Force, Navy and Marine Corps pilots and crews – especially those flying ground-attack missions – were brought down over enemy territory as were those flying high level operations such as the B-29 crews and the pilots of the F-84 Thunderjets and F-86 Sabres. Ideally, a disabled aircraft would head for the coast where those islands held by UN forces might provide an emergency landing strip and would be regularly patrolled by rescue amphibians. If the pilot were shot down close to the 'Main Line of Resistance' his squadron would form a 'RESCAP' or Rescue Combat Air Patrol above him to keep enemy troops away from him. They would then radio for a helicopter to rescue him. The problem arose if the pilot were brought down well inside enemy territory and had to make his own way overland to the coast. North Korean soldiers tended to shoot a downed pilot who was trying to escape, especially if he happened to be one of the hated T-6 Mosquito pilots who brought such devastation down on the heads of communist soldiers.

American aircrew were therefore carefully trained in escape and evasion techniques. All pilots had parachutes, 'Mae West' lifejackets and an inflatable dinghy. Each was equipped with an 'emergency vest', special kits containing a small transmitting radio, signal mirrors, a variety of knives and usually a handgun and ammunition. Some pilots favoured additional automatic weapons. All carried the so-called 'blood chit' which bore the pilot's photograph and the promise (written in Chinese and Korean) of a substantial reward to any one helping the pilot to escape. Towards the end of 1950 pilots were issued with 'barter kits' and these contained North Korean and Chinese money and the sort of possessions enemy troops and civilians coveted: fountain pens and wristwatches. The statistics are interesting for it is believed that 1,690 aircrew were shot down north of the 'Main Line of

Resistance.' Of these 999 were declared missing, believed killed. Some 175 were rescued and 263 were captured.

Of these 263 only three managed to escape from captivity and reach the south. One was Captain Ward Millar who after three months in hospital befriended a North Korean NCO who wanted to defect to the south and the pair of them signalled an aircraft that directed a helicopter to their position. Both safely returned to South Korea. Another was Captain William D. Locke, brought down and captured by the North Koreans. During the headlong flight of the communists in 1950, Captain Locke hid in Pyongyang until liberated by advancing UN troops. The third was 1st Lt Melvin J. Shadduck, a T-6 Mosquito pilot who was lucky to survive captivity and to experience a most extraordinary adventure.

Shadduck took off in his T-6 from K-6 air base south of Seoul on 23 April 1951 during the Battle of the Imjin River. He soon spotted literally thousands of enemy soldiers moving in to attack and fired smoke rockets to indicate their position to four Navy Corsairs circling overhead. He was fired on by an enemy machine-gun and he triggered his last smoke rocket to tell a waiting flight of Shooting Stars to napalm the position. Finally he dived on a mass of enemy soldiers, buzzing them to indicate to another Corsair flight where to unload their napalm. When his T-6 was hit by enemy flak and set on fire he had no option but to crash-land in the midst of the Chinese troop concentration. Despite a badly burned hand and a leg wound he managed to evacuate the aircraft, unsure what had happened to his observer. He began his escape run to the south, evading Chinese soldiers until he encountered half a dozen who took him prisoner. One officer confiscated his escape kit and was convinced that a photographic light-meter that Shadduck was carrying was a secret radio. He was then re-united with his observer, Sgt Gauldin, who had baled out of the T-6 at low-level. They then began the march north to a prison camp where, as the healthiest member, he acted as nurse and doctor. He struck up a very close friendship with three badly injured Americans and a Turkish soldier.

After 32 days of captivity, Shadduck was determined to escape. His four friends wished him luck – they were too sick to accompany him. He left the camp one night during a rainstorm – when communist guards tended to take shelter – and reached the Imjin River. Here he successfully evaded a military checkpoint and followed the river as it flowed towards the Yellow Sea, inadvertently walked into a minefield and then discovered a peasant's hut where the family bound his wounds and gave him food. They then hid him in a nearby cave until advancing UN soldiers appeared. Shadduck approached them – they were members of the Greek battalion. Against all the odds, Shadduck had passed through enemy lines, befriended a peasant family and reached a UN unit. He then persuaded a US colonel to organize 'Tank Task Force' to rescue his four sick friends. It was completely successful and was probably a unique operation during the war in Korea.

There was one other group of American aircrew who returned to the south without being captured. Colonel Albert W. Schinz was second-in-command of the 51st Fighter Interception Wing and on 1 May 1952 he was jumped by a flight of very experienced MiG-15 pilots. On fire and with a major hydraulic problem, his Sabre developed a mind of its own but was at least heading towards the coast, and near the island of Cho-do occupied by the UN.

At 1,500 feet above the Yellow Sea he ejected and managed to climb aboard his dinghy. He had lost his escape and evasion kit but still retained his radio and a couple of flares. He paddled towards an island, landed and built a fire using a Zippo lighter that had miraculously survived immersion in salt water. Schinz then discovered a deserted village near which he built a giant SOS out of raw cotton, later supplemented by a huge MAYDAY sign and an ambitious IM-USAF-P. A B-26 Invader flew over and Schinz tripped his flare which unfortunately exploded in his face. That night, in great pain, he was awakened by ROK soldiers who regularly patrolled the UN islands. They took him to Cho-do from which he was returned to his base in South Korea.

Captain Donald S. Thomas was a navigator-bombardier in a B-26 Invader investigating K-24 air base near Pyongyang on 14 January 1951. Hit by flak, the B-26 began to burn. The pilot headed towards the west coast in the hope of landing near a friendly Christian community. As flames engulfed him, Thomas baled out. He landed safely but with a badly burned hand. His escape gear included the new evasion barter kit, a .45 pistol and plenty of warm clothing. A party of civilians appeared, took him to a village, bound his hand and then pushed him in the direction of Seoul. In freezing weather he made his way to a house which he fervently prayed belonged to a Christian family. He handed the peasants his identity papers and his 'pointee-talkie' (statements written in English and Korean) and indicated 'I am a Christian.' One old man, Papasan, hid him in an ice-locked sampan and then took him to his son's house where he was fed and rested. Next day he was taken to a cave and then, later, to another. Papasan's plan was to wait until the ice melted and then sail Thomas out to sea on the family sampan.

On 26 March 1951 the entire family and Thomas boarded the sampan and sailed in search of a UN naval vessel. For several days they sailed, visiting islands to take on fresh water. Thomas made a huge sign AMERICAN ON BOARD and this was spotted by the British destroyer *Cockade* on 7 April 1951. He and the Korean family were taken on board and Thomas gave his blood-chit to Papasan so he could claim the reward for helping an American airman to escape. Later, when Papasan fell on hard times and had to sell the family sampan, the Americans tracked him down and rewarded him with the equivalent of 24 years' pay!

## THE PRISONER-OF-WAR ISSUE AT THE PEACE TALKS

The fate of over 13,450 UN prisoners-of-war and nearly 82,500 Chinese and Korean POWs would be decided by the outcome of the peace talks held first at Kaesong and then at Panmunjom. After the Soviet Union had proposed cease-fire talks on 23 June 1951, armistice discussions opened at Kaesong on 10 July but were soon suspended (5 August) when communist troops entered the neutral area surrounding the conference block. Talks had briefly resumed on 15 July but the communists flatly refused the UN Command's demand that the International Committee of the Red Cross should visit POW camps in North Korea. Admiral Joy, the senior UN delegate, had to concede this and the communists promptly demanded that all foreign troops should leave Korea. Joy refused to budge on this issue and Nam Il, the North Korean negotiator, suggested that this matter should be left to an international conference following an armistice. There then followed arguments regarding the precise armistice zone: the communists suggested the 38 degree Parallel while Ridgeway proposed the battle line on the day of the armistice: less attractive to the communists because at the time this battle line was mainly above the Parallel and in North Korean territory. Recesses and sub-committees were proposed and the talks broke down on 23 August after the communists accused the UN of bombing Kaesong.

Ridgway was determined that the UN would never again meet at Kaesong and proposed an alternative site. To save face the communists suggested expanding the Kaesong neutral area and shifting the talks to Panmunjom. Ridgway agreed to this on 21 October and the talks resumed in a tented site at Panmunjom on 25 October 1951 with an agreed agenda that included arrangements for the exchange and repatriation of prisoners-of-war. This was a matter complicated by ideological and political issues. Many of the prisoners held in UN camps were former Chinese Nationalist soldiers impressed into the communist army via the Lenient Policy. Such prisoners, argued the UN, should be given the chance to say whether or not they wished to be repatriated. Consequently, the UN took the view that there should be no enforced repatriation of prisoners-of-war. Emotions ran high in the United States during November 1951 when Colonel James Hanley of the US Eighth Army Judge Advocate Service stated that the communists had murdered 6,202 captured American soldiers. Later this figure was revised to 265 individual atrocities but the charges clouded American thinking for some time and encouraged hostility from the communist negotiators at Panmunjom.

Moreover, there was no agreement as to the precise number of prisoners held by both sides. America had reclassified some 16,000 Korean POWs as ROK citizens and released them as civilians. On 18 December both sides exchanged lists of POWs and on 2 January 1952 the UN formally proposed that the repatriation of all POWs should be on a voluntary basis. This was rudely received by the communists and the discussions on repatriation broke down. President Truman had no faith in communist attitudes towards 'all for all' repatriation – he recalled the fate of those forcibly repatriated by the western allies to the Soviet Union at the end of 1945. He supported the notion of 'screening' prisoners to discover their personal wishes and it was this 'screening' that gave the communist prisonerss on Koje-do an excuse for their riots during 1951–2.

During March 1952 the communists became a little more accommodating towards the exchange principles and suggested the exclusion of civilian internees from the final lists. Both sides were now keen to end the fighting in Korea and settling the POW issue would guarantee an early armistice. However, changes in UN lists of communist POWs meant that only 70,000 were available for repatriation, a figure that left the communists 'speechless'. This figure was an educated guess as the screening programme was incomplete. Unfortunately, the announcement coincided with the communist charges over germ warfare, so while the Chinese were prepared to accept the figure of 100,000 repatriates the damage was already done. The UN command fixed the figure of 70,000 as the basis of future discussions. This meant that both sides once more had reached an impasse. The communists would not readily change their position and were now prepared to continue the war indefinitely until the UN made concessions. Mao Zedong sent Zhou Enlai to Moscow in August 1952 to confirm that Stalin would increase his military aid to China. Stalin promised specific military assistance to China, especially anti-aircraft guns and radar. On 28 September the UN negotiators, now headed by America's General William Harrison, proposed a package deal involving the release of POW's through supervisory teams such as the International Red Cross. Predictably, the communists rejected this and on 8 October 1952 General Harrison suspended the peace talks indefinitely. In Washington, where Truman's presidency was coming to an end, Dean Acheson announced that the talks could resume as soon as the communists put forward acceptable proposals on the POW issue. However, Truman was determined that he would not leave the presidency with the future of American POWs compromised in any way. It was rightly assumed that the election of the Republican General Eisenhower as President of the United States in November 1952 would not see a weakening of US policies in this respect.

On 17 November India had made proposals for settling the POW issue – essentially that four 'neutral' countries, Poland, Czechoslovakia, Sweden and Switzerland, would take custody of POWs in a neutral zone and that there would no enforced repatriation of prisoners. On 3 December the United Nations General Assembly adopted what it considered to be a satisfactory compromise brokered by the Indians. The UN General Assembly then went into recess. President Eisenhower began his administration and immediately tried to frighten the communists. He stated that the US Seventh Fleet would no longer seek to protect mainland China from an attack from Taiwan; Republican supporters pressed for a blockade of China; and there was a distinct feeling that the United States would devise a new strategy for ending the Korean War. Mao Zedong was not impressed and vowed that China would fight on indefinitely. Then, on 5 March 1953, the international situation was transformed. Stalin died at his home in Kuntsevo just a few days after he had decided that Mao and Kim Il Sung would be well advised to seek a rapid armistice in Korea.

## OPERATION 'LITTLE SWITCH', 20 APRIL 1953

On 28 March real progress was made when the Chinese agreed to exchange sick and wounded POWs before the signing of a cease-fire. Zhou Enlai proposed that such a move could form the basis of immediate armistice negotiations at Panmunjom and, if a solution were accepted, could result in the final exchange of all prisoners. On 11 April both sides agreed to begin the exchange of sick and wounded on 20 April 1953 – Operation 'Little Switch' – and the peace talks were resumed. Some 684 UN POWs were brought by trucks from the North Korean camps to Panmunjom where they were welcomed by a military reception committee, including interrogators, medical teams and, more memorably, the ladies of the Women's Voluntary Service whose hands were gripped so tightly by wordless men who had not seen a white woman for years. Some of the released POWs were remarkably healthy and interrogation revealed that a proportion of these were progressives who had responded to communist re-education. The small number of UN prisoners released, including a mere 149 Americans, 471 ROK soldiers and 32 British troops, indicated that many more sick, wounded and disabled POWs remained in North Korea. Together with all the others, they could not be repatriated until the war was over.

# CHAPTER 12

# Naval Warfare, 1952–3

## THE CENTRAL INTELLIGENCE AGENCY IN KOREA

During the Second World War the Office of Strategic Services (OSS) provided the United States with its main source of overseas military intelligence. President Truman disbanded the OSS in 1946 and established the Central Intelligence Agency (CIA) in its place during 1947. Its work, then in the early stages of the Cold War, was primarily centred on Eastern Europe. Frank Wisner, a former OSS operative, headed a small CIA unit in Japan whose task was to set up the Office of Special Operations. He recruited Hans Tofte and Colwell Beers, both former OSS officers, and Marine Lt Col Vincent 'Dutch' Kramer. They established a training base at Cheju-do and a new headquarters at Yong-do with the title Joint Advisory Commission, Korea or 'JACK'. The intention was to carry out clandestine operations against North Korea and required the assistance of the US Navy. Tofte took charge of CIA covert operations; Kramer was in charge of CIA special operations in Korea.

The Navy responded by dispatching a much-modified destroyer, the *Horace A Bass*. It came equipped with four landing craft, a crew trained in clandestine operations, specialist marines and room to accommodate 162 raiders. Additionally, the Navy sent a submarine transport, the USS *Perch*, capable of carrying 110 raiders. Colonel Kramer decided that the *Bass* would operate along the west coast of Korea and the *Perch* would function in the deeper waters of the east coast. Up to this time, August 1950, there were no intelligence units operating in enemy territory. After the intervention of the Chinese and during the fluid nature of the war during 1950–1 it was impossible to conduct effective 'line crossing' operations to discover enemy intentions and resources. Eighth Army were of course as interested as the CIA in sending agents into enemy territory and many techniques were employed to insert the operators and, which was far more difficult, extricate them. Boat landings on the enemy coastline were the most effective and 41 Independent Commando Royal Marines had made two raids against the Hungnam-Chogjin railway from the USS *Wantuck* and *Bass* during October 1950. A third raid was made from the USS *Perch*. There were further landings from HMS *Ceylon* and HMS *Belfast* in May 1951. 41 Commando occupied Yodo Island in July 1951 but with the stabilization of the 'Main Line of Resistance' the unit was finally disbanded in February 1952.

Meanwhile, Eighth Army had decided to support an island base off North Korea on the island of Paengnyong-do in January 1951. Here guerrilla teams would be trained and inserted behind enemy lines. As the UN naval patrols dominated the Yellow Sea, the island would always be safe from Chinese or North Korean invasion. Air cover could be readily summoned if necessary. The island unit became known as 'Leopard' and the sub-units were termed 'Donkeys' and their clandestine activities continued throughout the war. It was in the furtherance of these that the UN navies engaged in many months of patrol warfare that became known as the Battle of the Islands.

## THE BATTLE OF THE ISLANDS

During 1951–2 some of the 'friendly' west coast offshore islands developed sophisticated resources; for example, airstrips, helicopter pads, Search and Rescue stations and radar facilities. Most islands were held by ROK marines and the guerrilla forces. Frequent firefights with their enemy opposite numbers occurred, especially after October 1951. Gradually, there emerged a special naval responsibility for the powerful Commonwealth and US naval forces now engaged in permanent patrol: the security of friendly islands from enemy attack. It was a difficult navigational task in the presence of ever-changing mudflats, ice-floes, fierce tides, floating mines and accurate shooting by skilfully camouflaged enemy shore batteries equipped with 105mm and 75mm guns. HMS *Constance*, engaged in close inshore bombardment, was hit just above the water-line by one of these batteries.

Communist attempts to seize some of the key islands began in

November 1951. They attacked in small patrol boats and motorized junks whose shallow draught enabled them to pass over the minefields laid by their compatriots. Under accurate covering fire from shore batteries, the communists assaulted Taewha-do in the Yalu Gulf. HMS *Cockade* intercepted the invaders and knocked out several junks and a patrol vessel, though the enemy bombardment killed one rating. At this stage the might of the combined navies moved into action: 4 aircraft-carriers, 4 cruisers, 8 frigates, 19 destroyers and 8 specialist ships. Britain's cruisers HMS *Ceylon* and *Belfast* were well to the fore as were the two American cruisers *Manchester* and *Rochester*. The USS *Fletcher, Porterfield, Taussig, Eversole* and *Gurke* were destroyers of Second World War vintage; the USS *Comstock* was a specialized high-speed Landing Ship capable of carrying small landing craft; and there were three rocket ships (401, 403, 404); and four tugs *Arikari, Abnaki, Apache* and *Yuma* invaluable for breaking up pack ice. British destroyers included *Constance, Charity, Cockade, Comus* and *Cossack*. Canada committed four destroyers: *Nootka, Sioux, Athabaskan* and *Cayuga*. Australia sent four more *Anzac, Bataan, Tobruk* and *Warramunga* – and the Netherlands contributed the *Van Galen*. Britain's frigates – *Cardigan Bay, Mounts Bay, Alacrity* and *Whitesand Bay* – were joined by New Zealand's *Hawea, Rotoiti* and *Taupo* and Australia's *Murchison*. Four light carriers provided air support: Britain's *Glory*, Australia's *Sydney* and the US Navy's *Badoeng Strait* and *Bairoko*. Though the composition of the force was constantly changing as ships were relieved or transferred for duties on the east coast, this level of naval power was maintained by the United Nations for the remainder of the war.

Naval policy by day was for the destroyers and frigates to bombard any target that presented itself under cover of the cruisers' big guns. Aircraft from the carriers would direct the naval shoots and, if necessary, employ their own firepower to take out enemy positions. When darkness fell and enemy troops and supplies were on the move, the fleet would illuminate the shoreline, the narrow channels and the numerous tiny islands with starshell and rocket flares. Warships then launched small boats to carry RM Commandos, US Raiders and ROK marines to individual islands or to investigate suspect junks and sampans that had been picked out by ship's radar and illuminated by searchlight.

## FLEET AIR ARM OPERATIONS

Britain's carrier *Glory* was relieved by HMAS *Sydney* (September 1951) and then, at the end of the Australian carrier's stint, by HMS *Ocean* (May 1952). *Ocean* had two Fleet Air Arm squadrons on board: 802 Squadron equipped with Sea Furies; and 825 Squadron with Fireflies. Before it took up its patrol position, four US airmen gave the aircrews a talk on escape and evasion, based upon their own experiences. Fleet Air Arm crews now collected together evasion equipment similar to that developed by the Americans: a .38 revolver, a Sten, escape maps, compasses, commando knives, flares, a 'blood chit', emergency rations and barter goods such as watches and fountain pens. The Sea Furies and Fireflies then went off to attack 'Leopard' targets on behalf of the guerrillas and bomb and rocket heavy gun positions along the Taedong Estuary. Low-level attacks became increasingly dangerous as the communists installed light anti-aircraft guns and formed hundreds of troops ready to put up barrages of machine-gun fire around likely targets.

US and British naval aircraft carried out a very heavy raid on Pyongyang (11 July 1952) and caused severe damage to the railroad marshalling yards and warehouses. Four days later *Belfast* and *Amethyst* bombarded the island of Changnin-do. ROK marines, covered by aircraft from the USS *Bataan* and the two Royal Navy warships, recaptured the island in a brief but bitter battle. MiG fighters appeared and damaged two of the Fireflies from HMS *Ocean*. Communist naval opposition was virtually non-existent and the UN fleet continued to dominate the west coast. During *Ocean*'s sixth patrol (5 May–8 November 1952) her Fireflies and Sea Furies encountered increasingly accurate ground fire. In an attack on an enemy gun site concealed on the Amgak peninsula, 14 May 1952, Lt K. McDonald radioed that his Sea Fury was hit and he died when his aircraft spun in from 4,500 feet. Flights of MiG-15s continued to challenge the Fleet Air Arm aircraft that were doing such immense damage to communist installations along the coast and further inland as far as Hanchon, Chinnampo and the North Korean capital. On 9 August 1952 eight MiG-15s attacked two sections of Sea Furies flying in battle formation. Highly manoeuvrable Sea Furies could always break and out-turn a MiG, even though the 802 Squadron aircraft were over 100 mph slower than the communist jets. Four MiGs sped past in head-on attacks as the Squadron diarist recorded:

> . . . a MiG came head-on to Lieutenant Carmichael and Sub-Lieutenant Haines – they both fired – it broke away to go head-on to Lieutenant Davies and Sub-Lieutenant Ellis – they both fired and registered hits . . . a MiG pulled up in front of Ellis with its air brakes on and he was amused to find the range closing. He gave a long burst and noticed hits on the enemy's wings. The aircraft then proceeded northwards with two other MiGs in company. Meanwhile, the flight, still in its battle formation, managed a dozen or more firing passes at MiGs head-on. The dogfight lasted 4–5 minutes and then the MiGs disappeared as quickly as they had arrived – as they departed an aircraft was seen to crash into a hillside and blow up. At first Lieutenant Carmichael thought it was one of his own flight and ordered a tell-off. However, when No. 4 came up 'loud and clear' it was realized that the Royal Navy had shot down its first communist aircraft. Lieutenant Carmichael is being credited with its destruction officially but the rest of the flight are claiming their quarter as well . . . This was indeed a fabulous start to our sixth patrol. What a day – Whew![1]

Lieutenant 'Hoagy' Carmichael was the first pilot of a piston-engined aircraft to shoot down a jet fighter.[2] A month later, on 10 September 1952, a Marine pilot flying a Corsair from the American carrier *Sicily* repeated the exploit. Captain Jesse Folmar and his wing man, Lt Daniels, were tasked with a strike on 300 North Korean soldiers located just south of the Taedong River. By the time they reached the target area the troops had disappeared and the two Corsairs continued on reconnaissance. Suddenly four MiGs swooped down to attack the Corsairs. The Marine pilots jettisoned their bombs and banked hard to avoid the tracer flashing slightly ahead of them. Captain Folmar opened fire on a MiG as it began its fatal climbing turn. As it started to burn, the MiG rolled over and its pilot ejected, his 'g' suit in flames. Captain Folmar was the second pilot of a piston-engined Second World War fighter to down an enemy jet. Almost immediately four more MiGs appeared and cannon shells ripped across Folmar's port wing. As the Corsair shuddered, Folmar baled out at 3,000 feet and was rescued in a matter of minutes.

## HMS *NEWCASTLE*

HMS *Belfast* departed Korean waters in September 1952. She had fired over 8,000 shells from her 6-inch guns and steamed more than 80,000 miles in the 404 days she had spent on active service. In her place came HMS *Newcastle*, commanded by Captain Crawford Rutherford DSO. *Newcastle* was a 'Southampton' class pre-war cruiser fitted with four turrets of triple 6-inch guns. In Korea *Newcastle* used these with devastating effect and was renowned for her fast-firing techniques and the accuracy of her massive bombardments. Capt. Rutherford had an onerous task and no illusions about the limitations of his command. As he put it,

> . . . we ourselves were on a shoestring basis taking over the entire running of the Naval War on the West Coast . . . I commanded *Newcastle* and a Task Element of 17 ships widely spread, guarded the UN garrisons on the main occupied islands and supported the guerrilla forces on the smaller in-shore islands. I had to provide a sizeable staff from ship's officers and my logistic backing was our own resources, a tanker, a rescue tug capable of diving, doing minor repairs and plating – and our native wit. The Government never admitted that we were at war and peacetime procedures were followed. I was actually re-buked by the Director of Stores, Admiralty, over the ex-penditure of electric light bulbs broken during bombardments . . . in Korea our presence was welcomed from the first and the Task Force which included other nations was a fully integrated set-up – we were commanded by Americans and, when required, we commanded Amer-icans, I found it an efficient and cohesive organization.[3]

## NAVAL WARFARE DURING 1953

This 'efficient and cohesive organization' continued its patrols and bombardments through the Manchurian-style winter of 1952–3. HMS *Glory* relieved *Ocean* in November 1952 and in January 1953 joined HMS *Birmingham* and the giant US battleship *Missouri* in a massive bombardment of communist guns that had been threatening the UN islands of Chodo and Sokto. HMS *Sparrow*, a modified 'Black Swan' class frigate with 6 × 4-inch quick-firing guns, tackled a number of batteries near Haeju and suffered light damage for her trouble; while in February the indomitable *Cockade* worked alongside the USS *Thompson*, a destroyer/minesweeper converted in 1944, in a successful shoot against targets near Chongjin. Snowstorms and ice floes made defence of the smaller islands more difficult. *Athabaskan* had problems forcing her way through the ice, as did the destroyer *Anzac* which managed to secure most UN islands and carry out bombardments when leading a mixed force of American, Dutch and British warships.

With the arrival of spring the cruisers could come closer in-shore in the bombardment role and undertake a major operation during May. On 15 May 1953 under the overall command of the new Senior British Naval Officer in Korea, Rear Admiral E.G.A. Clifford CB, *Newcastle* led a force including the American battleship *New Jersey* and the Royal Navy carrier *Glory* against communist shore targets. *New Jersey* stood out at sea steadily firing its 16-inch guns. *Newcastle* stood closer inshore ready to take out any Triple-A flak positions that might fire on spotter aircraft working from *Glory*. In a three-hour engagement she destroyed two Triple-A sites with her accurate broadsides without receiving any damage whatsoever. She had a similar experience on 28 May 1953 when she devastated enemy gun positions under cover of a smoke screen in company with Dutch and British warships. Chinnampo was the target for HMS *Morecambe Bay* and the USS *Thompson* on 2 June. HMS *Cossack* and the USS *Gurke* dispersed troop concentrations and damaged communist trains during 19–20 June 1953. Over the next month, as negotiations at Panmunjom moved rapidly to a conclusion, naval patrols continued both on the west and east coasts of Korea.

UN naval support on the east coast was usually in direct support of the ROK divisions that came under heavy communist attack during 1953. Admiral Joseph J. Clark, commander of the US Seventh Fleet, had decided on a new strategy for undermining the enemy's ability to fight. He would move away from air attacks on distant industrial and transportation targets, leaving these to the light and medium bombers of the US Air Force. Instead, his carrier aircraft would strike at the enemy on the actual battleline (now defined as the 'bombline' and its immediate approaches. Thus was born the policy of the 'Cherokee

Strikes,' a name chosen to mark Admiral Clark's descent from this accomplished Indian nation. By the end of 1952 Cherokee Strikes had become sophisticated modes of destruction. Intelligence assessments claimed that they had reduced or prevented several enemy infantry attacks along the 'Main Line of Resistance.'

For example, on 21 February 1953 US and ROK troops in the IX Corps area were tasked with regaining lost ridges from the enemy. Skyraiders from the US carrier *Valley Forge* flew parallel with the MLR and dropped their bombs on the Chinese side of the ridges. Three Skyraiders then systematically strafed the Chinese positions and a Mosquito pilot flew across the scene to assess battle damage. He reported that at least 16 bunkers were seriously damaged or wrecked and that many Chinese sheltering in caves had been killed. For the remainder of the war the United States assembled four carriers off the east coast. They were all ships of the 35,000 ton 'Essex' class each able to carry 90 aircraft: *Philippine Sea*, *Princeton*, *Boxer* and *Lake Champlain*. In March 1953, half of the sorties were dedicated Cherokee Strikes while in June all piston-engined squadrons were engaged on attacking the bombline.

To reinforce these efforts the US Navy allocated to the bombline the battleship *New Jersey*, the heavy cruisers *St Paul* and *Bremerton* and the light cruiser *Manchester* escorted by 12 destroyers. In the previous October the battleship *Iowa* had demonstrated how effective its 16-inch guns could be in battlefield support and now these heavily-armed warships were available to back up Admiral Clark's Cherokee Strikes. Between them, these warships fired 1,774 rounds of 16-inch shells, 2,800 8-inch shells, 700 6-inch and 13,000 5-inch, a colossal barrage that broke up several massed enemy assaults at the eastern end of the 'Main Line of Resistance' June–July 1953. One notable example, on 15 June 1953, was the bombardment of the much-disputed Anchor Hill (Hill 351) located some three miles inland, resulting in its capture by ROK forces.

## THE SIEGE OF WONSAN, 1951–3

Perhaps the most enduring single commitment on the east coast was the siege of Wonsan. America's intention was to deny to the Chinese and North Koreans the use of their most important port and railroad/highway centre on the east coast. Gradually, from the beginning of the siege on 16 February 1951, US ships had systematically swept mines that littered the harbour area so that destroyers and cruisers could work closer to the shore. Mineswept channels were then marked with prominent yellow buoys which communist gunners found useful for zeroing their own artillery. Wonsan was therefore a very dangerous posting and ships were damaged and crews suffered losses. Wonsan duty usually lasted 30 days before a warship was relieved.

Enemy artillery was always difficult to locate and destroy. Skilful camouflage and hide-outs in caves and in reverse slopes of hills gave good protection. Muzzle flashes and smoke were harder to disguise so the communists were quick to relocate their howitzers. Wonsan's gunners were also accurate and US ships had to keep steaming even at night as an anchored ship was invariably hit by enemy shells. For example, the destroyer USS *Brinkley Bass* suffered a direct hit amidships on 24 March, badly injuring one seaman; the Landing Ship Dock *Cabildo* was hit on 25 May 1952 and two men were injured.

One of the risks for US carrier aircraft was the prospect of being downed by Wonsan flak and being forced to ditch their aircraft in the harbour's unswept minefields. In May 1952 it was decided to build an emergency airstrip on the island of Yo-do, a task undertaken by the fleet's Amphibious Construction Battalion, the famous 'Seabees'. They built a 2,400 foot runway in 16 days and on 15 July 1952 it was first used by seven Corsairs low on fuel. Yo-do's presence so close to Wonsan infuriated the communists who made several unsuccessful efforts to destroy the airstrip. Finally the communists had to content themselves with desultory bombardments from the artillery based on Umi-do and Hodo Pando.

During the period December 1952–June 1953 the communists made their most vigorous attempts to drive the Americans from Wonsan harbour. Their well-directed fire fell on the blockade ships as well as the islands. During March-May communist gunners hit five destroyers and the cruisers *Bremerton* and *Los Angeles*. On 15 May 1953 they bracketed the destroyer USS *Bush* and on 11 June scored a direct hit on the destroyer USS *Wiltsie*. *New Jersey*'s reaction was first to destroy the howitzer caves on Hodo Pando, entombing the guns, and then on 11–12 July to hit the remainder with 164 16-inch shells. The guns on Hodo Pando never fired again.

The siege continued until the last day of the war, 27 July 1953. The minesweepers were still at work, the destroyers were patrolling inshore and the *Bremerton* was still firing broadsides at the battered infrastructure of Wonsan right up to the last minute of the armistice. In total the siege of Wonsan had lasted 861 days, the longest siege ever conducted by the United States Navy. It is difficult to evaluate its effect. It had certainly been conducted with determination and skill by the Americans; and the doggedness of the communist gunners in resisting the US warships and aircraft is unquestionable. The US Navy had virtually destroyed the city, forcing many of its industries to evacuate or 'go underground' while rail and road traffic had to bypass Wonsan. United Nations navies had provided the ground troops with shipborne artillery and aircraft in the offensive role and had guaranteed the security of their flanks. But the effort involved in maintaining this hugely expensive fleet outside Wonsan did not result in the halting of communist supplies from Manchuria to the front; nor did it have any more than a marginal effect on the *general* progress of the land war.

## SUPPLY AND MAINTENANCE OF THE NAVIES

Typical of the unsung heroines of the United Nations navies was the Royal Navy's aircraft-carrier HMS *Unicorn*. She was originally completed as an aircraft maintenance ship in 1943. During the Korean War, when she remained on station throughout hostilities, *Unicorn* functioned as a Repair and Ferry aircraft-carrier. Her main role was to ferry aircraft and equipment between Singapore, Hong Kong and Japan. In this way she kept supplied each of the five Commonwealth light aircraft-carriers that served in Korean waters. Occasionally, she accompanied these carriers on operations and thus provided a spare flight deck for aircraft in trouble. Replacement aircraft, of course, came from the United Kingdom and so *Unicorn* worked hand-in-hand with HMS *Warrior* ferrying aircraft from the UK to Singapore. *Unicorn* also acted as a troopship and brought 1 Middlesex to Pusan from Hong Kong in August 1950 and continued to take troops to and from Hong Kong and Japan throughout the war. She finally left the Far East to sail to the UK on 15 October 1953.

There were numerous oilers, tugs and ammunition ships vital to operations and, of course, the hospital ship *Maine*. *Fort Rosalie* and *Choysang* were ammunition ships; *Fort Charlotte* brought naval stores; while 12 oilers were required to support the ships in Korean waters: the *Echodale*, *Green Ranger*, *Brown Ranger* and nine of the

'Wave' class such as *Wave Chief* and *Wave Sovereign*. Including the two headquarters ships, *Ladybird* and *Tyne*, Britain committed no less than 52 naval vessels to the prosecution of the Korean War. When this total is added to the numbers of other UN ships and their naval air arms – the Fleet Air Arm and the United States Marine Division Air Wing – it represents a naval contribution greater than that which was allocated to North Africa or Burma in the Second World War.

# CHAPTER 13

# The Air War, 1952–3

## NEW STRATEGY AND TACTICS

Throughout the period 1952–3 discussions at the Panmunjom peace talks revolved around the prisoner-of-war issue, arrangements for a cease-fire and the precise location of the armistice line or demilitarized zone between the combatants. There was little or no mention of the air war and its conduct by the Fifth Air Force, its attached Australian and South African squadrons and allied naval carrier aircraft. Yet the use of air power during this period crippled the North Korean economy and certainly helped to persuade the communists to agree to armistice terms in 1953. Air power played a significant role in the overall UN strategy: the ground forces held the 'Main Line of Resistance' against savage communist attacks that peaked in 1953; the navies dominated the flanks; while air power employed its ever-increasing resources to wreck North Korea's industrial and agricultural infrastructure. In this way, attrition from the air helped to accomplish peace, a technique adopted by USAF in Vietnam during 'Linebacker II' operations in 1972 and by the NATO powers during the attacks on Serbia and Kosovo during 1999.

Creating a huge air striking force in South Korea in itself posed immense logistical problems. In a lecture to the Royal United Service Institution on 5 December 1951, Wing Commander P.G. Wykeham-Barnes DSO OBE DFC AFC, outlined some of the difficulties in the use of air superiority in Korea. It was relatively easy to assemble large numbers of fighter-bombers, interceptors and aircrews. It was less easy to operate them effectively in a country such as Korea where all hills looked the same and the rivers flowed in every direction. Then it was important for aircrews to have good high-grade radar and radio navigation facilities. These facilities arrived rather slowly and it was not long before the radar warning system, radar/radio navigational aids and homing beacons became over-used. Similarly, the problems of airfield construction were outlined by Lt Col Joseph I. Albert and Captain Billy C. Wylie in a paper in the US Air University *Air Quarterly Review*. Apart from the United States, no other UN force in Korea had its own Aviation Engineer teams. Korea's hills and mountain ranges were nightmares for airfield construction teams who were forced to lay out their strips in valley bottoms, most of which had been muddy paddy fields. Drainage was a constant problem. The use of Second World War pierced steel planking (PSP) was satisfactory for piston-engined fighters and air transports such as the C-46 Commando. But the blast from jet engines caused rapid deterioration in the PSP and eventually engineers found it easier to construct long solidly-based hard-surface airfields that could cope with the take-offs of heavily loaded jet fighter-bombers, Sabre jet interceptors and the giant C-124 Globemasters capable of carrying enormous loads. Two outstanding examples of airfields built by US engineers are still to be seen: at Taegu with its 9,000 feet concrete runway and at Osan, the 'superbase' known as K-55, still one of the most important of South Korea's air bases.

America's main medium bomber force, the B-29 Superfortresses, flew out of well-established airfields in Okinawa and Japan. Their night missions concentrated on bridges, marshalling yards and specific industrial targets such as the Orient Light Metals Company located at Yangsi on the Yalu River. Searchlights and Triple A fire – both radar controlled – plus roving MiG-15 night-fighters faced the crews on every mission. To combat these the Fifth Air Force painted the undersurfaces of their B-29s black in the style of RAF Bomber Command in the Second World War. They flew at altitudes where the tell-tail condensation trails were less likely to form while below them the B-26 light bombers attacked the searchlights and gun positions.

Ground-controlled MiG-15s presented a difficult problem. They were accurately vectored by GCI (Ground Controlled Interception) and locked on to the B-29 bomber stream. Initial attempts by F-94 Starfires to fly 'barrier patrols' between the MiGs and the bombers rarely succeeded and several B-29 formations suffered battle damage. However, in May 1952 the Marines received a dozen F-3D2 Skynights to escort the B-29s. It was an interesting aeroplane as the crew sat side-by-side. They had no ejection seats. Instead, they had a specially designed escape chute that enabled the crew to parachute from the bottom of the fuselage. Korea's first jet-versus-jet night combat took place on 2 November 1952 when a Skynight crewed by Maj. William Stratton and his radar-operator Master Sgt Hans Hoglind shot down a Russian aircraft identified as a 'Yak-15'. Skynights would shoot down four MiG-15 night-fighters, the Yak-15 and a wooden PO-2 'Bedcheck Charlie'. The night-fighter version of the MiG-15 was a formidable enemy with its own airborne radar. It had been a dangerous challenge to FEAF's bombing strategy prior to the advent of the remarkable Skynights.

To combat the night-fighter threat the B-29s devised a novel approach to the target. The aim was to reduce the 'compression' time between the beginning of the bomb run (known as the IP or Initial Point) and 'bombs away' over the target. It dispensed with a long period of formation flying, kept the enemy guessing as to the precise location of the target and made the task of vectoring night-fighters more difficult for the communist ground controllers. It meant that each B-29 would have to navigate its own way to the IP and then form up with the rest of the mission. Bearing in mind that the B-29s had to fly 800 miles from Okinawa and Japan, extraordinary accuracy was achieved with some missions forming up at the IP from all directions in a matter of 40 seconds or less.

During 1953 the versatile piston-engined B-29s carried out unrelenting attacks against bridges and the ten biggest communist airfields in North Korea. As the delegates debated the armistice terms at Panmunjom, it emerged that there would be a 12-hour delay between the announcement of a cease-fire and its implementation. FEAF feared that during these 12 hours the communists would transfer some of the hundreds of MiG-15s based in Manchuria to North Korean bases. It therefore allocated airfield strikes as a top priority mission to the B-29 Groups, and the bombers faithfully showered every runway and dispersal point with bombs up to the very last day of the war when Superfortresses wrecked recently repaired runways at Taechon and Saamcham airfields. A Superfortress engaged on photo-reconnaissance that day reported that all ten communist airfields were out of action. As far as is known not a single MiG-15 ever operated out of a North Korean base during the war.

## THE BOMBING OF NORTH KOREA'S
## HYDRO-ELECTRIC INDUSTRY

Between 1950 and 1952 it had been FEAF's policy to attack all industrial targets that contributed to the Chinese and North Korean war effort. This had considerable success in so far that metallurgical centres, arms factories and assembly plants were devastated by bombing. Learning from their mistakes in the Second World War, FEAF's target planners sent the bombers back to these targets time and time again in order that production could not resume. Despite this, the communists continued to manufacture weapons and the other paraphernalia of war by dispersing their industries to underground locations. These were immune to conventional bombing attacks. FEAF's planners therefore debated the possibility of striking at their sources of electrical power in order to disable production – the reservoirs and generating plants. They had before them the example of Bomber Command's extraordinary raids on the German dams in 1943. This, of course, would mean the destruction of electric power for the whole of North Korea – and part of Manchuria – with consequent civilian suffering. It could also lead to an unpredictable enemy reaction. Another thought paramount in the planners' minds was that, assuming that the United Nations occupied North Korea at the end of the war, their immediate need would be electric power to re-establish the country's peacetime economy. Knocking out the North Korean power sources that had taken the Japanese over twenty years to construct would confront an occupying force with an insoluble problem in the short term.

Overriding all these anxieties was the attractive notion that it would be more cost-effective to destroy North Korean industrial production by removing its source of electric power. It would mean the destruction of four major generating systems at Chosin, Kyosen, Fujon and Suiho. Production at these four centres amounted to some 1.7 million kilowatts during the Second World War. After 1947 the North Koreans had taken over the production and maintenance of these plants, now reduced in output after the Russian occupying forces looted two generators and three turbines in 1947. Even so, production was still relatively high: just over one million kilowatts in 1952. Transmission of electric power on the eastern side of North Korea was achieved through an elaborate array of sub-stations fanning out from Chosin, Fujon and

Kyosen. These fed Wonsan, Hungnam, Tanchon and Chongjin. Sui-ho's generators served the west coast – Chongju, Chinnampo and Pyongyang. Transmission lines also crossed the central mountains from Chosin and Wonsan. Up to 1948 South Korea was fed by sub-stations at Pyongyang.

Suiho was the biggest and most important of the four generating systems and was rated as the fourth biggest in the world. It was also the most modern as Japanese engineers were putting the finishing touches to the Suiho system in 1945. About one-quarter of its production fed Chinese industry in Manchuria in 1952. It was a tempting target and FEAF's planners arranged for the biggest raid of the war to destroy all four generating systems on 23 June 1952. It was a combined Navy-FEAF mission with 230+ aircraft flying off the US carriers *Bonhomme Richard, Princeton, Boxer* and *Philippine Sea.* Two Marine Air Groups and four Fifth Air Force fighter-bomber wings made up the remainder. Pilots were under strict instructions to avoid hitting the dam and to concentrate on the generators and transformers. At Suiho US Navy Panthers went in first to deal with enemy flak positions. These were followed by dive-bombing Sky-raiders and Panthers and 120 Thunderjets and Shooting Stars depos-iting several hundred tons of high explosives on these key targets. It was a great success. Suiho dam was untouched but the generating tagets were put out of action. Not one US aircraft was lost.

Simultaneously, carrier-borne Panthers, Corsairs and Skyraiders attacked the Kyosen system while Marine and Fifth Air Force fight-er-bombers hit the generators at Chosin and Fujon. By the end of the day, it could be fairly claimed that the electrical generating system of North Korea was temporarily out of action. Suiho was the most heavily disabled so the UN air forces concentrated their follow-up attacks on the other three. On 24 June the fighter-bombers returned to Chosin and Fujon; on 26 June these strikes were repeated; and on 27 June Chosin was raided so effectively that all production ceased. For the remainder of the year and up until the end of March 1953 the hydro-electric generating systems came under intermittent attack, sometimes by the Superfortresses that bombed Suiho on 12 September 1952 and sometimes by the Thunderjets that bombed and rocketed repaired sections of the plant on 15 February 1953. During this last attack the MiG-15s intervened and two were shot down by the escorting Sabres.

## THE CONTROL OF TERRITORY BY AIR POWER

During 1952 FEAF planners decided upon an extraordinary demonstration of UN air power designed to persuade the communists to move
towards a rapid conclusion of the Panmunjom peace talks. They
determined to deny part of North Korea to the communists. The area
chosen was the system of bridges crossing the Chongchon and Taeryong
Rivers at Sinanju and Yongmidong. These were approximately 100
miles north of the 'Main Line of Resistance' and represented the enemy's
primary supply route from Manchuria to the MLR. Sinanju-Yongmidong bridges were categorized as a 'choke-point'. If air power could
dominate even such a tiny area of some eight square miles it would be an
object lesson to the communists. They would realize that the United
Nations could control any part of North Korea simply by the use of
concentrated air power. Of course, the communists were well aware of
the importance of their Sinanju-Yongmidong bridge complex. They
located their most powerful anti-aircraft defences to protect the spans
that connected the supply routes from the Yalu to the Chinese and North
Korean soldiers on the 'bomb-line'. In fact, communist planners regarded not just this bridge complex but the entire zone north of
Pyongyang as the most vital in the whole of North Korea. That is
why their anti-aircraft guns stretched along the supply corridor back to
the Yalu.

These targets had been attacked consistently during 1950 and up to
the Autumn of 1952 by round-the-clock interdiction raids on enemy
transport. Undoubtedly these had seriously restricted the flow of
supplies from Manchuria to the MLR, perhaps as much as 80–90
per cent. Crippling though this was for the communists, there was no
great pressure on them to meet any crisis developing on the MLR.
After October 1951 no crisis ever did as far as the United Nations were
concerned. Eighth Army commander General Mark Clark and his
successors General Van Fleet and General Maxwell D. Taylor (appointed 11 February 1953) were under strict instructions to maintain
a defensive posture along the MLR. Thus the Chinese could initiate
localized offensives at their leisure at times influenced solely by the
position reached in the peace talks or as a particular reaction to an
unacceptable political development. But it is reasonable to assume that
the Chinese would have launched a major offensive during 1952 or
1953 and driven the United Nations out of the peninsula had not UN

F/O John Murphy in his F-86 Sabre when attached to the US 16th Fighter Interception Squadron in Korea, 1953

F-51D Mustang of the ROk Air Force taxiing out for a strike on NKPA positions

A MIG-15 bis in North Korean Air Force markings

Early propaganda leaflet air-dropped on North Korean troops (see text on p. 256).
Probably July/August 1950

Later propaganda leaflet air-dropped on Chinese troops
'Chinese Communist Officers and Soldiers: In the past two years, over
990,000 Chinese Communist troops have already died or been wounded
in the Korean battlefields. Just think, how heart-broken the parents of the
dead must have been! Who would look after their orphans and widows?
Why should the Chinese be cannon-fodder for the Soviet Russians?'

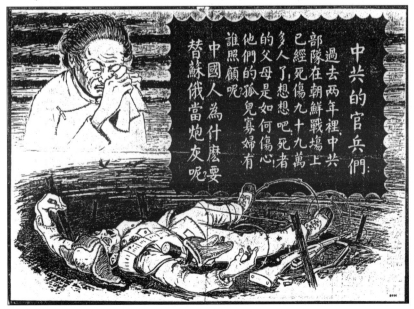

# Leaflets air-dropped on Communist troops, 1952

'Air cover! Arriving just when we need it! Whenever the Allied troops need it, planes will come instantly!'

'Air Cover??? Not a hint of it! Communist soldiers only hear the empty words of their leaders. Hurry up and free yourselves from your bondage! Run over here to the Allies side!'

Frozen rations eaten on the run.
Any moment he may have to run again,
to fight or die — and so may you.

Chinese leaflet fired at UN troops, c. 1951

# CHRISTMAS —
## HOME —
### HAPPINESS —

Those who love you want you back home, safe and sound.

*FIND A WAY OUT!*

## It's No Disgrace To Quit Fighting
## In
## This Unjust War!

傳單—11

Chinese leaflet fired at UN troops, c. 1951

Chinese propaganda poster attached to Commonwealth Division wire, 1953

The Hook, viewed from Sausage, 1953

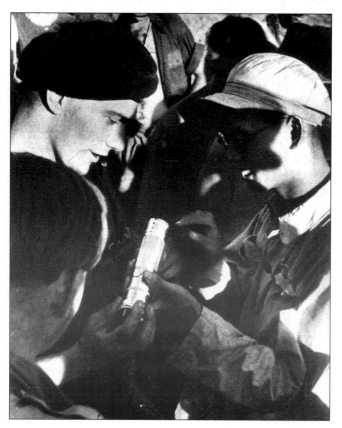

The first day of the truce, 1953. A Chinese officer discusses technicalities with British soldiers in front of the Commonwealth positions

air power rendered such an offensive impossible. So while the UN ground forces maintained a defensive stance throughout 1952–3 air power became the offensive arm of the United Nations, a fact well illustrated in the incredible assault that took place on the vital bridges at Sinanju and Yongmidong 10–15 January 1953.

During the late Autumn of 1952 UN intelligence revealed that the communists had succeeded in stockpiling war materiel in their bunkers on the reverse slopes of their MLR. Of special concern were the numbers of artillery shells, each one of which could have easily been brought south from the Sinanju-Yongmidong bridge complex on a peasant's A-frame. To counter this the UN resumed its attacks on the bridges. Attacks began on 9–10 January 1953 with a night raid by 18 B-29s flying from Okinawa and Japan. They dropped their bombs by radar and created general havoc along the railroads and among the local flak positions. On 10 January 300 fighter-bombers dive-bombed the bridges and the Triple-A positions, heralding four more days and nights of unrelenting attack on the eight square miles of North Korean territory. Simultaneously, B-29s and fighter-bombers patrolled north and south of the bridges, destroying every visible target. No less than 2,292 combat sorties were flown during those five days plus many more reconnaissance and rescue missions.

In the US *Air Quarterly Review*, pilots' reports indicated the level of 'envelopment' of territory achieved at the end of the fifth day of operations: '. . . Sinanju-Yongmidong lay smouldering, a reeking mass of gnarled steel, wrenched earth, and jagged chunks of concrete torn away and hurled hundreds of yards over the landscape. Trains, freight cars, and trucks caught between the Taeryong and Chongchon Rivers were wholly or partially buried under tons of earth thrown up by the impact of demolition bombs. Others, within or above or below the area, were sealed in the tunnels in which they were hiding or bottlenecked and destroyed by landslides. Reconnaissance pilots in post-strike interrogation reported the "entire area torn up, the approaches to the bridges, the bridges themselves and the area between." One pilot commented, "the bridges look like some giant hand picked them up and twisted them round like pretzels . . . it's a wonder if there is anything left.' "[1] Yet despite the number of sorties flown in the face of determined flak, only seven US warplanes were shot down and of these all but one of the pilots were rescued.

For over a fortnight the B-29s and the fighter-bombers between them denied the communists the use of the Sinanju-Yongmidong

bridges. After this, the Chinese and North Koreans used their in-
genuity and apparently inexhaustible reserves of manpower to begin
repairs, drive trucks across the frozen rivers and backpack supplies to
the front line. Moreover, it seemed that the communists were now
ready to ignore the ever-present fighter-bombers for they now began
moving supplies by road in broad daylight as well as by night, thus
presenting the fighter-bombers with easy, desirable targets. On the
'Main Line of Resistance' United Nations troops noticed a marked
reduction in artillery and mortar 'stonks' and assumed that the enemy
was either husbanding his stocks of ammunition prior to a major
attack or, more likely, was running short of shells and mortar bombs.

It was clear that the communists had been seriously hurt and to
hinder their recovery FEAF employed every type of munitions to deter
the reconstruction of the bridges. Dive-bombing from high altitude to
15,000 feet (just above the Triple-A flak limit) and the use of Variable
Timing (VT) fused and parademolition bombs rendered most of the
bridges unserviceable for the remainder of the war. All of Sinanju's
five bridge spans were defined as unserviceable in July 1953; and of
Yongmidong's seven major spans five were out of action and two were
being used by small numbers of vehicles. To make good some of the
shortfall, the communists surveyed and constructed a completely new
railroad 'bypass' connecting Namsi with Chasan-ni via Kunu-ri. They
laid the tracks at approximately a mile a day and in a couple of months
had re-established their link between Manchuria and the front line. It
was a prodigious effort and it served them well during the final battles
of the war. However, these would be bitter but brief as the armistice
was signed six months after the destruction of the Sinanju-Yongmidong bridges.


## ASSAULTING THE IRRIGATION DAMS OF NORTH KOREA

Having attacked the sources of hydro-electric power and the main
supply routes across the Taeryong and Chongchon Rivers, the fighter-
bombers turned their attention to the enemy's food supplies. This
meant attacking the paddy fields where rice, the staple diet of North
Korea, was grown. Some 20 dams, constructed from packed earth and
stone, fed the irrigation system of North Korea on which the rice
harvest depended. If this harvest could be interrupted it would cause
food shortages among both the civilian and military populations of

North Korea. An additional bonus would be the creation of flash floods that might inundate military sites and erode the foundations of bridges and railroad embankments. Towards the end of 1952 FEAF's planners began studying the main concentration of irrigation dams in the Haeju peninsula. They reported that there were two ideal times for interrupting the rice harvest: in May 1953 when the young plants had weak root systems and would be swept away by water; and in August 1953 when a flood would cover and kill the rice plants. As the dams were built from earth and stone they should be relatively easy to destroy. Among the planners' recommendations was the need to attack each dam simultaneously; otherwise, the communists would grasp FEAF's intentions and drain the reservoirs. Curiously, this factor was later ignored as the dams were attacked over a period of a month (May–June 1953) rendering the entire operation only 50 per cent successful.

FEAF's planners were prepared to risk the reaction of the communist propaganda machine for the UN would be immediately accused of causing civilian starvation and the destruction of peasants' homes. So UN counter-propaganda stressed that the communist régime requisitioned most of the rice crop anyway, leaving peasants under-nourished and critical of their government; and that many peasant haystacks and cottages concealed T-3485 tanks and self-propelled guns. Conscience appeased, the reservoirs at Toksan, Chasan, Kuwonga and Kusong were selected as the primary targets.

Toksan Reservoir was the first irrigation dam to be attacked. Located north of Pyongyang, it was a large packed earth and stone structure holding back a lake of some three square miles. F-84 Thunderjets bombed the dam on 13 May 1953. Pilots reported a trickle of water overflowing the dam. By the morning the trickle had becme a gushing torrent roaring through a breach over 140 yards wide. Bridges, railroads and a truck-bypass were badly eroded by flood water which stretched for 27 miles. When the Thunderjets targeted Chasan on 15 and 16 May they had less success and a third attack later on 16 May finally blew out the base of the dam causing flood water to exit through a 65 yard breach and sever a major rail link to Pyongyang. The bombing of Kuwonga was unsuccessful. When seven B-29s arrived on 22 May 1953 to destroy it the communists had already begun draining the dam; and when the Superfortresses returned a week later they found the reservoir completely drained. Similarly, the attacks on Kusong began on 13 June 1953 but despite the attention of 54 Thunderjets no bomb managed to breach the dam. On 16 June the

Thunderjets, supplemented by Marine Corsairs, almost scored a direct hit, after which the reservoir's headwater lapped dangerously close to the edge of the dam. The final attack on 18 June was too late. By then the communists had drained the reservoir. FEAF prepared for another campaign against the dams for August 1953 but the armistice in July rendered the plan redundant.


## STRENGTHENING THE SABRE FORCE

For almost a year (1951–2) the 4th Fighter Interception Wing had been the only unit equipped with the F-86A Sabre and had thus borne the brunt of the air superiority battles against the MiG-15. Most of the 102 MiGs shot down during that period had fallen to the guns of the Sabres. During the Autumn of 1951 the first of the up-rated F-86Es appeared but not all went to the 4th FIW. The hard-worked F-80 Shooting Stars were at last being replaced and the 51st FIW based at Suwon was allocated some of the new Sabres. The two Wings were very successful and shot down 375 MiGs during 1952. Other units received the new Sabres as soon as they were rushed off the production lines and transported to Korea. During 1953 the 18th Fighter-Bomber Wing, which had flown the F-51D Mustang piston-engined aircraft so effectively, received the new Sabres. After flying its last mission with the Mustang on 23 January 1953 it began converting to jets at Osan Air Base on 28 January 1953. By 25 February it was ready for action and undertook its first patrol along the Yalu River. It soon clashed with the MiGs and Major James Hagerstrom downed the 18th's first MiG in a dogfight that day.

At the same time, as has been noted earlier, the South African 'Flying Cheetahs' converted to the F-86E and specialized in using it as a fighter-bomber, as they had done with their Mustangs. The Flying Cheetahs flew their last operational sorties on the Mustang on 27 December 1952. Some impression of the intensity of their 10,373 ground-support sorties may be gauged from the fact that of the 95 F-51s originally purchased from the US government 74 were lost. South Africa's Flying Cheetahs maintained their reputation on the F-86 Sabre. They demonstrated to the many doubters that the F-86 was a first-class ground-support aeroplane. It could be adapted to carry bombs and napalm; and it was equally at home in high level inter-diction work and combat air patrols in 'MiG Alley'. Altogether the

South Africans flew 2,032 operational sorties on their Sabres and lost four of them. They certainly deserved the award of a US Presidential Unit Citation, the three Legion of Merit awards, the two Silver Stars and the fifty American Distinguished Flying Crosses among literally hundreds of individual honours accorded to South Africa's No. 2 Squadron.

Other fighter-bomber Wings converted to Sabres. Gradually, the 8th Fighter-Bomber Wing began to exchange its Shooting Stars for Sabres though individual squadrons continued to use the reliable F-80 until 30 April 1952. Sabres from the 8th FBW began their combat air patrols on 8 April 1952. If anything, the F-86E needed more power to chase – or escape from – the lighter MiG-15s. An uprated General Electric turbojet was fitted to a slightly modified Sabre known as the F-86F though it could never climb as fast as the MiG-15. Production lines were enlarged with new factories at Columbus, Ohio and in Canada, boosting the number of jets available for Korea. Thus by the beginning of 1953 substantial numbers of Sabres were available to deal with the ever-growing challenge from the MiG-15s. The Sabres faced one new and unexpected threat. Russian experts had installed anti-aircraft guns firing under radar control and capable of locking on to a high-flying aircraft and destroying it even above cloud. More than one Sabre was lost to flak firing through cloud.

## A POSSIBLE SOVIET THREAT

MiG-15s and radar-controlled anti-aircraft guns were not FEAF's sole anxieties. In 1953 FEAF's intelligence assumed a communist order of battle that not only included 950 MiGs but 100 Ilushin Il-28 'Beagle' jet bombers. Their relatively low speed, approximately 460 mph, meant they could be easily caught by fighter interceptors during daylight hours. But if they attacked at night with each one carrying a two ton bombload they would be a major threat to the UN. On 17 December 1952, in a somewhat ostentatious display, Soviet pilots flew two Il-28s along the northern bank of the Yalu, paralleling some Sabres flying along the southern bank. Fear of a Soviet build-up had been reinforced the previous month when, on 18 November 1952, during an attack by Task Force 77 on Hoeryong, some unmarked Soviet MiG-15s flew south from Vladivostok towards the fleet. Panthers from the USS *Oriskany* tangled with the MiGs and shot one down. According to the US Official History, General Mark Clark advised the Joint Chiefs of Staff that it would be unwise to release details of an aerial clash with the Russians.

Air superiority battles between the MiGs and Sabres intensified during June-July 1952 and on 1 August a skilful MiG pilot downed a Sabre flown by Maj. Felix Asla of the 4th FIW. Then on 1 September 1952 large numbers of MiGs flew south as far as Haeju where they intercepted fighter-bombers engaged in ground strikes. A pattern gradually emerged: the communist training cycle involved flying south of the Yalu at 40,000 feet to give new pilots a taste of combat flying; while experienced MiG fighter pilots (termed 'honchos' by the Americans) engaged the Sabres or flew low to attack the fighter-bombers. This meant that the MiGs could enjoy a tactical advantage over the Sabres whose combat time was severely limited by fuel shortages. Nevertheless, though the Sabres never enjoyed numerical supremacy they did carry a simple radar-ranging gunsight, far superior to the MiG's gyro gunsight.

In practice, the communists were developing a form of aerial ambush. After timing the Sabres on patrol or in dogfights (about 20 minutes), flights of MiGs would take off in Manchuria and fly south to the Chongchon River at 38–40,000 feet. Once the Sabre leader gave the call to head home, other MiG flights would begin to pursue the Sabres who, as they turned south, would be attacked by the 'Chongchon MiGs' diving down on their prey. To counter this threat, Sabres were then ordered to patrol under the direction of ground radar. The Sabre flights returning from MiG Alley would now withdraw over the Yellow Sea to avoid the ambush. In this way the air superiority battles became more complex but the advantage remained permanently with the Sabre squadrons.

This was proved by the combat scores of the Sabre squadrons. In September 1952 the Sabres shot down 63 MiG-15s for the loss of nine F-86 jets plus three more that crash-landed through lack of fuel. This ratio was maintained throughout October–December during which time new MiG-15 units arrived from the Soviet Union to take up position on the Manchurian air bases. These new units included many skilful Russian pilots who proved to be aggressive opponents during January 1953. Sabre pilots reported dogfights with a distinctive enemy squadron camouflaged in blue undersides and copper top surfaces. Their trick was to participate in the big formations flying south – the 'trains' – and then dive down four or eight at a time from 40,000 feet to surprise the Sabres. However, the new F-86F was happy at 40,000 feet and some of the MiG pilots were startled to find the American jets opening fire on them at their high cruising altitudes.

Scores mounted steadily and on 26 May 1953 three members of the 334th Squadron shot down four MiGs in a single mission. One was the first jet fighter ace in history, Major James Jabara, leading a flight that included Lt Bill Mailloux and Lt Richard Frailey. They intercepted a large 'train' of MiG-15s at a time when they expected the communist pilots to be low on fuel. The MiGs slowly turned towards the Yalu but took no evasive action. Jabara fired on two, destroying both; Frailey found himself flying alongside a MiG and turned into him, forcing the pilot to eject; Bill Mailloux shot down the fourth. Being numerically outnumbered rarely concerned the Sabre pilots. Odds of ten to one were common but in the experience of most the MiGs would either escape or turn away after a few seconds of combat. On 18 February 1953 a flight of four F-86s had engaged a communist train of 48 MiGs in the vicinity of the Suiho Reservoir. The Sabres shot down two while two more lost control during violent evasive action and crashed. Twenty-five MiGs were downed in February 1953 for the loss of two Sabres; in March the score was 34 MiGs against two Sabres; in April 29 MiGs were downed; in May, 58; in June, 78; and in July, 33. The last of these was destroyed by Lt Sam Young of the 51st Fighter Wing on 22 July 1953, five days before the armistice.

## ATTACHED PILOTS WITH THE SABRE SQUADRONS

Pilots from the US Marine Corps, the US Navy, the Royal Air Force and the Royal Canadian Air Force were attached to the Sabre squadrons during the Korean War. Their first kills came during 1950–1. Lt Commander Paul E. Pugh USN destroyed a MiG-15 on 22 December 1950; Flt Lt J.A.O. Levesque RCAF shot his down on 31 March 1951; Captain William F. Guss USMC claimed his first on 4 November 1951. Canadian pilots went on to destroy eight more MiGs, the highest scoring pilot being Flt Lt Ernest A. Glover who was credited with three confirmed kills. Most RAF pilots served with the 51st Fighter Wing based at Suwon (K-13). They included Flt Lt Timothy J. McElhaw and F/O John N. Murphy assigned to the 16th Fighter Interception Squadron (FIS); Flt Lt J. Dickinson and Flt Lt John E.Y. King posted to the 25th FIS; and Flt Lt Granville White who served with the 39th FIS. They had all converted to the F-86 in the United States and were designated as 'combat capable' on the F-86 Sabre.

F/O John Murphy was a Meteor pilot based at Horsham St Faith, Norfolk, UK. He was then attached to the United States Air Force and did his conversion and combat training at Nellis Air Force Base near Las Vegas. His comment was, 'Quite a posting!' He proved that the F-86E could dive at supersonic speed. As he put it:

> I pushed it down over the Nevada desert and read off the Mach numbers on the dial: Mach 1.1, 1.2, 1.3. I thought this was fast enough and pulled back on the stick. The hydraulics were beautiful in the F-86. Yes, it went supersonic which was something the MiG-15 could never do, not even in a dive, despite the stories that went around.[2]

Their skill was much appreciated by their fellow USAF pilots and none more so than by 2/Lt Robert D. Carter whose introduction to combat was as wing man to Flt Lt John Nicholls, an experienced RAF exchange pilot serving with the 335th FIS. Nicholls was flying the new F-model Sabre, slightly faster than Carter's E version. Nicholls pulled ahead, shooting chunks off a fleeing MiG-15. Carter was pursued by a determined 'honcho' and was a very worried pilot until saved by Nicholls and a distinguished US pilot, Captain Druen, who became a general in the USAF. Nicholls destroyed two MiG-15s in Korea and later became Air Marshal Sir John Nicholls commanding RAF Tactical Air Command. Flt/Lt Granville White shot down a MiG on 29 June 1953; while Squadron Leader Graham S. Hulse flying with the 336th FIS scored three victories between October 1952 and March 1953. Sadly, Flt Lt John King fell victim to radar-controlled flak firing through cloud.

## 'BED CHECK CHARLIES'

These were usually sturdy Second World War Polikarpov PO-2 bi-plane trainers supplied by Russia to the North Korean Air Force. Their role in Korea was to harass UN positions in 'nuisance raids' – night attacks, mainly behind the 'Main Line of Resistance.' Though their antiquity and slow-flying limitations were often derided, their North

Korean pilots achieved some surprising results and were carefully stalked by UN night-fighters. Based on Sariwon airstrip, two PO-2s bombed the Suwon air base and an Inchon vehicle park on 14/15 June 1951. On 16/17 June two PO-2s took off to attack Suwon and Inchon. Lt La Won Yung arrived over Suwon runway and was amazed to find the 4th Fighter Wing's air base brightly illuminated. He bombed the carelessly dispersed F-86s of the 335th Squadron, destroying one and seriously damaging four more.

Although the Bed Check Charlies were hard to intercept as they flew under the UN radar, US night-fighters had some modest success against these intruder aircraft. Captain Dick Heyman, piloting a B-26, flamed a PO-2 on 23 June while a Marine F7-F Tigercat shot down another on 30 June. Two more were destroyed between July and September. Later in the year the Americans armed T-6 Texans (the cherished mount of the Mosquito pilots) as a potential interceptor; and modified Lockheed F-94 Starfire night-fighters to combat them. One F-94 shot down a PO-2 but had throttled back to fire at the slow-flying biplane and stalled into the ground, killing its crew. Another Starfire had the misfortune to collide with a PO-2 and crash. Bed Check Charlies remained a threat for the remainder of the war. Their most spectacular success (using Yak trainers as well as PO-2s) was over Inchon in 1953 when the Bed Check Charlies destroyed a UN dump containing 5 million tons of fuel.

# CHAPTER 14

# Propaganda and Public Opinion

## THE LEAFLET WAR

On the 'Main Line of Resistance' propaganda leaflets were used by both sides to persuade the enemy soldiers to surrender and thus enjoy a happy and secure future away from the dangers of shot and shell. There was nothing new in the idea or in the forms adopted, both being commonly used in the two World Wars. While communist propaganda was designed to be far more insidious in that it tried to undermine the soldier's faith in his beliefs and values and then exploit his natural desire to return home to his family, the UN propaganda tended to stress the superiority of UN weapons and the inevitable death awaiting those who faced the rockets of the fighter-bombers or the cold steel of Turkish and Australian bayonets. Both sides swiftly re-discovered the golden rule of propaganda: it must be credible to those who actually read it.

## FORMS OF UN PROPAGANDA

This was well-illustrated shortly after the Chinese had intervened in November 1950. UN propaganda leaflets had been printed to show the devastating effect of a Turkish bayonet charge. They depicted a Turkish officer posed before a number of Chinese corpses. However, during the interval between printing the leaflets and their air drop on the Chinese, the Turkish Brigade had been severely mauled by superior Chinese forces. This Turkish defeat (and subsequent withdrawal for re-equipment and reinforcement) was well known to both the

Chinese and UN soldiers. Consequently, when Chinese infantrymen and grenadiers were captured in possession of these leaflets they asked their interrogators why the UN chose to print lies. It was difficult to persuade the captured Chinese that the statements had been true when they were printed! The lesson from this was that presenting a previous truth as a propaganda weapon is useless if the situation has undergone change. In other words, truth is not always a good propaganda weapon as it may lead to a loss of credibility in the eyes of the recipient! Thereafter the UN propagandists printed leaflets that showed a 'general truth' that obtained at any time: for example, that UN fighter-bombers, called down by ground controllers, could make life unbearable for Chinese soldiers.

   Other UN leaflets also misfired, notably one suggesting that Chinese soldiers had been propelled into the Korean War by Stalin and his puppet, Mao Zedong. The Chinese script, reading from left to right, proclaims that:

> *Chinese communist soldiers are pushed into the war on*
>   *behalf of the Russians.*
> *These are the Russian imperialists.*
> *This is the Chinese Communist Party.*
> *These are the Chinese soldiers.*

On the reverse, the UN propagandists actually printed the following:

> *Chinese soldiers, do not be misled by the Communist Party.*
> *The Russians are now in control of your homeland and*
> *have forced the Chinese Communist Party to join in the*
> *Korean War. Brave Chinese soldiers must now refuse to die*
> *for Russian imperialists. Oppose communism, resist the*
> *Russians.*

For the Chinese soldier reading this leaflet, the effect must have been both confusing and misleading. Most had already been persuaded by their political commissars that the United Nations were the aggressor and that UN troops had actually invaded China. Some prisoners-of-war captured in November-December 1950 firmly believed that they were still in Manchuria! Most were convinced that Stalin was their ally and a great friend of Mao Zedong. Had not the two leaders formed a great alliance? And had not Stalin promised as many tanks, aeroplanes and machine-guns as the People's Volunteers required? Again, this is an example where the propaganda failed to win credibility with its target audience.

## CHINESE PROPAGANDA: LEAFLETS AND BANNERS

The Chinese showed greater resourcefulness than the UN in devising propaganda themes. Their leaflets asked the American soldiers why they were risking their lives in Korea whilst the war profiteers had a good time with their girlfriends in the Florida sunshine; why they were shivering in the winter snows at Christmas time eating frozen rations, always on the lookout for an enemy attack, when their parents who loved them wanted them back home? The message was always the same: that American troops should surrender as there was no disgrace in quitting an unjust war. Chinese mortars propelled hundreds of these leaflets into the UN front line. Most contained a safe conduct pass with the phonetic forms of 'Surrender' printed in Chinese and Korean. All promised 'unconditionally' the main freedoms of the 'Lenient Policy': freedom from injury, maltreatment and abuse; medical treatment; and retention of all personal possessions.

Chinese propagandists waxed lyrical on the evils of American capitalism, on the 'fat cats' of the US armaments industry who profited from the war while ordinary GIs were dying in Korea. A rather gruesome form of this was painted on a canvas banner and, though it depicted dead American soldiers, it was placed in front of British positions on the MLR. It was captured by 2/Lt J.R.M. Keatley and his platoon of the Duke of Wellington's Regiment on Christmas Eve 1952. He later recalled that, 'We had moved into a position north of Seoul . . . Although the manoeuvre had been carried out in the utmost secrecy we were, nevertheless, 'welcomed' by the Chinese forces over a loudspeaker. I was called by one of my Section Posts who heard noises on the wire in front. I . . . had more machine-guns trained on the spot . . . In the morning the wire was festooned with banners, Christmas cards, badges and miscellaneous propaganda.'[1]

Christmas cards from the Chinese People's Volunteers often carried the usual pleading letter:

*Dear Soldiers*
*It is Christmas and you are far from home not knowing*
*when you will die. The big shots are home, enjoying*
*themselves, eating good food, drinking good liquor. Why*
*should you be here risking your life for their profits?*
   *The Koreans and Chinese don't want to be your enemies.*
*Our enemies and yours are those who sent you here and*
*destroyed your happiness. Soldiers! Let's join hands! You*
*belong back home with those who love you and want you*
*back, safe and sound. So we wish you . . .*
   A MERRY CHRISTMAS AND A HAPPY NEW YEAR
   *From the Chinese People's Volunteers*

Occasionally the Chinese hoped to divide the British from their American comrades with leaflets claiming that America was breaking up the British Empire, destroying its economy and wrecking British homes. These leaflets deplored the fact that Americans, General Mark Clark and General Matthew Ridgway, commanded British troops in Korea and Germany; and that 'Even the British Navy, pride of the British Empire – Rule Brittania, Brittania [*sic*] rules the waves' was commanded by Americans in the Far East and Europe. They assumed that British soldiers were concerned about or ignorant of the structure and purpose of the North Atlantic Treaty Organization and the United Nations Command. Colin Ross, who served in Korea, had very clear ideas: 'Ridgway was a soldiers' General and we knew he cared for men, unlike MacArthur . . .'[2] British soldiers, on the whole, were grateful enough for American food, transport, clothing and equipment not to take these Chinese statements seriously, though they may have been somewhat disgruntled by the following Chinese message:

*Brothels, exclusively catering for Americans, are operating*
*in Cambridge, Oxford, Norwich, Hunstanton, Newmar-*
*ket, King's Lynn . . . No decent women walking in the*
*Oxford streets can avoid being insulted . . . Housing is*
*given to Yanks while World War II veterans, who have*
*been on the waiting lists for five years and more, have to go*
*on waiting.*

Sometimes the Chinese deliberately exploited the racial discord that existed within the United States Army, especially after the unfortunate performance of the all-black 24th Infantry Regiment in the 25th Infantry Division whose three battalions represented the first complete US regiment to see service in Korea. It had arrived in Pusan on 12 July 1950 and just over six weeks later it came under heavy NKPA fire while guarding the approaches to Sangju. Most black private soldiers broke and ran, abandoning a great deal of equipment. The 24th was clearly ill-trained and prone to 'bugging out' when under fire – a situation, of course, that was not unique to the 24th Infantry. However, because of the desperate shortage of infantry soldiers the 24th was returned to action with its problems of discipline and respect for officers and senior NCOs ignored and unsolved. Later on it deserted again when defending Haman, returned to fight a second battle east of the suburbs where groups of black NCOs and private soldiers fought well against the NKPA. Nevertheless, the bulk of the 24th deserted in the face of the enemy. On 14 September two companies fled when attacked by NKPA units, by which time no military commander was prepared to employ the regiment in battle and even looked askance at the rest of the 25th Infantry Dvision.

These events encouraged the US Army to question its own policy on racial segregation. First, however, it was determined to punish the 24th Infantry and 36 black soldiers faced courts-martial for 'misbehaviour in the face of the enemy.' Black reaction in the USA was intense and the Chinese propagandists capitalized on this by accusing the Americans of 'Jim Crow' persecution of black soldiers in Korea. Their leaflets asked the blacks to be 'true to your race.' Claiming to be hostile to racial persecution and in favour of equality and mutual respect between the races, the Chinese urged black soldiers to abandon the war and fight 'Big Brass' and 'Big Business' in order to transform America into a world where all races would be equal. This argument echoed some Japanese sentiments during the Second World War when they sought to create their 'Co-Prosperity Sphere'.

In this case Chinese propaganda badly misfired for the US Army adopted racial integration in the face of all its traditions and deeply embedded prejudice. It was not achieved overnight but slowly, through rotating units and by the careful distribution of black reinforcements and replacements. Gradually, senior American officers came to appreciate that black and white soldiers in the same platoon or the same section would fight well if led by NCOs and officers for whom they had respect. They had before them the example of the 3rd Battalion (all-black) that fought well during the retreat to the Pusan

Perimeter side by side with its other two battalions (all-white) of the 9th Infantry Regiment. Black and white soldiers in the 9th Regiment appeared to enjoy mutual respect. This respect had to be founded on equal opportunities for blacks and whites alike – not an easy prospect for the many blacks whose educational and social potential had been so seriously neglected for decades. From this group in particular many recruits were drawn to fight in units in Korea and they forged an early comradeship with white GIs which would blossom among the 'grunts' in the horrors of Vietnam.

It is worth remembering that the first Congressional Medal of Honor awarded in Korea went to Private First Class William Thompson, a black GI serving in Company M of the 24th Infantry; and that Benjamin O. Davis, former commander of the all-black 332nd Fighter Group in Italy, had risen to the rank of brigadier-general. In July 1951 the Army, with the approval of the President, decided that full integration should proceed forthwith though it regretted that the 24th Infantry would have to be disbanded. Despite hostility from certain formations, particularly the National Guard Divisions, integration within the US armed services in Korea and elsewhere was achieved more quickly and more smoothly than in the rest of American society which was then on the edge of the great struggle for Civil Rights. Occasionally, the Chinese responded to political developments or changes of policy with a vigorous propaganda leaflet campaign. For example, when the possibility of atomic attacks on Chinese positions was mooted by the world's newspapers, a development that worried Mao Zedong and Stalin enormously, the response was to quote western statements out of context:

> *FRONTAL ATTACK?*
> *ATOM BOMBS?*
> *AMPHIBIOUS LANDING?*
>
> *NONE OF THEM CAN CRACK THE*
> *KOREAN AND CHINESE*
> *Here is what two American newspapermen say:*
> - *'A frontal attack on the existing Chinese line can not be considered since the line is now 20 miles deep and the enemy forces are much too well dug in.'*
> - *'For the same reason tactical employment of atom bombs in Korea would probably be fruitless.'*

- *In a landing, 'casualties can run up to 50,000 or more.' A landing force might be 'caught in a double envelopment and wiped out.'*
*You can't win in war, but you can have peace today . . .*

When in 1953 General Eisenhower became President of the United States and promised that he would bring an end to the war in Korea, the communists were perturbed at his willingness to escalate air, land and sea operations against North Korea. Their response was to denigrate the new President:

*DON'T LET IKE SEND YOU*
*TO DESTRUCTION!*

*He was eleced to bring peace in Korea, but he's landing you in endless war.*
*'WE WANT PEACE,' said Mao Zedong, leader of the Communist people on February 7 [1953]. We want to stop the war at once and leave other questions for later settlement. But the American imperialists prefer not to. All right then, we'll go on fighting them. We'll fight them for how many years they want to fight. We'll fight them till we gain complete victory. The Chinese mean what they say. Remember how Zhou Enlai warned MacArthur!*

*DON'T LET IKE SEND YOU TO DESTRUCTION.*
*DON'T FIGHT HIS WAR, AND HE'LL HAVE*
*TO CHANGE HIS TUNE*

*YOUR LIFE DEPENDS ON IT!*

## AN EVALUATION

Leaflet propaganda was supplemented by publications such as *PEACE*, a newspaper published by the communist Peace News Press and by western newspapers such as *The Daily Worker* in Britain. As far as the UN troops were concerned Chinese leaflet propaganda made little or no impact. Leaflets were discarded or kept as mementoes of the long days and nights spent at the 'sharp end'. If anything, the leaflet propaganda revealed more about the current Chinese mentality and its anxieties than the susceptibility of UN troops to communist arguments. Admittedly, the UN troops were not well-informed about world affairs or about the general war situation in Korea. Their different governments had provided booklets of information, usually issued before the troops departed for Korea. The British War Office produced *Notes on Korea* in August 1950. Part I explained why soldiers were posted to Korea, what had happened there and the current military situation. The *Notes*, bound in neat blue covers, emphasized in capital letters that British soldiers were going to Korea to help the South Koreans liberate their country from the invaders. They rammed home the point that the troops would be fighting for the Charter of the United Nations and to ensure that the world – not just Korea! – would in future be safe from those who wished to govern by force.

These stirring words were followed by a description and assessment of the enemy, his weapons and tactics. Part II described the country, the people, protection against disease; and gave hints on how to pronounce the Korean language when dealing with currency, measures and dates. The *Notes* were reissued in May 1952 under Code No. 10134 to accommodate the entry of the Chinese and to emphasize their skill and bravery in combat. Somehow, not all battalions received the updated *Notes*, for example the Royal Fusiliers. Undoubtedly, many soldiers were acquainted with the *Notes*; some of the doggerel verse that circulated in the battalions reflected their content!

On the whole, military information of this kind and enemy propaganda made little impact on the troops in the MLR. For most, the war was what was happening around their own hill or their own bunker. During combat, when the shells and mortars were landing on their positions and the sound of a Chinese bugle was only a few yards away, they were not even always sure who was on their left and right flanks. For the fighting men in any war, the 'big picture' is notoriously elusive. Information came to the soldiers through local brigade/divisional publications such as *The Circle*, *Crown News* and the American *Stars and Stripes*, through letters from home and out-of-date hometown newspapers. Occasionally they would hear rumours from drivers bringing up supplies from the rear, or news items from the American Forces Network radio broadcasting from Tokyo and picked up on the Signals radio truck. The fighting man in Korea, if he were well-fed, warm and equipped with effective weapons in a secure position backed by air support and protective artillery, was rarely susceptible to any form of propaganda. But, as ever, he was always prone to rumours of relief, 'Tokyo leave', better beer and the prospect of 'demob' and a quick return home.

## PUBLIC OPINION

For most of 1950–3 the effect of the Korean war on public opinion in the west was marginal, an extraordinary situation when it was, for the British at least, the third biggest conflict of the century. This lack of interest, the result of a paucity of information, contrasted strongly with the government propaganda issued by China and the Soviet Union. They were determined to keep their peoples abreast of the situation as reported by the communist press and radio. Such little research that has been done on this subject suggests that Korea's history in the past two centuries and even her geographical location meant little or nothing to most people in Britain and North America. It was just another 'faraway country of which we know nothing' as Czechoslovakia had been in 1938. For most people in Britain, Europe and the USA, *The Land of The Morning Calm* was virtually unknown. Few books on Korea were available in western languages immediately after 1945 and the country's difficulties were not a priority in an age of dangerous crises that flared between the west and the communist world. The Second World War and its immediate and stressful aftermath was perhaps too close for people to be concerned about events in the Far East. In 1948 attention focused on Europe where Germany and Austria were divided into occupation zones, where Berlin was a potential flashpoint and the scene of the famous airlift that persisted into 1949. There were problems within the failing British, French and Dutch empires and the inexorable advance of Mao Zedong's Chinese Red Army threatened the existence of Hong Kong.

Dr James E. Hoare has researched the prevailing attitudes among the British people during 1950–1. For his paper to the British Association of Korean Studies he drew on the Mass-Observation Archive presently lodged in the University of Sussex. Mass-Observation had been established in the mid-1930s as a means of defining characteristics of life in Britain, largely for the benefit of social scientists. Its method of asking standardized questions of ordinary people in relation to specific events was adopted by the government during the

Second World War and used to examine the state of public morale, especially in heavily-bombed cities such as Kingston-upon-Hull.

Mass-Observation moved into action as soon as the Korean War began and one of its first interviews was on a train with a young man travelling to London on 28 June 1950, three days after the North Korean attack. He said he had heard of the fighting and thought that it might be taking place in Karachi. At least he 'knew it began with a K.' A group of 'working class' people interviewed in London a little later held diverse views. Some were worried about another war and the possible use of the atomic bomb, a feeling that would persist throughout the conflict. Others thought that it was wrong to involve Britain in a struggle that seemed to be about the independence of the Korean people; or that, if Britain became too enmeshed, the fighting in Korea could turn into a world war. Women were especially terrified by such a prospect. So many had spent sleepless nights in air raid shelters during the last war fearing for their children and their husbands in the services. Some younger adults, however, had grown up in war and accepted it almost as a normal state of affairs. This was not restricted to men; young women believed that it was necessary to fight to stop aggression. Wasn't that the reason, they asked, why we had fought the Second World War?

There was also another problem regarding information circulated to the public that Attlee's Labour government never really solved. Though the Prime Minister and his Foreign Secretary were firmly behind the United Nations they did drag their feet before sending the Argylls and the Middlesex from Hong Kong to Korea. Moreover, they never truly explained Britain's precise military and diplomatic position. As North Korea was not an independent state recognized by the United Nations it was impossible for America or Britain or France to declare war. Thus for some time the conflict was described as a 'police action' and not a war. This quandary even beset the lexicographers of *Encyclopaedia Britannica* who were unsure how to classify the conflict.[3] Linked with this uncertainty was a tinge of British hostility towards the United States. Large numbers of British servicemen had been in action side-by-side with US troops or following up US operations, in North Africa, Italy and in France and Germany after D-Day. So when British troops had to rescue Americans from battles in North Africa, or suffer 'friendly fire' when the US Flying Fortresses missed the 'bomb-line' in Normandy, they understandably became critical of their transatlantic allies. This adverse criticism sometimes permeated the civilian population whose received view of American servicemen during 1942–5 was that they were 'Over paid, over sexed and over here.' Perhaps that was why one woman old enough to remember all this said that she 'hoped that they [the Americans] go down the pan until our boys get there.'

This last view largely disappeared once the North Korean advance threatened Pusan. However, doubts were expressed about the wisdom of crossing the 38 degree Parallel after the successful Inchon landings and the recapture of Seoul. Yet a general view persisted that the communists were the aggressors and that Britain should play a part in resisting them. Precisely how the £4.7 billion pledged for rearmament by the Labour government would be found at a time of rising inflation and a devalued pound was never fully explained. Public opinion resented increases in the cost of living unmatched by improvements in the quality of life and, when questioned, blamed the war in Korea. Nevertheless, the war itself and the reasons for British participation were not major issues in the 1951 general election which saw Labour's defeat and the return to power of Winston Churchill and the Conservatives. Yet the war made a direct impact on thousands of British families whose sons were conscripted into the armed forces from 1947 onwards. Initially, all young men were called up at 18 for 18 months National Service. Later, this was extended to two years. There was also a call for volunteers with previous military service to reinforce infantry battalions in Korea. This was K-Force. Almost all the volunteers had little or no interest in the rights and wrongs of the war in Korea. Bored with 'civvie street', they rejoined the Army for excitement. This struck the *Picture Post* as newsworthy and the magazine ran a feature on K-Force volunteers and their less willing comrades, the Z Reservists.

Throughout the war, *Picture Post* and *The Illustrated London News* were major sources of information and photographic coverage. Reports from *Picture Post's* Stephen Simmons and photographer Haywood Magee set the high standard followed by later war reporters, all of whom faced considerable personal danger. Simmons was later killed when the transport aircraft in which he was a passenger crashed. *The Times* and *Daily Telegraph* correspondents, Ian Morrison and Christopher Buckley, were both killed early in the war. James Cameron had a charmed life and gave a graphic account of the Inchon landings in *Picture Post*. So did General MacArthur's favourite reporter, Marguerite Higgins, the outstanding *Life* photographer and *New York Herald Tribune* correspondent. Yet despite their sacrifices and the high quality of their professional journalism, they were unable to sustain public interest in the conflict over the next two years. Some news items aroused public revulsion, notably the manner in which Syngman Rhee treated his political suspects and the propaganda surrounding the 'germ warfare' charges, but again public concern for such matters did not persist.

Lt Col A. J. Barker, in his account of the battles on the Hook, offered one explanation for British public reaction to the war. He maintained that people gave only 'fitful attention' to reports from Korea. Once they had heard stories of hordes of Chinese soldiers blowing whistles and sounding trumpets as they swarmed over 'our boys' positions in the dead of night they did not want to hear them again. Similarly, photographs of innocent people caught up in the maelstrom of a mobile war could make only limited appeal to a public hardened by pictures of Buchenwald and Belsen. Pathetic refugees did not win instant support in societies who had seen millions of them in the Second World War. Television, of course, was absent from Korean battlefields so that newsreel accounts of artillery bombardments and headlines proclaiming another advance or another retreat lacked the 'reality' and 'instant information' characteristic of modern visual coverage. Col. Barker argued that these news items represented just 'one more monotonous element' in the Britain of the early fifties. People were far more concerned with unexpected National Health charges for dentures and spectacles and in the exciting revelations of treachery by Guy Burgess and Donald MacLean than in another Asiatic conflict to which most could not relate. Public interest was only awakened by the heroic stand of the 'Glorious Gloucesters' in April 1951 but it was not sustained partly because of the publicity surrounding the Festival of Britain.[4]

This is perhaps a sad portrait to paint of public attitudes in the early fifties but it was true that when there were no set-piece battles or 'last ditch' heroics to report in the Press, people became bored; and once the peace talks began at Kaesong and the static war was fixed along the 'Main Line of Resistance', the media of the day offered very limited coverage of events in Korea. This was not peculiar to Britain. Norman Bartlett, in his *With the Australians in Korea*, observed that:

> The Press and public in Australia soon lost interest in this sort of warfare . . . patrol actions were as real and danger-

ous to men who fought through the static war as the advances and withdrawals experienced by the 3rd Battalion in the first years. The trouble was that one patrol, to the outside world, was very much like another. The public was interested in spectacular advances or catastrophic defeats. A war that just went on and on ceased to mean much in strategic terms, although the tactical importance of the many patrol actions was enormous.[5]

Canada's government was concerned about public opinion and in 1952 became highly agitated over the Koje Island POW affair and the bad effect events there might have on Canadian public opinion. Brigadier M.P. Bogert had issued the order for Baker Company, 1st Royal Canadian Regiment, to proceed to Koje-do to help restore order. In Canada the government was infuriated that there had been no reference by the UN Command to Ottawa before issuing that order. In fact the order came down the usual chain of command to Brigadier Bogert – from General Mark Clark through Eighth Army channels to the Commonwealth Division. The saga of Dodd and the Koje-do riots had been widely reported in the Canadian press and Prime Minister St Laurent believed that those reports highlighted American maladministration. To bring in Canadian troops to help sort out the problem was, in his view, a device to include Canada's soldiers in that maladministration and for them to share in the 'blame'. According to the *Official History of the Canadian Army*, revelations of this kind would have 'an unfortunate effect' on the Canadian people. General Mark Clark was mystified by this, assuming that it was a perfectly normal matter to ask UN soldiers to guard prisoners-of-war. After all, the men of 1 RCR had probably helped to capture some of those prisoners. Baker Company 1 RCR left Koje-do on 10 July 1952 having established excellent relations with both the prisoners and the US forces there. Far from being a public scandal, their success on Koje-do, which they shared with Britain's B Company 1 KSLI, was a remarkable and praiseworthy achievement.

Certain myths appeared during the Korean War and entered national and international folklore. Most enduring was the belief that Prime Minister Attlee's visit to President Truman in 1951 prevented the use of the atom bomb against China and North Korea. Reports of the actual discussions and their outcome were largely ignored as the media preferred simple but startling headlines, still characteristic of newspapers today. Yet little attention was given to the more active consideration of the use of nuclear weapons in the final year of the war. Prime Minister Churchill was often criticized for changing his mind about Korea, that he became increasingly sceptical about British participation there. For a time this was true but after his old wartime colleague General Eisenhower became President of the United States his enthusiasm for the fray increased in the genuine hope that the deadly air war being conducted by the Americans, plus the tenacious UN stand along the MLR, would force the communists to reach agreement in the peace talks and end the war. He was prepared to go to some lengths to achieve this. On 30 June 1953, when the chance of an armistice was being threatened by the obstinacy of Syngman Rhee, Churchill sent a personal telegram to 'Ike' via the British Ambassador. In it he expressed the thought that Syngman Rhee should either be arrested or dismissed as South Korea's President; and, if necessary, he was prepared to send an extra brigade of British troops from Egypt to Korea.[6]

Apart from South Korea, the United States made the biggest sacrifices in the Korean War. Public opinion hardened against the war after the dismissal of its wartime hero, General MacArthur, and there was opposition to the draft whenever there was news of heavy American casualties. During 1952–3 there was similar public opposition to National Service in Britain but for entirely different reasons, mainly linked to national expenditure on rearmament. Interestingly, neither the American nor the British soldiers conscripted for service in Korea were loud in their protests against the war. This amazed the communists who made every effort to convert POWs to their way of thinking. Certainly, some soldiers did confess that they had no idea what the war was about but that was probably due to the failure of their officers to make proper use of the relevant Army information publications that were issued to units at home and abroad. Publicity surrounded one soldier who stated on 'Radio Newsreel' that he had no idea why he was going to Korea. Worried by the bad effect this might have on public opinion, a major in the War Office asked the Foreign Office to take the matter up with the BBC. To his surprise, he discovered no-one was concerned; the BBC broadcast had already been cleared by the Army!

Col. Barker's charge against the public for its 'fitful attention' was echoed by most soldiers on the 'Main Line of Resistance.' By 1953 there was indeed a dearth of interest in the war, rekindled only when the horrors of those terrible battles on Pork Chop and the Hook were publicized. But the publicity remained transient as far as the national media was concerned. Local newspapers continued to cover the experiences of local boys and *The Scarborough Evening News* of 9 July 1953 was typical of journalistic reporting of the day. Under the headline NO HOLIDAY HERE, just above the advertisements for Quality Watches and the comic strip 'Here Comes Little Noddy . . .', Private George Jackson of the Duke of Wellington's Regiment is shown on look-out from his 'shell-spattered' communication trench gazing across No Man's Land to the Chinese positions. There is one sentence reminding readers of the recent Chinese attack on the Hook, one of the fiercest of the war.

When time-expired soldiers came back from Korea, many could hardly believe that they had been fighting on the other side of the world. No-one seemed interested in where they had been. No bands were playing. As one soldier put it, 'Returning home, one felt one had been on a trip to the moon.' When BBC TV reporters tried to interview returning POWs, they were steered away by the Army; and when it put on a programme about the war in Korea, the ratings promptly declined. Dr Hoare has argued, 'If no real attempt was made by the government to explain the war and Britain's part in it to the soldiers and sailors who went there, it is not surprising that little was done at home.'[7] This perhaps underestimates the value of the War Office *Notes on Korea* and the detailed accounts of the war provided by brigade newspapers. Yet the war must have had an impact on public opinion because the British Communist Party membership dropped from 43,000 in 1948 to 36,000 in 1952 and it did badly in the 1951 general election. Because of the lack of public knowledge and understanding Korea was not a well-remembered war and it soon became a forgotten war. In Britain, there was no national memorial until Her Majesty The Queen came to St Paul's to unveil the Korean War Memorial in March 1987. The first volume of the British Official History did not appear until 1990, 40 years after the war began; official accounts of the warfare itself had to wait until 1995.

# CHAPTER 15

# Canada, New Zealand and Australia: Their Special Contribution

## CANADA'S OVERALL CONTRIBUTION

Apart from Britain, Canada was the sole Commonwealth country to send a full brigade to fight the ground war in Korea. It mirrored Canada's generosity in the Second World War when she provided the RCAF aircrews for Bomber Command's 6 Group that flew Halifax and Lancaster bombers from Yorkshire and Durham against Germany. Very early in the Korean War Canada had dispatched three destroyers, HMCS *Sioux*, *Nootka* and *Huron*. Later they were relieved by *Athabaskan*, *Cayuga*, *Haida*, *Crusader* and *Iroquois*. All eight destroyers served with distinction in Korean waters. Twenty-two Canadian pilots saw combat service with the US Fifth Air Force. Flt Lt Ernie Glover flew with the 4th FIW at Kimpo in June 1952 and won both a Canadian and an American DFC. No. 426 Transport Squadron Royal Canadian Air Force carried freight and passengers from Washington State to Japan throughout the war. Several Canadian army officers flew as artillery observers in RAF Auster VI aircraft and American Texan T-6s.

However, Canada's particular contribution was the 'Canadian Army Special Force' announced by the Liberal Prime Minister Louis Stephen St Laurent on 7 August 1950. He promised a full infantry brigade to honour Canada's obligations under the United Nations Charter. This Special Force was to be composed entirely of volunteers and by the end of August applications to join exceeded 8,000. The three second battalions of three regular regiments formed the core of this new brigade: the Royal Canadian Regiment (RCR); the Princess Patricia's Canadian Light Infantry (PPCLI) and the Royal 22è Régiment (Vingt-Deux). Supporting arms included A Squadron of the 1/2 Armoured Regiment, 2nd Field Regiment Royal Canadian Horse Artillery, No. 54 Transport Company Royal Canadian Army Service Corps, a Brigade Signal Squadron, the 57th Royal Canadian Engineers, a Field Ambulance and a unit of the Provost Corps. Collectively, these units formed Canada's 25th Brigade.[1]

An advance party sailed from Seattle to Japan, expecting to establish a Canadian training ground on Okinawa. This was, however, changed to Korea so the Canadians did their battle training in the theatre of operations. The first battalion to reach Korea was the 2nd Battalion PPCLI, commanded by Lt Col J. R. Stone and they were posted to Miryang for training and sweeps against guerrilla forces. 2 PPCLI joined 27 Commonwealth Brigade on 17 February 1951 and in the hills flanking the Sangsok valley attempted the capture of Point 419. Their attack succeeded after 3rd Royal Australian Regiment provided support. At the end of the month the Canadians, together with the British, Greek, Australian, ROK and US forces, fought a series of unsuccessful hill battles against the Chinese 125th Division until, inexplicably, the Chinese withdrew along the entire front.

It was not long before the Chinese regrouped and launched their offensive against 27 Commonwealth Brigade just north of Kapyong village. In the battle that followed B Company of 2 PPCLI was rushed by 400 Chinese assault troops. Some ground was given but the Chinese were blasted by artillery and mortar fire and in a determined attack the PPCLI soon regained their lost positions. An air drop replenished ammunition, medical and food supplies and after a successful defence the Canadians counted their casualties: 10 killed and 23 wounded. Their success at Kapyong, contributing in no small way to the frustration of the Chinese advance on Seoul, won them a US Presidential Citation.

Meanwhile, the rest of the Special Force had assembled at Fort Lewis, Washington, and had been reconstituted as the 25th Canadian Infantry Brigade Group, commanded by Brigadier J.M. Rockingham. Three US troopships, *Marine Adder*, *President Jackson* and *General Patrick*, took the brigade to Japan and two ships docked at Pusan on 4 May 1951 and the other at Kure, Japan, on 6 May. They were part-equipped by the US Army, though the Canadians retained their Brens and small arms (Lee-Enfield rifles and Stens). Canadian armour was now represented by C Squadron Lord Strathcona's Horse and it had arrived at Pusan with its Achilles self-propelled guns, all of which featured somewhat vulnerable open fighting compartments. These were exchanged for American M-4 Sherman tanks. Similarly, the anti-tank platoons converted from their 17 pounders to American 75mm recoilless rifles. 2nd Regiment Royal Canadian Horse Artillery retained its 25 pounders and fired its first barrage against the enemy on 17 May 1951.

Three days later the Canadians joined in the general advance north, flanked by two US Regimental Combat Teams and just behind a battle group equipped with tanks. This was 'Task Force Dolvin' and its remit was to reach the 38 degree Parallel as quickly as possible. 25 Brigade advanced slowly up the Pochon valley and took up a position less than two miles from the junction of the Pochon and Yonpyong Rivers. Then, following on behind Dolvin Force, it held the high ground on the Parallel, backed by the 10th Philippine Battalion. The Strathconas and the Filipinos then crossed the 38 degree Parallel and advanced over six miles into North Korea. On 30 May 1951 the brigade was tasked with the capture of Chail-li and the capture of a series of hills in the Hantan valley. For the first time since they had entered North Korea they encountered determined resistance from the Chinese. The enemy were well dug-in with plenty of artillery and tank support, and the Canadians discovered that they were attacking on too wide a front and were devoid of adequate support. After losing six killed and 25 wounded the Brigade withdrew and Chail-li was eventually captured by the US 65th Regimental Combat Team on 5 June.

At this point 25 Brigade exchanged the 10th Philippine Battalion for its own 2nd PPCLI, previously under 28 Commonwealth Brigade's control. Then, within a few days, the 'Princess Pats' moved up to control the junction between the Hantan-Imjin Rivers and the rest of the brigade advanced to the outskirts of Chorwon which formed with Kumhwa the base of the famous 'Iron Triangle'. 25 Brigade now began a series of large-scale reconnaissance patrols, using Chunmasan as a firm base and moving north across a plain intersected by scores of streams and muddy ditches. They quickly discovered strongly-held Chinese bunkers and from here the enemy, part of the People's Volunteers' 192nd Division of the 64th Army, launched a fighting patrol against the Canadians on 18/19 July. This was repulsed by the Vingt-Deux. A much bigger attack during 19/20 July lasted three hours and the Chinese were forced to withdraw. Heavy rains and local floods made further operations impossible and the Canadians withdrew to firm ground south of the Imjin. Shortly afterwards 25 Canadian Brigade came under the command of General A. J. H. Cassels and was part of the first Commonwealth Division ever formed.

August was spent in patrols, all of which encountered opposition. In September, during Operation 'Minden', the brigade crossed the Imjin at Pintail Bridge and advanced to the 'Wyoming Line'. For Operation 'Commando', which began on 3 October, the Canadians advanced to the high ground overlooking the Nabu-ri stream, a tributary of the Samichon, to form the 'Jamestown Line'. They captured their objectives: Hills 187(a), 187(b) and Hill 159 on 4 and 5 October. This was their contribution to the 'Main Line of Resistance' for these were to be basically static positions until the end of the war. General Cassels favoured offensive raids against the enemy and the 25 Brigade Commander, Brigadier Rockingham, selected Hill 166 as the Vingt-Deux objective while Hill 156 and associated features went to the RCR and PPCLI.

Meanwhile, Chinese assaults were coming in at roughly battalion strength. The 2nd Princess Pats had already lost two killed and seven wounded on 12 October and it was important to deter them. Covered by the Sphinx Bofors guns firing over open sights, the RCR and the PPCLI reached the enemy bunkers and booby-trapped them. The Vingt-Deux had a tougher time when it ran into Chinese machine-gunners but close support from tanks and artillery ensured partial destruction of bunkers on Hill 166. Five Canadians were killed and 21 wounded in these patrol clashes which, over the next year, would become much more sophisticated and deadly in the paddy fields of No Man's Land.

However, the next attack on 2/3 November was a major assault on 25 Brigade's front and was stoutly resisted. Then came the Chinese attack on the adjacent 28 Brigade – the Chinese were clearly determined to capture Hills 217 and 317 – and persistent rushes against the 1st Princess Patricias. 25 Brigade responded by counter-attacking Hill 166 on 9 November with squads drawn from the Vingt-Deux. They reached the top of 166 but withdrew after stirring up enemy fire. Further Chinese attacks were directed at the crucially important Hills 227 and 355. Slopes on both hills changed hands several times during 22/23 November but the Vingt-Deux held on to its precarious positions on 227. Outposts were lost temporarily but men of the calibre of Corporal Major DCM, who was leading the Scout & Sniper Platoon, held on until 300 Chinese threatened to swamp his defences. He withdrew a few yards and called down mortar fire on the Chinese. Under accurate battalion fire, the Chinese advance stalled and then withdrew. For this display of leadership and heroism Corporal Major won a bar to his DCM. Altogether, seven Chinese attacks were directed against the Canadians. Almost all were at night but the Chinese were held on every occasion, thanks to the accuracy of the tank guns, the 81mm mortars and the artillery.

Armistice talks at Panmunjom resulted in an agreement on a demarcation line between the two sides (adopted 27 November), designed to endure for at least 30 days. For a time there was no offensive activity, just desultory artillery exchanges along the Canadian sector. Then on 10/11 December the Patricias attacked Hill 227 and the RCR sent a fighting patrol to 166 mainly to ascertain the latest state of Chinese defences that had been strengthened during the temporary lull. In January 1952 the 25th Canadian Brigade was relieved by 28 Commonwealth Brigade and for the next six weeks was held in reserve. It then returned to the Samichon positions and resisted a heavy Chinese attack on 25/26 March 1952. Rotation of Canadian soldiers occurred during March-April 1952 with the 1st Battalion of the RCR (Lt Col P.R. Bingham) and the 1st Battalion Vingt-Deux (Lt Col L. F. Trudeau) replacing the 2nd Battalions. The 37th Field Ambulance replaced the 25th; Brigadier Rockingham returned to Canada and was succeeded by Brigadier M.P. Bogert. The 23rd Royal Canadian Engineers replaced the 57th; the 1st Royal Canadian Horse Artillery replaced the 2nd; and B Squadron of the Strathconas replaced C Squadron.

During the Spring of 1952 the UN engaged in a series of 'snatch patrols' designed to capture live prisoners. 25th Brigade's special target was a Chinese-held feature known (from the shape of its contours) as the 'Boot'. On 20 May it fell to the 1st Patricias to launch a 'snatch' patrol against the Boot. An unusually large patrol commanded by Lt D. A. Middleton, 32 men in all, was split into a firm base squad, a covering fire group and a fighting patrol. They carried two radios and the fighting patrol had two Bren groups and two assault groups armed with Stens, grenades and coshes. Plenty of brigade firepower would back them up: 25 pounders, the Strathcona's tanks and heavy machine-guns. As the fighting section clambered up the hill, Chinese machine-gunners opened fire and several men, including Lt Middleton, fell wounded. Corporal Dunbar led the withdrawal and all patrol members, including the wounded, returned to their lines but without any prisoners. A similar raid by the Royal Canadian Regiment led by Lt A. A. S. Peterson on 31 May 1952 again failed to produce any prisoners. Lt Peterson had taken his patrol through the enemy trenches unopposed and reached the crest of Point 113. Suddenly Chinese troops poured out of their bunkers below and the patrol was lucky to be able to extricate itself with only four men wounded.

Throughout May and June 1952 the brigade devoted itself to patrol work. Each day the Canadians on the MLR suffered a Chinese artillery 'stonk' that seemed to be increasingly accurate and intense. Casualties in this period were not negligible: 21 Canadians killed, over a hundred wounded and one man taken prisoner. It was therefore with relief that the Canadians went into divisional reserve at the end of June and did not return to the line until 8/10 August 1952. During May-July Baker Company of the 1st Royal Canadian Regiment had been detached to serve side by side with B Company 1 Battalion King's Shropshire Light Infantry on Koje Island where they swiftly restored order and established a respectful – almost friendly – relationship with the prisoners.

Heavy Chinese shelling continued throughout August-October 1952 as the Canadians persisted with their 'snatch' patrols. Chinese patrols, determined to ambush the Canadian raiders, moved out of their bunkers and several fire-fights developed in No Man's Land after which both sides retired to lick their wounds but with little else achieved. Much more serious were the Chinese bombardments of Hill 355, 'Little Gibraltar', guarded by 1 RCR. On 1 October 1952 913 artillery shells and mortar bombs landed in the battalion area; next day Chinese shelling destroyed 'Vancouver' outpost (the Canadians had adopted the American system of outpost defence) and for the next three weeks the battalion as a whole came under heavy fire. The Canadian infantry stood-to every night expecting an attack but the Chinese seemed strangely reluctant. 1 RCR's War Diary noted that all they did was to throw stones!

B Company was determined to retaliate but was promptly ambushed on the night of 12/13 October. This persuaded the Canadians to limit their patrols to their more exposed outposts in the west. Vancouver was abandoned and was now known as 'Old Vancouver'.

Outpost 'Calgary' was strongly held and protected by a thickened minefield. B Company 1 RRC, commanded by Major E.L. Cohen, was in position on Hill 355 on 22/23 October 1952 and subjected to heavy shellfire and probing patrols from the Chinese. On 23 October shells and mortars deposited 40 or 50 rounds a minute on B Company. These wrecked all of B Company's bunkers, smashed the communication and fighting trenches and buried many weapons and ammunition. The scale of the bombardment had shattered the morale of several B Company soldiers. For a few more minutes the radios survived and B Company could keep in touch with Battalion HQ. Then they resorted to runners who had to pick their way across the debris of shattered communication trenches. At 1820 hours the most concentrated Chinese shelling yet experienced descended on B Company who estimated that the Chinese had increased their firepower in excess of 100 rounds a minute. Following on the edge of this barrage swarmed several hundred Chinese infantrymen and grenadiers, estimated at battalion strength. These troops attacked the remnants of the Canadian position. Smoke and dust obscured the fighting but Captain Doug Caldwell, the Forward Observation Officer for A Battery, 1 Royal Canadian Horse Artillery, brought down accurate fire just in front of B Company's battered bunkers. By 1836 hours Lt John Clark of 4 Platoon reported to Battalion HQ that his men had been overrun and just over an hour later Major Cohen and 5 Platoon managed to reach A Company, bringing in as many wounded as they could find. Cohen had no idea what had happened to 5 and 6 Platoons. B Company had disintegrated as a fighting force.

1 RCR, still uncertain about the enemy's precise intentions, decided to mount a counter-attack primarily to investigate the current situation among the outposts. Preceded by tank and mortar fire on the former B Company position, D Company's platoons moved forward just before midnight. They suffered a few casualties but reached their objective as planned early on 24 October. The situation, according to the RCR War Diary, was restored. All the Chinese had vanished, removing their wounded as usual, but a few 'dead' RCR men sprang to their feet! Led by Lt Gardner, the survivors of 5 and 6 Platoons had fought until they ran out of ammunition and then played dead as the Chinese overran them. For the RCR it had been a terrible night and foreshadowed the fighting that was to characterize the last eight months of the war. The battalion had suffered 75 casualties: 18 men killed, 43 wounded and 14 believed captured by the Chinese.

Over the next few days, RCR's patrols searched out several Chinese bunkers and these were destroyed by sappers. Their tour on the 'Main Line of Resistance' had cost 25 Brigade dearly. 1 RCR's total casualties were 191; the Patricias suffered 18; and the Vingt-Deux had 74.

25 Brigade was now withdrawn from the line. 1 PPCLI was replaced by the 3rd Patricias, commanded by Lt Col H. F. Wood, so that the 25 Brigade was now, on 3 November 1952, composed of:

1 Royal Canadian Regiment
1 Royal 22è Regiment
3 Princess Patricia's Canadian Light Infantry.

From now until 31 January 1953, when the Commonwealth Division was placed in reserve, the brigade settled down to a winter in the vicinity of that the all-important feature, the Hook. Canada's 23rd Field Squadron (it had replaced the 56th) began to restore, deepen and extend the Hook's defences, adopting the Chinese technique of deep tunnels in which infantry and artillery alike sheltered during heavy shellfire. The Canadian sappers had the help of the British infantry (The Black Watch) and Korean labourers. Korean engineer squads formed part of the Korean Service Corps (KSC) and these often included homeless or orphaned children who were given uniforms and badges to show the regiment or company they were serving. They usually functioned as 'domestics', cleaning out rear echelon bunkers and doing the washing. Some soldiers became greatly attached to these children and maintained contact after the war. Korean interpreters and liaison officers proved invaluable and by the Spring of 1953 every battalion in the Commonwealth Division, plus the engineers, could draw on 1,000 'KATCOMS' or *Korean Augmentation to the Commonwealth* troops. Three hundred joined the 25th Brigade, trained with Canadian smallarms and then were attached individually to a 'buddy' in the rifle companies. The Americans had already adopted the *Korean Augmentation to the USA* or 'KATUSAS' and all played an important role in the final battles of the war.

25 Brigade returned to the line with the rest of the Commonwealth Division during 6–8 April 1953 and during 19/20 April endured the last major Chinese assault on Canadian positions. It was holding the central sector of the Commonwealth Division front with 28 Commonwealth Brigade on its right and 29 Brigade on its left. Once more it

was the RCR – this time the 3rd Battalion – that was the main Chinese target. Lt Col K.L. Campbell carefully disposed his battalion on 187, a complex hill feature with B and C Rifle Companies holding the spurs jutting into the valley of the Nabu-ri and A and B Companies holding the high ground in the rear. Most exposed was C Company, located east of the largely destroyed village of Chinchon at which it received more than its fair share of Chinese shelling. The company numbered 130 including 22 Katcoms. Some 40 KSC personnel were strengthening the bunkers and digging tunnels while 20 more acted as porters bringing up ammunition, food and water.

Lt Col Campbell had no indication on 2 May that the Chinese were preparing to rush his positions. His appreciation of the situation was that Chinese mortars and field guns were sending over the usual 'stonk'. Enemy patrols, however, were unusually active in No Man's Land. His main fear was enemy infiltration between his battalion and the Patricias. Campbell therefore despatched an A Company ten-man patrol at 2030 hours in the direction of Chinchon to ambush any Chinese on their nightly forays. A Company's patrol slipped quietly through the gaps in the wire and minefields and for two hours met no opposition. Suddenly they were fired on by three groups of Chinese soldiers who killed or wounded half the patrol. Lt Col Campbell ordered the survivors to return and No. 8 Platoon was sent out to cover their retreat. Before long 8 Platoon was attacked and during their firefight the Chinese saturated C Company's bunker defences on Point 97. While the Canadians struggled to regain lost ground, three groups of Chinese infantry rushed C Company's positions, concentrating on Point 97 and Lt E.Y. Hollyer's No. 7 Platoon. Hollyer immediately called down air-bursting Variable Timed (VT) fire on the Chinese and directed the shellfire with the aid of a Royal Canadian Signals officer, Lt L. G. Colé.

Artillery saved the situation for C Company. No. 8 Platoon fended off a twin-pronged push against its position just behind No. 7 Platoon. Divisional shellfire now rained down on the Chinese. The enemy bombardment had numbered 2,000 shells. The brigade and divisional guns replied with 8,000 rounds that landed on the Chinese assault squads. Canada's own 81st Field Regiment worked non-stop, firing 4,300 rounds. Shortly after midnight the Chinese began to retreat from their footholds on Point 97, the artillery lifted its fire and Lt Hollyer's platoon chased off the last of the Chinese. Lt Col Campbell pulled out C Company and sent it into reserve for a well-deserved rest.

D Company replaced it and as the 3rd Vingt-Deux had just arrived it took over D Company's bunkers.

Intense fighting such as this had cost the enemy well over 80 dead. Canadian and Korean losses were relatively heavy: 25 RCR infantrymen killed, 28 wounded and 7 captured by the Chinese. Two Patricias and two gunners died under the Chinese barrage and seven more were wounded. Thirty-five Koreans were killed or wounded. But for the widespread use of the new armoured vest, introduced in July–August 1952, casualties during the 'Battle of Point 97' would have been even heavier. For the remainder of the war 25 Brigade was engaged in patrol work, carried out under persistent enemy shelling. A further 17 Canadians died during this period. Total deaths in Canada's 25 Brigade were 309 killed in action, 1,101 wounded and 32 taken prisoner. One hundred and one men suffered other injuries in Korea and 90 died. Proportionate to her population, Canada had made a bigger contribution than most other countries that sent ground forces to Korea, forces that had integrated with other Commonwealth countries to form the unique Commonwealth Division. It had marked the willingness of Canada to contribute to the high principles of the United Nations and a readiness to make sacrifices in the name of international peace and security, a process that remained of paramount importance for the remainder of the century. In the field, the Canadian soldiers may have seemed to other units in the division as more 'American' than 'British'. That may have had its root in envy of better Canadian rates of pay, better sleeping bags, better rations and plentiful supplies of better beer, notably 'Anniversary Ale,' 'A Gift to Canadian Troops in Korea From *Labatts*'! Their literature also seemed more American, especially the *Combat Kelly* comics written for USA consumption and popular with Canadian soldiers. But ever since the 2nd Battalion Princess Patricias had arrived in Korea, respect and admiration among Commonwealth and American troops for the fighting ability of Canada's 25th Brigade had never wavered.

NEW ZEALAND'S 16th FIELD REGIMENT, KOREA 1950–4

Britain, Canada and New Zealand all sent Field Regiments of Artillery to serve in Korea. The experience of the New Zealanders' 16th Field Regiment was typical of the artillery regiments and underlined their immense importance throughout the conflict. New Zealand's response to the United Nations' call for help to South Korea was to advertize for a thousand men to form the New Zealand 'Kayforce'. Six thousand – including many Maoris – responded and Brigadier R.S. Park was appointed to lead an expeditionary force to Korea. On 27 October 1950 the 16th Field Regiment, Royal New Zealand Artillery, came into being and its 25-pounder guns and heavy equipment left New Zealand aboard the freighter *Ganges* in November and headed for Pusan. The gunners left Wellington aboard the *Ormonde* on 10 December 1950 and reached Pusan on 31 December. United with their guns, they moved up to the training area at Miryang to calibrate the 25 pounders. During this move they suffered their first casualties. A battery sergeant major and his driver took the wrong turning in their jeep and ran into a guerrilla ambush. Both were killed, mutilated and robbed of their possessions.

A week later the 18th Field Regiment, commanded by Lt Col J.M. Moodie, drove north to join 27 Commonwealth Infantry Brigade. It relieved the American gunners equipped with 105 mm howitzers and on 29 January 1951 the regiment's 24 guns, located on frozen paddy fields, fired their first rounds into enemy positions near Naegon-ni. During February 1951 the Regiment's batteries fired in support of 1 Middlesex (Peter Battery), 1 Argyll and Sutherland Highlanders (Queen Battery), 3 Bn Royal Australian Regiment (Roger Battery) and the newly arrived 2 Princess Pats (Baker Battery). Two New Zealanders won decorations when spotting for 1 Middlesex during a Chinese attack in mid-February whilst 1 Middlesex was leading the brigade in its bid to relieve the Americans and French troops holding out in embattled Chipyong-ni. Captain A.A. Roxburgh, aided by wireless-operator Lance Bombardier H.K. McGubbin, was Forward Observation Officer (FOO) with A Company. Both came under attack from Chinese grenadiers who overran much of the company area. They remained at their post directing 18th Field Regiment's barrage, protected their equipment and killed several Chinese. Captain Roxburgh won the Military Cross; Lance Bombardier McGubbin the Military Medal.

The New Zealanders joined in the pursuit of the fleeing Chinese and gave support to ROK, US Infantry and Marine divisions. In April, when the Chinese made their two major thrusts towards Seoul and central Korea the regiment lay directly in front of the Chinese thrust along the Kapyong valley. There on 24/25 April 1951 the New Zealanders fired in support of the 3rd Royal Australian Regiment, the Middlesex and 2 PPCLI as they resisted Chinese attacks along the Kapyong. Chinese pressure was intense and the regiment, aided by US tanks and artillery, poured fire into the advancing Chinese ranks who appeared to ignore their hideous casualties. 3 RAR bore the brunt of the hand-to-hand fighting and they and the gunners between them inflicted over 4,000 casualties. On 25 April, ANZAC Day, 500 dead Chinese were piled in front of the Australians. They had stemmed the Chinese advance. President Syngman Rhee awarded his Unit Citation to the Regiment:

> The President takes profound pleasure in citing for excep-
> tionally meritorious service and heroism the 16th New
> Zealand Field Regiment . . . Its performance in the April
> enemy offensive merits the highest praise . . .

At the end of April, with the departure of the Argyll and Middlesex and the arrival of 1 King's Own Scottish Borderers and 1 King's Shropshire Light Infantry, 27 Brigade became 28 Brigade. The New Zealanders were now attached to 28 Brigade and supported the Commonwealth Division (formed 28 July 1951) for the remainder of the war. Each battery moved closer to the front line when giving covering fire to patrols, and during Operation 'Commando' advanced north of the Imjin to give support to the infantry as they took the high ground that would become the 'Main Line of Resistance.' No less than 72,000 rounds were fired by the regiment's 25 pounders during this operation. Until then there had been few casualties but as the Chinese brought in heavier guns their shelling hit the regiment's own positions. The most vulnerable, however, were the FOOs and their assistants in the forward observation posts (OPs).

It was in this context that the only New Zealand POW was captured. On 17 November 1951 Gunner N.G. Garland was spotting for a company of 1 KSLI during an attack on 'John', one of the so-called 'Four Apostles', the hills occupied by the Chinese behind 355. From the gunners' point of view Hill 355, 'Little Gibraltar', was of crucial importance because they could maintain two OPs on the crest and keep the Chinese under constant observation. The Four Apostles were frequently the target for ground and air attack and the infantryman's approach to these was via the infamous 'Bowling Alley.' Garland came under fire from a Chinese SU-76 self-propelled gun and his OP was overrun by enemy infantry. Recovering from the assault,

Garland met up with two KSLI soldiers and the three tried to evade the Chinese and head for Company HQ. They were almost through the first concertina wire obstacles when several Chinese appeared and levelled their burp guns at the three soldiers. There was no option but to surrender and Gunner Garland remained a prisoner of the Chinese for the next 21 months.

On 4 November FOO Major P.F. King MC won the DSO and his wireless operator, Gunner D.E. Rixon, won the DCM when spotting for C Company 1 KOSB. Chinese infantry were attacking and Major King and Gunner Rixon called down defensive fire (DF) and for a time the Chinese were held. Then they charged through the smoke, hurling grenades and spraying the OP with their burp guns. Maj. King and his wireless operator continued to direct fire until a grenade smashed the radio set. Both then picked up weapons and fought the Chinese in hand-to-hand combat. After two hours both were badly wounded and when C Company withdrew Gunner Rixon carried his officer to safety.

In December the regiment was put in reserve with the rest of 28 Brigade and returned to the line on 21 January 1952. A routine quickly developed with OPs established in forward positions for 12 weeks on and six weeks off. Interspersed with the live rounds were the propaganda shoots, showering enemy positions with leaflets urging them to surrender. In October the New Zealand batteries shelled Chinese assembly points during the Royal Canadian Regiment's struggle on Hill 355; in November it covered the Black Watch on the Hook; and in December its barrages gave some protection to the Royal Fusiliers during Operation 'Pimlico'.

The Commonwealth Division went into reserve just after Christmas 1952. It received many Christmas cards from the Chinese People's Volunteers and the Royal Fusiliers even had a tree! The New Zealanders remained on duty, supporting the Americans during February, when both sides engaged in numerous fighting patrols, and in March when the regiment fired thousands of shells against Chinese troops attacking the slopes of Little Gibraltar. One New Zealand gunner, W.L. Clarke, was evacuating wounded GIs from a position that was under Chinese attack. There were many stretcher cases and Gunner Clarke made several trips under enemy shellfire back and forth to the aid station. Each time he returned to the front line he brought back grenades and ammunition. His bravery led to the immediate award of the Military Medal.

On 8 April 1953 the Commonwealth Division returned to the line where it would face some of its toughest battles. During the Battle of the Hook which began on 28 May the regiment fired over 4,500 rounds. Later it supported the ROK units when the Chinese turned to attack them. And throughout this period the Chinese persisted in their attempts to destroy the OPs on the major hills – especially on Hill 159. This was much lower than 355 but it jutted out into the Chinese front lines and was an ideal assembly point for Commonwealth and US reconnaissance and fighting patrols. For a time a spare Centurion tank lived on 159, crewed by New Zealanders, to protect the vital OPs. When the war ended on 27 July 1953 the regiment was still in action, firing its last round at 0530 hours. In all, it had fired 800,000 shells – the highest tally of any Field Regiment in Korea. After the armistice, the regiment remained in Korea until October 1954. Most gunners then returned to New Zealand though some remained behind with the Royal New Zealand Army Service Corps. Sadly, 16th Field Regiment then ceased to exist. It had provided a remarkably consistent level of artillery support in a kind of war that was beyond previous experience. Those New Zealander gunners had served in combat for 2½ years and, as one Australian soldier said, 'They were always welcome.'

## THE OVERALL AUSTRALIAN CONTRIBUTION

The remarkable exploits of No. 77 Squadron Royal Australian Air Force have already been described, but it is worth recording that the squadron had just completed its tour of duty in Japan on 23 June 1950, two days before the NKPA crossed the 38 degree Parallel. Flying the remarkable Second World War Mustang, 77 Squadron had perfected air-to-ground gunnery, low-level rocketry and 60 degree dive-bombing techniques. The squadron had not been back to Australia since 1943 and the Mustangs were about to be crated and returned home. That they stayed to fight made them invaluable during the defence of the retreating ROK and American forces and, later, the Pusan Perimeter. 77 Squadron lost their first pilot, Squadron Leader Strout, on 7 July 1950. Just over a year later, 77 Squadron converted to the RAF's Gloster Meteor 8 jets and was the first to take this twin-jet into action against the MiG-15s on 29 August 1951. At the end of that year the squadron had lost 25 per cent of its pilots killed or captured. By August 1952 the Meteors had flown 8,000 sorties and several RAF pilots came out to Korea to gain combat experience on the Meteor. Six were killed during 1952–3. When the war ended the Australians had flown 18,872 sorties, lost 37 pilots killed and 7 captured.

From the beginning of the war Australia readily allocated her warships in Japanese and Pacific waters for service under General MacArthur's command. HMAS *Shoalhaven*, a frigate, and the destroyer HMAS *Bataan* became available on 29 June. HMAS *Warramunga*, another destroyer, would follow shortly to replace *Shoalhaven*. Australia's warships first saw action when *Bataan* engaged a shore battery – a role that would face the later Australian warships *Murchison*, *Anzac* and *Tobruk*. Australia's unique contribution was HMAS *Sydney*, a light aircraft-carrier that served in Korean waters from 30 September 1951 to 27 January 1952. Flying off her Sea Furies and Fireflies, *Sydney* averaged 55 sorties on each of the 43 flying days and lost 3 pilots, 8 Sea Furies and 9 Fireflies. Her achievements during her seven patrols, remarked Admiral Scott-Moncrieff, were 'quite excellent'. Nine Australian warships eventually saw service in the Yellow Sea and the Sea of Japan; their crews totalled 4,507 Australians.

The men of the 3rd Battalion The Royal Australian Regiment, sailed from Tokyo aboard the USS *Aiken Victory* bound for Pusan on 27 September 1950. On board were 960 volunteers drawn from Australia itself or from the units on occupation duties in Japan. Each man was selected for his physical fitness and his previous service as an infantryman. In a sense, these were all professionals, forming an élite battalion commanded by a veteran of the New Guinea battles, Lt Col C.H. Green. They joined the first two British battalions to arrive in Korea and took part in the invasion of North Korea. It was their misfortune to lose their colonel immediately after their victorious battle at Pakchon on 24 October 1950. In April 1951 3 RAR was one of the four units – the other three being 2 PPCLI, Company A US 72nd Tank battalion and the New Zealand gunners – defending Kapyong. Nowadays regarded as a model rearguard defensive action followed by a fighting withdrawal, Kapyong saw these units hold up the Chinese advance to Seoul. After their extraordinary defence at the Battle of Kapyong the battalion received its US Presidential Citation. Then came the saga of Maryang-san. Brigadier Coad later described 3 RAR the 'finest fighting battalion he had ever seen.' 3 RAR fought the battles on Hill 355 and soldiered on until they were joined by 1 RAR in 1952.

The 1st Battalion The Royal Australian Regiment commanded by Lt Col I. Hutchison DSO MC joined 28 British Commonwealth Brigade and relieved the Leicesters in June 1952. Thereafter, Australians commanded 28 British Commonwealth Brigade: Brigadier T.J. Daly 1952–3, Brigadier J.G.N. Wilton 1953–4 and Brigadier I. T. N. Murdoch 1954. 1 RAR served in Korea until March 1953 and was then replaced by the 2nd Battalion RAR, commanded by Lt Col C. F. Larkin. On 4 May 1953 it relieved 1 Royal Fusiliers and was promptly welcomed by the Chinese propaganda loudspeakers. Rainstorms seemed more of a menace than the Chinese and hindered any hope of a major action. Instead, 2 RAR engaged in numerous patrols until it went into reserve on 16 June.

The battalion came back in July to take over the battered features of the Hook and became involved in one of the last Chinese offensives of the war when the Marines and Turks on 2 RAR's left came under attack. Three positions ('Reno', 'Elko' and 'Vegas'), part of a series of ouposts called the 'Nevada Complex', were lost to the Chinese and this exposed the Hook as a salient jutting out into Chinese-held territory. One of the heaviest artillery barrages put down by the Chinese killed 5 Australians and wounded 24, including several KATCOMS, but the determined resistance put up by the Medium Machine-Gun Platoon machine-gunners led by Sgt B.C. Cooper on 24 July helped beat off the enemy attacks. Next night Lance Corporal K.H. Crockford heroically defended his bunker, called down VT fire and on several occasions crossed No Man's Land to pass information about enemy dispositions. Both soldiers received the Military Medal.

There were many such deeds among the Australians during the last battles around the Hook on 24/25 July 1953 and not least was the bravery shown by Lt P.O.G. Forbes, in command of the 2 RAR Assault Pioneers. His task was to repair the Hook defences and especially check the minefields in front of the forward trenches. Working at night and exposed to Chinese fire, he and his pioneers ensured that the Chinese attacks on 24/25 July were blunted by the defences he had created. For this Lt Forbes was awarded the Military Cross. It was estimated that over 2,000 Chinese dead lay in front of the Marine and Australian defences in a battle that had gained nothing of strategic importance for the enemy. Thirty minutes before the ceasefire eight Chinese soldiers advanced towards a 2 RAR outpost. The

Australians prepared to open fire but the Chinese made no effort to attack. For them the war was over.[2]

The contribution of Australia to the war in Korea, the bravery of her fighting men and their achievements in battle on land, sea and in the air were endorsed by all. Possibly the Korean War marked a new maturity in Australian political thinking. Undoubtedly, many saw a communist threat to an East Asian country as a menace to Pacific Rim security, an anxiety that persuaded both Australia and New Zealand to send armed forces to fight in Vietnam. Australia's leadership in the Pacific therefore has its roots in the Korean War and this was underlined when she spearheaded the United Nations Force that landed in East Timor during 1999.

# CHAPTER 16

# The Battles of the Hook
# and Pork Chop, 1952–3

## THE STRATEGIC IMPORTANCE OF THE HOOK

During 1952–3 the hill position known as 'the Hook' overlooked the Samichon valley and controlled the two main crossing points on the Imjin River. If the Chinese captured the Hook there was no immediate fall-back defensive line for the United Nations Forces, necessitating a retreat of at least five miles to the first high ground south of the Imjin. Such a retreat would leave the Chinese free to mop up the western sector of the US Eighth Army held by the Turkish Brigade and a single division of the US Marine Corps. From the UN positions on Yong Dong, a hill on other side of the Samichon River, the crescent-shaped Hook and its three related strongpoints on hills known as 'Sausage', Point 121 and Point 146 could be clearly seen; together with the Chinese position called 'Pheasant' from which most enemy attacks came. For the Chinese, the easiest approach to the Hook was along the ridges and their preferred route was 'Green Finger', one of three approach ridges. There were two alternative lines of attack: along 'Seattle' and 'Ronson' or, further east, along 'Long Finger'.

Over the months, as each battle flared, many compared the forward defences with those of 1916. Unlike the First World War, however, the UN troops did not construct the support and reserve trenches that used to run for miles behind the front lines on the Western Front. Plentiful resources such as the UN enjoyed enabled them to transport reserves to danger spots and make elaborate earthworks in the rear redundant. This was in marked contrast with the complex Chinese trench systems. Because the UN dominated the air, the Chinese built communication trenches to protect the movement of reserve troops into the MLR from some 20 miles away. In one way it was possible for the Chinese to exploit this unusual battlefield scenario militarily and politically. They could assemble large infantry forces and artillery batteries at a key point such as the Hook or Little Gibraltar, attack and occupy all or part of a vital hill. This would force the UN to contain the Chinese with air strikes and artillery barrages; and then face the unpalatable fact that the only way to regain lost ground was to send in the infantry and suffer casualties as a result. The Chinese saw this as a means of weakening the political leaders of the nations contributing forces to the UN; or perhaps they would become sickened by the endless conflict. Their peoples would call for an end to the war and press for a peace settlement that would be advantageous to the communists. Such was the reasoning of the Chinese leadership when they ordered a major attack on the US Marines entrenched on the Hook.

On 26 October 1952 the Hook was held by the Colonel M. Delaney's 7th US Marines who had created a simple defence system around the ridge as far as Sausage. Marine riflemen had dug a shallow firing trench and installed 158 heavily sandbagged bunkers for their automatic weapons every 30 yards. In front of the trenches, barbed wire and minefields were disposed to stop enemy attacks before they reached the rifle companies. Early that day an intense and accurate Chinese artillery bombardment began the disintegration of the barbed wire and exploded the minefields. As the barrage crept forward to the trench-line and the bunkers, the Chinese infantry advancing up Green Finger swept through the gaps to attack the bunkers. Here a terrible carnage ensued as Chinese soldiers kept coming forward, irrespective of their losses, to engage the Marines in hand-to-hand combat in the trenches and bunkers.

It was not long before Delaney realized that the Hook was the prime objective of a typical Chinese enveloping attack. On both sides of the main Marine defences the Chinese were trying to capture the ridges and break through the UN defence line. Here and there Marines were either killed in their bunkers or driven out by Chinese grenades and mortar bombs. Delaney now called down a Mosquito T-6 to direct an air strike. Fighter-bombers quickly appeared and their rockets and napalm caused more horrifying casualties among the Chinese. Then as soon as the aircraft had climbed away UN artillery barrages fell on their dazed survivors. In went the Marines, forcing the Chinese back to their assembly points. Despite their 200 casualties, the Marines had held the line and regained every position. On 27 October 1952 they were very happy to hand over the Hook to 1 Battalion the Black Watch, commanded by Lt Col D. Rose.

David Rose was none too impressed with his inheritance. He spoke with Delaney who compared his Marines' experience on the Hook with the Pacific War battles on Guadalcanal and Saipan. Rose determined to refortify the Hook and requested 800 Korean labourers and a Sapper Troop to help build tunnels, brand new bunkers and a system of weapon pits that would provide defence in depth. On 14 November 1952 the Black Watch formally relieved the US marines and a new fighting plan was implemented. As soon as the Chinese infantry attacked in force, company commanders would call down VT fire on their own positions. As the artillery air bursts showered the Chinese with red hot steel, the Black Watch would shelter in the bunkers. At the right moment they would emerge and drive off the Chinese with, Rose hoped, minimum casualties to his soldiers.

At 1900 hours on 18 November 1952 two Chinese companies left Pheasant and made their way up Green Finger. Warnings of their approach were signalled by a doomed Black Watch patrol on 'Warsaw', well forward of the Hook. The Chinese split into three fighting groups led by grenadiers. Down came the VT fire supplemented by Vickers machine-guns from the Duke of Wellington's Regiment based on Yong Dong who fired across the Samichon River to protect the Black Watch. It was a wildly illuminated scene as searchlights from five Royal Inniskilling Dragoon Centurion tanks, bursting starshells, tracer rounds, flares and a full moon picked out the charging Chinese infantry. Here and there they gained a footing on the Hook and a Centurion tank that climbed the Hook to fire down on the Chinese was quickly put out of action by a Chinese rocket launcher.[1] A bayonet charge led by 2/Lt Roig failed to dislodge the Chinese and as first light appeared on 19 November the enemy troops were still there. However, they were not prepared to fight in daylight and began to fall back. As they retired the Black Watch looked on in amazement as the Chinese medical teams came out at 0500 hours to clear the battlefield of their dead. Several Black Watch soldiers had been captured and one or two managed to escape. Private Graham was one of these; he had killed his Chinese guard with his bare hands.

By 0530 hours the battle was over and shortly after this a company from the reserve battalion of Canada's Princess Patricias relieved the Black Watch who had lost 12 of their number and possibly 15 who had been taken prisoner. Seventy-three had been wounded but the defence systems instituted by Col Rose had proved their worth and undoubtedly saved the lives of many Black Watch soldiers. Then, on 31 January 1953, the 2nd US Division arrived to defend the Hook, allowing the Commonwealth Division to go into reserve – apart from the artillery which stayed in the line to support the Americans. They endured numerous Chinese attacks during February–March 1953. Both the Hook and Little Gibraltar (Hill 355) saw scenes of bitter close-quarter fighting and US positions on both these crucial hills changed hands several times. Typical of the Chinese assaults was the platoon attack during the night of 3 March 1953. Heralded by massive stonks by Chinese 122mm guns and heavy mortars, the Chinese overran one of the 38th Infantry Regiment's outposts on Warsaw. Colonel A.W. Stuart, commanding the 38th, ordered down VT fire and then sent in a company to regain the lost ground. Next month the Commonwealth Division was back in the line (8 April) and the Black Watch returned to their familiar positions on the Hook.

It was spring and the heavy rains reduced patrol activity. At stand-to times the soldiers were no longer as cold as they had been during their November battle. Col Rose had produced a new defence plan with his four rifle companies located on 121, the Hook, Sausage and 146 with the last hill supported by a company from the Duke of Wellington's Regiment. Across the paddy fields came the sounds of 'Loch Lomond' and 'There's No Place Like Home' as the Chinese propaganda units serenaded the Black Watch over loudspeakers, later warning the Scotsmen not to go out on patrol. Facing the Black Watch were four major artillery emplacements on the hills named 'Betty Grable' 'Rome', 'Goose' and 'Pheasant'. Their big 122mm guns were housed in deep tunnels, safe from UN fire. When in action they were rolled to the tunnel lip and and then quickly returned to their secure positions. After some devastating fire on 7 May an RAF Auster, acting in the role of a Mosquito, tried to locate each tunnel mouth so that the UN artillery could zero in on these and possibly destroy the trouble-some guns. Chinese ground fire brought down the Auster but the pilot and his observer parachuted safely only to land in enemy lines.

Chinese guns continued to fire and the Americans brought in their 8-inch Persuaders in retaliation. At first it seemed that 72 deep-penetration shells had disheartened the Chinese, but at 0200 hours,

8 May 1953, the Chinese began to advance along Ronson. Searchlights and flares revealed the enemy, many of whom were cut down in crossfire from 121 and the Hook. This temporarily stopped the Chinese who now set up a mortar counter-bombardment position. This move attracted the full power of the Commonwealth Division's artillery. As the 20th Field Regiment now had plenty of VT shells, the 25 pounders proved devastating. 4.2-inch and 3-inch mortars added their contribution and when the main Chinese advance moved to Seattle the Turkish Brigade joined in the general bombardment. It therefore seems incredible that Chinese grenadiers could approach within a few yards of the perimeter wire round the Hook. The Black Watch, firing Brens and several recently acquired Browning Automatic Rifles (BARs), held them there for a time while the Directed/Defensive Fire (DF) fire was exploding a mere 20 yards in front of the Black Watch positions.

Through the smoke and the fire, and amidst general confusion, Colonel Rose was able to assess that the Chinese were still on Ronson and ordered a counter-attack to clear the ridge. It fell to 2/Lt Ian Baillie to take his platoon forward to accomplish the mission. They were also told that a bottle of whisky awaited the man who brought back a *live prisoner*. The platoon reached Ronson safely but thereafter encountered several groups of Chinese burp-gunners. Before long they were involved in a hand-to-hand combat with Chinese infantry. Above them exploded the VT shells, behind them were bursts of DF. Baillie had no hope of clearing the Chinese and Col Rose ordered a smokescreen and a rescue patrol. Baillie brought his soldiers back to safety; 2/Lt D. Haugh died leading the rescue patrol. Another subaltern, 2/Lt Alec Rattray MC, was killed. It was definitely becoming a subaltern's war.

The battle was over and the now-customary Chinese medical teams appeared to clear the battlefield. The Black Watch had lost two subalterns and three men killed. A reconnaissance patrol to Green Finger found two wounded Chinese and anticipated not only the whisky but perhaps a few day's R & R in Tokyo. But they were frustrated; both Chinese simply died. They were not pleased when the Chinese loudspeakers announced that there would be a full-scale attack on 13 May. Colonel Rose had the benefit of Intelligence Corps radio intercepts. Messages indicated that fresh Chinese troops were assembling in the hills facing the Hook and there was news that thousands of Korean porters had replenished the ammunition of the enemy guns and brought a huge stock of grenades from the north. Brigadier Kendrew, 29 Brigade commander, had already determined that the Black Watch had done enough and that the Royal Scots, still on their troopship, would eventually replace them. Meanwhile, the Duke of Wellington's Regiment, commanded by Lt Col Ramsey Bunbury DSO, would act as immediate relief. This occurred on 13 May 1953, the night when the Chinese had threatened to attack. C Company went to Sausage, B held the Hook, D Company took over Point 121. A Company was in reserve. The 'Dukes' were ready for action.

## THE THIRD BATTLE OF THE HOOK, 28/29 MAY 1953

The Dukes reached Korea during October 1952 just after the arrival of two other battalions, 1 Battalion The Durham Light Infantry and 1 Battalion The King's Regiment. These had already seen action and had made a name for themselves for their excellent patrol work and the effectiveness of their 'snatch squads'. General Sir George Cooper GCB MC, then a Sapper officer, recalled the situation on the Hook just before the Black Watch left. His sappers, 1 Troop 55 Field Squadron, were in support. 'As a result of continuous shelling and mortaring, the forward trench linking up the various weapon pits was virtually untenable. In place of the deep, sandbagged trench along the forward slope was a wide and shallow 'V,' along which it was impossible to move in daylight without attracting enemy attention. There was no other cover, the scrub and bushes having all disappeared in the shelling until the hill looked like a World War I scene. It was a thoroughly unhealthy place.'[2]

His troop had already helped turn the Hook into a fortress but much of that had been destroyed during the battle between the Black Watch and the Chinese. Nor had it benefited from the recent US occupation, when the Chinese had shelled the Hook almost every day. Cooper had begun a tunnel along Green Finger and now he continued to develop this each night. His sappers could not work on the forward slopes during the day as any movement attracted enemy fire. 'Every vestige of cover had long disappeared and the ground was littered with all the debris of war: tangled barbed wire, bent pickets, shattered timber, torn sandbags, scattered ammunition, enemy stick grenades and the odd dead Chinaman stuck in the wire.'[3] Because of the heavier shells now favoured by the Chinese, George Cooper decided to build new-style bunkers with concrete embrasures to protect the section posts.

> These bunkers were dug out of the forward trench, lined with heavy baulks of timber and with interlocking concrete lintels at the front, the whole covered with 3 to 4 feet of earth and rocks. These lintels, each weighing 600–800lbs, were constructed in the Field Park and had to be dragged over the top of the Hook, through the shell craters and debris, and into their forward positions. This could only be done on the darkest of nights and the local Korean labourers displayed great courage in carrying out this hazardous work. It is not always easy to teach a Korean that the safest thing to do when a flare lights up the surrounding area is to 'freeze' – there is an almost overwhelming desire to run![4]

With the enemy so close this feeling was not entirely confined to the Koreans.

Simultaneously, the Dukes were dispatching standing patrols every night into No Man's Land from the section weapon pits on Ronson, Green Finger, Warsaw and Long Finger. On the night of 17/18 May the Chinese seemed to be preparing for an assault. Lance Corporal Herbert Bailey won the Military Medal for his courage and leadership when his standing patrol (including two KATCOMS) on Long Finger encountered 12 Chinese infantrymen. There was a furious firefight during which the KATCOMS, unable to comprehend Bailey's orders, returned to the lines. Bailey covered his soldiers' withdrawal, grenaded the enemy and put them to flight. There seemed to be so many Chinese patrolling that the Dukes half-expected a full scale assault. But further patrols that night simply clashed with their Chinese equivalents; there was no sign of a massive attack.

Next morning an unarmed Chinese soldier named Hua Hong of 2nd Battalion 399th Regiment, Chinese People's Volunteers, surrendered to an 8 Platoon OP on Sausage. Hua Hong seemed unhappy with his lot on Pheasant and brought with him the news that all five positions occupied by the Dukes would come under simultaneous attack from five assault companies drawn from the 397th, 398th and 399th Regiments. They would outnumber the Dukes five to one and would approach via the ridges and stay under cover before rushing the bunkers. Lt Col Bunbury took the news very seriously. Active Chinese patrolling began on 19

May, tested the Duke's defences and actually 'snatched' one of the Duke's patrol commanders on Warsaw. During 20–22 May the Chinese seemed to have vanished. Warsaw was clear and so was Green Finger. By 23 May, General West had reinforced Lt Col Bunbury: 1 Royal Fusiliers came to the Hook and the Black Watch was brought in on 27 May to hold Yong Dong in place of 1 King's. The King's had already been in action on 24/25 May when they had sent strong patrols to attack Pheasant. They had to cross the Samichon and one patrol led by 2/Lt Caws blundered into a minefield and had to be rescued under accurate artillery protection, for which every soldier gave thanks.

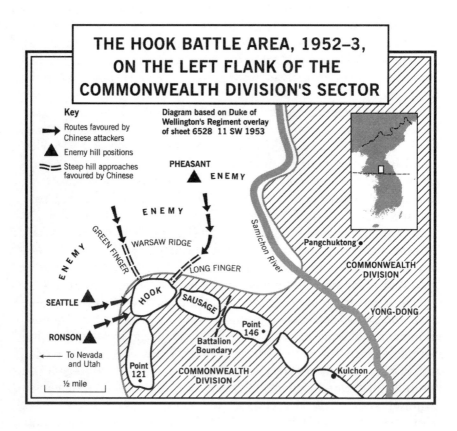

**THE HOOK BATTLE AREA, 1952–3, ON THE LEFT FLANK OF THE COMMONWEALTH DIVISION'S SECTOR**

Key

➤ Routes favoured by Chinese attackers

▲ Enemy hill positions

〓 Steep hill approaches favoured by Chinese

Diagram based on Duke of Wellington's Regiment overlay of sheet 6528 11 SW 1953

PHEASANT ▲ ENEMY

ENEMY

GREEN FINGER

ENEMY

WARSAW RIDGE

LONG FINGER

Samichon River

Pangchuktong ●

COMMONWEALTH DIVISION

SEATTLE ▲

HOOK

SAUSAGE

Point 146 ●

YONG-DONG

RONSON ▲

Battalion Boundary

← To Nevada and Utah

Point 121 ●

COMMONWEALTH DIVISION

Kulchon ●

½ mile

Unusually, the Chinese had not interfered in the King's raid but resumed their shelling of the Hook on 25 May. More patrols returned to report that the usual Chinese assembly points were unoccupied. Clearly, intense shelling was designed to destroy the wire fence systems that now ran up the front of the Hook and actually roofed many of the bunkers, thanks to 2/Lt John Stacpoole and his Assault Pioneers. Men of B Company on the Hook had been standing-to ever since 18 May and were now very tired. Brigadier Kendrew arrived and ordered them to change places with Captain Edward Emmett's D Company on Point 121. John Stacpoole's Assault Pioneers finished off the wiring on 26/27 May despite the fact that it was a moonlit night with very little cloud or wind so that noises would carry to the Chinese lines. Lt Col Bunbury had drawn up a detailed artillery fire plan involving all 72 guns of the Divisional Field Regiments, the heavy mortars, plus the guns of the US Marines and the Turkish Field Regiment. He had also incorporated the firepower of an American battery of 8-inch Persuaders firing 200lb shells. This was an awesome array of guns to defend the Hook; and it included the ability to fire the deadly VT proximity air-bursts immediately above the Dukes' defences. Attacking Chinese would surely be blown to pieces as the Dukes remained safe and sound in George Cooper's bunkers.

After the Americans had ranged their Persuaders on the Chinese on 26 May the enemy gunners responded with barrages directed against Sausage, the Hook and Point 121. Shellfire prevented D Company from putting the finishing touches to their wire defences. Again, the Chinese were firing very heavy shells of which they seemed to have a very great supply. Next day, 27 May, the battering continued and the Dukes' standing patrols suffered casualties. One listening patrol was crucial. It was to cross No Man's Land to a shallow hiding place and warn the Hook defenders by radio of the lines of 'silent' Chinese infantrymen moving across to the caves at the bottom of the hills. Captain Colin Glen and Corporal Duncan Taylor formed the patrol and in the early hours of the morning of the 28th they spotted hundreds of Chinese wandering in all directions making quite a lot of noise!

At 1030 hours the Chinese heavy guns began blasting the Hook defences. Some weapon pits and several of the carefully prepared bunkers were badly damaged and in some cases men were buried alive. Yet no Chinese soldiers appeared and Captain Glen had nothing to report. However, Brigade Intelligence was certain that a major attack was brewing as Chinese radio chatter indicated the assembly of several assault battalions. The battle began at 1950 hours and Captain Glen whispered 'This is it!' into his radio as the Chinese scurried past his hideout. Three minutes later the Chinese were halfway up Green Finger when the shelling suddenly stopped. They were in the bunkers and tunnels before the dazed Dukes could emerge. Chinese appeared in tunnel entrances carrying shrouded torches and hurling stick grenades. Behind them came the burp-gunners, raking the interior with automatic fire. When the Dukes retaliated by lobbing their own grenades and firing their Brens and Stens from the dark interior, Chinese satchel-charges sealed the tunnel and entombed the soldiers.

By-passing the tunnels, other Chinese soldiers continued to charge up Green Finger but the shell-wrecked hillside plus the mass of grenades and rifle fire coming from the Dukes slowed them down, making them vulnerable to VT air-bursts and heavy machine-gun fire from the Turkish and Black Watch positions. In the midst of this, Colonel Bunbury ordered smoke to help Glen and Taylor escape across No Man's Land. Glen did not survive but Taylor managed to reach the King's positions next morning. At 2045 hours the Chinese switched their attacks to Warsaw. Captain Edward Emmett, commanding the Duke's D Company on the Hook, urgently needed reinforcements. Chinese troops were less than 30 yards from his command post and Bunbury ordered a platoon from Point 121 up to the Hook. 2/Lt Michael Ryder led a 1 King's platoon to fill the gap in 121 just as the Chinese attacked it. Caught in the open, the Chinese were slaughtered. Again the Chinese switched their main assault, concentrating on 146 and once again the Chinese soldiers, devoid of cover, were mown down. UN gunfire was decisive that night and even managed to pulverize a battalion of Chinese still forming up on Pheasant. The only grumble the Dukes and Kingsmen had was that the heavy rain clouds were causing some VT shells to detonate above *their* heads. At 0030 hours 19 May the Chinese committed their last company to a final attack up the hills named Betty Grable towards Ronson. They had to cross in front of Point 121. A hail of fire descended on them. Most were probably killed; later 30 bodies were found on the wire. The Dukes were still on the Hook; only dead Chinese soldiers marked the failure of the biggest communist assault on a Commonwealth position during the entire Korean War.

In the morning light the Dukes could survey the devastation on the Hook. It was unrecognizable. They had lost 28 men killed; another 121 were wounded or captured. Some 250 Chinese died in their attacks on the Hook and at least a thousand must have been wounded. Men buried alive by the bombardment were dug out at first light while the sappers of 55 Field Squadron Royal Engineers repaired as much of the wire and weapon pits as they could under cover of a smokescreen. The same morning, 29 May, 1 Battalion Royal Fusiliers relieved the Dukes. No-one could be sure that the Chinese would not repeat their attacks; after all, they had been keen to dislodge the Commonwealth troops for weeks. One way to prevent this would be to destroy newly-dug enemy tunnels used for forming up troops prior to an attack. These were located on the reverse slopes of Warsaw 250 yards from the Hook. About 15 tunnels had been or were being built and these were hidden behind three re-entrants named 'Rip', 'Van' and 'Winkle'. Brigade had decided to raid them on the night of 3/4 June 1953 and destroy all 15.

Captain George Cooper's tunnel expertise was again needed and the raid was so important that C Company 1 King's would accompany a Sapper officer and 14 men from No. 1 Troop, 55 Field Squadron. Two 8lb charges of plastic explosive plus two 2lb tamping charges fitted neatly into conventional lightweight issue haversacks. Careful rehearsals were held and reconnaissance parties checked out the best route to follow. They quickly returned having discovered some of the tunnels were still occupied by Chinese! On 4 June 1953 the raiders formed up at Kulchon and followed the track towards Pheasant, turning westwards along the valley to attack the enemy in the rear. Corporal F.L. Smith, 1 King's, recalled that, 'The night wasn't completely dark, slightly moonlit, with fast moving clouds; visibility would be about ten to fifteen yards.'[5]

Early on the raiders suffered casualties from a Chinese grenade and then one soldier stepped on a mine killing three men and wounding twelve. From a firm base a smaller raiding party now concentrated on Rip, covered by an artillery barrage supplemented by rounds from Centurion tanks dug-in on Yong Dong – designed to distract the enemy while the raiders, now divided into two sections, tackled the caves. They laid explosives in two tunnels despite a hail of enemy grenades from above. Corporal Smith saw two caves blown: 'the sections were given the order to 'Bug out,' taking up the wounded as they went. The patrol moved down the hillside, proceeding across the valley floor before rejoining the firm base . . . On the following day it was reported that the raid had been a total success.'[6] Although the raiders had not destroyed all the tunnels they had caused heavy casualties among the enemy. Significantly, the Chinese abandoned the Warsaw re-entrants and never again launched a frontal attack on the Hook.

## THE BATTLES ON PORK CHOP HILL, APRIL–JULY 1953

That a small hill 600-feet high in No Man's Land, 50 miles north of Seoul, could possess such tactical and strategic significance to justify hundreds of deaths in a series of bitter battles is hard to accept. Its name derived from its shape; its tactical value, (apart from removing a salient between the Chinese on Old Baldy and Chink Baldy and their strongpoints on Snook and T-Bone Hill), was primarily as a propaganda weapon. Were it to be captured by the Chinese People's Volunteers then their propagandists would deride the determination and ability of US fighting men to hold 'vital' ground; while its capture would strengthen the arguments of their delegates at a delicate stage of the negotiations at Panmunjom. American willingness to risk men's lives to defend Pork Chop was simply to frustrate the communists' ambitions.

There had already been many battles on and around Pork Chop and on 16 April 1953 its defence was the responsibility of the 31st Infantry Regiment of the 7th US Division. Pork Chop was on the US I Corps front close to the boundary with IX Corps and White Horse Hill. Less than a mile away was Old Baldy held by the Chinese, having been capured by them in the previous month. Pork Chop and its adjacent hillocks were guarded by outposts, two of which were known as 'Erie' and 'Arsenal'. Erie was well-defended by two platoons from Easy Company, 31st Infantry Regiment, plus a rifle platoon from George Company and the 81mm mortar platoon and heavy machine-gun section from How Company. Arsenal had two rifle platoons numbering 95 men. Both outposts were isolated from the 'Main Line of Resistance' but linked with it via a trackway for food and ammunition supplies. Each outpost was surrounded by barbed wire and minefields and had deep bunkers in which troops could shelter during friendly bombardments against enemy attacks. Plentiful reserves of food and ammunition were stored in each outpost.

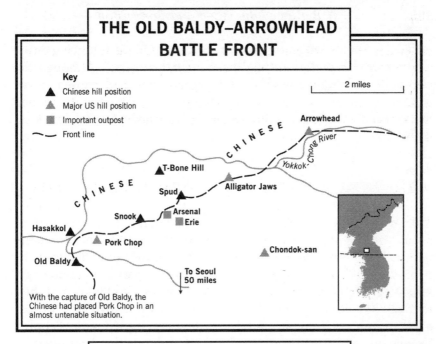

## THE OLD BALDY–ARROWHEAD BATTLE FRONT

**Key**

▲ Chinese hill position
▲ Major US hill position
▨ Important outpost
– – Front line

2 miles

CHINESE

Arrowhead

Yokkok-Chong River

CHINESE

▲T-Bone Hill

Spud▲ Alligator Jaws

Snook▲ ▨Arsenal
▨Erie

Hasakkol▲

▲ Pork Chop

▲Chondok-san

Old Baldy▲

To Seoul
50 miles

With the capture of Old Baldy, the
Chinese had placed Pork Chop in an
almost untenable situation.

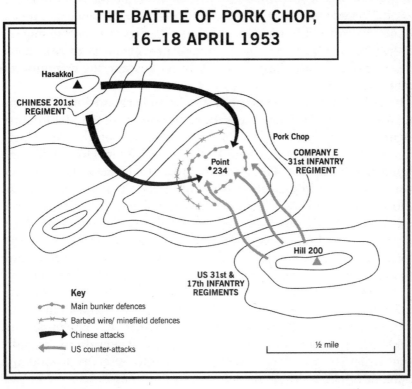

## THE BATTLE OF PORK CHOP, 16–18 APRIL 1953

Hasakkol▲

CHINESE 201st
REGIMENT

Pork Chop

COMPANY E
31st INFANTRY
REGIMENT

Point
•234

Hill 200▲

US 31st &
17th INFANTRY
REGIMENTS

**Key**

Main bunker defences
Barbed wire/ minefield defences
Chinese attacks
US counter-attacks

½ mile

During the morning of 16 April there were rumours of a heavy Chinese attack due to start that day and these rumours were taken seriously by Regimental HQ. At 1730 hours Chinese artillery shells began exploding on Arsenal and one particularly accurate gun cut pathways through the outer defences. Unknown to the defenders, parties of Chinese skirmishers were now around the wire and preparing to climb the hill. Inside Arsenal the Americans were trying to cope with fires that were flaring inside the OP tunnels and the Command Post. Other Chinese guns simultaneously zeroed on Alligator Jaws, White Horse Hill and Hill 327. Chinese grenadiers managed to annihilate the How machine-gunners and then were immediately killed by their own artillery fire. Other Chinese began penetrating the rifle squad bunkers only to be cut down by Corporal Kinder on a light machine-gun (LMG). When he was wounded Private First Class Ramon Angel took his place. Behind them more Chinese gathered in the paddy fields in another attempt to take Arsenal from the rear. Two privates, Wolzneak and Crane, stopped them with an LMG and a BAR and thus averted a disaster. At the same moment 'flash fire' dropped to surround Arsenal's outer defences in smoke, fire and shrapnel. High explosives and VT shells fired by the US 48th Field Regiment arrived at the rate of two per second and lasted for four minutes. For a moment there was silence. Cautiously the defenders of Arsenal and Erie peered out of their bunkers – and unbelievably the Chinese were attacking again, hurling their grenades and firing their burp guns directly at the bunker slits.

Once more the Americans showered the Chinese with VT fire and this finally drove the attackers away. Amazingly, only eight Americans had been killed and 17 wounded. Both Erie and Arsenal had defied the Chinese but at great cost of their defences. Other outposts were not always so lucky. 'Dale' was one such post, the responsibility of Baker Company's well-armed 3rd Platoon commanded by 2/Lt Ryan A. Bressler. Located on a small hillock, Dale was less than 400 yards from the Chinese lines and overlooked by enemy-held hills. Bressler had placed 12 of his men outside Dale, hiding in 'listening posts' and connected by telephone with their Command Post. As Arsenal and Erie were under bombardment, two platoons of Chinese soldiers slipped past the listening posts at Dale and swamped the defences from two directions. For once the artillery was nonplussed and when the guns finally fired illuminators to warn of impending VT fire the flares went wide of Dale. As the Chinese overran Dale, Bressler was wounded and put out of action. Grenades and mortar fire collapsed his bunker, pinning him down under heavy beams. He managed to order Private Pfaff, a wounded squad leader who had fought the Chinese hand-to-hand, to leave the outpost and find help. Pfaff escaped, reached Company HQ and made his report. He believed that Dale outpost had fallen to the Chinese and was unsure about the fate of 2/Lt Bressler.

31st Regimental HQ required the recapture of Dale and transmitted this order to Lt Col George L. Maliszewski, commanding 3rd Battalion. He decided to retake the outpost by means of an enveloping operation with infantrymen drawn from Item Company. His attack was not well organized and the squads working their way uphill faced withering fire from two well-concealed machine-guns from bunkers located near the summit. Men hugged the ground to avoid the deadly tracer and were not inclined to move. Lt Hemphill resolved the situation in an act of personal bravery. Though wounded by grenade fragments, he crawled with a rocket launcher within 30 yards of the machine-gun bunker and then fired point-blank, killing the entire crew. The second gun position was assaulted by Lt Col Maliszewski's platoons. A stick grenade took off the colonel's foot and he was stretchered from the hill. His squads carried on a fierce firefight in front of the enemy-occupied bunkers and, after the battle, found all eight Chinese soldiers who had been firing the second machine-gun dead at their posts. Chinese survivors were scurrying back to their own lines and Dale outpost was suddenly American again. It had been a confused and disorganized military operation saved by acts of great personal heroism. Casualties in Item Company were amazingly light: four Americans had died and thirty-one were wounded in a battle that had been fought through the night of 16/17 April.

On Pork Chop Hill itself Easy Company gazed upon the mighty Chinese hill called 'Hasakkol'. Their Korean interpreter had told Lt Thomas V. Harrold that the dirge-like sounds his men could hear were in fact Chinese soldiers singing a death-song from the depths of their bomb-proof tunnels. He was well aware of the report that the Chinese were going to attack Pork Chop that night; and was mightily conscious that he had only 96 men of Easy Company to defend not only the 44 well-built bunkers and extensive trench works surrounding the hill but the ten outguards and listening posts as well. Extraordinarily, none of the outguards seem to have spotted the two companies of Chinese infantry padding silently into the attack even though the American posts were some 20 yards beyond Pork Chop's perimeter. Undoubtedly, some were killed by the Chinese assault squads for only seven of the 20 men in the outguards survived the night of 16/17 April 1953. There was no preliminary bombardment, no covering barrage. Before the Americans realized what was happening the Chinese had reached their outer defences.

On cue, the Chinese gunners blasted the perimeter defences a few yards ahead of their own troops. Lt Harrold called up the listening posts and Battalion HQ but the telephone lines were dead. He sent up a red flare to signal that Pork Chop was under attack and a few moments later the US artillery fired its own flares to indicate that flash fire was imminent. Down came the VT shrapnel: the Chinese infantry halted and the Americans retreated into their bunkers. Chinese grenades killed many Americans while they were still taking cover; other US soldiers, such as company clerk Riepenhoff and Sgt Midgeley, systematically slaughtered the Chinese as they entered their fortifications. The Pork Chop meatgrinder had begun. Inevitably, the outnumbered Americans lost bunkers to the Chinese who now installed themselves in these until they controlled more than half of Pork Chop Hill.

When at last Lt Harrold managed to raise Regimental HQ on a radio and passed on the bad news, Battalion HQ assumed that Pork Chop had fallen and despatched platoons from Love and Fox Companies to reinforce the remains of Easy Company. King Company was ordered to support the counter-attacks. Harrold's own command post now came under direct attack. He had been wounded by a grenade pushed through the sandbags so he resolved to seal himself in the bunker and await relief. In the meantime, he endeavoured to command any of the surviving troops who managed to contact him by radio. King Company, led by Lt Joseph G. Clemons, arrived to face the prospect of having to attack former American bunkers now filled with Chinese soldiers. As they began this difficult task, many more enemy grenadiers and burp-gunners filtered across the shell-pocked plain from Hasakkol to reinforce their comrades fighting around and on top of Pork Chop Hill. King Company employed flame-throwers and 3.5-inch rocket launchers but even with these they were unable to break up the enemy resistance.

Dawn came, heralding a bright cool day. Unusually, the Chinese decided to fight on in daylight. More reinforcements from the 17th Infantry Regiment arrived until there were sufficient riflemen to challenge the Chinese in an exchange of fire that killed more and more men on both sides. From the American standpoint, the defence of Pork Chop Hill had become a national issue. However, as no more companies would be sent into the meatgrinder pending the outcome of a conference at I Corps HQ, King Company (18 killed and 71 wounded) and the remnants of Easy, Fox, George and Love would have to soldier on until someone reached a decision. It came at 1800 hours on 17 April 1953. Maj. General Bruce Cooper Clarke at I Corps promised that Pork Chop would never be surrendered and that reinforcements would arrive.

Fox Company now deployed a platoon to the trench line while Love Company faced an imminent attack from yet more Chinese soldiers emerging from Hasakkol's tunnels. VT fire showered the enemy with shrapnel, forcing him to take cover. Seemingly, this enraged the Chinese gunners who fired salvo after salvo on Fox Company positions, killing 15 men even before they had engaged the infantry. After midnight – it was now 17 April – the 17th Infantry Regiment sent in another company, also with the name of Easy. By 0250 hours the Americans were pushing the Chinese off the summit and dealing with groups of snipers and burp-gunners who rose from the shattered trenches and wrecked bunkers. Able Company from the 17th arrived to join the fray and when the day ended the Chinese had had enough and began drifting away. The Battle of Pork Chop fought from 16–18 April 1953 was over. It has gone down in history as one of the greatest artillery duels ever recorded. On the first day of the battle the American Field Battalions had fired in excess of 37,600 rounds in their efforts to preserve Arsenal, Erie, Dale and Pork Chop. On the second day of battle, when the fate of Pork Chop hung in the balance, the gunners fired over 77,000 rounds. All this effort was expended to preserve a little hill that jutted into No Man's land in the middle of Korea.

Pork Chop was not destined to remain in American hands even though the victory was followed up with a series of fighting patrols. Notable was one provided by the Ethiopian Battalion on 28 April 1953. Led by Lt Wongele Costa, an Ethiopian fighting patrol set out to establish a firm base at Alligator Jaws from which they would ambush enemy patrols and attempt to capture prisoners. To his surprise, he found he had disposed his force barely 15 yards from the enemy and an extraordinary firefight lasted for 15 minutes before the Chinese withdrew. Wongele Costa called for flares to illuminate the scene and in their light he spotted a Chinese patrol coming in to attack *behind* him. He called down VT fire from the 48th Field Battalion deputed to support the raid and the artillery broke up enemy attacks developing to his front and rear. When the barrage was over the Chinese had fled, leaving 22 dead behind them. Wongele Costa had captured two badly wounded Chinese and returned to his battalion lines, bringing all his own casualties home. He had led the new Kagnew Battalion's first patrol, for it replaced the old Kagnew Battalion that had served its year in Korea. It was a remarkable tribute to the quality and determination of Ethiopian soldiers who were more expert in night-fighting than any other combatants during the Korean War.

While these fighting patrols were testing the enemy strength the US 7th Division gradually rebuilt the bunkers, ramparts and fighting trenches on Pork Chop Hill. Every day the Chinese gunners intervened to disrupt the work of the American engineers but enemy infantry did not retaliate until, significantly, the Fourth of July. On that day a fighting patrol was testing the enemy's will to defend Old Baldy when it ran into a Chinese ambush and retired with heavy casualties. Propaganda loudspeakers welcomed Able Company of the 17th Infantry by name and invited it to surrender immediately. Otherwise, all the company would die as the Chinese People's Volunteers were now prepared to capture Pork Chop Hill even if they had to 'wade through blood.'

There followed a battle as intense as that fought by the Dukes on the Hook. Hundreds of Chinese took part in charge after charge, their political officers screaming slogans and prodding them on with burp guns. The usual whistles and bugle calls added a surreal atmosphere to the bursting VT shells and exploding mortars. As at the Hook, the fighting was hand-to-hand with individuals slamming steel helmets into Chinese faces. Unlike the Hook, the Chinese forced Able Company off the crest of Pork Chop. Lt Richard Shea regrouped the survivors and fought back to the top of the hill where he was killed, a posthumous Medal of Honor winner. There was no end to the killing: a Chinese shell landed on the company aid station and everyone inside was killed. By 10 July 1953 the reserves were in position. Five battalions of infantry were ready to hold Pork Chop Hill; while the Chinese had brought in an entire division to take it! Mercifully, the United Nations Command decided that the killing there must stop. Pork Chop was not worth another American life. All units were evacuated from the hill in the expectation of an early armistice.[7]

# CHAPTER 17

# Partisans and Guerrillas: the Covert War in Korea

## PROBLEMS OF COVERT OPERATIONS IN NORTH KOREA

Considerable money and effort, plus many lives, were expended in this, one of the more curious aspects of the Korean War. Partisans and guerrillas existed in North Korea even before the North invaded in June 1950. Thereafter, the US Eighth Army, the United States Air Force and the Central Intelligence Agency grappled with the task of training and leading guerrillas to detect enemy plans, disrupt communications and, where possible, assassinate local communist leaders. There was no shortage of keen recruits for many had already taken revenge on their communist enemies during the UN invasion of North Korea in 1950. Once the Chinese intervened these guerrillas either hid in the mountains or escaped to one of the numerous west coast islands. Some were young men evading the North Korean Universal Military Service Act (1947). They had refused to join the armed forces and were hunted down by the North Korean People's Field Police as well as by Soviet and North Korean soldiers. Others had lost their farms to local communists. Typical of these was Kim Yong Bok whose land had been commandeered by the communists before the Korean War. He had hidden in the mountains and taken part in anti-communist raids. As the UN troops retreated in 1950 and again in 1951, Kim was at risk from anti-guerrilla sweeps conducted by the Chinese. He was aware that Chodo-do was a refuge for partisans and in February 1951 he escaped by fishing boast to meet the groups assembled by American guerrilla leaders in the base code-named 'Leopard'.[1]

He found that Chodo-do was one of the American covert war centres that co-ordinated anti-communist guerrilla raids and that these had been operating since August-September 1950. Far East Command (FECOM) had discovered that General Willoughby, the staff officer in charge of intelligence, had made recommendations to MacArthur on the basis of flawed or outdated intelligence. It was therefore vital to co-ordinate sources of information and a new Far East Command Liaison Group (FECLG – pronounced Feckleg) was formed. Parallel with this was CCRAK (See-crack), the Combined Command Reconnaissance Activities Korea agency designed to control all partisan operations in the north. There had been two major operations already. The first took place during 31 August–8 September against three islands held by North Korean forces: Yonghung-do, Taebu-do and Taemuui-do. These guarded the entrance to the Flying Fish Channel, the approach chosen for the attack on Inchon. Supported by HMS *Jamaica* and HMS *Charity*, Royal Marines and guerrillas led by Lt Eugene F. Clark, USN, occupied Yonghung-do and Taebu-do without any resistance. After questioning the local police chief, it emerged that the enemy had built bunkers on Taemuui-do, probably for artillery capable of hitting the Inchon invasion fleet. Clark's guerrillas landed while *Jamaica* blasted the bunkers. Within a few minutes the last North Koreans had been killed and the third island had been successfully liberated, removing a major problem that had worried the planners of Operation 'Chromite'.

Less successful was a raid conducted on the east coast while the Inchon landings were in progress. The intention was to create a bottleneck in the North Korean supply route and an ideal spot, the village of Changsa, was chosen for the guerrillas to ambush enemy trucks coming down the twisting mountain road. On 14 September 1950 a guerrilla battalion, led by 1st Lt William S. Harrison and Sgt Frederick D. Cooper, landed from an LST. They had gunfire support from the USS *Endicott* and the few NKPA troops in Changsa retreated into the hills. Recuperating in the high ground just above Changsa, and quite unknown to Harrison, was the 12th Regiment of the NKPA 5th Division. These troops began to mortar the defensive positions set up on the beachhead by Harrison to protect his beached LST. He desperately needed help and asked *Endicott* to shell the enemy. In turn, *Endicott* asked Admiral Hartman's task force for support. Amazingly, Hartman knew nothing of the operation – he was in the midst of shelling Samchok, 70 miles to the north. Hartman steamed south at full speed and launched a helicopter to reconnoitre the beachhead. The news was not good. Harrison and Cooper were both wounded and the seas were too rough for *Endicott*'s boats to rescue the guerrillas. Under heavy fire, the helicopter took two wounded Americans back to Hartman's flagship, the USS *Helena*, for treatment. Just in time, the task force fired barrages off the beachhead to keep the NKPA at bay. When the weather improved the US Army tug Lt 636 landed engineers to place explosive charges on the LST. In all 725 guerrillas were rescued and their abandoned LST was left a burning wreck. The raid had been a total failure and there was a clear need for improved communications between the US armed forces before any more guerrilla operations were launched.

The changed military situation in January 1951, when the Eighth Army had established an emergency 'Main Line of Resistance' south of the 38 degree Parallel, emphasized the need to exploit any guerrilla activity in North Korea to relieve pressure on the United Nations. General Ridgway was impressed by the news that 10,000 partisans were operating in Hwanghae Province. He discussed this with Colonel John H. McGee, his expert on guerrilla warfare, and authorized assistance. McGee appoined Major William A. Burke to command operations based first on Paengnyong-do and then on Yonpyong-do and Chodo-do. These islands were chosen for four reasons: easy radio transmissions provided a reliable radio-net with each other and with forces on the mainland; their sandy beaches permitted C-47s to land with supplies; they could readily summon naval and air support if they were attacked by communist forces; and they were out of enemy artillery range. Later Nam-do was added as a major base and became the training centre for guerrilla fighters.

Training and equipping partisans became Burke's special duty as commander of 'Task Force Able'. In this capacity he travelled to many other islands to meet partisan leaders in an effort to evaluate their strengths – their expression 'regiment' could mean six or seven hundred men – and their needs. Most partisans were using old Japanese and Russian rifles, North Korean and American machine-guns and a few ex-American carbines. Burke arranged training programmes and equipped small boats with powerful diesel engines so they were capable of towing junks filled with guerrillas. Eventually, the bases became known as 'Leopard' and the guerrilla units despatched on operations were coded 'Donkeys.'

Whilst guerrilla training was in progress on the islands, McGee planned the first of numerous air drops over North Korea. He trained his paratroopers at the Eighth Army Ranger School on K-3 air base near Pusan. Nearby was a sabotage school for special agents run by Captain Ellery Anderson, a former SAS officer. He picked four Rangers to join his Korean paratroopers to carry out an operation coded 'Virginia I' and on 15 March 1951 they parachuted from a C-47 near their target, a rail tunnel at Hyon-ni. Waiting off-shore was HMS *Alacrity*, its boats ready to pick up the raiders. Unfortunately, the tunnel at Hyon was full of Chinese railroad repair engineers. The raiders then made for their alternative target, the tunnel at Samdae-ri. This was being used as an air raid shelter! Deprived of targets and in the midst of a Siberian storm, the unhappy members of Virginia I were now short of food while their radios began to fail because of the intense cold. Luck had not deserted them, however, and they managed to radio a Mosquito controlling an artillery shoot. The Mosquito called up naval support and three helicopters from *Coral Sea* and *St Paul* began the rescue of Virginia I. Communist troops had virtually surrounded the raiders and their ground fire brought down one helicopter. Corsairs attacked the enemy with bombs and rockets and the two surviving helicopters, one with winch problems, rescued two of the Americans. The rest decided to break-out and reach friendly lines. The Koreans disappeared and the other two Americans, Watson and Thornton, became prisoners. Although they suffered harsh treatment in the prison camps, their fortitude and courage enabled them to survive. During the 'Big Switch' exchange of prisoners, Watson was the last American PoW to walk into 'Freedom Village'.

## DONKEY MISSIONS

Donkey 1, 38 men strong, was commanded by Chang Chae Hwa. It set out in March 1951 to liaise with sympathetic villagers, harass the enemy in every way possible and capture enemy weapons. Their first target was the police station at Buchong-ni where an area meeting of communist officials had been called. They crept up to the building, attached plastic explosives, blew it up and tossed two fragmentation grenades into the smoking interior for luck. They killed 35 communists and acquired burp guns, ammunition and grenades and plenty of food. All was transported in ox-carts liberated from the communists and Donkey 1 set off to its next target, a truck assembly point at Sinchon. This was destroyed and Chang found he had recruited local guerrillas so that his force was now 100 strong. He therefore decided to make a major attack on Sinchon where 1,700 civilians, some very ill, were being held in a group of warehouses. They rescued 400 civilians but the rest were killed when Chinese troops unexpectedly appeared. Enemy soldiers harried the partisans as they withdrew and many died in a series of firefights. The survivors continued to make raids, notably an attack on a monazite mine that was being worked by 800 civilian captives. Donkey 1 attacked on 10 May 1951 and then withdrew to the hills when Chinese soldiers arrived.

Chang now ordered Donkey 1 to split into small groups and to assemble at a rendezvous near Changyon prior to an escape to the coast. On 23 July Chang managed to cross the mud flats with 20 survivors and reach the tiny island of Yuk-do, then held by Donkey 4. Donkey 1's success was measured not just in terms of the destruction it had carried out but also by the fact that the NKPA had been compelled to allocate three divisions (30,000 men) to assist the Chinese in their anti-guerrilla sweeps. News of their success did not filter back to Burke in time to prevent Donkey 4 from setting off on a similar operation on 6–7 March. Donkey 4 was well-equipped to carry out a raid close to Buchong-ni but unfortunately ran into strong enemy patrols seeking Chang's guerrillas. They succeeded in escaping but lost most of their stores and equipment and seemed unable to live off the land as Donkey 1 had always done. To add to their misfortune, nearly half of their members deserted.

Burke therefore sought better quality recruits and managed to bring in the Ac-do Regiment commanded by Kim Ung Su. Unfortunately, no-one on Cho-do knew they were coming and promptly opened fire on a convoy of junks containing the partisans. Ac-do Regiment then moved to Sok-do and landed in North Korea on 27 March 1951 where it displayed remarkable military skills. Kim Ung Su ambushed an NKPA heavy weapons unit and stopped a tank attack. He used these captured weapons to good effect in a raid on another monazite mine on 3 April. When the Ac-do Regiment returned, Burke split it into Donkeys 13, 14 and 15.

## ENEMY REACTION

Donkey operations intensified during the summer of 1951 and inevitably the communists attempted some form of counter-attack. Yuk-do, then being held by Donkey 4, was their prime target and the defenders were well-prepared. Elaborate bunkers strengthened with scores of sandbags hid heavy machine-guns, barbed wire ringed the island and hidden under the sand were five gallon drums of napalm and a maze of anti-personnel mines. On 6 September 1951 the defenders could see NKPA troops setting up mortars to bombard their bunkers while infantry struggled across the wide mud flats towards them. A terrible massacre followed as enemy soldiers were blown up by the mines, frizzled by napalm and then subject to an intense machine-gun cross-fire. The day did not go so well for Donkey 8 on Yongui-do, less easy to defend because of its shape and size. On 6–7 September the NKPA assault troops arrived in boats on the high tide and landed some 200 men before the defenders were aware of their existence. Donkey 8 withdrew and Yongui-do fell to the enemy.

Enemy intelligence was very good and the Chinese were aware of plans by Donkeys 13 and 15 to attack Simni-do on 13 October and destroy an NKPA observation post at Tongdam-dong. Chinese troops secretly landed on Simni-do and laid an ambush for the two Donkey units arriving in sail junks. It was nearly a disaster for the partisans but one Chinese soldier accidentally fired his rifle and alerted them just in time. They drew off after suffering 40 casualties. This was the last major conflict in the western islands during October 1951 due to poor weather conditions, but on 6 November the Chinese resumed the offensive. After a week of fighting against Chinese amphibious forces, Donkeys 13 and 14 were driven off their islands (15 November). Five days later Chinese aircraft began strafing guerrilla island bases. On 1 December 1951 the Chinese captured Tachwa-do, defended by the partisans who had returned with Donkeys 14 and 15. HMS *Black Swan* managed to rescue the survivors. Next the Chinese and North Koreans turned their attention to islands below the 38 degree Parallel. A battalion of NKPA soldiers landed on Yongho-do on New Year's Day 1952, killing 32 guerrillas and wounding 40 more. The Donkeys clung to their base on Kiri-do and were gradually reinforced and re-equipped by Leopard. Before long they were strong enough to recapture all the lost islands and to re-establish a strong partisan threat to Hwanghae Province.

## THE LIMITATIONS OF GUERRILLA ACTIVITY

There was a tendency to misuse guerrilla forces during 1952–3. This was due partly to the character of the Americans who were taking the lead in more and more guerrilla operations. For example, Master Sergeant Roy Meeks, an ex-Ranger, commanded a revitalized Donkey 1. He led his Donkey on missions against much larger enemy forces but it is doubtful that Meeks' 'hit and run' raids achieved anything of consequence. Moreover, as guerrilla units became much larger and much better equipped, they were tempted to fight as ordinary combat soldiers. In a raid on Pongyong, 29 October 1952, Meeks led 200 Donkey 1 partisans ashore amidst a rolling fog that swept in from the sea. Almost immediately he was engaged in a firefight with a company of NKPA troops backed by Chinese forces. The fog prevented fighter cover and gunfire support from warships, but the tenacity of Meeks and his determined grenade charges against the enemy enabled his force to retreat back to the beaches. Suddenly the fog lifted and Fleet Air Arm Seafires machine-gunned the enemy who retreated only to be blasted by a naval bombardment. Donkey 1 suffered ten men killed in a mission that had failed even to reach its target. Consolation came with the announcement that the enemy had lost at least 200 dead.

Some of the original Donkey units were now transferred into a new guerrilla force known as 'Wolfpack'. These were organized in exactly the same manner as the earlier Donkeys but in every case contained at least one American. Their first missions were very successful and were ideal examples of guerrilla work: reporting the location of enemy units and calling down air strikes to exterminate the enemy. Yet once again Wolfpack Command repeated the mistakes of Leopard by sending in large units to fight conventional battles against the enemy. On 28 September 1952, 475 guerrillas led by four Americans tried to carry out a reconaissance mission. It failed largely due to its size and suffered heavier casualties than was expected.

American expectations from covert warfare actually increased during 1952–3 when estimates of the ideal size of the total guerrilla force ranged from 22,000 to 40,000. Units were now termed Partisan Infantry Regiments (PIR) but were actually small groups tasked with

# ROYAL MARINES/GUERRILLA RAIDS AGAINST NORTH KOREA, 1950–3, AND THE ARMISTICE DEMARCATION LINE, JULY 1953

Chongjin

NORTH KOREA

Suiho Reservoir

OCTOBER 1950

Antung

Mapyong-ni  Chosin Reservoir

Hagaru-ri

Koto-ri

Unsan

Changgo-dong

Yalu River

Taedong River

Hamhung

Hungnam

APRIL 1951

KOREA BAY

Wonsan

SEA OF JAPAN

Pyongyang

SOK-DO
CHO-DO

Sariwon

Imjin River

Sinchon

Changyon

HWANGHAE PROVINCE

Kaesong

38°

PAENGNYONG-DO

YONGPYONG-DO

Panminjom

Kapyong

Uijongbu

Hongchon

Inchon

Seoul

Suwon

12–15 SEP. 1950
Diversionary raid prior
to US Marine landings
at Inchon
15 September1950

Samchok

Pyongtaek

Han River

YELLOW SEA

Naktong-ni

Andong

Yongdok

Key

Chasan

Pohang-Dong

Kum River

Waegwan

Taegu

Armistice line 1953

Raids by Royal Marines

Kunsan

Donkey operations in
Hwanghae Province

Chonju

Territory gained by
North Korea

SOUTH KOREA

Naktong River

Territory gained
by South Korea

Chinju

Masan

Pusan

Kwangju

Sunchon

Makpo

TSUSHIMA

75 miles

specific missions. These PIRs became expert at 'snatch' tactics and armed with silenced Sten guns, as were 2 PIR on 13 November 1952, proved capable of capturing valuable prisoners. In the same month, a specialist team from 2 PIR used their flame-throwers in an assault on enemy positions. By March 1953 the PIRs were operating on both coasts of the Korean peninsula and were positively dismayed to receive news of the impending cease-fire. Some deserted and went inland to carry on fighting after the armistice was announced. At least one unit was operating in North Korea on 3 November 1953 and was not declared defunct until 28 February 1954. However, irrespective of certain clandestine evacuations of US agents from North Korea during February 1954, America's official position was that all partisan units should be disbanded and, where appropriate, be encouraged to join the ROK Army. The run-down was fairly rapid and the US-backed guerrilla organization was formally abolished on 30 April 1954. Equipment, including assault boats and recoilless rifles, was still being handed in during July 1954.

Was the clandestine warfare of benefit to the UN Command? Undoubtedly, it administered a number of uncomfortable pinpricks to the communist forces and killed large numbers of the enemy. It also committed the communists to deploy many thousands of troops in extensive anti-guerrilla campaigns and thus marginally reduced the forces confronting the UN troops on the 'Main Line of Resistance.' The inherent weakness of the covert war was that the partisans, as organized by the Americans, could not strike at the most crucial targets of all – the communists' 'Main Supply Route' (MSR). Apart from the east coast railroad the MSR travelled via Pyongyang and into central Korea, well away from partisan activities. On a fair basis of comparison, therefore, the guerrilla operations against North Korean military targets never achieved the level of success won by the French Maquis and Tito's partisans against German occupation forces in the Second World War.

# CHAPTER 18

# The Armistice and After

Numerous battles, of which Pork Chop and the Hook are the best known, flared along the 'Main Line of Resistance' from March to early July 1953. All were initiated by the Chinese as they fought to gain a superior bargaining position across the green cloth-covered tables at Panmunjom. General Maxwell Taylor, who had ordered the withdrawal from Pork Chop Hill, was unwilling to sacrifice further lives in pointless defence of a hill or outpost that he could safely abandon.

For example, during May 1953 the Nevada City outposts near Bunker Hill in the US 25th Division sector were held by the Turkish Brigade. Located about ten miles to the north-east of Panmunjom and 25 miles west of Old Baldy, they were about 1,500 yards beyond the MLR. These outposts had witnessed much bloodshed in the past. On 27 March the Marines had fought a major battle against 3,500 Chinese who assaulted the outposts in front of Bunker Hill. By sheer weight of numbers the Chinese captured several outposts though all were later retaken by the Marines. Now it was the turn of the Turkish Brigade to face another mass assault and in the late evening of 28 May a battle began comparable with the struggle on Pork Chop. Under the usual artillery barrage, some 2,000 Chinese soldiers attacked the outposts named 'East Berlin', 'West Berlin', 'Elko', 'Carson' and 'Vegas'. After three hours of hand-to-hand fighting – at which the Turks always excelled – the Chinese withdrew. Their depleted battalions were replaced with fresh troops and these resumed the attack at 1100 hours on 29 May. At this stage, Divisional HQ ordered the Turks on Elko to return to the MLR. A similar battle was fought on the slopes leading to the Vegas outpost. This did not end until 2300 hours on 29 May when the Turks on Vegas were ordered back to the MLR. Chinese disregard for human life faltered at East and West Berlin. For two hours the Turks kept them at bay until the Chinese gave up and withdrew. The Turks had lost 104 of their men; 324 were wounded. Three outposts had been surrendered but the 'Main Line of Resistance' remained intact. For this slight territorial gain the Chinese had suffered 2,200 killed and over a thousand wounded.

When the Chinese began a fresh offensive against ROK II Corps on 10 June they employed two full divisions and supporting battalions from other units (35,000 men) in an attempt to force the South Koreans to abandon their defences around Kumsong. Their attack along the Pukhan River began the Battles of Capital Hill and the Kumsong Bulge, posing the threat of a major Chinese breakthrough and raising the spectre of China's rapid advances of 1951. General Maxwell Taylor therefore decided to create a new 'Main Line of Resistance' in the ROK II Corps sector, some two miles to the rear. His acknowledgment of a modest Chinese victory was triumphantly exploited by the communist delegates at Panmunjom. In an attempt to capitalize on their success the Chinese unwisely attacked the outposts thrown up in front of the new MLR only to be frustrated partly by ROK resistance and partly by the exhaustion that had overtaken so many Chinese soldiers. By 20 July 1953 the fighting had almost ceased after appalling casualties on both sides, largely the result of artillery fire. These major Chinese offensives had extended along a wide front from the Kumsong River, through Heartbreak Ridge to Capital Hill. Casualties on both sides were higher in the so-called 'static war' than in the war of movement during 1950.

All along the line, soldiers' expectations of a truce had been lifted and then cast down ever since the armistice talks had begun at Kaesong. Political events over which they had no control always led to an intensification of warfare in which men died. A serious complication developed on 18 June when President Syngman Rhee unilaterally released 25,000 prisoners from his own POW camps. These were the so-called anti-communist 'non-repatriates' who did not wish to return to China or North Korea. His action threatened the entire peace-talks programme and the battles that flared along the MLR were in no small measure related to his implacable belief that the two Koreas must be reunited and that this was no time to sign an armistice. He underlined his point by releasing a further 2,000 'non-repatriates' over the next few days. Syngman Rhee ordered the news to be broadcast over Radio Seoul; commanded the ROK police to help the former prisoners; and urged the people of South Korea to care for them in their homes. In the opinion of General Mark Clark, Rhee's action betrayed the United Nations' promises to the communists regarding the orderly exchange of prisoners and gave the communists every reason for delaying the peace talks.

President Eisenhower and Prime Minister Churchill agreed. Syngmann Rhee's reckless release of prisoners and his much-publicized hostility to an armistice seemed calculated to undermine the delicate position of the United States at the peace negotiations; while Britain was concerned for the welfare of Commonwealth prisoners in communist hands. General Mark Clark indicated that although the ROK army fought under his command, he had no control over the actions of Syngman Rhee's government. President Eisenhower therefore sent his personal representatives to Seoul to seek an assurance from the South Korean leader that such unilateral action would never occur again. The seriousness of the matter can hardly be over-emphasized. The one issue that had plagued the Korean armistice negotiations had been the Chinese insistence that every prisoner-of-war must be returned to his home country, by force if necessary. This was something the United Nations could not accept and progress in the talks had been based upon careful numerical assessments of each class of prisoner involved. Screening prisoners to detect their political affinities and their personal preferences had been grist to the communist mill and much propaganda had emerged from these processes as the war dragged into the Spring and Summer of 1953. However, as the days passed and the hard-fought communist offensives resulted in some tangible 'real estate' prizes for the Chinese, their delegates seemed anxious to end the war. Chinese front-line troops – those that had survived – were tired and the escalating air raids on their road and rail communications plus the bombing of their hydro-electric dams and generators reduced the fighting capacity of the Chinese People's Volunteers. Moreover, Mao Zedong could no longer count on generous Soviet aid. New leaders emerging in the Soviet Union, fronted by Georgi Malenkov, desired peace and were unlikely to back Mao Zedong in a protracted conflict.

On 19 July the delegates met for their 158th session at Panmunjom where the communist delegates accepted American assurances that President Rhee's action would not be repeated. General William K. Harrison, the senior UN negotiator, suggested that the armistice date should be 24 July but procedural difficulties put it back to 27 July. All fighting would cease twelve hours after the signing of the armistice. On 27 July General Harrison arrived by helicopter at Panmunjom. General Nam Il, the senior communist negotiator, drove to the site in a jeep. Both entered the hall, specially constructed by the communists, where the armistice would be signed. Formalities were brief. Immediately after he had signed copies of the truce in English, Korean and Chinese, Nam Il glanced at his watch and strode out of the building. It was just after 1000 hours. Commonwealth representatives had witnessed the ceremony: Major General West GOC for Britain; Brigadier Allard for Canada; Brigadier Wilton for Australia and Brigadier Park for New Zealand. Later the documents were removed to General Mark Clark's advance headquarters at Munsan-ni for signature by him on behalf of the United Nations, by Marshal Kim Il Sung for North Korea and General Peng Dehuai for the People's Republic of China. Meanwhile, after General Mark Clark and the US ambassador had visited President Syngman Rhee, the South Korean government promised not to obstruct the peace and trusted that an international conference would soon settle the problems of a divided Korea. In New York the Canadian President of the United Nations General Assembly, Lester Pearson, arranged a special political conference for 17 August to address this specific issue.

The armistice agreement's opening statements were crucial:

> A Military Demarcation Line shall be fixed and both sides shall withdraw two (2) kilometres from this line so as to establish a Demilitarized Zone . . . a buffer zone to prevent the occurrence of incidents which might lead to a resumption of hostilities.

Over the radio came instructions from Pyongyang ordering all communist troops to obey the terms of the truce. Off the Korean coast, the United Nations naval forces withdrew to a distance of two miles. In the air a B-26 Invader dropped the last bombs on North Korea at 2136 and just before 2200 hours another B-26 completed the final reconnaissance mission. All UN aircraft now withdrew three miles behind the 38 degree Parallel to respect a new 'no-fly' zone.

## THE TROOPS HEAR THE NEWS

The truce had been signed at 1000 hours local time and became effective 12 hours later at 2200 hours. Signals corporals up and down the line reported the news to the soldiers. Was the war over? Nearly, but it was still business as usual until 2200 hours. There had been so many false alarms that the troops on the 'sharp end' were resigned to the possibility that there might be another hitch in the negotiations and that the fighting would resume. So the patrols went out as usual that night, the outposts remained at full alert and the message was that if the 'Chinkies,' or 'gooks' (and these terms were anything but signs of disrespect) were encountered, shoot them as usual. Standing patrols were therefore delighted when shortly before 2200 hours their radios crackled with the order, 'Able Charlie Fox, this is your Sunray. You can come in now. I say again, come in now.' Gunners and infantry soldiers vied with one another to claim they had fired the last shots in the war. Opposite the Hook, Chinese loudspeakers urged the Australians to come over and fraternize. Flares and tracers soared high into the air; mortars loosed off their Very lights. 20th Field Regiment, Royal Artillery, projected red, white and blue air bursts and 107 Battery, which had fired more rounds than either 12 or 45 Battery, was given the order to fire the parting shots. Major F. S. G. Shore MC was delighted. 'I shall always remember my final order to the Battery's loaded and waiting guns: "For the last time in action in Korea. One round gun-fire . . . FIRE!" Heaven alone knows what the target was. It didn't matter.'[1] Then up and down the line the buglers sounded Cease Fire and Last Post.

Shortly after dawn, on 28 July 1953, Chinese soldiers appeared on the hills, their bunkers garlanded with banners and paper decorations. One or two came across to the UN lines to meet their former opponents and a few intrepid souls made their way to the Chinese hills to report that at least their beer was good. However, there was little time for pleasantries. In front of the Canadians many thousands of Chinese soldiers emerged from their camouflaged bunkers, moving backwards and forwards across the paddy fields to demonstrate their overwhelming numerical superiority. Elsewhere, small groups of unarmed Chinese walked towards patches of quick lime that covered the bodies of their comrades and quickly recovered their dead. UN troops had three days to pull out of the line, three days to pack up the heavy equipment, roll up the signal wire and dismantle the bunkers. Then, shouldering their unloaded weapons, they marched down the reverse slopes to the waiting trucks, leaving forever the hills they had defended since 1951. Behind them were signs proclaiming 'Keep Out – Demilitarized Zone.' Down rumbled the tanks and artillery: the Centurions, the Pattons, the Pershings, US tractors towing howitzers, Royal Artillery quads towing limbers and 25 pounders. Last to leave were the sappers who had set charges and exploded the remains of the static war defences.

Coincidental with the armistice, 27 July 1953, the United Nations Command in Washington issued a statement endorsed by all 16 member states who had contributed military aid to the Korean War. All supported the terms of the armistice and promised to help the UN create a united, independent and democratic Korea. Moreover, they categorically stated that if any aggressor resumed the war in defiance of United Nations principles they would resist with military action and warned that such action would not necessarily be confined to Korea. This is generally referred to as the 1953 Sixteen-Nation Agreement, underlining the UN commitment to a peaceful Korea.


OPERATION 'BIG SWITCH'

The United Nations forces prepared for a possible resumption of hostilities and began constructing new defence works across Korea in case hostilities were resumed. Despite these precautions, it seemed that the armistice would hold and during August 1953 Operation 'Big Switch' – the prisoner exchanges – began. It had been agreed that this would take place within 60 days of the truce and the operation was controlled by a Neutral Nations Repatriation Commission composed of Sweden, Switzerland, Poland, India, and Czechoslovakia and chaired by Lt General K.S. Thimayya of India. Prisoners who did not wish to return to their home country were the responsibility of the 190th Indian Infantry Brigade, the special custodial force. This question of 'non-repatriates' had been one of the most difficult areas of disagreement at Panmunjom and it was not fully settled for some years. General Thimayya resolved the bulk of the problem by the beginning of 1954 and many Chinese were sent to Taiwan, while captured South Koreans, forced into the communist armies, remained in the south. The Indians finally left Korea in 1954.[2]

The overwhelming majority of UN personnel captured by the communists were eager to return home. Many who arrived at Freedom Village were seriously ill and certainly should have been repatriated in the earlier 'Little Switch'. They had many stories to tell and Fusilier Kinne's was not untypical. Once he heard the news that the armistice had been signed he applied to the Chinese commander to be released as one of the sick and wounded. He was told he was being held for his own good! Enquiring why, Kinne was informed that because he had been a 'difficult' captive those fellow prisoners who had been 'good students' might now wish to kill him! Kinne replied he was willing to take the risk! Eventually, he was deemed suitable for release and he travelled to a transit camp near Kaesong in a cattle truck. Just before he was driven to the exchange point, a Chinese soldier snatched from his hands a list of his fellow prisoners' names scribbled on an empty pack of Red Cross cigarettes. For a moment he thought his release would be stopped but the truck moved on to Freedom Village.

Senior officers of all nations were there to greet their newly-liberated countrymen though for the British troops the sight of the WVS ladies must have been the most welcome. Two WV, 'acting as barmaids, put down a glass of frothy ice-cold beer (courtesy of the NAAFI) in front of each returning POW and the light in their eyes will always be remembered by the WVS ladies involved.'[3] Sick and wounded were given immediate attention and were then usually flown for hospitalization in Japan. Altogether, 12,755 United Nations prisoners were released by the communists during Big Switch between 5 August and 6 September 1953; while the UN released 70,183 North Koreans and 5,640 Chinese. The combined totals of Little Switch and Big Switch involved the exchange of 82,493 communists for 13,457 UN personnel.

## RETURNING HOME

There was no mass evacuation of United Nations forces from South Korea. It had been customary for the American Eighth Army to rotate its soldiers back to the States at the conclusion of each tour. British Commonwealth troops were usually relieved in battalions, though individual reservists and National Servicemen would depart their units as their demobilization date drew closer. Consequently there had grown up a regular trooping operation between Pusan and the United States and Pusan and the United Kingdom. This was supplemented by trans-Pacific aircraft such as the speedy Constellations and the huge Globemasters, ideal for transporting the critically wounded back for hospitalization in the US. Most British troops, having had their two Korean War medal ribbons sewn on their uniforms, came home by ship. One reason, it was widely believed, was to give time for any dreadful diseases picked up in Korea to manifest themselves! In fact, there was no alternative to the troopship as Britain did not possess a fleet of long-range air transports. A sea-voyage in the sun was usually enjoyable after leaving the Seaforth Transit Camp at Pusan.

Norman 'Taff' Davies took the troopship *Empire Longford* to Kure, Japan, and then came home in the *Trooper*: 'As we pulled away from the docks the inevitable American Negro band was there to play us off. They must have been a permanent fixture on that dock side and I swear I saw the same musicians that greeted me eighteen months previously.'[4] Ron Larby heard the same band as he was leaving Pusan. However, the Americans were not playing for him but for the Royal Norfolks who were bound for Hong Kong for a spell of garrison duty. His troop transport was the *Orwell*, a fast ship that would take him to the UK before his two years of National Service expired. For a moment his thoughts were elsewhere: 'As land slips away, a silence falls on the men crowding the ship's rails. Most are lost in private thought. Everyone has known someone who would not be coming home, who would be staying forever in the Land of the Morning Calm.'[5]

When they arrived in the UK, usually at Southampton, there were no bands playing; just a few anxious relatives, wives with babies their husbands had never seen – and the Customs and Excise. These officials scanned each disembarking serviceman for the two tell-tale ribbons that would show the wearer had served in Korea. Because so many had seen action at the 'sharp end' it was correctly assumed that some would try to smuggle souvenir carbines, burp-guns and Colt .45s as well as the usual watches and cameras bought in Tokyo's PX. John Martin had visited the PX and spent $800 on '. . . a Rolex Oyster, $15 \times 70$ binoculars, a tiny jewel-encrusted Longines lady's dress watch, a hundred pairs of nylons, a thousand cigars and cigarettes and the latest model Winchester pump-action shotgun, plus shells . . .'[6] He had three kit-bags and, hidden in a ship's locker, a .45 Colt automatic and a Thompson sub-machine-gun. The weapons went over the side and are presumably still immersed in Southampton's mud. Excise and Customs found everything else – apart from the lady's watch – and he had to pay duty on his bargain purchases.

## THE GENEVA CONFERENCE 1954

Negotiators representing the United Nations Command had grown accustomed to the communist technique of inserting political issues into conference discussions and thus delaying the moment of decision. They therefore accepted the communist proposal that all political issues should be on the agenda of a post-armistice conference. This was written into Article 60 of the Armistice Agreement:

> In order to ensure the peaceful settlement of the Korean question, the military Commanders of both sides hereby recommend to the governments concerned on both sides that, within three months after the Armistice Agreement is signed and becomes effective, a political conference of a higher level of both sides be held by representatives appointed respectively to settle through negotiations the questions of the withdrawal of all foreign forces from Korea, the peaceful settlement of the Korean questions, etc.

On 26 April 1954 the Geneva Conference assembled to debate these matters together with the growing crisis in French Indo-China. Its members included the 16 nations that had given military aid to the United Nations during the Korean War, together with the Soviet Union, the People's Republic of China and North Korea. Its primary object had been the the reunification of Korea, though this was overshadowed by the developing conflict in French Indo-China. UN negotiators must have known that their proposals for a reunited Korea would fall on deaf ears. They insisted that the United Nations was a competent authority to deal with the problems of reunification; and that, until the new Korea could demonstrate that it had full civil backing and was ready to conduct democratic elections under UN supervision, then UN troops must remain in Korea. Communist delegates rejected the authority of the United Nations, arguing that the Korean War had been a civil war, deliberately enlarged by UN intervention. For them, the withdrawal of foreign troops was a precondition for elections in Korea. There was no meeting of minds at Geneva in 1954 as far as Korea was concerned and on 15 June 1954 the conference announced that it had failed to solve the Korean problems. Five days later the conference dispersed, having made its decisions on Indo-China. All the 16 nations could do was to reissue their declaration of 27 July 1953 to show their commitment to South Korea.

Thus the document that both ends the Korean War and preserves the existence of the *two* Koreas remains the armistice agreement. Article I enshrines the Military Demarcation Line and the Demilitarized Zone and its main points are summarized below:

(a) A Demilitarized Zone shall be established as a buffer zone to prevent the occurrence of incidents which might lead to a resumption of hostilities.

(b) The waters of the Han River Estuary shall be open to civil shipping of both sides. Civil shipping shall have unrestricted access to the land under the military control of that side.

(c) Neither side shall execute any hostile act within, from, or against the Demilitarized Zone.

(d) No person, military or civilian, shall be permitted to cross the Military Demarcation Line unless specifically authorized to do so by the Commander into whose territory entry is sought.

There have been several incidents along the Demilitarized Zone since 1953, some of which are described in the final chapter, but in every case all have been resolved without involving either of the Koreas in open warfare.

## GUARDING SOUTH KOREA

On 8 August 1953 the United States signed the Mutual Defense Treaty with South Korea. Syngman Rhee promised to abide by the terms of the armistice if America would continue to defend and give aid to the Republic of Korea. The Americans also wished to impose some conditions and the final treaty (endorsed in January 1954) stated that in the face of a 'common danger' South Korea and the United States would react according to their constitutional processes. This treaty, which survives today, guaranteed a US military presence of some 40,000 personnel stationed in Korea. Other UN members gradually whittled down their forces. The Turks had provided the fourth largest infantry force during the Korean War and had rotated three brigades during the war. A fourth brigade arrived in July 1953 and remained in Korea until May 1954. Australian troops remained in South Korea until April 1957 when the last infantry section withdrew. Canada's 3rd PPCLI left in 1953 after being relieved by the 2nd Black Watch (Royal Highland Regiment) of Canada so that a full brigade remained intact in Korea up to 8 November 1954. Thereafter, the Canadians gradually reduced their forces: the Queen's Own Rifles of Canada enjoyed a brief stay but then returned to Canada in April 1955; just one battalion remained in 1956. Britain continued to rotate infantry battalions through Korea. These were the 1st Battalions of distinguished regiments. Four arrived in 1953 and served until 1954: the Royal Scots, the Essex Regiment, the King's Own Royal Regiment and the North Staffordshire Regiment. The Northamptonshire Regiment and the Royal Irish Fusiliers stayed barely six months (July–December 1954) while the Dorset Regiment (1954–5) was relieved by the Queen's Own Cameron Highlanders (1955–6). Then on 15 July 1957 the Union Jack was lowered for the last time at the Royal Sussex Regiment's base on the Imjin River, close to Gloster Hill. In the autumn of 1957 the last combat elements of the British Army embarked at Inchon and left The Land of the Morning Calm forever.

# CHAPTER 19

# Perspectives on the Korean War

In the west, the Korean conflict is usually assessed as a 'just war' fought by 16 nations and their 7 non-combatant allies to halt a communist aggressor and for no other reason. They had responded to a United Nations call to preserve world peace and this they had achieved. But the simplicity of this aim in 1950 was gradually fogged by the nature of the war that developed on the Korean peninsula during 1951–3. Because there had been no formal declaration of war on North Korea or on China and because there were no easily identified objectives it became impossible to focus prolonged public interest on anonymous battlefields in a distant land. For the United States in particular it was not a popular war. The heavy casualties suffered by infantry units offended the American people and made them hope for an early end to what was, in their eyes, the pointless carnage in Korea.

But there was no concerted plea for peace once the one slight chance of ending the war had been lost in November 1950, following the Chinese 'disappearance' into the mountains of North Korea. Both the United States of America and the People's Republic of China had decided on a military solution to the Korean problem; and both underestimated each other's military capacity and determination. There was never any formal diplomatic exchange between the two powers; all suggestions were fed through third parties either at Panmunjom or in neutral capitals. Historically, the Chinese felt they had every right to intervene in Korea. In January 1593 they had crossed the frozen Yalu to oppose a Japanese invasion force that had occupied Pusan, Seoul and Pyongyang. Thereafter Korea had been a Chinese 'tributary state' until defeat in the Sino-Japanese War of

1894–5 had forced China to recognize Korea as an independent kingdom. As there was no doubt in their minds that current Chinese military policy was appropriate to the situation, the Chinese government was not inclined to engage in diplomacy. Instead, China would drive the UN out of North Korea, and this they successfully accomplished during December 1950. Thus Britain's well-intentioned proposal for a buffer zone emerged too late in 1950 to have any significant impact. Yet in 1953, after tens of thousands had died, both sides accepted a four kilometre-wide 'buffer' or demilitarized zone across Korea that would persist into the next millennium.

## JAPAN PROFITS FROM THE WAR

The prolongation of the Korean War was of immediate economic and political benefit to the Japanese people. Japan had emerged from the atomic horrors of 1945 as a defeated, occupied nation. Though administered by General MacArthur, Supreme Commander Allied Powers (SCAP) as their military ruler, the Japanese people retained Emperor Hirohito as their Head of State. MacArthur and his advisers envisaged the gradual creation of a new democratic Japan, economically viable with a strong consumer market. This notion was boosted by the demands of the Korean War. An influx of United Nations troops provided an instant consumer market and a new source of foreign currency. The military needed air and naval bases, elaborate training areas and leave centres for the troops. Japanese workers found plenty of well paid-jobs within the UN military machine. Military contracts flooded into Japanese firms and previous talk of abolishing the former industrial giants (the *zaibatsu*) vanished. Mitsui, Sumitomo and Mitsubishi were not only preserved, they were expanded by US investment and advised on the latest production methods and quality control techniques by imported experts such as W. Edwards Denning. It was the demands of the war that revitalized Japanese heavy industry, especially ship-building, the pharmaceutical industry, beer production and oil-refining. It was all financed by the American Special Procurements system whereby the US armed forces in Japan and Korea were authorized to purchase goods locally produced. During 1950 Special Procurements totalled $149 million; by 1953 they reached $809 million. Between 1950 and 1953 Japan's Gross Domestic Product increased by 10 per cent each year. Her exports increased by 53 per cent, all explained by the massive American spending in Japan totalling nearly three billion dollars between 1950 and 1954.

Typical of the Japanese experience were the stories of Toyota and Sony.[1] Toyota's president, Shotaro Kamiya, was anxious to produce Ford cars under licence in Japan as his own products were selling at barely 300 trucks a month. He arrived in the USA on the same day that the North Korean invasion began. Ford turned him down and a disconsolate Shotaro went back to Japan where he found the industrial world being turned upside down by the Americans. They desperately needed trucks of every description. Shotaro was besieged by contracts and Toyota began its spectacular rise to prosperity, confirmed when America's General Motors approached the company to make small automobiles in California! Two engineers, Ako Morita and his friend Ibuka, produced an entirely new consumer product based on Second World War German experience, the new American Wilcox-Gay tape recorder, and the tape produced by the Minnesota Mining and Manufacturing Company (now called 3M). Before long the two engineers had found work using their new tape-recorders with the American Forces Radio Service and the Fifth Air Force. From such small beginnings grew the high-technology firm called Sony.

The existence of army, navy and air force bases in Japan, plus the fact that the UN commander had his headquarters in Tokyo, gave the United Nations a 'sanctuary' just as valuable as Manchuria would become for the communists. There was also active Japanese support for the UN forces though it was not publicized during the Korean War. Japan's Special Minesweeping Flotilla under the control of Admiral Takeo Okubo did invaluable work for the UN during its major amphibious operations; while Japanese workers helped to crew landing craft and provide labour in the ports occupied by the UN in Korea.

Such unstinting Japanese support for the UN war effort in Korea undoubtedly influenced the American decision to sign a peace treaty with Japan, something for which Prime Minister Shigeri Yoshida had actively campaigned since 1950. In 1951 he signed the San Francisco Peace Treaty and the Japan–US Mutual Security Treaty. Japan regained her sovereign independence and the formal Allied occupation of Japan ended in 1952. San Francisco allowed the United States to retain military bases in Japan, control the Ryukyu Islands and maintain a major base on the island of Okinawa. Neither the Soviet Union nor the People's Republic of China attended the peace conference and consequently Japan was unable to regain four islands to the immediate north-east of Hokkaido which had been occupied by the Soviet Army in 1945: Habomai, Shikotan, Kunashiri and Etorofu. Clause IX of the San Francisco Treaty forbade Japan to have any armed forces, other than a Self-Defence Force. Between 1952 and 1954, this Self-Defence Force began to grow into a small army, navy and air forces. Of all the great trading nations in the late 1950s Japan was notable in having only a tiny proportion of her GDP – around one per cent – devoted to a defence budget.

As a direct result of the Korean War the United States had funded Japanese economic expansion on condition that Japan became capitalism's eastern bulwark against Russian and Chinese communism. Although the Japanese Lower House had voted for the restoration of trade with China, US funding implied that Japan would *not* revive her pre-1938 trade links with China but would seek her markets in the 'Pacific rim' of Asian countries that were non-communist, and in particular Taiwan, South Korea, Indo-China, India and Indonesia. American paternalism also foreshadowed the time when Japan would become a 'defensive shield' against communism, a desirable role from the point of view of the Americans who were currently applying the same logic to the revitalization and rearmament of West Germany.

## THE EFFECT OF THE WAR ON THE UNITED STATES

At Panmunjom, China (and by implication the Soviet Union as well) and the United States had promised to defend the armistice line against future attack by either of the two Koreas. So a fundamental principle, the sanctity of frontiers, had been enshrined in an agreement between capitalist and communist countries. It should have augured well in the solution of other problems that beset the world in the 1950s. In August 1953 the Soviet Premier Georgi Malenkov had spoken of 'peaceful coexistence' between the superpowers. Briefly, Moscow assumed that future conflicts might be solved through negotiation and not by military force. The new Soviet leadership must have been impressed by the fact that the three-year war in Korea, essentially a bloodthirsty struggle between infantry soldiers using 'conventional' weapons, had been contained within the peninsula and terminated without recourse to atomic bombs. America and her allies had intervened in Korea much more strongly and effectively than the Soviets had ever thought possible.

However, the United States armed forces drew very little comfort from this. They had never wished to fight another war, especially a war that they could not claim to have won outright, with obsolete weaponry and under strict political limitations. Most of all, they were bitterly conscious that the North Korean invasion of 1950 had caught everyone unawares and that the most technologically advanced nation in the world had been hard-pressed to save the perimeter around Pusan. Additionally, the Truman Doctrine requiring the 'containment of communism' had heavily restricted the military, for it implied that America's armed forces must always be reactive when faced with a communist threat. The military had chafed under the President's political and military limitations, notably his refusal to allow them to bomb the Manchurian airfields from which the Russian MiG-15s had operated so effectively.

Under the Republican leadership of President Eisenhower the military expected things to change. General Mark Clark had told a Senatorial subcommittee in 1954 that Americans should always fight to win and should be permitted to adopt tactics to ensure a certain victory. Admiral Joy, General Van Fleet and Air Force General George E. Stratemeyer warned the same subcommittee of the dangers inherent in a 'limited war'. It was soon apparent that the Eisenhower administration was prepared to be more 'hawkish' than Truman's. It was already taking credit for forcing the communists to agree to an armistice in Korea following Eisenhower's veiled threat that he might authorize nuclear strikes if a peace formula could not be agreed. The received view was that America must rearm and, through the creation of a new military-industrial complex, develop weapons capable of dealing with any communist threat. From this the doctrine of 'massive retaliation' swiftly evolved, particularly among the Air Force generals who enjoyed strong Republican support. The first tangible sign of America's ability to launch a 'full retaliatory response' came with the formation of Strategic Air Command equipped first with propeller-driven B-36 bombers and then with subsonic B-47 Stratojets. Strategic Air Command's jet bombers carried nuclear weapons and were soon on perpetual patrol from air bases in the USA and around the world. As nuclear weapons were inappropriate against peasant armies America's defence policy was gradually modified by military thinkers such as General Maxwell Taylor. He defined the concept of 'flexible response:' the United States must judge the best approach to crises that emerged in Europe and the Third World and then select from its vast armoury and its highly trained combat teams the best way of dealing with them. This approach was supported by those US Army and Navy leaders who foresaw limited rather than unrestricted warfare developing in the post-Korea world.

There were two more immediate issues confronting Americans as a consequence of the war in Korea. The first was the distasteful affair of an uncertain number of 'turncoat prisoners' and the 21 American non-repatriates who had chosen to go to China. Most of the 21 later returned to the USA. Undoubtedly, some had collaborated with communist political officers in the prison camps. A few had actually informed on their fellow prisoners or committed more serious crimes. These genuinely feared that if they were exchanged with other prisoners their lives would be in danger. During 1953–4 the US government identified about 75 'Manchurian candidates', that is those former prisoners who might represent a threat to the American way of life. It chose to prosecute a few but in the main preferred to publish denials or 'recantations' by prisoners who had under pressure signed confessions relating to, for example, the use of germ warfare. The media of the day chose to concentrate on why Americans would betray their fellow countrymen and explained this away by saying that these were Americans who had either 'gone soft on communism' or had been subject to brain-washing and thought control. Long after public interest had faded the film *The Manchurian Candidate* was released, starring Frank Sinatra and Laurence Harvey.

The second issue that dominated national interest during and after the Korean War was the 'witch-hunt' launched by Senator McCarthy against suspected communists, the so-called 'Second Red Scare' during 1950–4. A tradition of unearthing subversives in the US government had existed since 1938 through the work of the Senate's House Un-American Activities Committee. In 1950, investigations led to the arrest of Klaus Fuchs in Britain and Julius and Ethel Rosenberg in the USA, all charged with passing atomic secrets to the Soviet Union. The Rosenbergs were executed on 19 June 1953, the first spies in America to be sentenced to death in peacetime. Once the Korean War began, General MacArthur had purged the Japanese Press of its Communist Party members and banned the Japanese pro-communist newspaper *Akahata*. In the United States Congressman Richard Nixon and the Wisconsin Senator Joe McCarthy cast an even wider net to catch suspected communist agents. Public opinion had already been shocked by the revelations concerning Alger Hiss, President of the Carnegie Endowment for International Peace and former secretary of the United Nations Charter Conference. He had been accused of passing state documents to the Russians and, after a mis-trial, was convicted on a lesser charge in 1950. The public, subjected to much media hysteria, were left wondering if more members involved in the nation's admin-istration might be guilty of communist sympathies.

It was this feeling that Senator McCarthy exploited during the Korean War, though his pose as an anti-communist predated it when he spoke at Wheeling, West Virginia (February 1950), claiming to hold in his hand a list of communist sympathizers working in the State Department. When he was asked to provide those names he havered and eventually mentioned Owen Latimore, a well-known expert on East Asia, working at the John Hopkins University. Enquiries showed MacCarthy's allegations to be false but this did not stop the Senator. He simply produced more names and called for their investigation. In all, he hounded hundreds of suspects from the media, the universities and the arts, especially the film industry. Government departments and even General George C. Marshall became favourite targets. Congress was persuaded to pass the 1950 McCarran Internal Security Act which made it illegal to 'combine, conspire or agree with any other person to perform any act that would substantially contribute to . . . the establishment of a totalitarian dictatorship.'

After General Eisenhower won the Presidential election in 1952 it was expected that McCarthy would reduce his campaign to 'expose' communism in America. In fact, his accusations grew wilder and his targets became even more unreal. His ultimate charge was to accuse the United States Army of communist sympathies and he suffered ridicule on television during 1954 when the US Army counsel exposed his fraudulent evidence. Senator McCarthy never unearthed a single communist conspirator in the United States government or its armed forces, though he managed to smear the names of hundreds of innocent people. On 2 December 1954 the US Senate voted to condemn McCarthy and his methods. The Senator died in 1957.

By then the Korean War had been consigned to history, largely forgotten and the sacrifice made by its veterans rarely acknowledged by either side. A new American-backed defence perimeter evolved in the Far East as the 1954 South East Asia Treaty Organization (SEATO), a pale imitation of the 1949 North Atlantic Treaty Organization (NATO). SEATO was a collective military defence organization comprising the USA, France, Britain, Australia, New Zealand, Thailand, Pakistan and the Philippines. Associated states were Laos, Cambodia and Vietnam. There was no formal alliance with Japan. The 1960 Treaty of Mutual Co-operation and Security promised that Japan would contribute to bilateral security with the USA.


## THE EFFECT ON THE PEOPLE'S REPUBLIC OF CHINA

Outwardly, China's successful offensives in 1950–1 and her resistance to the United Nations in the static war 1951–3 defined her as a new world power. Following Mao Zedong's announcement of the creation of the People's Republic of China in Beijing on 14 October 1949, the People's Liberation Army (PLA) had defeated the Chinese Nationalists, forcing them to take refuge in Taiwan. On 7 October 1950 the PLA invaded Tibet, causing the Tibetan Cabinet to ask for assistance from the American and British governments. None was forthcoming and the PLA fought a terrible mountain war against the fierce nomadic Khambas in northern Tibet where it lost some 5,000 troops during 1950–1. This was coincidental with Chinese intervention in Korea. Her belief in her military power was unshakeable and caused a costly over-estimation of China's capacity to drive the United Nations from the Korean peninsula. For that was always her aim: Zhou Enlai had reiterated the consistent Chinese position in December 1950: peace in Korea required that, 'all foreign troops must be withdrawn from Korea and Korea's domestic affairs must be settled by the Korean people themselves. The American aggression forces must be withdrawn from Taiwan. And the representatives of the People's Republic of China must obtain legitimate status in the United Nations.'

None of these objectives had been secured by the time the Korean armistice was signed in 1953. The issue of Taiwan was complicated when Japan signed the 1951 peace treaty and agreed to relinquish all claims to Taiwan and the Pescadores. However, she did not actually cede them to anyone. Georgi Malenkov was inclined to the view that Taiwan belonged to China and with his assurance of communist solidarity PLA gunners began shelling the offshore islands of Quemoy and Matsu in 1954, while Chinese aircraft bombed the Tachen Islands. When PLA soldiers invaded the tiny island of Yikianshan, they escalated the possibility of yet another war in East Asia. US sent military aid to Taiwan; several PLA divisions appeared on the coastline facing Taiwan. But the threat came to nothing, possibly because Zhou Enlai wished to speak at the forthcoming Third World Bandung Conference to be held in Indonesia in April 1955.

There was probably another reason. China was in no position to mount a war against Taiwan, the United States and her SEATO allies. In an interview between John Robert Young and General Sir Anthony Farrar-Hockley, the General gave his assessment of the PLA after their grievous losses during 1950–3:

> The Korean War changed the whole basis of the PLA, inasmuch as it went into Korea as Mao's obedient tool and came out three years later disenchanted with his leadership. This was because they had been told that weapons were not the first matter of importance, but men, and above all, men's spirit and attitude. They had lost hundreds of thousands of men because they lacked the right equipment and weapons. They had also lost the best of their political officers who had been killed or severely wounded in battle. The result was that they never again trusted Mao or were his absolutely reliable servants.
>
> There was a rising movement in the services that was quick to see that there had to be a change once Mao had gone and the era of the Little Red Book was over. So Zhou Enlai was secretly in favour of improvements in weaponry in all the main services and when Deng Xiaoping came to power he was of the same opinion.[2]

There were other factors too. The rapport between Mao Zedong and Stalin did not persist into the Khruschev and Brezhnev years and there was a widening gap between the political philosophies of the two great communist powers. When the popular Marshal Peng Dehuai argued at the 1959 Party Conference that links between Russia and China were vital to the PLA's modernization programme, Mao's jealousy of China's greatest soldier exploded. His attitude to Peng Dehuai exceeded Stalin's jealousy of Marshal Zhukov in 1945. Mao arrested Peng, tortured him and he died in 1974. By then China had confronted Russia in an armed clash at the 'Battle of Damansky Island' (1969), exploded her own atomic and hydrogen bombs (1964 and 1967) and become a member of the United Nations (1971).[3] Taiwan remained under Chinese Nationalist rule; the two Koreas remained divided.

## THE EFFECT UPON BRITAIN

During the Second World War President Roosevelt and Prime Minister Churchill had cemented a 'special relationship' between the United States and Britain. Although Churchill had been defeated by Clement Attlee and the Labour Party in 1945, the uncertainties of the 'Cold War' and the mutual interests of Britain and America made the 1941–5 alliance equally important in the post-1945 world. Britain viewed US military and economic support as paramount if she were to remain a world power, and both countries saw in the Soviet Union the greatest threat to international peace. That is why Attlee's Foreign Secretary, Ernest Bevin, was so anxious to create the North Atlantic Treaty Organization in 1949 to give teeth to President Truman's determination to contain communism. For the first time, traditionally isolationist America had made a commitment to the defence of Western Europe for which Britain was deeply grateful. The fact that America now dominated the Atlantic alliance did not trouble the Labour government which made its own substantial contribution by committing the British Army of the Rhine to bases in West Germany. Bevin was careful to maintain smooth working relationships with Secretary of State Dean Acheson and placed great reliance on an expert on foreign relations, the British ambassador in Washington Sir Oliver Franks. Bevin also kept a firm grasp of military developments in the United States and its spheres of interest through the British Joint Services Commission based in the USA.

Apart from the forces allocated by the United States and South Korea, Britain made the largest contribution to the Korean War. The 'special relationship' was as strong as ever though it was no longer a partnership of equals. British actions were now largely subject to American decisions and though Labour ministers often flew to Washington to confer with the President of the United States their views and their ambitions almost always had to defer to American decisions. So when the first British naval and land forces went to war against North Korea in 1950 they were fighting not for South Korea but to demonstrate the reality of the Anglo-American alliance and its determination to resist international communism. That is why, when

Syngman Rhee's soldiers and police committed horrific atrocities, or when British troops were sent to guard communist prisoners on Koje-do, Britain would voice her protests in Parliament but never reduce her commitment to the United States of America. Throughout the war, Britain accepted that American commanders in Korea took their orders from the Pentagon and not from the United Nations; and that British forces in Korea were under the command of American generals and admirals. Admittedly, loud protests came after the Chinese intervention in the winter of 1950 and there was a very real fear that America might widen the war in Korea. However, it was soon clear that Attlee's flight to Washington, and the subsequent myth that he had stopped America from using atomic weapons, had satisfied the British.

Initial costs of funding naval and military operations in and around Korea had been reluctantly accepted by most shades of opinion in the Labour Party. Labour's Party Conference in October 1950, where opposition might have been expected, endorsed government policy. The £4.7 billion allocated to rearmament would, however, bite into sums reserved for the health and welfare services of which Labour was so proud. It was something that Aneurin Bevan, Minister of Labour, could not stomach and his resignation on 22 April 1951 was really a protest against the way in which Attlee and the rest of the Cabinet had become the slaves of American foreign policy. For example, unlike America Britain had recognized the sovereign power of the People's Republic of China on 6 January 1950, months before the outbreak of the Korean War. In 1951 Foreign Secretary Herbert Morrison and Chancellor of the Exchequer Hugh Gaitskell visited Washington to expose their anxieties about America's intentions with regard to China. They wished for guarantees that American would not bomb Chinese airfields, introduce Chinese Nationalist troops from Taiwan or widen the war in any fashion. The Americans offered general assurances but did not allay the British fears. At the same time Clement Attlee decided on a General Election, though the Korean War never emerged as a significant issue. After winning a narrow victory in October 1951, Winston Churchill returned as leader of a Conservative government with a majority of 20 seats in Parliament.

Conservative attitudes to the Korean War differed little from Labour's own policies. Churchill and his Foreign Secretary, Anthony Eden, made the ritual flight to Washington in January 1952 but both found that they could do nothing except underline the policies established by Ernest Bevin. They discovered the then secret contingency plans America had for ending the war and proposed to announce these to Parliament on their return. Acheson, shocked by the willingness of the British to betray American secrets about future bombing plans just to score political points against the Labour Party, persuaded Churchill to relent. When the bombing of the North Korean hydro-electric plants began Anthony Eden dutifully appeared in Parliament to defend American actions just as Foreign Secretaries before him had done.

After General Eisenhower won the US Presidential election on 5 November 1952 Churchill hoped for a renaissance of the old 'wartime spirit' that had existed between the two men during 1944–5. Eisenhower visited Korea in December 1952 and had returned convinced that firmer action would have to be taken against the communists. He did not rule out the use of atomic weapons if there was no other way of ending the conflict and was not afraid of publishing his views to the communists. British pressure on the United States made no effect whatsoever; it was the death of Stalin in March 1953 that proved decisive. After Zhou Enlai returned from Moscow, where he had been a pall-bearer at Stalin's funeral, his attitude was transformed and he sought to hasten the peace process. Despite the hostility of Syngman Rhee and his irresponsible political actions, Operations 'Little Switch' went forward smoothly. Britain briefly paid homage to the heroism of her troops during the final battles of the war but was not party, except as a witness, to the armistice signed by an American and a North Korean.

In a sense, this symbolized the lesser status enjoyed by Britain as a world power. Despite her efforts and pretensions, she never managed to determine the way in which America fought the Korean War. Britain was capable of crushing the communist rebellion in Malaya and the Mau Mau revolt in Kenya because in both cases no other nation state intervened in the fighting. Three years after the Korean armistice Suez proved decisive in redefining Britain's status. During 1956, when Britain conspired with France and Israel to topple President Nasser by invading Suez, no support was forthcoming from the United States. In American eyes, the Franco-British attack was an unwarranted action to prop up the last vestiges of empire, a view endorsed by the Soviet Union. The decline of Britain as a world power had become apparent in negotiations over Korea and was sharply underlined by the fiasco of Suez. By 1962 Britain had reluctantly accepted that world peace depended on US monetary and defence policies in Europe, the Middle East and Asia.

## THE TWO KOREAS SINCE 1953

The war was an unmitigated disaster for the Korean people. Tens of thousands of civilians died in North and South Korea as a consequence of shelling and air attack or at the hands of murderous Korean police and soldiery. By 1953 fatal casualties probably ran into 1 or 2 millions, though detailed figures have never been compiled. The war ended as it began, with the two Koreas divided though not precisely on the 38 degree Parallel. South Korea gained a modest increase in territory as the armistice line snaked into the south-east corner of North Korea. Neither country has secured general international recognition. Britain, for example, had maintained a legation in Pusan during 1950–3 while the abandoned diplomatic compound in Seoul had reputedly been used as a mess-hall first by Chinese and then by UN soldiers. A renovated embassy opened in 1957 with Sir Hubert Evans as British ambassador.[4]

Under the leadership of Kim Il Sung (1912–94) North Korea's watchwords were nationalism and self-reliance. With the backing of the Soviet Union and the People's Republic of China, Kim created a Stalinist state, a 'cult of personality' and basked in the title of 'Great Leader'. Kim Il Sung combined the post of head of state with that of party secretary, and guided the regeneration of heavy industry and mechanized agriculture in war-shattered North Korea. Stalinist philosophy influenced Kim Il Sung's agricultural policy and farming did not prosper in the post-1953 years. The disappearance of the Soviet Union and declining aid from China contributed to North Korea's predicament but the decisive factors were climatic and demographic change in the 1990s when North Korea encountered the twin problems of famine and a declining population. Successive years of drought followed by floods in 1994 created famine, disease and emigration. Some estimates state that North Korea's population fell from 24 million in 1994 to 22 million five years later. Many must have died but significant numbers have migrated to China and Russia.

Relations with South Korea remained tense after 1953 and both North and South seemed anxious to destabilize the other. However, South Korea's remarkable economic development and the strength of her armed forces presented a reality that Kim Il Sung could not ignore, and he attempted to achieve some sort of parity by building nuclear weapons and urging closer co-operation between the two Koreas. After becoming a member of the United Nations in 1991 (simultaneously with South Korea), North Korea signed a non-aggression pact with South Korea. Families divided by the cease-fire line were to be reunited and a hot-line between the two capitals was set up to avoid border crises. In 1992 the two Koreas promised to ban the manufacture and deployment of nuclear weapons and North Korea signed the Nuclear Safeguards Agreement by which nuclear powers allow UN inspectors to visit their nuclear sites. Few promises were kept by either side.

Kim Il Sung died suddenly on 8 July 1994 immediately prior to a planned summit meeting with South Korea's President Kim Young Sam. His successor was his son, Kim Jong Il, who regarded his father as 'president in perpetuity'. He therefore took the title of Chairman of the National Defence Committee and was known as the 'Dear Leader'. He had to face the problem of food shortages. International aid agencies helped him to some extent but he looked to the United States for massive supplies of grain. These depended on proof that North Korea was not in breach of the 1994 anti-nuclear pact. Ever since a North Korean rocket missile overflew Japan in 1998 to land in the Pacific both Japan and the United States were distinctly cool in their relations with Kim Jong Il. The Japanese were convinced that this was a prototype Taepodong I ballistic missile with a range of nearly 800 miles. They also had evidence that North Korea was developing Taepodong II with a range of 3,800 miles.

In South Korea the dictatorial regime of Syngman Rhee sparked off a student rebellion and he was forced to resign on 27 April 1960. Chang Myon became the constitutional prime minister but was overthrown by General Park Chung who became the elected president in 1965. In 1971 US troops began withdrawing from their defence positions south of the Demilitarized Zone, a process completed in 1991. The 'front line' in South Korea was thereafter held by ROK Army forces in the expectation that South Korea would remain stable under the stern rule of a popular military leader. Following the assassination of President Chang in 1979 South Korea was placed under martial law and President Chun Doo took office on 1 September 1980. Political disorder sparked by discontented trade unionists and students in 1987 led to promises of democratic elections and President

Roh Tae Woo came to power. Both he and Chang were later accused of bribery, corruption and treason but were released after the payment of heavy fines. Despite these charges, they had shown some commitment to democratic, constitutional government and genuine progress towards this goal was made after the Democratic Liberal Party, formed in 1990, won an elected majority.

President Kim Young Sam (1992–7) and his successor Kim Dae Jung faced the most serious trading crisis to sweep the tiger economies of East Asia. South Korea had prospered through first American and then Japanese investment and shared with China, Taiwan, Singapore, Malaysia and Hong Kong the excellent profits from its high technology exports. Investment capital modernized heavy industry and South Korea became a specialist ship-building nation, a major exporter of automobiles worldwide and an investor in China's special economic zones. Huge manufacturing conglomerates known as *chaebol* (comparable with Japan's *zaibatsu*) had prospered though, unlike the Japanese, South Korea's *chaebol* such as the automobile manufacturer Hyundai exploited their workforce by demanding long shifts and paying low wages. Then during 1996–8 an economic crisis caused by reckless lending by irresponsible banks to the *zaibatsu* and *chaebol* rocked East Asia. The value of South Korea's currency, the *won*, collapsed in 1997 and the government went cap in hand to the International Monetary Fund and asked it to shore up industry with $57 billion. Naturally, the IMF sought guarantees requiring South Korea to carry out financial reform and make her industrial sectors more efficient. Massive job losses resulted and union pressure forced President Kim Dae Jung to boost pay awards to those remaining in work. Consequently, during 1998–9 South Korea's industrial workforce enjoyed the second highest wages in East Asia; while out of a workforce of some twelve million, between one and two million were unemployed.

While the economies of both Koreas were in a parlous state, their border relations remained fraught with danger and potential crisis. Incidents along the Demilitarized Zone were all too common, culminating in the 1967 clashes when the ROK Army resorted to artillery fire. During 1974–5 the UN Command revealed that two infiltration tunnels under the DMZ had been constructed by the North Koreans and in 1976 the infamous 'axe murders' caused the deaths of two US officers within the DMZ. In the air the North Koreans shot down an American E-C 121 reconnaissance aircraft on 13 April 1969 and a helicopter in August the same year. Several clashes ocurred around the coasts involving North Korean 'commando' raids, and in 1968 North Korean warships captured the USS *Pueblo* when it was engaged on intelligence work. There were also two 'submarine incidents' involving North Korean vessels. The first was in 1996 when a North Korean submarine ran aground on reefs and ROK soldiers killed 24 of the crew.[5]

Then in June 1998 a North Korean submarine became entangled in fishing nets and the North Koreans later admitted that it had been on an intruder mission. Perhaps the most serious incident was the battle in the Yellow Sea fought on 15 June 1999 during which a North Korean torpedo boat was sunk. For several days North Korean fishing boats had tried to cross the demarcation line into South Korea's rich crab-fishing grounds. On 15 June North Korean gunboats opened fire on South Korean boats and this led to the ten-minute 'Battle of the Yellow Sea'. It was an event taken very seriously by the United States and all ROK and US combat units along the DMZ were put on alert. The USS *Vincennes*, armed with guided missiles, then arrived to patrol the area. The North Koreans then accused the South of deliberately provoking war; the United Nations Command held emergency meetings with the communists in Panmunjom. It was not a good omen for the resumption of talks between the communists and President Kim Dae Jung over the emotive issue of families still separated by the DMZ. Fortunately, as in the case of all other crises since 1953, relations between the North and South did not ultimately worsen.

## CONCLUSIONS

The Korean War was the first ever to be fought by the United Nations in response to an act of aggression by a communist state. To the extent that it preserved the territorial integrity of South Korea from a communist take-over, it was an undoubted success. Its ramifications, however, conditioned much of world history for the remainder of the century. America's experience amidst the war-ravaged hills of Korea led her to militarize the Cold War and to construct her own weapons of nuclear deterrence. This in turn compelled the Soviet Union to compete in a new and punitively expensive arms race that involved the exploration of space and the construction of inter-continental ballistic missiles. Ultimately, that arms race exhausted the resources of the USSR, a major factor in the collapse of Soviet communism in 1991.

The Korean War also witnessed the emergence of the People's Republic of China as a world power and as an ally of North Korea. Simultaneously, it regenerated an independent Japan destined to become the second most powerful capitalist economy in the world. It was therefore unwise for North Korea to have fired a ballistic missile over Japanese waters in 1998 for it threatened the fragile stability of East Asia. It certainly prompted the Japanese to question whether they should amend their constitution which limits the size of their Self Defence Forces. Britain enjoyed a less buoyant economy and perceived a somewhat misty future linked with Europe. Nevertheless, she was still wedded to the notion of a 'special relationship' with America and accepted that the war began her subordination to the world view of the United States. For the Korean people the three-year conflict was a colossal human tragedy leading to a permanently divided peninsula in which ten million people remain separated from their families. It was once thought that the Berlin Wall would never fall or that the two Germanies would never be united. Perhaps one day the common needs of the Korean people will surmount the obstacles of ideological division so that all may agree upon a common understanding of that elusive concept, democracy.

# Endnotes

## 1. THE OUTBREAK OF WAR (pp. 1–17)

1. William Stueck *The Korean War – An International History*, Princeton University Press, Chapter 1.
2. James Chase, *Acheson*, Simon & Schuster 1998 p 186.
3. Stone I. F., *The Hidden History of the Korean War*, Turnstile Press 1952 pp 1–6.
4. Kolko G., *The Politics of War*, Random House 1968, and with Kolko J., *The Limits of Power*, Harper & Row 1972.
5. Bruce Cumings has written extensively on the Korean War and its political antecedents. See especially his Princeton University Press publications *Child of Conflict: the Korean-American Relationship 1947–53* and *The Origins of the Korean War 1945–47*.
6. Her letter in *The Listener* 4 April 1985.
7. Transcripts and Documents, Peter N. Farrar collection (Trans & Docs PNF).

## 2. THE DEFENCE OF THE PUSAN PERIMETER, 1950 (pp. 19–36)

1. Trans & Docs PNF. For a full account of the US predicament see Edwin P. Hoyt, *The Pusan Perimeter*, Stein & Day 1984, Chapter 5.
2. Documents on British Policy Overseas, (DBFPO) Section II, Volume IV, *Korea 1950–51* No. 27.
3. Hoyt, *op cit* pp 231–2.

## 3. THE HAMMER AND THE ANVIL: INCHON AND BEYOND (pp. 37–53)

1. For a good illustrated account of MacArthur's achievements in the Second World War see S. L. Meyer *MacArthur*, Hamlyn 1981.

2. For a first-class account of Inchon see Robert Debs, *Victory at High Tide*, J. B. Lippincott, New York 1968, and Leo Cooper UK 1972. The story of MacArthur's intoning of The Lord's Prayer is on p 255. For a British interpretation see Michael Langley, *MacArthur's Last Triumph*, Batsford 1979.


## 4. THE INVASION OF NORTH KOREA (pp. 55–71)

1. See an account of 1st Middlesex in J. N. Shipster, *The Diehards*, especially Chapter 2. It is printed by Austin Reed plc and the second edition (1983) has a foreword by Colonel Andrew Man. The text includes personal reminiscences of his service in Korea.


## 5. CHINA DEFEATS THE UNITED NATIONS (pp. 73–98)

1. Quoted from S. L. A. Marshall, *The River and the Gauntlet* 1987, p 307 by permission of The Battery Press, Nashville.
2. See Volume 2 of Harry Truman's Memoirs, *Years of Trial and Hope 1946–1953*, Doubleday NY/Hodder & Stoughton 1956, p 417.
3. Quoted from Captain John G. Westover's *Combat Support in Korea (1955)*, p 55, by permission of Combat Forces Press, Washington DC.
4. Not all American authorities agree with this type of operation. Though there is universal admiration for the Royal Marine contribution and the conduct of Task Force Drysdale, US commanders tended not to encourage small scale Task Forces thereafter.
5. Quoted from Russell Spurr, *Enter the Dragon*, p 267 by permission of Macmillan Publishers Ltd.
6. Trans & Docs PNF.
7. Truman, *op cit* pp 419–20.
8. DBFPO, No. 86.


## 6. THE CHINESE WINTER OFFENSIVES AND THE UN RESPONSE, JANUARY–APRIL 1951 (pp. 99–117)

1. Trans & Docs PNF.
2. Under United States General Order No. 16 the Department of the Army recognized the 'extraordinary heroism' of the volunteer French battalion by the award of a Presidential Unit Citation. It recorded that most of the enemy dead were found in front of the French position; and that as a result of the defence of that position the attack by the Chinese 373rd Infantry Regiment 'was routed.'
3. Quoted from *With the Australians in Korea*, editor Norman Barclay, 3rd edition 1960, p 74, by permission of the Australian War Memorial, Canberra, copyright the Australian Government.

## 7. THE CHINESE OFFENSIVES, APRIL–MAY 1951 (pp. 119–37)

1. Quoted from *Red Winds from the North*, Able Publishing 1999, p 94 by permission of Norman 'Taff' Davies.
2. Quoted from *K-Force: To the Sharp End*, Korvet Publishing 1999, p 42, by permission of John Martin.
3. Martin *op cit* pp 48 and 54.
4. Quoted from *The Royal Ulster Rifles in Korea* pp 70–71, by kind permission of the Trustees of the Royal Ulster Rifles Regimental Museum.

## 8. TALKING AND FIGHTNG, MAY–NOVEMBER 1951 (pp. 139–51)

1. Private Pat Knowles, quoted from *Something Extra, 28 Commonwealth Brigade* by Hamish Eaton, Pentland Press 1993, pp 51–2, by kind permission of Mary Eaton.
2. Lt Pembroke, quoted Eaton *op cit* p 52–3.
3. Tom Carew, *The Korean War: The Story of the Fighting Commonwealth Regiments 1950–1953*, Chapter 14, Pan Books Ltd, 1970.
4. Major Tadman's address is quoted from *The Borderers in Korea* by Major General J. F. M. MacDonald CB, DSO, OBE by kind permission of the Trustees of The King's Own Scottish Borderers Regimental Museum, The Barracks, Berwick-on-Tweed.

## 9. LIFE AND DEATH ON THE LINE, 1951–2 (pp. 153–79)

1. Davies, *op cit* p 70.
2. Carole Carr's memories are quoted from General Sir A Farrar-Hockley, *The British Part in the Korean War Vol. I, An Honourable Discharge*, Appendix I 1995 by permission of The Cabinet Office, Her Majesty's Stationery Office.
3. Correspondence with Colin Ross, September 1999.
4. Quoted from *British Forces in the Korean War* (BFKW) edited by Ashley Cunningham-Boothe and Peter N. Farrar 1997, p 107 by permission of Ashley Cunningham-Boothe.
5. BFKW pp 114–8.
6. Quoted from *The Morning Calm* (MC) No. 20 April 1989 by permission of the editor, Reuben Holroyd.
7. Conversation with the author, June 1986.

## 10. NAVAL AND AIR OPERATIONS IN THE KOREAN THEATRE, 1950–1 (pp. 181–205)

1. These extracts from Ed Murrow's broadcasts (CBS 6 February 1950) are reproduced by kind permission of the 6147th Tactical Control Squadron, the Mosquito Association of America.

2. Captain Robert Thresher's description of his air combat over Korea is to be found in Aerospace Publication's *Wings of Fame* Vol. I pp 21–22 and is reproduced by kind permission of the author, Warren Thompson.
3. In the hands of a skilful pilot, the Meteor F8 was capable of besting a MiG-15 in combat. On 1 December 1951 14 Meteors tangled with 40 MiG-15s and F/O Bruce Gogerly shot down 77 Squadron's first MiG kill. On 7 May 1952 P/O Bill Simmonds showed that at low level the Meteor could down a MiG-15. Accounts of these combats may be found in Osprey's *Korean War Aces*. During 1952–3 77 Squadron's Meteors were tasked mainly with ground-attack missions.

## 11. PRISONERS-OF-WAR (pp. 207–26)

1. MC 19 October 1988.
2. MC 27 October 1992.

## 12. NAVAL WARFARE, 1952–3 (pp. 227–37)

1. The log of 802 Squadron, Fleet Air Arm, is quoted by permission of the Fleet Air Arm Museum Records and Research Centre.
2. Carmichael's victory was the first in Korea. Several pilots of piston-engined aircraft had claimed victories over jet-propelled Me 262s during the Second World War.
3. Correspondence with the author 1982.

## 13. THE AIR WAR, 1952–3 (pp. 239–54)

1. Colonel James T. Stewart, *Air Power: The Decisive Force*, Van Nostrand 1957 pp 159–160 by permission of Ayer Company Publishers, NH, USA.
2. Telephone interview, September 1999.

## 14. PROPAGANDA AND PUBLIC OPINION (pp. 255–69)

1. Brian Catchpole, A Map History of China, Heinemann 1988, p 133.
2. Correspondence with the author, September 1999.
3. I am grateful to Dr Elfride Bickersteth, a former lexicographer, for this information.
4. For Colonel Barker's views, see his *Fortune Favours the Brave*, Leo Cooper 1974, pp xiv–xv.
5. Bartlett, *op cit* p 141.
6. John Halliday & Bruce Cumings, *Korea: The Unknown War*, Viking 1988, p 95.
7. I am grateful to Dr J. E. Hoare for permission to quote from his *British Public Opinion and the Korean War* and for his permission to make use of his research work.

## 15. CANADA, NEW ZEALAND AND AUSTRALIA: THEIR SPECIAL CONTRIBUTION (pp. 271–87)

1. For Canada's organization of her Special Force see *Canada's Army in Korea – A Short Official Account*, published by the Historical Section, General Staff, Army HQ, Ottawa; and for Canada's role post-1945 see Godspeed, *The Armed Forces of Canada 1867–1967*, published by the a/m Historical Section, 1967.
2. For a full account of Australian military operations in Korea, see Robert O'Neill, *Australia in the Korean War*, Vol. II Combat Operations, The Australian War Memorial and The Australian Government Publishing Service, 1985.

## 16. THE BATTLES OF THE HOOK AND PORK CHOP, 1952–3 (pp. 289–307)

1. See Chapter 9 for details of the Centurion tanks involved in the Black Watch battle. Lt Anstice commanded the Centurion that climbed the hill. Though his Centurion caught fire, his gun continued to shoot. He was awarded the Military Cross. During this battle the Centurions were in action for six hours.
2. BFKW p 34.
3. BFKW p. 35.
4. *ibid.*
5. MC 30.
6. MC 30.
7. The most absorbing account of this battle is S. L. A. Marshall, *Pork Chop Hill*, William Morrow, NY, edition published in 1956. It was later published in the UK by Panther, 1959. It was made into a film (United Artists – *Pork Chop Hill*) starring Gregory Peck and Harry Guardino).

## 17. PARTISANS AND GUERRILLAS: THE COVERT WAR IN KOREA (pp. 309–17)

1. The most readily available source for these operation is E. Evanhoe, *Dark Moon: Eighth Army Special Operations in the Korean War*, Korvet 1995. It was published simultaneously with the US edition by the US Naval Institute Press, Annapolis, Maryland. For raids by 41 (Independent) Commando Royal Marines see James D. Ladd, *By Sea By Land*, pp 277–287.

## 18. THE ARMISTICE AND AFTER (pp. 319–29)

1. In correspondence between Ashley Cunningham-Boothe and Peter N. Farrar.
2. *The Times* paid tribute to General Thimayya and his 190th Infantry Brigade (23 October 1953) for dealing with this 'thankless task' with tact and patience.
3. BFKW p 52.

4. Davies, *op cit* p 138.
5. Larby, R. *Signals to the Right, Armoured Corps to the Left*, Korvet 1993, p 165.
6. Martin, J. *op cit* p 192.

## 19. PERSPECTIVES ON THE KOREAN WAR (pp. 331–47)

1. For Toyota see Martin Walker, *Cold War*, Fourth Estate 1993 pp 78–80. For Sony see Akio Morita, *Made in Japan*, William Collins 1987/Fontana Paperbacks 1987.
2. Young, J. R., *The Dragon's Teeth: Inside China's Armed Forces*, Hutchinson 1987. This extract is quoted by permission of the Random House Archive and Library.
3. For details of these events see Brian Catchpole, *Map History of China*, Heinemann 1988, Part VII.
4. For details of the embassies in Korea see J. E. Hoare, *Embassies in the East*, Curzon 1999, Part 3: Korea.
5. The most significant coastal and border incidents to 1998 are listed in J. E. Hoare and S. Pares, *Conflict in Korea: An Encyclopaedia*, ABC–CL10 1999.

# APPENDIX I

# An Explanation
# of Common Korean Suffixes

| | |
|---|---|
| bong/pong | Usually describes a large hill or mountain |
| chon | Denotes a small river (e.g. Samichon), a tributary of a larger river |
| dan/tan | Indicates a point |
| do/to | An island |
| dong/tong | A small village or isolated settlement |
| gang | A larger river e.g. Imjin Gang = Imjin River |
| gap/kap | Another term for a point |
| gol/kol | Sometimes a village in a valley or gorge; or can denote the gorge itself |
| li/ni/ri | Denotes an area, a widespread township or several villages |
| lyong/nyong/ryong | A series of hills or mountains or a pass through high ground |
| maul | A village |
| nae | A stream |
| namdo | North province |
| pukto | South province |
| san | A high mountain |

# APPENDIX II

# Korean War Casualties United Nations Forces 1950–3 The Sixteen Nations

| | KIA | Wounded | MIA | POW | TOTAL |
|---|---|---|---|---|---|
| Australia | 291 | 1,240 | 39 | 21 | 1,591 |
| Belgium/ Luxembourg | 97 | 350 | 5 | 1 | 453 |
| Britain | 710 | 2,278 | 1,263 | 766 | 5,017 |
| Canada | 291 | 1,072 | 21 | 12 | 1,396 |
| Colombia | 140 | 452 | 65 | 29 | 686 |
| Ethiopia | 120 | 536 | – | – | 656 |
| France | 288 | 818 | 18 | 11 | 1,135 |
| Greece | 169 | 543 | 2 | 1 | 715 |
| Netherlands | 111 | 589 | 4 | – | 704 |
| New Zealand | 34 | 80 | – | 1 | 115 |
| Philippines | 92 | 299 | 57 | 40 | 488 |
| South Africa | 20 | – | 16 | 6 | 42 |
| South Korea (includes civilians) | 392,000 | 230,000 | 330,000 | 85,000 | 1,037,000 |
| Thailand | 114 | 794 | 5 | – | 913 |
| Turkey | 717 | 2,246 | 107 | 219 | 3,349 |
| United States | 54,246 | 103,284 | 8,177 | 7,000 | 172,707 |

# APPENDIX III

# Principal US Civil and Military Personnel who Served During The Period of the Korean War

PRESIDENT OF THE UNITED STATES AND COMMANDER IN CHIEF
Harry S. Truman                    12 April 1945–20 January 1950
Dwight D. Eisenhower               21 January 1953–20 January 1961

SECRETARY OF STATE
Dean G. Acheson                    21 January 1949–20 January 1953
John Foster Dulles                 21 January 1953–22 April 1959

SECRETARY OF DEFENSE
Louis A. Johnson                   28 March 1949–19 September 1950
George C. Marshall         21 September 1950–12 September 1951
Robert A. Lovett           17 September 1951–20 January 1953
Roger M. Kyes                       2 February 1953–1 May 1954

SENIOR DELEGATES UN COMMAND TALKS AT KAESONG/PANMUNJOM
Vice Admiral C. Turner Joy          10 July 1951–22 May 1952
Lt General William K. Harrison      22 May 1952–27 July 1953

US AMBASSADOR TO THE REPUBLIC OF KOREA
John J. Muccio                      7 April 1949–8 September 1952
Ellis O. Briggs            25 November 1952–12 April 1955

SUPREME COMMANDER ALLIED POWER JAPAN (SCAP)
General of the Army Douglas MacArthur    15 August 1945–11 April 1951
General Matthew B. Ridgway                11 April 1951–28 April 1952

COMMANDER IN CHIEF UN COMMAND
General of the Army Douglas MacArthur      8 July 1950–11 April 1951
General Matthew B. Ridgway                11 April 1951–9 May 1952
General Mark Clark                        9 May 1952–5 October 1953

## COMMANDER US EIGHTH ARMY, KOREA

| | |
|---|---|
| Lt General Walton H. Walker | 3 September 1950–23 December 1950 |
| Lt General Matthew B. Ridgway | 26 December 1950–14 April 1951 |
| Lt General James A. Van Fleet | 14 April 1951–11 February 1953 |
| Lt General Maxwell D. Taylor | 11 February 1953–25 March 1955 |

## CHAIRMAN JOINT CHIEFS OF STAFF

| | |
|---|---|
| General of the Army Omar N. Bradley | 16 August 1949–15 August 1953 |

## FAR EAST AIR FORCES COMMANDER

| | |
|---|---|
| Lt General George E. Stratemeyer | 26 April 1949–21 May 1951 |
| Lt General Earl E. Partridge | 21 May 1951–10 June 1951 |
| General Otto P. Weyland | 10 June 1951–31 March 1954 |

## COMMANDER FAR EAST NAVAL FORCES

| | |
|---|---|
| Vice Admiral C. Turner Joy | 27 August 1949–21 May 1951 |
| Vice Admiral Robert C. Briscoe | 4 June 1952–2 April 1954 |

## COMMANDER SEVENTH FLEET

| | |
|---|---|
| Vice Admiral Arthur D. Struble | 19 May 1950–28 March 1951 |
| Vice Admiral Harold M. Martin | 28 March 1951–28 March 1952 |
| Vice Admiral Robert P. Briscoe | 28 March 1952–20 May 1952 |
| Vice Admiral Joseph J. Clark | 20 May 1952–1 December 1953 |

# Bibliography

## JOURNALS AND PUBLISHED PAPERS

'British Commonwealth Naval Operations during the Korean War', Parts I–VI, *Journal of the Royal United Service Institution* 1950–3.

Wing Commander P. G. Wykeham-Barnes, 'The War in Korea with special reference to the difficulties of using our air power,' *Journal of the Royal United Service Institution*, May 1952, No. 586.

Farrar P. N., 'Britain's Proposal for a Buffer Zone South of the Yalu 1950', *Journal of Contemporary History*, (Sage) Vol. 18, 1983.

Hoare J. E., 'British Public Opinion and the Korean War,' Papers of the British Association for Korean Studies, No. 2, 1992.

Friedman E., 'Nuclear Blackmail and the End of the Korean War,' *Modern China*, (Sage) Vol. I No 1, January 1975.

Holroyd, Reuben ed. 'The Morning Calm,' *Journal of the British Korean Veterans Association*.

Henderson J. B. 'Defence of the Knoll,' *British Army Review*, December 1983.

Warren Thompson, 'Air Combat over Korea' in *Wings of Fame* Volumes I–IV, Aerospace Publishing, 1995–6.

16th Regiment 1950–4, Royal New Zealand Artillery, undated.

## UNPUBLISHED PAPERS

Documents and transcripts, the Peter Farrar collection.

## PUBLISHED TEXTS

Akio Morita  *Made in Japan*, Collins 1987.

Anon  *The Battle of Maryang San*, Royal Australian Rifles, 2–8 October 1951, Headquarters Training Command 1991.

Anon  The Royal Ulster Rifles in Korea, Belfast 1953.

Badsey S.  *Korean War*, Bison 1990.

Barclay C. N.  *The First Commonwealth Division*, Gale and Polden 1954.

Barker A. J.  *Fortune Favours the Brave*, Leo Cooper 1974.

Bartlett N.  *With the Australians in Korea*, Australian War Memorial, 3rd edn. 1960.

Bishop C.  Ed. *The Aerospace Encyclopaedia of Air Warfare*, Vol. II '1945 to the present' 1998.

Blair C.  *Beyond Courage*, Jarrolds 1956.

Brown B.  *The Battle of Kapyong*, Australia Headquarters Command 1992.

Boyne W. J.  *Beyond the Wild Blue*, St Martins Press, NY 1997.

Catchpole B.  *Map History of Modern China*, Heinemann 1988.

Clark M.  *From the Danube to the Yalu*, Harrap 1954.

Cleveland W. M.  *Mosquitos in Korea*, Peter E. Randall 1991.

Corr G. H.  *The Chinese Red Army*, Osprey 1974.

Crawford S.  *Battleships and Carriers*, Dempsey Parr 1999.

Cumings B.  *The Origins of the Korean War*, Princeton University Press 1981.

Cunningham-Boothe A. & Farrar P.  *British Forces in the Korean War*, (BKVA) 3rd ed. 1997.

Davies N.  *Red Winds from the North*, Able 1999.

Davies S. J.  *In Spite of Dungeons*, Hodder & Stoughton 1954.

Dorr R., Lake J., Thompson W.  *Korean War Aces*, Osprey 1999.

Dunston S.  *The Centurion Tank*, Osprey 1991.

Eaton H. B.  *Something Extra, 28 Commonwealth Brigade 1951–74*, Pentland Press 1993.

Evanhoe E.  *Dark Moon: Eighth Army Special Operations in the Korean War*, Korvet/US Naval Institute Press 1995.

Farrar – Hockley A.  *The Edge of the Sword*, Frederick Muller 1954.

– *British Part in the Korean War*, Vol. I, HMSO 1990.

– *A Distant Obligation*, Vol. II, HMSO 1995 (British Official History).

Fehrenbach T. R.  *Crossroads in Korea: The Historic Siege of Chipyong-ni*, Macmillan, New York 1966.

Forty G.  *At War in Korea*, Ian Allen 1982.

Foss M.  *The Royal Fusiliers*, Hamish Hamilton 1967.

Futrell R. F.  *The United States Air Force in Korea 1950–53*, Office of Air Force History 1983 (Official History).

Goodspeed D. J.  *The Armed Forces of Canada 1867–1967*, Canadian Forces HQ, Ottawa 1967.

Grey J.  *The Commonwealth Armies and the Korean War*, Manchester University Press 1988.

Gugeler R. A.  *Combat Operations in Korea*, Office of the Chief of Military History, US Army 1970.

Halliday J. & Cumings B.  *Korea: the Unknown War*, Viking 1988.

Hammel E.  *Chosin*, Vanguard 1981.

Hastings M.  *The Korean War*, Michael Joseph 1987.

Heinl R. D.  *Victory at High Tide: the Inchon–Seoul Campaign*, T. P. Lippincott, NY 1968.

Hess D. E.  *Battle Hymn*, Peter Davies, 1957.

Hickey M.  *The Korean War*, John Murray 1999.

Higgins R.  *United Nations Peacekeeping 1946–1967*, Documents & Commentary, Vol. II, OUP 1970.

Hoare J. E.  *Embassies in the East*, Curzon Press 1999.

Hoare J. E. & Pares S.  *Conflict in Korea*, ABC-CLIO 1999.

Hoyt E. P.  *The Pusan Perimeter*, Stein & Day 1984.

Isby D. C.   *Jane's Fighter Combat in the Jet Age*, HarperCollins 1997.
Jackson R.   *Korean Combat*, Arthur Barker 1983.
– *Air War Korea 1950–1953*, Airlife 1998.
Kim Chum Kon   *The Korean War*, Kwangmyon Publishing 1973.
Kinne D.   *Wooden Boxes*, Frederick Muller 1953.
Kolko G.   *The Politics of War*, Random House 1968.
Kolko J. & Kolko G.   *The Limits of Power*, Harper & Row 1972.
Knox D.   *The Korean War: Uncertain Victory*, Harcourt Brace Jovanovich 1972.
– *The Korean War: Pusan to Chosin*, Harcourt Brace & Co. 1985.
Ladd J. D.   *By Sea and by Land: The Authorised History of the Royal Marines Commandos*, HarperCollins 1998.
Langley M.   *Inchon: MacArthur's Last Triumph*, Batsford 1979.
Lansdown J. R. P.   *With the Carriers in Korea*, Crécy 1997.
Larby R.   *Signals to the Right, Armoured Corps to the Left*, Korvet Publishing 1993.
Large L.   *One Man's War in Korea*, William Kimber 1988.
Lee Hyung Suk   (Chairman War History Compilation) *The History of UN Forces in Korea*, Vol. V, Ministry of Defense, Korea 1976.
Linklater E.   *Our Men in Korea*, HMSO 1952.
Lowe P.   *The Origins of the Korean War*, Longmans 2nd edn. 1998.
Lunt J.   *The Duke of Wellington's Regiment*, Leo Cooper 1971.
MacDonald C.   *Britain and the Korean War*, Basil Blackwell 1990.
MacDonald J. F. M.   *The Borderers in Korea*, privately printed and undated.
Malcolm G. I.   *The Argylls in Korea*, Thomas Nelson 1952.
Marshall S. L. A.   *The River and the Gauntlet*, Battery Press 1987.
   *Pork Chop Hill*, William Morrow, NY 1956.
Martin J.   *K-Force: To the Sharp End*, Korvet Publishing 1999.
McGuire F. R.   *Canada's Army in Korea*, Queen's Printer, Ottawa 1956.
Melady J.   *Korea: Canada's Forgotten War*, Macmillan of Canada 1983.
Mescio J.   *Armour in Korea*, Squadron/Signal Publications 1984.
O'Neill R.   *Australia in the Korean War 1950–53*, Vol. I, 'Strategy and Diplomacy.' Vol. II, 'Combat Operations Australian War Memorial 1981/1985 (Official History).
Porschall R.   *Witness to War: Korea*, Perigree/Berkeley Publishing 1995.
Peacock L.   *North American F-86 Sabre*, Salamander 1991.
Polak T.   *Stalin's Falcons*, Grub Street 1999.
Portway D.   *Korea: Land of the Morning Calm*, George Harrap 1953.
Proctor R. T.   *Radio Jeeps in Korea*, Mosquito Association 1994.
Rees D.   *Korea: the Limited War*, Macmillan 1964.
– ed. *The Korean War: History and Tactics*, Orbis 1984.
Ridgway M. B.   *The War in Korea*, Barrie & Rockcliff 1968.
Roetter C.   *Psychological Warfare*, Batsford 1978.
Sandler S.   *The Korean War: No Victors, No Vanquished*, University Press of Kentucky 1999.
Shipster J. N.   *Diehards in Korea*, printed by Austin Reed plc, 2nd edn. 1983.
Smithwaite D. & Washington D.   *The British Soldier in Korea 1950–53*, The National Army Museum 1988.
Spurr R.   *Enter the Dragon*, Sidgwick & Jackson 1989.
Stanton S. L.   *Ten Corps in Korea*, Presidio Press 1996.
Stewart J. T.   *Airpower: The Decisive Force in Korea*, D. Van Nostrand 1957.
Stone I. F.   *The Hidden History of the Korean War*, Turnstile Press 1952.
Stueck W.   *The Korean War: An International History*, Princeton University Press 1995.

Tindall G. B. & Shi D. E.   *America: A Narrative History*, W. W. Norton, NY 4th edn. 1996.

Truman H.   *Years of Trial and Hope*, Hodder & Stoughton 1956.

Wagner E. W.   ed. *Korea Old and New*, Harvard University Press 1990.

Walker M.   *The Cold War*, Fourth Estate 1993.

Westover J. G.   *Combat Support in Korea*, Combat Forces Press, Washington DC, 1955.

Whiting, C.   *Battleground Korea: The British in Korea*, Sutton Publishing 1999.

Winchester S.   *Korea: A Walk through the Land of Miracles*, Grafton Books 1990.

Yasamee H. J. & Hamilton K. A.   ed. *Documents on British Foreign History*, Series II, Vol. IV, 'Korea' HMSO 1991.

# Index

DATE DUE